The Brainiac's Puzzle Book

The Brainiac's Puzzle Book

by
Frank Longo,
Fraser Simpson,
Terry Stickels &
the National Puzzlers' League

Sterling Publishing Co., Inc.
New York

10 9 8 7 6 5 4 3 2 1

Published by Sterling Publishing Co., Inc.
387 Park Avenue South, New York, NY 10016
This book is comprised of material from the following Sterling titles:
Cranium-Crushing Crosswords © 2002 by Frank Longo
Hard-to-Solve Cryptograms © 2001 by National Puzzlers' League
Cunning Mind-Bending Puzzles © 2002 by Terry Stickels
101 Cryptic Crosswords © 2001 by The Condé Nast Publications, Inc.

© 2003 by Sterling Publishing Co., Inc.
Distributed in Canada by Sterling Publishing
c/o Canadian Manda Group, One Atlantic Avenue, Suite 105
Toronto, Ontario, Canada M6K 3E7
Distributed in Great Britain by Chrysalis Books
64 Brewery Road, London N7 9NT, England
Distributed in Australia by Capricorn Link (Australia) Pty. Ltd.
P.O. Box 704, Windsor, NSW 2756, Australia

Designed by StarGraphics Studio

ISBN 1-4027-0875-0

Contents

Cranium-Crushing Crosswords

Introduction

We'll come right out and say it: This section isn't for everybody. Sure, many people enjoy solving crosswords—in fact, it's America's #1 pastime. But most crosswords are of average difficulty, a pleasant diversion during a lunch break or a lazy Sunday afternoon.

However, let it be known: the puzzles in this section are diabolically difficult! Only if you are, or very well might be, a brainiac who loves incredibly challenging crossword puzzles, will these puzzles be for you.

The answers are almost all common words or phrases. The difficulty lies in the clues, where there is ample use of misdirection, trivia, puns, vagueness, and other trickery in an attempt to beguile you. But we believe that ultimately, once you solve them, you'll agree that these puzzles are eminently fair. Cruel, but fair.

A few "easier" puzzles along the way are meant to build up your self-confidence, which will be severely tested by the last ten puzzles. These last ten, which we like to call "The Dastardly Decade," are the hardest in the bunch. (So, unless you're a real glutton for punishment, this section is probably not one that you would want to work in backward order.)

You'll also notice that many of these puzzles were created with very wide-open and often unusual grids, with few black squares and large chunks of white. Grids like this are very difficult to create. But creating them was worth the effort—just to give you these cranium-crushing crosswords.

Are you ready to play?!

1

ACROSS

1 2001 Hollywood Walk of Fame star recipient
9 1-Across offering
15 Turquoise
16 ___ Éireann (Irish parliamentary house)
17 Injure irreparably
18 There may be a cap on it
19 Like some pleas
20 Some speculative commodities
21 Superlatively slippery
22 "Very funny"
23 Two-time U.S. Open winner
27 It specializes in old pictures
30 Galba's God
31 Locke of the Harlem Renaissance
32 Trucks
35 Character in the Septuagint
36 ___ maté
37 Goldfinger's first name
38 Sci-fi royal
40 How the wind may blow: Abbr.
41 Grinned and bore it
45 Josephine Tey's Brat
46 Fogies
50 Actor Brimley
52 Expect to get back
53 "My Cup Runneth Over" musical
54 Encounters
55 Less loaded
56 In ___
57 Pillars of the community
58 Object of Solveig's affection

DOWN

1 Iris Murdoch and others
2 Like some proportions
3 "Back in the Saddle Again" singer
4 *Phantom Lady* costar
5 Least bumbling
6 Dressed down
7 Camel waste
8 "___-haw!"
9 See to it
10 Passing anniversary
11 Like some lessons
12 Late
13 Not be apathetic
14 Dreyer's, east of the Rockies
20 Star's stack, perhaps
22 Arrogance
24 Be conscience-stricken
25 Spare fare?
26 Wear away
27 Melvillean mariner
28 Spreckelsville locale
29 Baseballer who initiated free agency
33 Prepared to roast, perhaps
34 Portrayer of Detective Sorenson
39 Senator D'Amato
42 Overthrows, e.g.
43 It may be gummy
44 Orchestral activity
47 Hall of fame
48 Add
49 Weasel with a black-tipped tail
50 Dissolve alternative
51 Tiki, e.g.
52 Friction reducer
54 Hammer's sound

ANSWER, PAGE 241

2

ACROSS

1 Ace
9 Match collection
15 ~~Wax producer~~
16 Strengthen
17 Foreigner's state
18 Scalping, say
19 Wheelman?
20 Went home, perhaps
21 New walker
22 Aquanaut's abode
23 Hideki of the diamond
27 One of the Ten Attic Orators
30 It has sympathetic strings
31 Parisian pronoun
32 It may follow less
33 Like a lamb
34 Immature newt
35 Top of the Catholic Church

36 Golf's "Champagne Tony"
37 Heart
38 One perfecting
39 Boston's style
41 Wallace's costar in a 1981 Louis Malle film
42 Where to find the filament
43 Kind of grass
45 Court defendant of 1925
46 Crack investigator's concern?
51 Hip boots, e.g.
52 From a helicopter, perhaps
53 For one
54 People who are udderly talented?
55 Upset
56 Word in a cover letter

DOWN

1 Shellac
2 ~~Granada greeting~~
3 Letterhead?: Abbr.
4 Some construction bar shapes
5 Intrinsically
6 Utah's ___ Mountains
7 F–, e.g.
8 Computer ___
9 Cosmic units
10 Like some garages
11 Exposure to the sun's rays
12 In the immediate vicinity
13 Gossip
14 Olympic racer
22 Inhabiting Inchon
23 Sicilia, e.g.

24 Painting of nature, perhaps
25 Wilbur Smith bestseller
26 Tropical castaway?
28 Certified letter?
29 It may get the game
35 Ann Marie, to Don Hollinger
37 Like vinyl records
40 Impose a fine upon
44 Composer who was one of "Les Six"
45 Love-letter letters
46 ___ City, Florida
47 Subtitle of a Belafonte hit
48 Some blight victims
49 Protected, in a way
50 *Middletown* sociologist

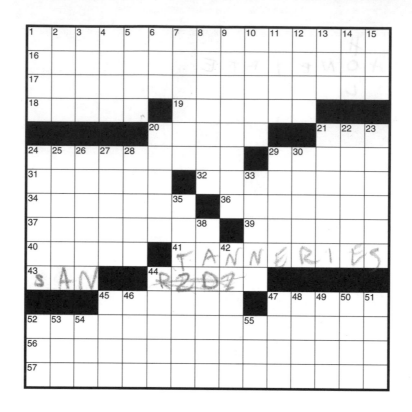

3

ACROSS

1 Vancouver is on it
16 Place of change
17 River through Franklin, North Carolina
18 Very heavy
19 Tater Tots producer
20 Biotite and muscovite
21 Doña ___ (New Mexico county)
24 Potential hiree's hurdle
29 Meet collection
31 Figure skater Grinkov
32 *Providence* actor
34 Ann's twin
36 Dangerous current for a small boat
37 Calling convenience
39 Profits
40 Body double?
41 They produce leather
43 Cabo ___ Lucas, Mexico
44 Threepio's pal
45 Comment after failing
47 *Semiramide* librettist
52 Deserts
56 Whitney Houston hit
57 Commission receivers, perhaps

DOWN

1 1944 ETO battleground
2 Chi paper
3 Minimum wage, e.g.
4 Farm team?
5 Ferry destination, perhaps
6 One all, e.g.
7 Emperor during Benedict VII's papacy
8 Comparatively cutthroat
9 Left base, in a way
10 Del of the diamond
11 Paper page
12 Dickens's Dartle
13 Grunts
14 Elephant follower
15 Had a date
20 11th-century year
21 When Romeo slays Tybalt
22 It may get under your skin
23 Valuate
24 *Compromising Positions* novelist
25 It may be planetary
26 Moon of Neptune
27 Instigate
28 *Peg Woffington* novelist
29 Star of 1998's *Rear Window* remake
30 Roddy Doyle's ___ *Called Henry*
33 Lotto variety
35 Outhouse relatives
38 Sails on a dhow
42 Acknowledges, in a way
44 Therapy preceder
45 Shania Twain's "The Woman ___"
46 General ___ chicken
47 India's Lakshmi Bai, e.g.
48 Twice tetra-
49 *In Living Color* number
50 A little
51 Supermodel Sastre
52 How-___
53 Article in *La Repubblica*
54 Sem. focus
55 Zippo competitor

ANSWER, PAGE 245

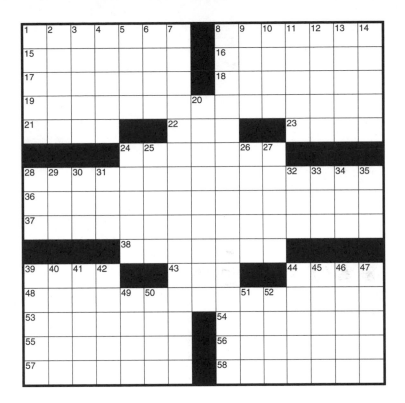

4

ACROSS

1 Spinning wheel attachment
8 Locale of the Hale telescope
15 Ward of Miss Havisham
16 Igneous rock constituent
17 Cooperatively
18 Slates, to Caesar
19 Site of a core problem?
21 1949 medicine Nobelist
22 The *Eagle* that landed, e.g.
23 They may meet
24 Paddled, perhaps
28 Glycogenosis and others
36 Investment options
37 No greenhorn
38 Not quite huge
39 Time or life follower

43 Ted Lewis's "Somebody Stole My ___"
44 Hermosillo hibernators
48 Shared the life and fortunes of
53 Makes a judicial decision about
54 One with a manager, maybe
55 Tending to bounce back?
56 Keened
57 Like some weather
58 Times for egg rolls?

DOWN

1 Curtains, so to speak
2 See 52-Down
3 They may be seen after a header
4 *Idée* sources
5 Helm position
6 Cheat
7 Reason to rush home from work early

8 Showy façade masking an embarrassing situation
9 Range of the Tien Shan Mountains
10 Ad-___
11 Embryo sac container
12 Fabio's birthplace
13 Indian chess grand master
14 Thin things
20 It's rarely pumped anymore
24 John Paul II's given name
25 Satellite launcher
26 1952 Newbery Medal winner for *Ginger Pye*
27 Submariner's concern
28 Yearbook sect.
29 Airport terminal?
30 Hiroshima's river
31 ___ *de veau* (calf sweetbreads)
32 Bass, for one

33 Org. of which 14 U.S. presidents have been members
34 Bambi's aunt
35 W-2 info
39 It's turned by a carpenter
40 King of Greece, 1947–64
41 Lion of C.S. Lewis's "Narnia" tales
42 Mushroom cloud producer
44 Baby boobook
45 One who can't keep a secret
46 Wolverine's cousin
47 Casts off
49 Bone: Prefix
50 Sam Spade stories, say
51 ___ *vez* (again, in Almería)
52 With 2-Down, telephone identity phrase

5

ACROSS

1 Audrey's sitcom costar
7 One purifying naphthalene, perhaps
15 Flute inventor, as legend has it
16 Three numbers in parentheses, perhaps
17 French fop's collection
18 Was irresponsible with waste
19 *The Defense Never Rests* author
20 Seat of Randolph County, North Carolina
21 Maintained
23 Hi-___
24 Possible result of a hung jury
25 Broccoli servings
29 Nitty Gritty Dirt Band's dancer
31 "Ahem" alternative
35 Mounted
36 End of an annual song
37 Carefully crafted comment
40 They may be balanced
41 Move back
46 ___ Lingus
47 Glove producer
48 Emblems
52 Grape greenhouse
53 Knocker alternative
54 Missing nothing
55 Being displayed ostentatiously
56 Relatively rare
57 Santa Clara Valley city
58 Brown-coated ermines

DOWN

1 Abdul-___ (Alcindor, now)
2 Base directive
3 Levi's stopper
4 *42nd Street* star
5 Meantime
6 Sitting duck
7 Mealtime mix-up?
8 *Mitla Pass* author
9 One of the Marches
10 Eventually
11 Bow breakers?
12 With a dour disposition
13 German river
14 Emendation
22 They may be on the table, in more ways than one
25 Products of glacial erosion
26 Some off-road vehicles
27 It may indicate perfection
28 One way to travel: Abbr.
30 Chiwere speaker
31 Highly toxic pollutant
32 Moo ___ pork
33 Crush and Surge
34 Hit by the Original Dixieland Jazz Band
38 They have two hemispheres
39 Fabric resembling wool
42 Is entirely unacceptable
43 New York native
44 Good ratter
45 Fast-food restaurant equipment
47 Some are tropical
48 One on a pedestal
49 One in front?
50 Electee's prize, perhaps
51 Ray of Hollywood

ANSWER, PAGE 249

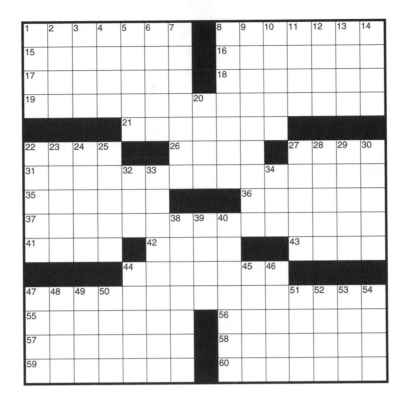

6

ACROSS

1 Psychotic character
8 Psychotic character?
15 Robusta alternative
16 *Fear of Flying* anti-heroine
17 Pump alternative
18 Like some maps
19 People who are good at IT
21 Kind of fishing
22 Dollar alternative
26 Seed enveloper
27 Part of WATS
31 The Williamsburg Bridge leads to it
35 Domain of José Eduardo dos Santos
36 Associated with
37 Roosevelt had one
41 Shooting sites
42 They may be made of shells

43 Like some jeans
44 Nerd's favorite newspaper section, maybe
47 What deadlines create
55 Thinner, perhaps
56 They may appear in the mist
57 One who does body work?
58 Submits just before the deadline
59 Matrimonial state
60 Some stanzas

DOWN

1 Metallica drummer Ulrich
2 Deuterium discoverer
3 Track long shots
4 Lean against
5 Like some walls

6 Part of a famous tripartite claim
7 Shower gift, perhaps
8 Makes one's attendance official
9 Gilgal camper
10 Boxer Ali
11 Purl
12 Shakes' opposites
13 Allowance after deduction for tare
14 Resting places for mice
20 ___ Harbor (Guam port)
22 Lay up
23 Oklahoma Air Force Base
24 Mint bar
25 They're done in bars
27 Like a good guard
28 Wave catcher?
29 Script word

30 Festoon, e.g.
32 Key abbr.
33 Rocket components
34 Master, eventually
38 People concerned with net results?
39 Webmaster's concern
40 Dangerous dipterans
44 Where Scottish kings were once coronated
45 Neanderthal
46 Displays, in a way
47 Chihuahua chow
48 Trash can, at times
49 Insignificant
50 It was founded in 1440
51 Cynical remark
52 Winning margin, maybe
53 Needle
54 IRS info

7

ACROSS

1 Didn't quit
9 Pancho's cover-up
15 Immigrant's state
16 He played McBride in *DeepStar Six*
17 1994–1995 news-magazine satire
18 Not old
19 Is linked with
20 Astaire's *Yolanda and the Thief* costar
21 People running in
23 Do to do, to Donizetti
24 Votes against
25 Like some problem skin
27 Basque for "game"
29 Superlatively slab-sided
30 Container in the dairy section
34 Gluck opera
35 ___ acid (intermediate in B-complex vitamin synthesis)
36 Dakota Indian
37 Solo
39 War film, when tripled
43 Tons
44 Place of habitual confinement and drudgery
47 It may be attached to a shark
49 Quality of some birds?
50 Inveighed
51 Boxing moniker
52 Garfield's gal pal
53 Trapped, perhaps
54 *Lie Down in Darkness* novelist
55 Using vowel rhyme

DOWN

1 *Corky Romano* star Chris
2 TV's Mistress of the Dark
3 Evergreen grove of a sort
4 Increases the volume of, in a way
5 No pros
6 Poison
7 Peter & Gordon tune
8 High-reaching men?
9 Ivanjica inhabitant
10 Opposite of until
11 Dieter's snack, perhaps
12 People in your class, e.g.
13 Judge, sometimes
14 Break in show business?
22 Astronomical phenomena
26 Breathing anomaly
27 William Barr's successor
28 Closeout caveat
30 ___ *de richesses*
31 *Urban Legend* costar
32 How a pessimist views things
33 One hugging, perhaps
38 *The Secret World of Alex Mack* star Oleynik
39 Some metalworkers
40 Iroquoian tongue
41 Fix the exterior surface of
42 OK
45 Region in northwest Asia Minor
46 San Francisco Bay college
48 It's at the tip of the Arabian Peninsula

ANSWER, PAGE 253

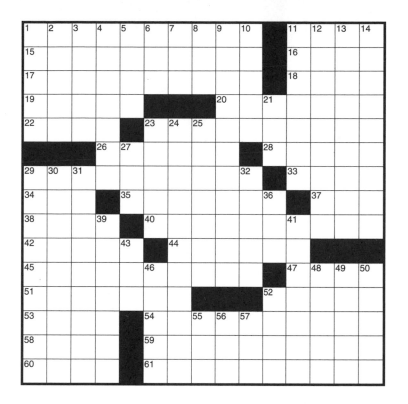

8

ACROSS

1 National monument near the Gila
11 Give up
15 Oralism advocates
16 Defendant, in canon law
17 Suspect's claim, perhaps
18 Maui music makers
19 Parcels
20 "___ without justice"
22 God's little acre?
23 Walleye
26 Fonzie's cousin
28 Short partner?
29 Behaving insincerely
33 Dr. Zhivago
34 Quoits peg
35 Like a junior
37 HHS division
38 Room offerers
40 Slapstick prop
42 Sergius II's successor
44 Mesquite or mimosa, e.g.
45 Bug killers
47 It may be needed for the present
51 Slugger Manny
52 Buenos ___
53 "___ in Calico" (1946 hit)
54 It may indicate alkalinity
58 M.'s other half
59 Not taking "no" for an answer
60 Shambles
61 Compliment, perhaps

DOWN

1 Weather conditions
2 Part of CAD
3 Treat maliciously
4 Passion
5 ___ du monde (society leaders)
6 Rubbish relisher
7 Throw in
8 Prefix with romantic
9 19, in Canada
10 These, in Toledo
11 Sadist's satisfaction source
12 Reggae artist who's a scream?
13 The natural order of events
14 Like some fatty acids
21 ___ de bourrée
23 Ebenezer's ghostly partner
24 Bringing out of latency
25 Worked out with a bar, perhaps
27 Stable stock
29 Party-switching senator
30 Lucky Lindy, with "the"
31 Deviants
32 Yucca, for one
36 Butter in the meadow
39 Some comparisons
41 Clothing sizes
43 Husband: Latin
46 Whoopi's role in *The Color Purple*
48 Ain't the way it should be?
49 Fish, in Florence
50 Oleate, e.g.
52 Memo starter
55 "General" of Chinese cuisine
56 Film starring Smith and Jones, for short
57 It gave Hope to GIs

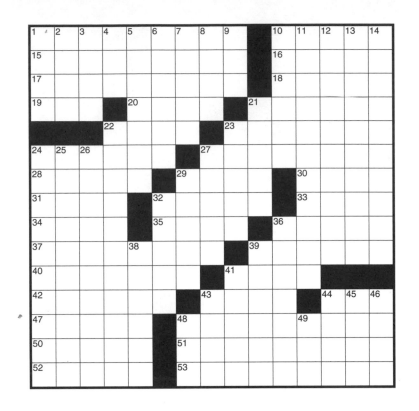

9

ACROSS

1 You're looking at it
10 Score symbol
15 Statisticians' tools
16 Relatively robust
17 Bleeped
18 Laura's *Jurassic Park* role
19 Tibetan milk source
20 Make a touchdown
21 Accouters anew
22 "___ nome" (Verdi aria)
23 Doesn't sell, perhaps
24 Units of about three grains
27 Bizet's "L'amour est un oiseau rebelle," e.g.
28 ___ citato
29 Tag datum
30 What some singers perform in
31 ___ Harbor, Guam
32 Characteristic carriers
33 Not fancy in the least
34 Pullulate
35 English horn, e.g.
36 Holder of the Host
37 Hotel employees
39 Least healthy-looking
40 Gordon Lightfoot's Ontario birthplace
41 You may do it with a clicker
42 Noninvasive med. test
43 One may draw from it
44 Kin of -oid
47 Japanese stringed instruments
48 *Midnight Cowboy* costar
50 *I Hated, Hated, Hated This Movie* author
51 Has dinner delivered
52 Forked-tailed fliers
53 Opening aid

DOWN

1 Be a good dog
2 Zip
3 Quarterback Kramer
4 Dramatic division
5 Having pincerlike claws
6 Control-tower systems
7 Black Bears' home
8 It may be ear-piercing
9 Mach-2 traveler
10 Easton of pop
11 Cream alternative
12 Write a tongue twister, maybe
13 Keeps saying
14 Photo-op arranger, perhaps
21 Choir attire
22 Stick-to-your-teeth snack
23 Knocked for a loop
24 Place for a hand on a cold day
25 Seem
26 Get back on the roll
27 Top tapper
29 "Adios!"
32 Kind of muscle
36 Places to play games, perhaps
38 Lets have it
39 1955 role for Lemmon
41 ___ message to
43 Modeled
44 Helper with a hump
45 Feng ___
46 URL opener
48 Molecule
49 Novel ending

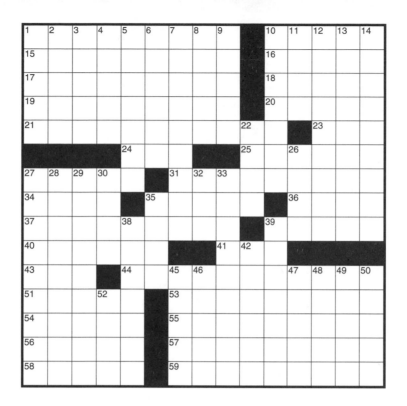

10

ACROSS

1 Come out of denial
10 Struck with the feet, in a way
15 Like a .22
16 *Zigeunerliebe* composer
17 Washer of a sort
18 Stem
19 Buster's activity
20 Score, essentially
21 What a caret might indicate
23 EW workers
24 End of a race?
25 Inexperienced surfer, maybe
27 Some seafood
31 They may make people break up
34 Driving tool
35 Record groove, e.g.
36 Four before V
37 Public transportation
39 B-board biggie
40 Source of many bark varieties
41 Pitch preceder
43 Ode conjunction
44 Guitarist killed in a motorcycle accident at age 24
51 David's 1977 sci-fi role
53 100 centavos, until 1963
54 Davis of movies
55 Curbing
56 She was under Kirk
57 Bulbous roof ending in a sharp point
58 Created striking sentences?
59 Puts back on the payroll

DOWN

1 Polaris or Procyon
2 What makes *il mondo* go round?
3 Blue Grotto locale
4 Dame Terry
5 Used nylon thread, perhaps
6 Goes down
7 Doesn't oversee alone, perhaps
8 Italian city on the Adige River
9 Two-time French Open winner Bruguera
10 Like some pregnancies
11 Saab model
12 Great Lakes species
13 Became familiar with gradually
14 Gets ready for church, perhaps
22 Ready to serve
26 Like some canine coats
27 Revealed
28 Not shot a lot
29 They follow the leader
30 Oldman's *Romeo Is Bleeding* costar
32 It may be picked out
33 Jock's other half
35 He was under Kirk
38 Arousing hairstyle?
39 Your current activity
42 Spread out atop
45 Execrate
46 Who might be to blame
47 Hunt of Hollywood
48 Armageddon combatant
49 Some cartoons
50 Vespers preceder
52 It may be slashed

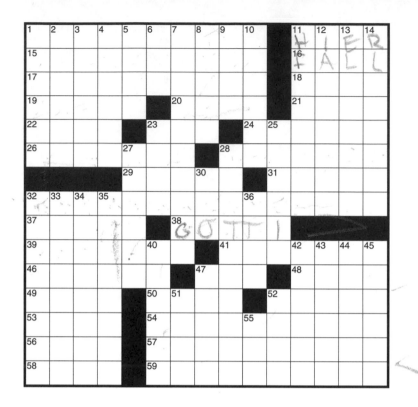

11

ACROSS

1 Exasperated cry
11 German senior
15 Headaches
16 Spring's opposite, in a way
17 *People of the Lie* author
18 She played Donna on *Beverly Hills 90210*
19 Complex community of a sort
20 Scale segment
21 Believers
22 It may follow ye
23 Dumas's *La Dame ___ Camélias*
24 Hawaiian's "thank you"
26 Goat's activity
28 Suffered from a bad stroke, perhaps

29 Hausa home
31 Sierra spur
32 It's strengthened by rowing
37 Gage title character
38 Big name in organized crime
39 Husky, e.g.
41 Full seriousness
46 They may be rubbed out
47 Young newt
48 Not had by
49 Elvis's rival at Nagano
50 Exiting exclamation
52 Evaluate
53 Gernreich of fashion
54 Like a fox
56 Buffalo hunter
57 Truck model until 1996
58 ___ vaccine

59 West Indian entertainment

DOWN

1 Romp
2 Store, in a way
3 Write in C, e.g.
4 No slowpoke
5 Suffix with hydro- or electro-
6 Stable particle
7 Depriving of juice?
8 Mountaineer's aid
9 Yellow Hats, e.g.
10 Edmonton gridder
11 Lucky Jim, e.g.
12 "More Than I Can Say" singer
13 Sweet little treats
14 *Star Wars* follower
23 Spanish liqueur
25 Moroccan port

27 Like some pitches
28 Muscle
30 Roxette records for it
32 Gene Kelly musical
33 Hymnal interjection
34 Britney Spears, e.g.
35 Lettering liquid
36 Assists, say
40 *Titanic* booty
42 Cosa ___
43 Flag
44 Released by breaking the cask
45 People playing
47 Words on a Wonderland cake
51 Pauline Kael's *I Lost ___ the Movies*
52 V.S. Pritchett's ___ *at the Door*
55 Pucksters' org.

ANSWER, PAGE 244

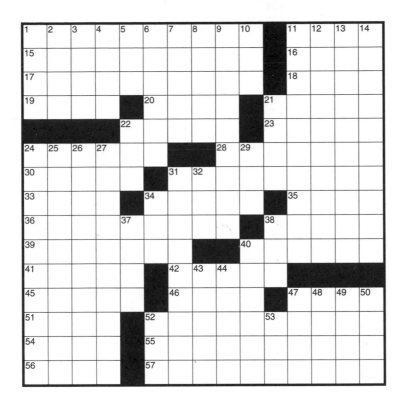

12

ACROSS

1 Ben & Jerry's boycotted it in 1990
11 1-Across product
15 Controls completely
16 Do some combining
17 How many possible beginning deals there are in bridge
18 McMillan of the court
19 Preacher's concern
20 Using signs, perhaps
21 ___ to go
22 Travis of country
23 Emphatic agreements
24 Biblical wind
28 Pay back
30 Hot flowers?
31 Where Shah Jahan mourned
33 "___ plaisir!"
34 MIT's ___ School of Management
35 Kind of column
36 Truthful
38 Painter Andrea del ___
39 Body language?
40 Moosehead rival
41 *The Shanghai Cobra* star
42 Hanged Irish revolutionary
45 Gay
46 Water under the bridge, perhaps
47 Its current name was adopted in 1935
51 Shape wood, in a way
52 Be driven by strangers, perhaps
54 Riddle middle?
55 Star witness?
56 St. Louis's ___ Bridge
57 Turned upright

DOWN

1 Christogram components
2 Bassist Pastorius
3 Alphabet bit
4 Catch but good
5 Tie indicator
6 Less afraid
7 Less emotional
8 "Prosit!" kin
9 Bestowment
10 Cricket sides
11 Houseplant
12 Bumps in the road?
13 Destroying gradually
14 What hunters look forward to
21 First name among sitarists
22 More, in Madrid
24 Business before the Civil War
25 Really don't know
26 Coated so as to conceal
27 Ease
29 Suffix with Mozart
31 Philosophers' stone seeker
32 District annexed by India in 1961
34 Cheer starter
37 Tabloid fodder
38 Elbow-bender
40 Stanislavski System, with "the"
43 Company creation
44 Very large
47 Good driver
48 Winter coat?
49 Near East port
50 Exam enthusiast, maybe
52 Cries of triumph
53 "I'll take that as ___"

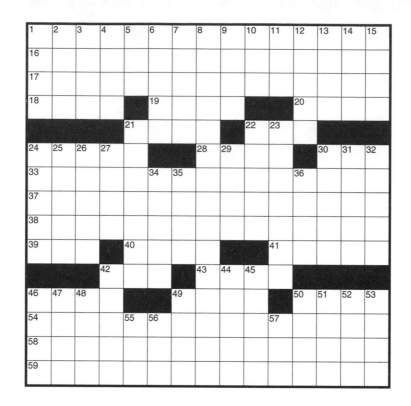

13

ACROSS

1 A dip needle indicates its direction
16 Quite advanced
17 Clients of foreign banks, maybe
18 Rolled pair, perhaps
19 Take to Sardi's, say
20 Polish language
21 Check
22 Music to Manolete's ears
24 In no more
28 More
30 Through
33 Some close encounters
37 Bookstore subcategory
38 Rolling Stones album that followed *Some Girls*
39 George's veep
40 Org. abbr.
41 Jazz vibraphonist Roy
42 Cut collector: Abbr.
43 Tobacco curer
46 Dell alternative
49 Ludlam's Vep
50 ___ Linda, California
54 Batman and Robin, e.g.
58 Post pooh-poohs it
59 Isn't funny, perhaps

DOWN

1 Beauregard Burnside's better half
2 Cry on a deck
3 Parent's contribution
4 Highland head shakes?
5 Dreyer's partner in the ice cream business
6 Words before joke or story
7 "___ to see the humor"
8 Emulated a loser?
9 Cousin of -trix
10 Richard Feynman book
11 It may be fair
12 Margaret Whiting's "___ in the Meadow"
13 Seven up, e.g.
14 Actor Katz
15 Balance
21 Creator of many illusions
22 He wrote lyrics for Richard's music
23 Cry at the table
24 Cut back
25 1941 title role for Dorothy Lamour
26 Kids do what he says to do
27 Parking place?
29 Break
30 Kind of recital
31 Arouse
32 Jacks, e.g.
34 C.P. Snow's ___ *of Varnish*
35 Deflected
36 Paris suburb
42 "You ___ Home" (song from *The Scarlet Pimpernel*)
44 Lifeless, old-style
45 More together
46 Eagerly expectant
47 Spreadsheet unit
48 Irish-born poet Young
49 Common contraction
50 She played WKRP's Jennifer
51 Designer for Jackie
52 Engage, as gear teeth
53 Kind of dir.
55 Duct
56 Kamoze of reggae
57 Nutrition std.

ANSWER, PAGE 248

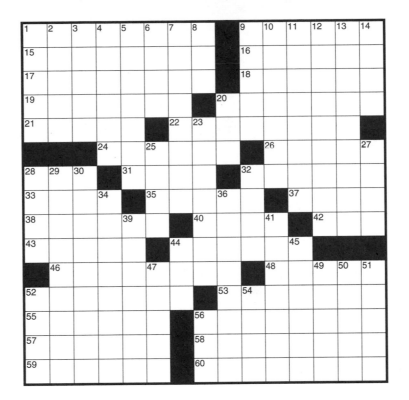

14

ACROSS

1 It may stick to your ribs
9 Enjoy, as a pleasant situation
15 He played Kyle McBride on *Melrose Place*
16 Dramatic beginning
17 Party animal
18 Fleers
19 Last word in the title of a documentary about The Who
20 Keeps in stock
21 Arcturus, e.g.
22 User's option
24 Chase of the court
26 Salon stock
28 Tolkien's Gorbag, e.g.
31 Prison part
32 She played Kelly on *Beverly Hills 90210*
33 Court target

35 São ___
37 Buckled
38 Part of the Quad Cities
40 ___ Lang (Superboy's girlfriend)
42 James Fenimore Cooper's ___ *Myers*
43 Trial figure
44 Muddles
46 Object of Diomedes's affection
48 *Stars & Stripes*, e.g.
52 Angler's activity
53 Song after "There Is Nothin' Like a Dame"
55 Kovalenko of the NHL
56 Express sententious opinions
57 Superlatively Solomonic
58 Exceeds
59 Falls hard?
60 Course requirements?

DOWN

1 See 44-Down
2 Flax seed vessels
3 Arcade introduction of 1983
4 Brown drawings
5 Shade yellower than lichen green
6 Box Elder locale
7 Of a constellation between Lupus and Vela
8 1970s–1980s seminar subject
9 Kind of metabolism
10 Grow together
11 Rushing
12 "Global Compact" proposer
13 Catching
14 Promontory
20 USMC E-4
23 Clutched?
25 Shipping address?
27 Bad thing to go to

28 Impedance units
29 Extraction alternative, perhaps
30 *Christabel* writer
32 Folk forename
34 Turpentine source
36 Social butterfly
39 Maximally meddlesome
41 It breaks down starches
44 With 1-Down, discovery by a record producer, perhaps
45 One sparring, maybe
47 Pets
49 Kind of cream cheese
50 Belittling brother
51 Arena arrangement
52 Pitch that's low
54 *Alfred* composer
56 Evan S. Connell's ___ *Bridge*

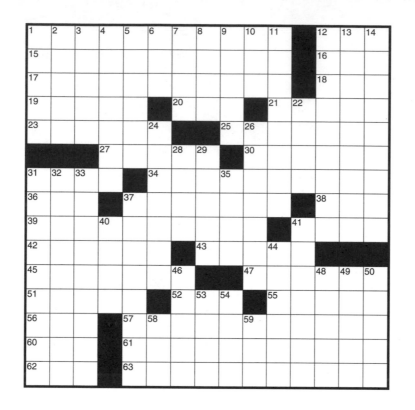

15

ACROSS

1 Story of choreographer Joe Gideon
12 Site for sweaters
15 *On the Pulse of Morning* author
16 Z key neighbor
17 Man whose career was stunted?
18 Buff
19 No ordinary ballgoer
20 Painter Bartolommeo
21 Lexicographer's concern
23 It may follow sound
25 They may come from the bench
27 Pollutes, in a way
30 It might be moving
31 Jabber?
34 Philanthropist's focus
36 Retrospective focus
37 Like trees, at times
38 On, in a way
39 Binary system
41 Member of U2
42 Captivate
43 Pensive piece
45 Not too bright
47 Site of some ancient revelations
51 Like some skeletons
52 Sumac of Peru
55 Driven up the wall
56 How, in Hamburg
57 Like many a telemarketer
60 Spots on the tube
61 1925 Globe Theatre debut
62 Before all is done
63 Nostalgia elicitor

DOWN

1 Slide presentation?
2 Flows against, as a river
3 *Principles of Geology* author
4 Petronas Towers descriptor
5 "The Dream" of basketball
6 Mezzo Murray
7 Shout before you're off, perhaps
8 Display derision
9 Architect Aalto
10 One of the Muppets
11 Natal territory
12 Fort Concho locale
13 Ready to be turned on, perhaps
14 Substantiates
22 Give rise to
24 They may say "Say when"
26 Spoke
28 Serengeti herd
29 Strike down
31 Dissolved
32 Magnetic tape coating
33 Like the best beefcake?
35 Roster abbr.
37 Grain farmer's chore
40 Kind of release
41 Like most magazine articles
44 Latin-class topic
46 Sleep in front?
48 *Oro's* partner
49 Infamous miser Green
50 Inventive Parisians get them
53 It may be set for a date
54 Noted *New Yorker* cartoonist
58 Sound from a Brahman
59 He dethroned Botvinnik in 1960

ANSWER, PAGE 252

16

ACROSS

1 Age, e.g.
5 City north of Kazan
10 Bon ___
14 Orthicon, e.g.
16 Draft drawers
17 Was part of the cast of
18 Shot sources
19 Some conservationists' concern
20 Move through mud
21 Banished colonist Hutchinson
22 Prince played by Carter
23 Convoy, perhaps
27 Dropped
29 Members of the genus *Branta*
31 Information information
35 Seat of Hot Springs County, Wyoming
36 Lapse
37 Spanish valentine phrase
42 Indian, e.g.
43 Year in John XVIII's papacy
44 It has spin 0
45 Single
51 Shut in
52 Part of the New York State Barge Canal system
53 On a par, in Orléans
54 It has five feet
55 Bank
56 Hazlitt piece
57 Pharmacy stock

DOWN

1 Iconic insect
2 Pitcher Kevin
3 Intensifying, briefly
4 Adolescent
5 Big name in corn syrup
6 Aqueduct of Sylvius, e.g.
7 Like an interrupter
8 Japanese bands?
9 Let out
10 Where people work
11 Esters in some vegetables and nuts
12 Like Romeo and Juliet
13 Positively
15 WWII flyboys
22 Break down, in a way
24 One-time delivery people
25 Los ___, California
26 Centers' actions
27 One way to behave
28 Nintendo name
30 Flap
31 Large, robust person
32 Film in which martial law is imposed upon New York City
33 Like some airports
34 Way for a knight to travel
38 Badge
39 Use a joystick, maybe
40 Exploited
41 Spill sources, perhaps
45 Schlemiel
46 Parts of most binaries
47 Shoot
48 Rocker Ford
49 Forever's partner
50 Pickup option

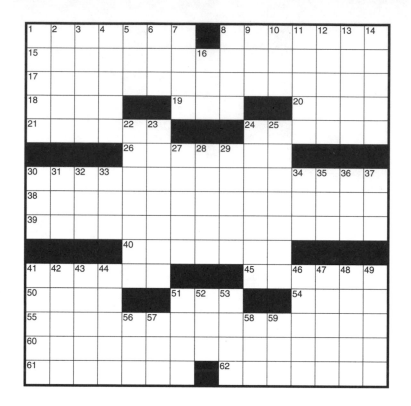

17

ACROSS

1 Bad-mouth
8 Co-host with Star, Lisa, Meredith, and Joy
15 Series set in Mayfield
17 Change of heart?
18 Flew
19 When all is said and done
20 He played Paco in *Bad Boys*
21 Part of an I rhyme?
24 Take stock?
26 Where something sweet may develop
30 They're smaller than their African cousins
38 Catholic University was its champion in 2001
39 Things to talk about on a first date, perhaps
40 Guiding group
41 Dickens duo

45 Director and star of *On Deadly Ground*
50 Sleipner's rider
51 It's got game
54 Hollywood's Wood
55 Film with the song "Have Yourself a Merry Little Christmas"
60 Knot-tying need?
61 Pigeonholes
62 Experienced hand

DOWN

1 ___ Airlines
2 Stroke of the pen
3 *Love Me Tender* actress
4 Shake
5 Kricfalusi's dog
6 Prepare to be painted, perhaps
7 Angers auxiliary
8 No nemesis
9 Some are chiseled
10 GWB, e.g.

11 Barnyard collection
12 Stop order?
13 Kind of calculus
14 Rip's role on *The Larry Sanders Show*
16 Get darker, in a way
22 Where the Colts play
23 They may be chipped
24 Old thrusters
25 Defeat
27 Brown of baseball
28 Gathering of information via radar, e.g.
29 Trattoria topping
30 *BusinessWeek* alternative
31 D.S.M. recipient, maybe
32 Impede
33 Cartesian conclusion
34 Hydrocarbon suffix
35 Former Serbian capital

36 "___-Willow" (song from The Mikado)
37 Boom preceder
41 *Murder, She Wrote* character
42 They may be put into your head
43 Zuppa inglese features
44 Opening
46 First-aid flora
47 Hardly healthy looking
48 Member of the carrot family
49 CD player component
51 Sharp changes of direction
52 Eagle's bill?
53 Where the Storting sits
56 Peace: Russian
57 Work on the side
58 Kay Kyser's "___ Reveille"
59 Kind of screen

ANSWER, PAGE 256

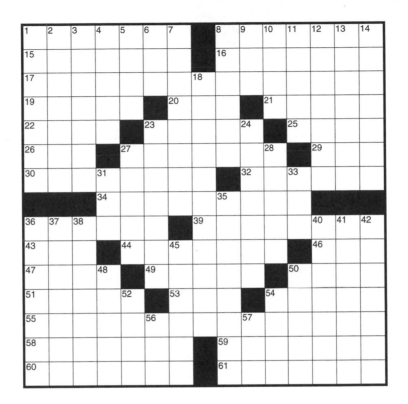

18

ACROSS

 1 Snub
 8 Contest with shells
15 Accept
16 Patterned after
17 *Funny Girl* subject
19 *Fried Green Tomatoes* director
20 Global positioning abbr.
21 *Purgatorio* author
22 Complete
23 Holding one's piece
25 Tooth component?
26 Fizzle
27 Like some engines and basements
29 She played June in *Henry & June*
30 One may go around the world
32 Push
34 Out in left field
36 Ford of the '20s
39 Ford of the '90s
43 Subject follower
44 Words to the unwelcome
46 Periodic-table ending
47 Where to find Edam and Gouda: Abbr.
49 It may arouse you
50 Demond's sitcom costar
51 Dismal
53 Swing voter, perhaps: Abbr.
54 Greased
55 Frankie Carle's theme song
58 "Anything for You" singer
59 Novelist Arturo Pérez-___
60 Abounding things
61 Cut

DOWN

 1 Things to watch out for
 2 Concessional comment
 3 British colony, until 1974
 4 *The Science of Logic* author
 5 Significance
 6 Had a gut reaction?
 7 Where the going rate is charged?
 8 Emulated Huck Finn
 9 *Another Green World* composer
10 Ambitious thing to go for
11 Place holder?
12 Contrive
13 When to start shooting
14 John Brown raid target
18 *Major Payne* star
23 National capital replaced by Astana
24 Good form
27 Is of the opinion
28 Interdiction introduction
31 Letter run
33 British Midgets, e.g.
35 Gets more of, in a way
36 Attitude
37 Make clichéd
38 Thaw
40 Haberdashery stock
41 Enlarged
42 Wapiti's smaller look-alike
45 Bigheaded bunch?
48 Women's room
50 Ancient letters
52 Abounding
54 Clothier Strauss
56 Corsica's neighbor: Abbr.
57 Remote abbr.

ANSWER, PAGE 258

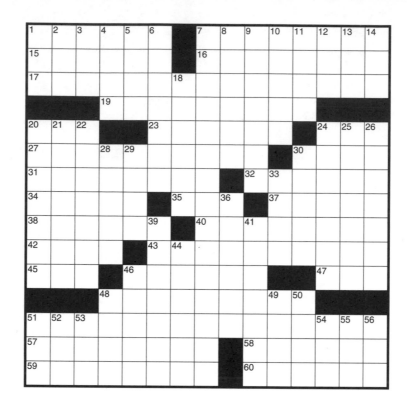

19

ACROSS

1 They may have stilts
7 They may have stilts
15 Quaint attention-getter
16 Clingy one
17 "The way it appears to me..."
19 Follows
20 Masseuse's need
23 Products of glaciation
24 Stink
27 Product stamp of a sort
30 "Hurry it up!"
31 "Jammin' Me" singer
32 One of the Dionn quintuplets
34 Bellows
35 Mall convenience
37 Circles
38 Andersen's birthplace
40 Intimidates like a bushmaster
42 Word on a supermarket checkout sign
43 Do as told
45 5,000-fingered piano teacher of film
46 Comparatively cross
47 Limit
48 A long time
51 Survivors may attend it
57 Make sour
58 Macaulay's kid brother
59 Holds with
60 Caesar's body?

DOWN

1 Single dance move?
2 Guitarist Dudek
3 No exemplar of elegance
4 Finish filming
5 "Stoned Soul Picnic" composer
6 Aromatherapeutic additive
7 Don't risk being penalized, perhaps
8 Leave
9 Way to storm off
10 Frank and others
11 Refuse visitors
12 Setting of a camel execution
13 45 inches, once
14 *Poivre's* partner
18 Sheets
20 Flattened
21 Like some affairs
22 Most abundant in calcium oxide
24 Like some trauma patients
25 County whose seat is Las Cruces
26 Rag of a sort
28 Court contests
29 Costner character
30 Word Perfect producer
33 Spray holder
36 High hats
39 Thomas Arne, for one
41 Cackles
44 Put away more than
46 Balkan republic, in combination
48 Phone's lack, maybe
49 Where I-79 ends
50 Cinematographer Nykvist
51 G3 or G4
52 *The Role of the Reader* author
53 They're moved in games
54 Roth ___
55 One kept in the bag?
56 Chemical ending

ANSWER, PAGE 241

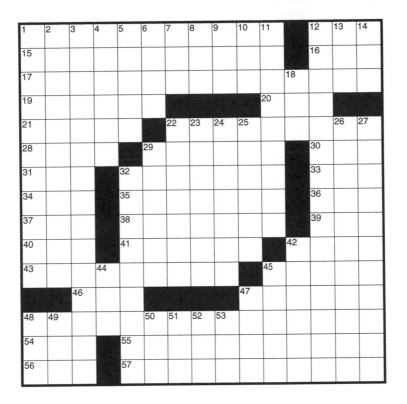

20

ACROSS

1 Where to find faults
12 Chestnut
15 "You Got It" singer
16 Score quickly?
17 Bad things to breach
19 Bind, in a way
20 Tablet holder
21 What a joke may evoke
22 Chicken Little
28 Cheek
29 One who may have made a mark?
30 V.P. under GRF
31 German pronoun
32 Trattoria treat
33 D-Day transport
34 Former Quaker cereal
35 Jazzman Coleman
36 End of some URLs

37 It may be in the air
38 Jason, e.g.
39 Hoover, e.g., for short
40 Chemical suffix
41 Like some glass
42 Unintentional habit that gives away a poker player's hand
43 First to be credited, perhaps
45 "Did I Shave My Legs for This?" singer Carter
46 Canada's Campbell
47 Some pizzas
48 1979 Henry Kissinger book
54 Unit in astronomy
55 Not yet proven
56 Early bird?
57 Snakebite fighters: Var.

DOWN

1 Very hard to shake, perhaps
2 Public soft-drink dispenser, e.g.
3 Like Liberia
4 History
5 Great-___
6 Eliot title character
7 Frodo's foe
8 Eastern way
9 Bolivian export
10 He had 1,860 RBIs
11 WA high point
12 1977 L.T.D. hit
13 Show piece?
14 Survey choice
18 A bandit may have one
22 Emblem of victory
23 Mr. Maserati
24 Envelop

25 Like anchovies, often
26 Part of the parasympathetic system
27 People may consider all the angles in them
29 It may be pressed in the kitchen
32 Vanguard University locale
42 Approximately cylindrical
44 Morse click
45 "A ___ the Life"
47 Majesty lead-in
48 Bit modifier
49 Take all of
50 Barbarian
51 Elect
52 Wire org.
53 King, e.g.: Abbr.

ANSWER, PAGE 243

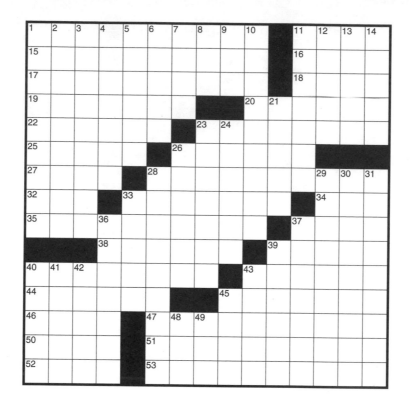

21

ACROSS

 1 *Show Boat* director
11 Lick makeup
15 Like some ships
16 It may be retractable
17 Followed suit
18 Span creator
19 Echo
20 Shampooing step
22 Ravigote ingredients
23 Twang producer
25 Quiet
26 Chesapeake Bay vessel
27 Junk, e.g.
28 Successfully completed
32 Atlanta Hawks coach Kruger
33 Descriptor for Hartsfield Airport

34 36th prime number, to Nero
35 They may make pupils shrink
37 Kind of orchard
38 Wildlife
39 Set up
40 Is a bad player, perhaps
43 Of a zodiacal constellation
44 Helen of Troy portrayer of 1953
45 Trace
46 Chisholm Trail city
47 Cause of some long lines in 1973
50 Spacious yard, perhaps
51 Shooting effect
52 Storied speakeasy raider
53 Reassures

DOWN

 1 Apt to be tried
 2 *A Girl Like I* autobiographer
 3 Thought ahead, in a way
 4 Beg
 5 *Boys Town* screenwriter
 6 Stimulates
 7 It may transport air
 8 One of Knute's successors
 9 Writer Stanislaw
10 It grows high in the Alps
11 Mowed, in a way
12 "Hi, Ho!"
13 Wordsworth, Coleridge, or Southey
14 Weenie
21 To date

23 Case studiers
24 Ornamental plume sources
26 Maximally mean
28 Transected
29 Tanks in a zoo, perhaps
30 Yardbirds?
31 Rubber giant
33 One way to play
36 Rubs down
37 Turn the hand, in a way
39 Wired woman
40 It's in Wow! chips
41 Air Force Base located in Oklahoma
42 Some heads of state
43 Headword
45 Gym set
48 Ending for Brooklyn or Manhattan
49 Good deal

ANSWER, PAGE 245

22

ACROSS

1 City devastated by a January 1999 earthquake
16 Boxers may develop them
17 It's earned in two years
18 Singer in R.E.M.
19 Davis of Hollywood
20 Slams gratuitously
26 Added gratuitously
27 Field goal?
31 Chips Ahoy! alternative
32 Mark for life
36 Debussy's dream
37 *Muchachos y muchachas*
38 Mozart's "Rondo ___ Turca"
39 Epigone
40 Sans significance
41 Diner in a Suzanne Vega song
42 Doesn't give any stars, perhaps
43 Ham-and-___ (bum)
44 Yesterday, so to speak
45 Equilibrium maintainer
46 Gives forth
47 Scale pair
48 Grace periods?
50 Stir
51 Baio's sitcom costar
52 Superlatively stingy
54 Appraise
56 Like some diseases
57 Proves
58 In
59 Cops, at times

DOWN

1 In ___ (immobilized, sort of)
2 One with dreaded hair?
3 Berlin Orchestra output
4 Bond on the run
5 Least like Legree
6 Tony Toni Tone's "___ Had No Loot"
7 Like
8 Rollaway alternative
9 Have a loan from
10 Chaired
11 Where the John Day flows
12 "Let ___ this straight ..."
13 Reveals
14 *Faerie Queene* character
15 "Have ___" (host's exhortation)
21 Mountebanks
22 Joseph R. Biden's successor
23 In the minority?
24 Became ecstatic upon seeing
25 Cross cats, perhaps
27 Taj Mahal attractions
28 Lender's expectation
29 Dressed and stuffed in advance, perhaps
30 Human resources department
32 Idled
33 Track nail-biter
34 Source of old school ties
35 Irritability
49 It's good for the long haul
51 Philip I's birth date
53 Childhood bedroom sharer, maybe
55 Her third husband was Frank

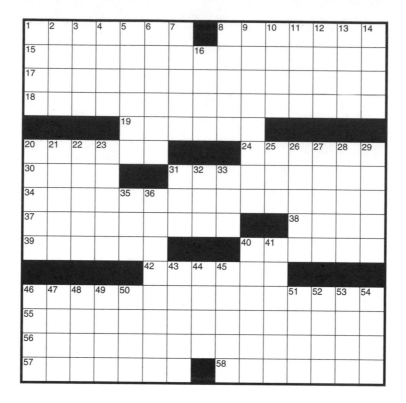

23

ACROSS

1 It gives some baked goods a kick
8 Like some bookcases
15 Concern of Wade and Giles
17 T cells and B cells are involved in them
18 People who benefit the most, maybe
19 Abode of the wretched
20 Out, in a way
24 Like some cases
30 "Breaking ___ Hard to Do"
31 Over 5, in a way
34 Military rule
37 Kind of commuter program
38 Playwright's dream
39 Milano of movies
40 Their work may be on the house
42 Yeshiva staff
46 Eliciting a flood of thank-yous
55 Economist's concern
56 They cause some expansions
57 Matisse work
58 Expressed disdain

DOWN

1 End of Gregory the Great's papacy
2 Wistful words
3 Flanges
4 Nobelist novelist Hamsun
5 Crawfish
6 All gone
7 Have coming
8 Tack up, perhaps
9 Public figure not recognized by the government
10 Oistrakh or Ozim of the violin
11 *Terre* orbiter
12 *Pure Luck* director Nadia
13 Janet Jackson's "___ Lonely"
14 Stack part
16 Spring stretch
20 One of the Barkleys on *The Big Valley*
21 Turn into a brat?
22 Jitterbug variety
23 He ran with Adlai in 1956
25 Crib sheet user?
26 Chorus section
27 Billy Blanks's brainstorm
28 Florida Air Force Base
29 Take-out orders?
31 Forerunner of rock steady
32 Burnable computer data holder
33 Weed, in a way
35 It may be burdened
36 Gets ready to write with, perhaps
40 Native of Hijaz's capital
41 Pungent Italian cheese
43 Lederer who's known as Ann Landers
44 Gas-operated machine gun
45 They may do stern damage
46 Grinder
47 Fit for the forces
48 Amberjack relative
49 *"Shana ___!"* (Hebrew "Happy holidays!")
50 Revival comeback
51 Monkey
52 Shade
53 Wagon attachment?
54 Acronym for a disk drive

ANSWER, PAGE 249

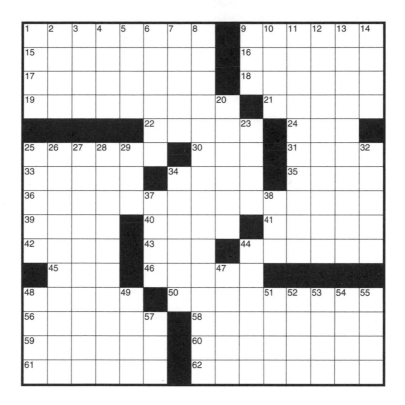

24

ACROSS

1 "Queen of Soul"
9 Queen of literature
15 "Lost in Emotion" singer
16 Lake Erie feeder
17 Shakes up
18 Haunt
19 Links hazard
21 Play, in a way
22 One whose targets may be electric
24 Lady's man
25 Cat, e.g.
30 Davis was its pres.
31 Soviet attack submarine
33 No exemplar of erudition
34 Oom Paul or Jan Smuts
35 Motorist's misery
36 Stumping schemes
39 Hilton Coliseum locale
40 The Beatles' "___ Pony"
41 Bank buildup?
42 Shirt-tag irritation point
43 It may appear before long
44 Soprano Stratas
45 Diddly
46 1942 Preakness winner
48 *Die Fledermaus* maid
50 Connected stores, perhaps
56 Time out
58 Working together
59 Not inclined
60 Blade sharpener
61 Moral
62 Retirees may use them

DOWN

1 Design problem
2 Baryshnikov's birthplace
3 "___ happens ..."
4 Newton of the NFL
5 "*Alles* ___" ("Understood," in Ulm)
6 One may pick from it
7 Grenoble's department
8 Cold development
9 First name in zany comedy
10 Test sites
11 Really wants
12 Food Network hit
13 Comes up again
14 Huck Finn's affirmative
20 Spanish mint product
23 Uncommon, to Ulpian
25 Puerto ___
26 Fall figures
27 They have hands and faces
28 They fly off the shelves
29 Greek figure
32 One way to be lost
34 Tavern temptresses
37 Boardroom presentation
38 Key, in Cannes
44 They bear no interest
47 Becker on *L.A. Law*
48 Lake ___ (Amu Darya's outlet)
49 Sinclair competitor
51 Raid target
52 Bad news for the king
53 In a swivet
54 Anatomical expander
55 Wine-vat waste
57 Clinton, e.g.: Abbr.

25

ACROSS

1 Features of some PCs
11 Kind of suit
15 Shot from the sky
16 Fresh
17 New face on base, perhaps
18 Brogna of baseball
19 First Lady before Florence
20 Picky people?
22 *Grand Illusion* director
24 Union contract
25 Beezers
29 Portrayer of Midge in *I'm Not Rappaport*
30 Fuel efficiency abbr.
33 It's symbolized by the loon
35 *Kanthapura* novelist
36 Pontiac and others
37 Marshaled
38 Still-unresolved issues
40 Bears make them
41 Silvery fish
42 Niggled
44 Oddsmaker's calculation
46 Looked at, with "out"
50 Screening procedures for tuberculosis
54 Peter Allen's "I Go ___"
55 Sickeningly smelly
56 A question of blame
58 It smells
59 Kind of firearm
60 Song ending
61 They'll get back to you

DOWN

1 Check writer, in part
2 Val ___ (Texas county whose seat is Del Rio)
3 Creator of a small whirlpool
4 They're spotted on ranches
5 Really reproving
6 Tanner family visitor
7 Pianist Jean-___ Thibaudet
8 Colleen's land
9 Fall back
10 Compass
11 Most cutting
12 Spice-rack selection
13 Was a service provider?
14 Some motors
21 Sample showing all characteristic parts
23 They may be showing
26 Some kind of nerve
27 "More ___ Woman" (Tavares hit)
28 No pleasant workplace
30 Vessel volume units
31 Handy computer?
32 Refurbish, in Reading
34 Irritates
39 Parasite
43 Jigger
45 Flask-inventing chemist
47 Destruction preceder
48 Goldeneye relative
49 They may be cracked
51 *Leaving Las Vegas* costar
52 Body art, slangily
53 Wire word
57 Brown of the WWF

ANSWER, PAGE 253

26

ACROSS

1 It's a shore thing
5 Sound from the litter
8 Schubert's "___ Militaire"
14 *Namouna* composer
15 North Yorkshire river
16 Attic areas
17 Very little
18 French flower
19 Shock successfully, perhaps
20 No perfect couple
22 Love: German
23 Only New World monkey with a short tail
24 Cry from the fold
26 Cry from the fold
28 Humored
31 Russ Westover heroine
32 Cannes cordial flavoring
33 Paralleling
38 Wind in a pit
39 Yield
40 Step toward perfection?
46 Nursery purchase
47 On ___ (similarly valued)
48 Place for *películas*
49 Convolution
51 Apple tree
53 Madonna's "___/Ashtangi"
54 With 30-Down, 1977 role for Alec
55 "Only ___" (Oingo Boingo title track)
56 Older version of "Yo, dude"
57 Hearing aid?
58 Bit
59 Leblanc's Lupin
60 Ordinal ending
61 Kind of mocha

DOWN

1 Stop speaking
2 Spokewise
3 Willow locale
4 2000 PGA Championship runner-up
5 Combined curricula
6 Cager Montross
7 Activists' assertion, maybe
8 "The Boys in the Back Room" singer
9 Unstoppable process
10 Proceed peripatetically
11 Plagiarism
12 "Dig in!"
13 Race conclusion?
21 Feature of the Rockies
25 Monks, in Marseilles
27 Facetious phrase of comprehension
29 Member of the genus *Lama*
30 See 54-Across
33 Heat
34 Start of a Coen comedy title
35 Catwalks may be next to them
36 Fun, for short
37 Smaller picture, perhaps
41 Trews material
42 It may be on a torpedo
43 Not straight, in a way
44 Hardly plain
45 Became careless
50 Etta James's "Trust ___"
52 It may contain funeral plans
53 First "word" of "Get a Job"

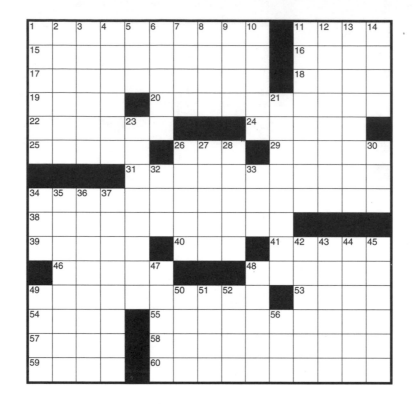

27

ACROSS

1 Hearty approval
11 People making physical contact?
15 #1 hit of 1941
16 About
17 Flack
18 Racket
19 Off to one side
20 Khamenei's successor
22 Academy Awards array
24 Flat parts
25 Pathetic
26 Shock treatment: Abbr.
29 Deceive
31 #1 hit of 1977
34 Achim von Arnim's *Des Knaben Wunderhorn* collaborator
38 Pastoral activity
39 "My Eyes Adored You" singer
40 Milk, in prescriptions
41 *The Hot Zone* topic
46 Word before well or water
48 Boodles
49 *Blues Suite* choreographer
53 It may follow a proposition
54 Hold
55 Emulate Kenny Lofton
57 ___ *Reader*
58 1952 literary debut
59 Skilled canner, perhaps
60 Workout formation

DOWN

1 Influence
2 James's *Dead Silence* costar
3 Anatomical interstice
4 One who says grace incorrectly?
5 Part of U.N.L.V.
6 They may be faced
7 Figure skater Markova
8 Place to run aground
9 Travel guide listing
10 Kazan resident
11 Having no common elements, as two sets in math
12 Being shot
13 The Shadow's alter ego
14 Rig
21 Not anymore
23 Not accidentally, perhaps
26 Henry's son
27 Mongoose's quarry
28 Like a doughnut
30 John Lennon's middle name
32 Soldier on the hill?
33 Spumco cartoon character
34 Year in Sergius III's papacy
35 Having a predisposition for
36 Stimulates
37 Dinar divisions
42 Seat of Cochise County, Arizona
43 Half a Beatles title
44 Like some cars
45 Trembling flora
47 Moderates
48 One way to be chosen
49 Rub-___
50 "... ___ a puddy tat!"
51 Literally, "injured"
52 "Peach" preceder
56 Patrick or Peterson: Abbr.

ANSWER, PAGE 257

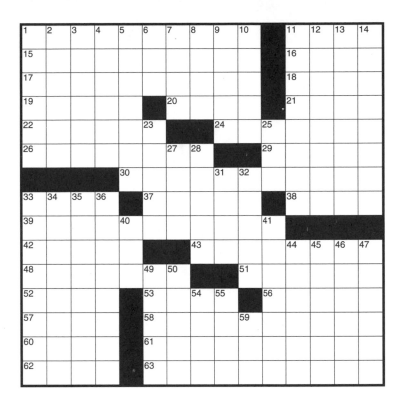

28

ACROSS

1 It may be pulled
11 It may be pulled
15 Radially symmetric creature
16 Paper section
17 Enters
18 Good opponent?
19 Angelou's *Still* ___
20 It may be prepared meunière
21 Satisfying start?
22 Least certifiable?
24 Like some disturbances
26 News source since 1992
29 She replaced Dixie on *Entertainment Tonight*
30 One on the slopes, perhaps
33 Cantonese caregiver
37 What some dogs do
38 Nature
39 Unchoosable
42 All together, in scores
43 Expression said before a bold act
48 Very quickly
51 Twisted
52 Tiffing
53 What blood may do
56 Senator from Texas
57 Mystery writer Faye Kellerman's Lazarus
58 Body image?
60 Gulf of ___
61 *Lady Be Good* star
62 Lyre player, perhaps
63 They're often sheeted

DOWN

1 Umbrian town
2 View badly?
3 Gloria Estefan, e.g.
4 He nationalized the Suez Canal
5 Overruns
6 Prefix with science
7 Cigna offerings
8 Gulch biter
9 Organic compounds
10 Taylor of movies
11 Iron-fisted people?
12 #1 hit of 1964
13 One who exercises
14 Car for the course
23 Emulate Frank Slade in *Scent of a Woman*
25 Stevedores' org.
27 Cock-a-leekie, e.g.
28 Mower's creation
31 It's mold-ripened
32 Locker room collection
33 Like some violence in the Middle East
34 Cretan high point
35 Reaching one
36 Put a lid on it
40 *Ladders to Fire* novelist
41 Historic London prison
44 Measures around
45 Emulates Cicero
46 Creator of Maximum Bob
47 Poet Arthur
49 Presidential middle name
50 City southeast of Bombay
54 Lacks entity
55 It may appear before we forget
59 Craggy crest

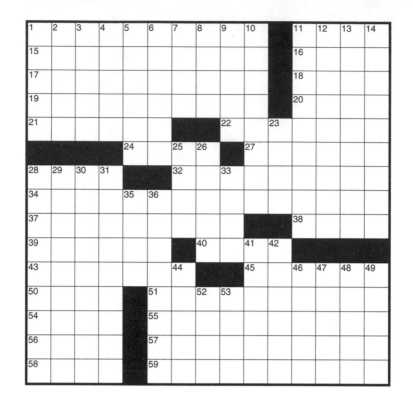

29

ACROSS

1 Unreal
11 Han ___ (river in China)
15 One may go around the world in it
16 Alpine pool
17 Way around for the well-to-do
18 Such-is linkup
19 Things that are heat-driven?
20 You may experience it on the road
21 Rack unit
22 *Death in Venice* composer
24 Scene of heavy WWI fighting
27 Disney's "Lucky Rabbit"
28 It may be in a locker
32 It's north of Newfoundland
34 It may require shifting
37 Some Numic speakers
38 One of a matching pair, perhaps
39 Young or Brown
40 Rather follower
43 Do
45 Start to steam
50 Prefix with protein
51 Pick up
54 Ben Hecht's ___ *Dorn*
55 Examined more closely
56 No pan
57 With bounce
58 Ranger, e.g., briefly
59 Successful people, often

DOWN

1 *Where's ___?* (1970 George Segal film)
2 Iroquoian tongue
3 Inclined
4 Author Shute
5 She played Carol on *Growing Pains*
6 Late bloomers
7 Kind of sheet
8 Goya's *La ___ vestida*
9 Limy?
10 Todd Beamer's 9/11/01 rallying cry
11 Instruction opener
12 Tries, with "of"
13 James Randi book subject
14 People who plan
23 "Gotcha"
25 Israeli foreign minister, 1966–1974
26 Roll back, say
28 Hegira
29 Fleeting
30 Transfusion specification
31 One who's made final preparations?
33 Grateful Dead bassist
35 Saturn satellite
36 *Hopscotch* novelist Julio
41 Bright
42 Must
44 ___-Car
46 Like some cases
47 Niger-Congo language branch
48 Kwajalein, for one
49 *Love and Human Remains* director Arcand
52 Ignition system component
53 *Fashion Emergency* host

ANSWER, PAGE 244

30

ACROSS

1 Protestant theologian Arminius
8 Many a middle-schooler
15 Earth, e.g.
16 It may follow a big win
17 Where malmsey is made
18 Hardly hostile
19 Way to raise your voice
20 One of a *Clueless* bunch
21 Superlatively swampish
22 Field hockey term
23 Took part in an operation
25 Nag
27 Nigerian natives
29 Conductor Lehman
30 Nodding acquaintance, perhaps
36 Quarterback image?
37 Star burst
38 A matter of *Time*
40 Some heroes
46 Serengeti sight
48 Jack Kirby collaborator
49 Zip
50 It may come out of the woodwork
51 Some triathletes
52 Breakout planners, perhaps
53 Most sharp
54 Superlatively submissive
55 Holds
56 *El Túnel* novelist Sábato

DOWN

1 Veronica's role on *Daniel Boone*
2 Grammy winner Morissette
3 David Guterson's *Snow Falling on ___*
4 "Damien" follower
5 Cloths made of natural undyed wool
6 Having slept fitfully
7 Got to
8 Nannies' burdens, in Birmingham
9 Be left
10 No saint
11 *The Naked Truth* star
12 Gerry for whom "gerrymander" is named
13 City north of Nuremberg
14 Putin's veto
24 "It'll ___ now"
26 Antiquity, in antiquity
28 Kills two birds with one stone, perhaps
30 *Coup de ___* (gun discharge, in France)
31 Aquarium minnows
32 They do the lighting
33 Fashionable woman
34 Recruit
35 Snap, e.g.
39 Least buggy
41 Opera set in Seville
42 Destroy
43 Influential groups
44 School makeup
45 Handles
47 Revival sites, sometimes
49 Actress Talbot

ANSWER, PAGE 246

31

ACROSS

1 University of Tasmania city
16 Fogerty hit
17 Like some disorders
18 Like some Mass recitations
19 Nucleoside involved in carbohydrate metabolism
20 Some deer
21 Business letters
23 Haggadah recitation occasion
24 She corresponded with Henry
26 It's hardly heart-healthy
36 It's in SHAPE
37 Be creative
38 Source of night sweats?
42 Rooting part
43 A sister may get into it
48 Tossed mail, maybe
49 "Slave, I have set my life upon ___" (*Richard III*)
54 Old floral crowns
56 Charcoal holder
58 Having no dearth of delegates
60 Quiddity
61 It may be carefully folded

DOWN

1 One may be played
2 It may display subtitles
3 2000 Republican primary candidate
4 Stop: French
5 Crosses
6 Kind of concerto
7 Kind of dye
8 Ginseng relative
9 Its capital is Castries
10 Wrestler of Elli
11 Kelly's co-host
12 Bear
13 French play by Pierre Corneille about a Spanish hero
14 Lacking a point
15 "Inferiority complex" coiner
22 Photographer Goldin
24 Golden ___
25 High-stepper's need?
26 Laughing sound
27 Gertrude's Broadway costar
28 "Still ___" (1999 rap song)
29 Sinbad's transport
30 Go (for)
31 Self-help author LeShan
32 Wolf's creation
33 Iowa symbol
34 Fossil finisher?
35 Court ruling?
39 Confused
40 It may be filleted
41 Heaps
43 *Our Mutual Friend* actress Keeley ___
44 "___ of robins ..."
45 Tree of the bombax family
46 Goldbrick
47 Mackerel gulls
49 Cross as ___
50 The Cure's "Why ___ Be You?"
51 Carry on
52 First name in sex research
53 They fall periodically
55 Physical starter
57 First word of "Send in the Clowns"
59 1986 movie about BMX racing

ANSWER, PAGE 248

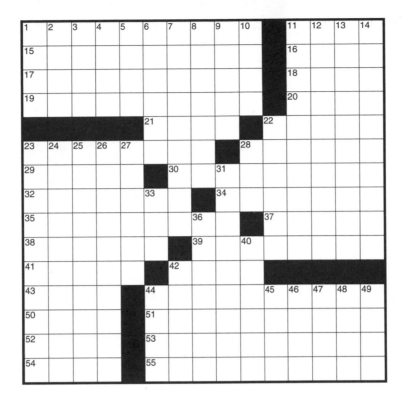

32

ACROSS

1 Barbershop tops?
11 Excited
15 Did novel work?
16 ___-dieu
17 Phrase of projection
18 Barrage
19 Like a one-way sign arrow
20 Shortening
21 Take ___ view of
22 Block
23 Judge wrongly
28 Foolish remark
29 Beneath, in Brunswick
30 Larks
32 Ovation offerer, often
34 Mooning group
35 Slowpokes
37 Rung
38 Hospital doctor, perhaps
39 Got into
41 Shows respect, in a way
42 Genesis figure
43 Bionomics: Abbr.
44 Enjoying a white bed?
50 *Licence to Kill* actor
51 Stoppage
52 The Wildcats beat them in 1998
53 Kind of monosaccharide
54 Set of a sort
55 Ruler of Scotland, 1306–1329

DOWN

1 Clement Moore poem opener
2 *Ben-Hur* costume designer
3 Kid's punishment, perhaps
4 "Sign ___ Times" (Prince title track)
5 Means of control
6 Bavarian river port
7 People known for cutting remarks?
8 Band aides
9 Venerated emblem
10 Program, briefly
11 Patisserie products
12 Genius's output
13 Teapot Dome, e.g.
14 Throw something on
22 Oust
23 Summoned
24 Put under the table?
25 Takes it from the top
26 "Perspiration," vis-à-vis "sweat"
27 Passions
28 Spoiled
31 Like a waterfall
33 A as in Austria
36 Enters cautiously
40 Moving arrow, maybe
42 Lacquer resin
44 Lake Oahe loc.
45 "___ happens ..."
46 Spread, as plaster
47 *A Loss of Roses* playwright
48 I-77 runs through it
49 *Goldfinger* portrayer Fröbe

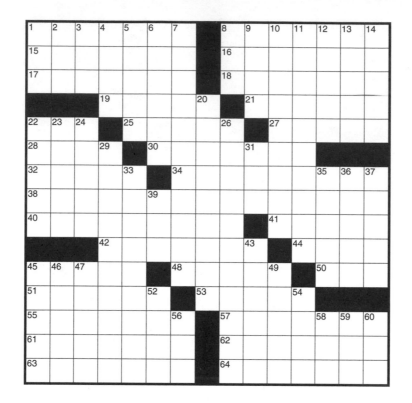

33

ACROSS

1 Capital of Georgia
8 Capital of Georgia
15 Working parent's morning stop, maybe
16 Fast time for Muslims?
17 One risking a citation
18 Pancreas production
19 Exorcism target
21 Far from flustered
22 Truncation abbreviation
25 Caftans
27 Isn't active
28 Rhythmic swing
30 Kind of comb
32 Construction-site sight
34 Red-headed comedian Scott Thompson's stage name
38 Terminal precautions?
40 Jaybird's state?
41 Meal in which knaidlach are eaten
42 Billet-doux beginner
44 Contemporary of Alvar and I.M.
45 Astrologer Sydney
48 Any of five pontiffs
50 Troubled telegraphy
51 Texas-Louisiana border river
53 Takes ten in a tub
55 Haberdashery purchases
57 How partners work
61 Fujimori of Peru
62 *Raising Cain* director
63 Like some peanuts
64 Bugs Bunny, self-admittedly

DOWN

1 Show stoppers
2 Surveillance set-up
3 Leaching product
4 Didn't merely pass
5 LaDuke ran with him
6 Earth mover?
7 Intestinal tract residents
8 Centennial opener
9 They may be lifted
10 "No joke!"
11 Small European evergreen
12 Hangs out
13 One may be a patron
14 Weaver's portrayer on *ER*
20 Corporation concern
22 González in 1999 news
23 It articulates with the talus
24 Bob Cratchit, e.g.
26 Quality assurance concerns
29 CD-R alternatives
31 Compass-drawn line, e.g.
33 20th-century busts, e.g.
35 Daily risers
36 Its seat is Alamogordo
37 People who love lighting?
39 It's stranded in the body
43 China ensemble
45 Picture prize
46 Thomas of TV
47 Addis ___
49 Giraffidae family member
52 Ranch add-on?
54 Friend of Eric, Kyle, and Kenny
56 Settlers' building material
58 Four-legged bugler
59 Simone's soul
60 Spoil

ANSWER, PAGE 252

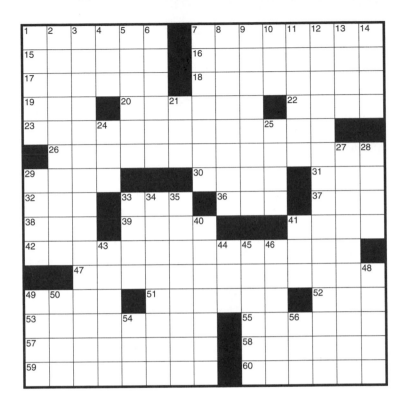

34

ACROSS

 1 They're usually found in floats
 7 Man of letters?
15 A-frame, perhaps
16 Protein granules in the seeds of cereal plants
17 Source of a light, soft wood
18 Bad thing to drive over
19 The Diamondbacks, on scoreboards
20 Generic
22 Soon enough
23 A dove may be a part of one
26 Disk drives, e.g.
29 Kind of alert
30 She ranks in Raipur
31 With 42-Across, how some statistics are calculated

32 Maxwell Anderson's *High ___*
33 *Cosmo*, e.g.
36 Letters on some MLB caps
37 CCCLXVII tripled
38 Web address ending
39 "Bloom County" character
41 *Diary of ___ Housewife*
42 See 31-Across
47 "Gladly!"
49 King's civil-rights gp.
51 Shred
52 1979 accident scene: Abbr.
53 Light bulb component
55 Hold a follow-up conference
57 Being there
58 Dentist's supply
59 Left for good

60 South Carolina river or beach

DOWN

 1 Junk
 2 Continuation segue
 3 Auto-parts store stock
 4 TV ET
 5 Pulitzer winner for *The Beak of the Finch*
 6 Cell's supporting framework
 7 Conference
 8 Shady walks
 9 Slums sight
10 Opposite of *nord*
11 Big name in fashion
12 Bipartisan appointments
13 Year in Caesar's reign
14 Very sensitive
21 It may be taken in during the holidays

24 No big wheel
25 One of two forces
27 Covering
28 Didn't merely think
29 F follower
33 Town near Arches National Park
34 Eagerly desirous
35 PG part
40 Kept in print, in a way
41 Olive relative
43 Music holder of a sort
44 Relief map info: Abbr.
45 *The Devil's Dictionary* author
46 "My thoughts exactly"
48 "My thoughts exactly"
49 Dirty Harry's gp.
50 Wax: French
54 Debussy subject
56 When Bush took office

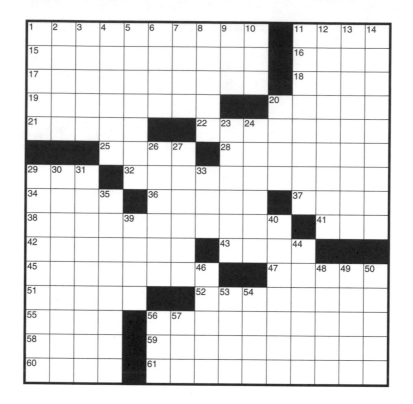

35

ACROSS

1 Song on the album *The Who By Numbers*
11 Jack took his title in 1919
15 Member of the genus *Carica*
16 Forerunner
17 Like some competitive athletes
18 Word in many Mannheim Steamroller album titles
19 Yakov Smirnoff and Emil Gilels, by birth
20 Period of *douze mois*
21 PLO's Al ___
22 Pioneering automotive engineer
25 Terry's role in a 1939 classic
28 Gallimaufry
29 Finish a letter, perhaps
32 Some suits
34 Phrase from a dictator?
36 "Copperhead Road" singer
37 ___ potential (electrical measure)
38 Symbol of the industrial revolution
41 Be on the bottom?
42 ___ Cross
43 It may appear ahead of time
45 Hindered
47 Soda flavor
51 Violinist Morini
52 Tune from *Beatles For Sale*
55 Menu item
56 Personal watercraft choice
58 "That's clear"
59 Parentless people
60 Melanie Griffith's *Working Girl* role
61 Repaired metal objects, maybe

DOWN

1 Send up
2 Seminar part, perhaps
3 Rock
4 Wears down gradually
5 Sight
6 *The Jeffersons* actress Cully
7 Neighbor of Windsor Castle
8 Lively
9 It's full of citations: Abbr.
10 Indicates a choice, in a way
11 Humanitas International founder
12 High stations
13 Where some buffalo roam
14 Scorns
20 Art Garfunkel's "___ Know"
23 Social reformer Bloomer
24 Evangelical exhortation
26 "Period"
27 Santa Ana's county
29 Smear
30 Going up
31 Essays
33 Centimeter-gram-second unit
35 They may be caused by altitude adjustments
39 *Mississippi Masala* director Nair
40 Robert of *A Nightmare on Elm Street*
44 Football player ___ Gadsden
46 They may get high onstage
48 He played Richards's boss
49 Gall
50 Slipped
53 Message from upstairs, maybe
54 Shrinking Asian sea
56 Dove's dislike
57 Gator's tail?

ANSWER, PAGE 256

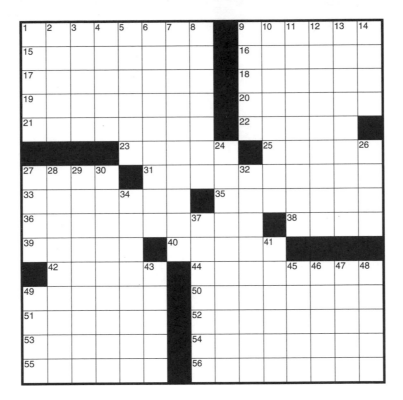

36

ACROSS

1 Yore
9 Like some rules
15 Aphrodite's golden apples distracted her
16 *The Ransom of Red Chief* author
17 Befitting an old man?
18 One that makes a noticeable impression?
19 It may be found on trattoria tables
20 *The Big Parade* costar
21 Failure to sign up
22 Came out of a slump?
23 Dash devices
25 *La Dolce Vita* actress Gray
27 Carriage

31 Philosophical book supposedly written by Lao-tzu
33 Whose guess it may be
35 City on the Susquehanna
36 Film about a group of artistes in 1926 Paris
38 They sometimes clash
39 Van ___
40 *Queen Kelly* costar Owen
42 Bagel alternative
44 Wises
49 Feathers, in zoology
50 Perth suburb
51 Big blasts
52 People of Indian descent, in Africa
53 Elton's songwriting partner
54 Signifies

55 Some destructive acts
56 Machines, tools, and mechanical devices

DOWN

1 Strike lightly and repeatedly
2 *Confessions of Zeno* novelist Svevo
3 Early-morning
4 Pupil with *une plume*
5 Excuse writer
6 Like a study Bible
7 You may take them down
8 It may arouse the hounds
9 They're kept behind bars
10 1910 Matisse painting
11 Washoe County airport

12 Gate-crasher's activity
13 Become evident gradually
14 Cornwall whitewall
24 Producer of monumental works?
26 "What ___!"
27 It's full of problems
28 Denizen
29 Some come in pencils
30 Exasperated refusal
32 Pitfall's purpose
34 Like the Greek alphabet, e.g.
37 Make it easier to read between the lines?
41 Versace competitor
43 Approves
45 Wyoming peak
46 Four Hundred
47 More like Nelly
48 Wise, in a way
49 Sunscreen ingredient

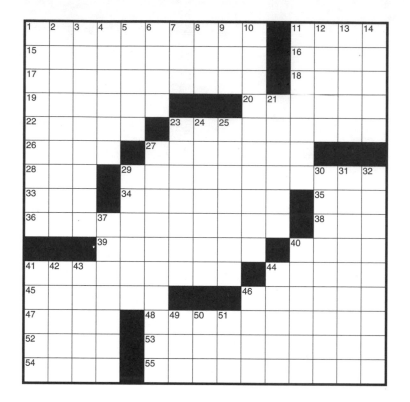

37

ACROSS

1 Breakfast brand
11 Breakfast brand
15 *Rudolph the Red-Nosed Reindeer* uses it
16 Deep blue
17 Vonnegut novel featuring the religion Bokononism
18 One third of a 1970 war epic
19 Releases, in a way
20 *The Robots of Dawn* author
22 Notre Dame splits it
23 Bad taste
26 Piz Bernina and others
27 *Suite for Flute and Jazz Piano Trio* composer
28 Fluffy wrap
29 Sports drink, e.g.
33 Fail to keep up with
34 Wild-animal tracking aids
35 Good feller
36 Minneapolis suburb
38 Set a setter on, say
39 Wedding parties?
40 Tut's relative
41 Avocational
44 Dancer's guider
45 Jack Lemmon comedy
46 Feature of some sloping roofs
47 Fauré's *Après un ___*
48 Icing over
52 Shell team
53 1950 Preakness champion and Horse of the Year
54 Disrespect, in a way
55 Doesn't straddle the fence, perhaps

DOWN

1 Like a perp
2 As many as can be carried, perhaps
3 "Hush Hush, Sweet Charlotte" singer
4 They cause the disintegration of bacterial cells
5 Act introducer
6 Rattles
7 One-time filler
8 *El ___* (1961 epic film)
9 *___ Nidre* (Yom Kippur prayer)
10 Entering through a window, perhaps
11 Ingesta
12 Guardian of the earth's treasures, in folklore
13 Copters' forerunners
14 Several Norse kings
21 *Truman* star
23 Five-star
24 Never greater
25 Less doubtful
27 Makes a fork decision?
29 Kind of performance
30 Is thinking of
31 Philosopher's topic
32 Plugs in overnight, perhaps
37 Airer of an *Overnight* show
40 "The Return of ..." alternative
41 People who deal with traffic violations?
42 ___ barrel
43 Places for pews
44 Skyrockets
46 Minor market downturns
49 *Skylight* Tony nominee Williams
50 Having a high pH: Abbr.
51 Key: French

ANSWER, PAGE 241

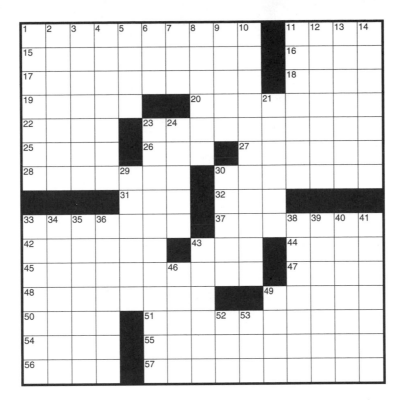

38

ACROSS

1 On-line game, perhaps
11 Its capital is Singaraja
15 Red flag alternative
16 Like some tempers
17 "You'll regret it!"
18 Jazzy ostinato
19 Robert Baden-Powell, for one
20 Let up
22 Danube feeder
23 Makes understandable, perhaps
25 Object in a wild goose chase?
26 She turned Tithonus into a grasshopper
27 Long Island horse-racing venue
28 Bills may be stuffed in it
30 Gives
31 Weather report abbr.
32 You may have a tun of it
33 Throws caution to the wind
37 Dress part
42 Spots
43 Beginning of creation?
44 It joins the Fulda
45 Earned credits, perhaps
47 Bad thing to be under
48 Like the Yupik language
49 Yield of some orchards
50 WWI fighter plane
51 Emma Peel portrayer
54 Point at the table
55 Dunlop product
56 Snick-a-___
57 Providing pull

DOWN

1 Making a painful connection
2 Rap sheet collection
3 No permanent resident
4 Mail man?
5 Cole Porter's "I ___ Love"
6 Rose's network
7 Boxer in the house, e.g.
8 Pack with packs, perhaps
9 *Boswell* novelist
10 Dangerous swarm
11 Italian province or its capital
12 One may raise a flap
13 One of two side boundaries
14 Uses as a host
21 Starving
23 Where some stroking occurs
24 He may help you find the right word
29 It runs up one's leg
30 *Zapped!* star
33 Second chances for students
34 Baryonic property
35 Expo '74 locale
36 "I've Got the Music in Me" singer
38 Cite
39 He was exiled to Saudi Arabia
40 Lamborghini's birthplace
41 One trillion cycles per second
43 London locale
46 Football Hall-of-Famer Hunt
49 Hungarian sheepdog
52 Trigeminal neuralgia
53 It may be banded

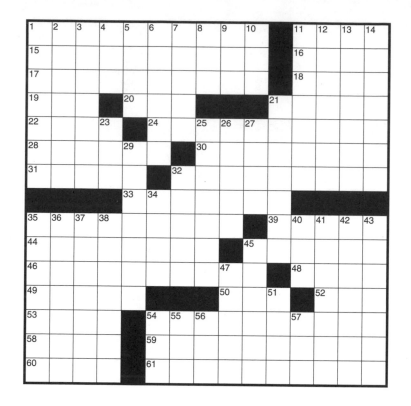

39

ACROSS

1 It features "The Style Guy"
11 Attention attractor
15 Repugnant
16 Canard
17 Entering gingerly
18 Automatic advancements of a sort
19 Aurobindo Ghose's title
20 People in a mess
21 Mathematical grouping
22 The Ponte Vecchio crosses it
24 He played Hamlet
28 Finest examples
30 Unsheltered, in a way
31 Choice
32 Drivers may swing them down
33 People who get the goods, legally
35 Turned over again
39 *American Song* poet Paul
44 One putting the screws on
45 Kind of plane
46 Contents of a picture book?
48 ___ cow (flipped)
49 Like some New Testament passages
50 It may symbolize loss
52 Jazz cornetist Adderley
53 *Einstein's Monsters* author
54 He exposed Uri Geller
58 Ten mills
59 A fee may be charged for it
60 Cube component
61 Annual gift for Czar Alexander III

DOWN

1 Loses it
2 Words, so to speak
3 Exodus setting
4 *Exodus* hero
5 Side in a war, perhaps
6 New Mexico State team
7 City near Utrecht
8 Attractive little thing
9 Loony
10 Pamplona pronoun
11 Vessels like McHale's
12 Response to a dubious assertion
13 More streamlined
14 People giving final warning?
21 Deck furniture
23 Leaving
25 Trucks, at times
26 Like wheat
27 She played Sidney in *Scream*
29 New Yorker alternative
32 They may be historic
34 Uffizi pieces
35 Cover for
36 Brought to light
37 Fireman's job
38 Way of salting
40 Highest
41 Ma of a ma
42 Terhune book
43 More than pleasing
45 Private reply?
47 Product of glaciation
51 Some people perform in it
54 Peter Pan rival
55 Memorable saying, say
56 1997 blockbuster, briefly
57 Got something down

ANSWER, PAGE 245

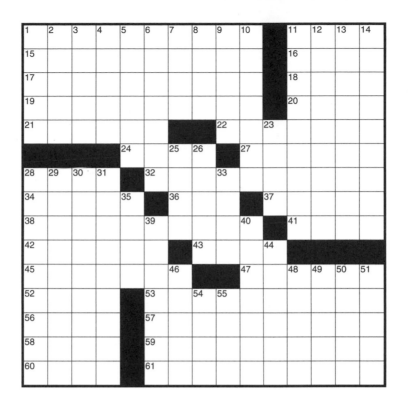

40

ACROSS

1 Guy with a stunted career?
11 Houlihan portrayer
15 On the beach
16 You may turn from it
17 Subject of Stanley I. Kutler's *Abuse of Power*
18 Silents star Nielsen
19 Visiting national parks, e.g.
20 Wearer of iron gloves
21 Quest alternative
22 Exhibits nervousness, perhaps
24 La Salle of *ER*
27 Having an association with
28 Dummy
32 Epworth League or Komsomol
34 Some lacquered metal pieces
36 Part of *la familia*
37 Acclimate
38 Mace targets
41 Cooper's costar in *The Wedding Night*
42 Octave, e.g.
43 It may be blue-winged or green-winged
45 People making connections?
47 ___ Law (criminal registry statute)
52 Others at the forum?
53 Monty Python sketch subject
56 Prosperity
57 Registered with
58 8, for O
59 Some Winter Olympians
60 Baseball's Eddie "The Walking Man" ___
61 They're very attractive

DOWN

1 ___ Addiction
2 Adventuress of literature
3 Guitarist Graham
4 Berry farm founder
5 Pass over
6 Creek
7 Toast
8 They have their reservations
9 "Give it ___!"
10 Monkees guitarist
11 Slovenly women
12 Weary
13 More than suffering
14 Attacks, as a long-awaited piece of mail
23 Shoe-endorsing dog
25 Drop
26 Yvonne Dionne, e.g.
28 Secrete
29 Hardly sympathetic of
30 Albert Schweitzer and others
31 Was quite important
33 Dryden's *Absalom and Achitophel* collaborator
35 Tag info
39 Lubricant for cutting tools
40 Hewitt beat him in 2001
44 Found out
46 Watercolor painting on dry plaster
48 Spanish-American flamenco dancer
49 Revlon rival
50 Word in a Hugo title
51 German artist Veit ___
54 Served well
55 Zoot suiter, say

41

ACROSS

1 I-635, familiarly
11 Forget, perhaps
15 Pen name
16 Exhibit edginess, in a way
17 Concourses
18 Biblical plot
19 Represent
20 Lilith, e.g.
22 Prurient peek
23 Was similar to, in a way
25 Alligator ___ (avocado)
27 *The Case Against Hillary Clinton* author
28 Antonym: Abbr.
31 Puritanical person
34 Way to go
35 Astronomical cover-ups?
38 States may be ruled by them
39 Split: Prefix
40 Jack, e.g.
41 Forgives
43 Footballer Ewbank
45 *The Spy Who Came in from the Cold* spy
48 Madame Bovary
52 Heed
53 Rub it in
54 Game ending
55 Young target
58 *Idée* producer
59 They're often dyed
60 Expert in futures?
61 Matching comb, brush, and mirror, e.g.

DOWN

1 Like some briefs
2 Orthopedist's order
3 Georges Seurat's *Grand* ___
4 Feature of some keys
5 Tony-winning *Nicholas Nickleby* star
6 Believe a fallacy, e.g.
7 Queen's label
8 Sticks with power
9 French photographer Eugène
10 Agreeable guys?
11 Control system with no self-correcting action
12 Union label?
13 Pair for pairs
14 Masseuse's concern
21 Scent
23 Where Mammy worked
24 Ovule growths
26 James, for one
28 Tuxedo accompaniers
29 *Barb Wire* star
30 It's offered to creditworthy bank customers
32 Flash
33 It's unstressed
36 Less predictable
37 Can't stand, perhaps
42 Saw, e.g.
44 Portrayer of Detective Munch on *Homicide: Life on the Street*
46 Essential oil
47 Code name
49 Some synthesizers
50 Veterinary diagnosis
51 SALT I concern
53 *King David* star
56 Where-at connector
57 Jennifer Lien's *Star Trek: Voyager* role

ANSWER, PAGE 249

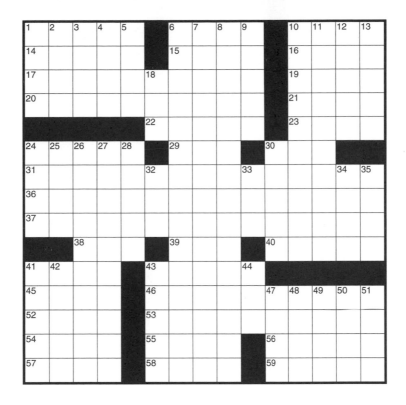

42

ACROSS

1 Asteroids producer
6 Symbols of safe passage
10 Lift of a sort
14 Truman's Missouri birthplace
15 *Waiting for God* author
16 It may be full of hot air
17 Choice in designer shoes
19 Its capital is Beauvais
20 It's rigorously enforced
21 With 29-Across, it may be traded in
22 Contemporary of Freud
23 Three in a match, maybe
24 Turning point
29 See 21-Across

30 ___ chi ch'uan
31 Perception qualification
36 "This Day in History" day
37 Top
38 Ending for two
39 Dehydrated dinner, perhaps: Abbr.
40 Grasp, informally
41 Gp. concerned with ratings
43 "Pat-a-Pan" and others
45 Frontier figure
46 Eppie Lederer, familiarly
52 Others, to Ovid
53 Convert for computer use, in Canterbury
54 China's Xiaoping
55 "Bad Reputation" singer
56 Living things
57 Significant stretches

58 North Carolina county
59 Hole in one's head

DOWN

1 Father's clothing
2 Limey?
3 Manchurian border river
4 Royal in a sari
5 Sporty Dodge Daytona
6 Match followers
7 Not particularly potent
8 Hypothetical space-based weapon
9 Comparatively vulpine
10 Small part
11 Northwest Nazarene University site
12 Height, to a cager
13 Bagpipe duet?
18 Transportation inits.
24 Den ___, Nederland
25 Yes's "Yours ___ Disgrace"

26 First Formula One champion
27 Test targets
28 Former Albanian premier ___ Hoxha
30 Member of the weasel family
32 Neophyte socialite
33 It's past *due*
34 Neapolitan, e.g.: Abbr.
35 Incline
41 Opponent of Lee
42 Relatively light
43 1994 vampire movie
44 Was in a stall
47 Catches
48 Year in Vigilius's papacy
49 Bailey who played Jann Wenner in *Almost Famous*
50 V lead-in
51 They may be rough

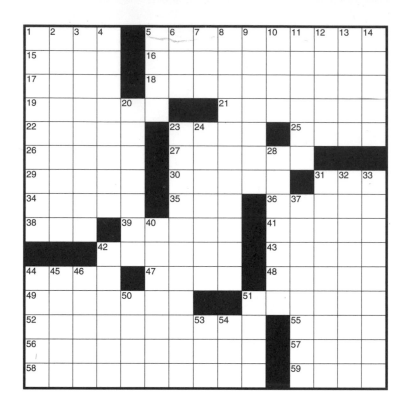

43

ACROSS

1 Ran
5 Rang
15 Range
16 Words of empathy
17 At odds with, in oaters
18 Mercury, e.g.
19 *Le Morte d'Arthur* author
21 Like Russia, partially
22 Invest
23 Shoots satisfactorily
25 Hunter ___ of soaps
26 How a group may act
27 Early Internet advocate
29 Wall unit
30 Graff of *Mr. Belvedere*
31 What "1" may mean: Abbr.
34 Outhouse cutouts
35 Start of South Carolina's motto
36 Dig, in a way
38 Like Bacon and Lamb: Abbr.
39 Unconventional
41 "Shut your trap!"
42 Conditional
43 Match point?
44 E.g., e.g.
47 See 7-Down
48 Apartment alternatives
49 Apartment alternative
51 Makes over
52 Jacopo Robusti, familiarly
55 Apropos of
56 Not foreign
57 Free of sexist language, perhaps
58 Perished
59 Impedes

DOWN

1 Like a photograph
2 1976 sci-fi film
3 Sin
4 Hardly praise
5 Difficult to make out, maybe
6 Prefix with politics
7 With 47-Across, item on a hospital bill
8 Blowup
9 Continue
10 Half in front?
11 Animal tallow salt
12 Unlike a slob
13 On-line malls and such
14 ___ Remy (manufacturer of electrical car components)
20 Smells strongly like
23 Was enough to make ends meet
24 Is attractive
28 Make more modest, maybe
31 *Coming Home* costar
32 Temporarily
33 Company concern
37 Sent up
40 Given vent
42 Ophthalmological case
44 Top-flight destination?
45 Steep, in a way
46 Sea south of the Moluccas
50 Opera box
51 Rambler, e.g.
53 Excessively
54 It has a certain ring to it

ANSWER, PAGE 253

44

ACROSS

1 "Honest!"
9 Doesn't tip
15 "I wish I had thought of it!"
16 One of a mythological ennead
17 Cat with a very short, curly coat
18 Look at
19 African whose lips are pierced and stretched around flat disks
20 Made
21 Palms, e.g.
24 Standing order?
25 Outed?
26 *7th Heaven* actor Andrew
27 MacArthur wanted to unite it
29 Lead-in for house or wife
30 High one in Europe
33 Don't wait to heat
35 *The London Spy* author Ward
36 12 deniers, once
37 Derby neckwear
38 Sour
40 Place for bulk buying
47 Do a favor for
48 *Jurassic Park III* costar
49 Position
50 *Topkapi* director
51 Good for the figure, perhaps
52 Runs away from it?
54 Opening on Broadway
55 President Ali Abdullah Saleh, e.g.
56 Hybrid bottoms
57 Judges incorrectly

DOWN

1 Cause
2 Driving area
3 Pundit
4 Concurrently
5 With 22-Down, Hemlock is one of them
6 Recurring role for Talia
7 Cheer leader?
8 Encumber
9 One barely running?
10 They were pursued by Colonel Lynch
11 Words of accord
12 He didn't believe in bad boys
13 It may be held to raise money quickly
14 Blue
22 See 5-Down
23 Least expeditious
28 Tabulae ___
30 Once
31 He had 938 stolen bases
32 Enter with a vehicle
33 Almost due, perhaps
34 "Be My Baby" group, with "the"
39 Abet in dishonesty, perhaps
41 House keepers?
42 Theseus, to the Minotaur
43 Aviation pioneer Clyde
44 Flipped
45 Eastern Christian
46 Jags
52 *Quartet in Autumn* novelist
53 It hangs on Ho

ANSWER, PAGE 255

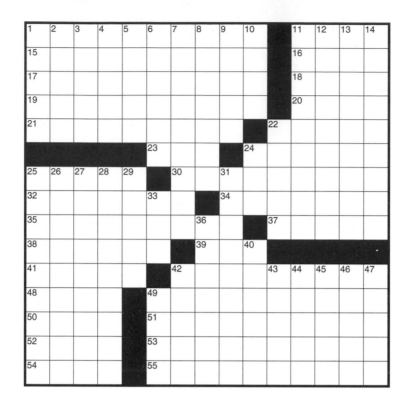

45

ACROSS

1 Like many a footnote
11 Silver skates pursuer Brinker
15 Ship whose foremast is square-rigged
16 Zeno of ___
17 *Purple Noon* star
18 Not made up
19 In a frugal way
20 Young of Rocky films
21 They're bound to bound
22 San ___ Bridge
23 When DST begins
24 May of sci-fi
25 Like some tails
30 Some minivans
32 Floor
34 Rapprochement
35 Last of the Capetians
37 Figure skater Cohen
38 He played Lilith's husband on a sitcom
39 Ant's drinking source, perhaps
41 Future furniture, perhaps
42 Tube for some viewers
48 Radiation units
49 They often contain bread crumbs
50 Esau's wife
51 Arrival
52 Gaston of the diamond
53 Cary Grant's costar in *The Awful Truth*
54 More than suspected
55 Men may keep them

DOWN

1 Sunning
2 Jumping game similar to Chinese checkers
3 It may have a diner
4 Stretching (out)
5 Car or Cop lead-in
6 Jawaharlal's daughter
7 Office Depot stock
8 ___ Trout (character in several Vonnegut novels)
9 Hydroxyl compounds
10 Opposite of admit
11 It's usually not caffeinated
12 Bidarka builders
13 Kind of asteroid
14 Imperial Valley lake
22 They're not optional
24 Lord of Deep Purple
25 Cover the same ground, in a way
26 Preceded
27 Draw
28 Paints may be displayed in it
29 Holiday times
31 Back-mutated gene
33 Marshal at Waterloo
36 Emulates a creative director
40 Comparatively cunning
42 He studied cultures
43 Atmospheric probe
44 *The Myth of Sisyphus* essayist
45 They may run on gas
46 Tubes on the table
47 Pitcher Shawn
49 Really hurt

ANSWER, PAGE 257

46

ACROSS

1 Brian Piccolo portrayer
10 Bays
15 Early
16 Strain at ___
17 You can bet on it
18 Word of concurrence
19 Turns away
20 *Feast of St. Nicolas* painter
21 Something to shake on
22 Kitchen drawer?
24 Weapon for *un soldat*
25 Hedy Lamarr played her
28 Some Bantus
32 *Objet* ___
33 Its president is Charles Taylor
34 Sharp turn
35 Primed
36 Couldn't take
37 1996 Juliet portrayer
39 "Santa Baby" singer
40 Grade-schoolers do them
41 Locks in a den?
45 Juvenile dragonfly
47 Fortified with a stake fence
50 Go over the top, in a way
51 Jim Croce song
52 Resilience
53 Storied ladies?
54 No bruiser
55 They're open to a Brit's interpretation

DOWN

1 Vigorous, emotional crusade
2 Iguana's cousin
3 Arnold's wife
4 Corsair or Pacer
5 *My Life as an Explorer* author Hedin
6 Jay & the Americans' "___ Mia"
7 Asian Turkey
8 Capitulates
9 *Les Misérables* star
10 Rolls tightly
11 Firebrands
12 Break off
13 You may not be up for it
14 Hit for Barbra Streisand
23 Move a bit
25 Position filler
26 They're in
27 Popular side
28 Reason to reprimand an employee
29 He was known as "the Red"
30 Surgical removals
31 Risks getting lost?
34 17th century English theater manager Philip
36 Vandal, e.g.
38 Chiseler's skill
41 House of the lord
42 "To woo so fair ___ to be his wife": Shakespeare
43 Temple of Zeus locale
44 Elysiums
46 Moist
48 Start of a Brian Hyland song title
49 *Final Destination* star Devon ___

47

ACROSS

1 Video game adventuress
10 1-Across portrayer
15 1977 Pulitzer winner
16 Massey of movies
17 Althing member
18 Bill producers
19 Hats may symbolize them
20 Maid hirer, maybe
22 *Billy Budd* captain
23 Gave guff
25 Begin et al.
27 Punch of a sort
29 Light locale, in a Silverstein title
30 Possible result of a hearing problem
35 One earning won
37 Pollen bearers
38 Voix ___ (organ stop)
39 Not a lot

40 Like some funds
41 Monkey
42 Spanish queen
43 Unheedful of the tenth Commandment
45 Hit lightly
51 Groundbreaking discoveries?
52 Member of the family Troglodytidae
54 Tenor Bergonzi
55 *eXistenZ* actor
57 One's backside?
59 Make up
60 Disappear without a trace
61 Private instructor?
62 Romanced, in a way

DOWN

1 Kennels
2 Maryville's twin city
3 Lurches

4 Car components
5 *The Dukes of Hazzard* highlight
6 Worked
7 Aurora producer
8 Ache, perhaps
9 No pros
10 Runner Ryun
11 Mediterranean drupe dropper
12 Most bleak
13 Knotty
14 Moves with great care
21 It may squeal as you stop
24 Milk source
26 Midway, for one
28 The Talking Heads' "And She ___"
30 Scratch
31 Fiancée, e.g.
32 Try to reach

33 Program opener, often
34 On again
36 Nancy Drew's Nickerson
38 The 1900s, e.g.: Abbr.
40 Rate
43 Sonata sections
44 They may be irresistible
46 Follow
47 City on the Shatt-al-Arab
48 Kale
49 Opposite of deject
50 Portioned
53 Problematic for a presbyopic person
56 Shoe designation
58 One who swings a good deal

ANSWER, PAGE 244

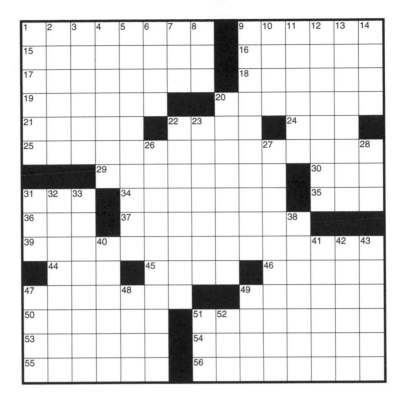

48

ACROSS

1 Run-down movie theatres
9 "Take your time"
15 First-down gain
16 Words before the public
17 Far from traumatic
18 Busted
19 PETA president Newkirk
20 Some Tetons
21 River to the Baltic Sea
22 Elroy's mom
24 Long-jawed swimmer
25 It's celebrated on a September weekend
29 Heavy rainfall
30 In-flight announcement
31 Workout target
34 Like some breezes
35 Moonshine
36 Shofar source
37 Arms, ammunition, and equipment
39 Globetrotters may use them
44 Ramakrishna's title
45 Hand over
46 *Jack London* star
47 Followed
49 ___ 'Ali Mirza (Baha'i founder)
50 Bellyached
51 Sort of
53 Arch coverer
54 Members of Quark's race, on *Star Trek: Deep Space Nine*
55 Some characins
56 Contrarian's comment

DOWN

1 Sending from a remote PC, perhaps
2 Relatively rawboned
3 Person of contradictory character
4 *The Virtue of Selfishness* author
5 Mom or pop
6 Angered
7 Conversion preceders, briefly
8 Lottery org.
9 Branded
10 It symbolizes bad luck
11 Packs differently, as groceries
12 Took the edge off?
13 Zinc ___ (waterproofing compound)
14 Masons' troughs
20 Small and insignificant
22 *The Painter's Family* painter
23 Army of Hollywood gossip
26 They deal with crime and punishment
27 High hideouts
28 Plane problem
31 Prints and such
32 Some bachelors are into it
33 Superlatively saucy
38 Palliates
40 Strive to get
41 Redress?
42 Adds to the database
43 Least likely to be put away
47 Some
48 Troubadour Adam ___ Halle
49 Last name in spydom
51 George Strait's "___ Know Me"
52 Bushranger Kelly

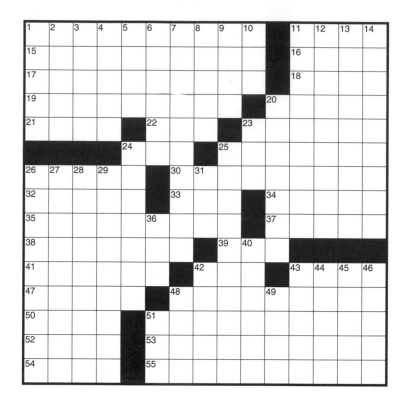

49

ACROSS

1 People on night watch?
11 *Monastère* head
15 Tiny parts
16 Metal ash
17 Owner's words?
18 Smart
19 Plants
20 Italian province or city
21 Gets to
22 It's connected by canal with Lake Biel
23 Basic metaphysical entities
24 Merger-blocking org.
25 When the kids are out
26 Fuming
30 Gets moving
32 Cathartic drug
33 N.Y.C. tube
34 Actress Gimpel
35 Framing
37 New Jersey county
38 Level
39 Free
41 North of the screen
42 Stop start?
43 Wingless insects
47 Ma's cello, e.g.
48 Cantina fare
50 Camaro model
51 Good thing to save for
52 Straight
53 New Jersey birthplace of Dionne Warwick
54 Some dropouts get them: Abbr.
55 Book ends, perhaps

DOWN

1 Video store category
2 David's daughter
3 Wildly
4 Stops bowing, perhaps
5 Don't skip
6 Ancient debarkation location
7 Each consists of 30 degrees
8 Radio commentator Davis
9 Old Portuguese money
10 It has an adjustable nose
11 Sparrow look-alikes
12 Dinar spenders
13 Nursery rhyme trio
14 Whiskey Rebellion prompter
20 Best player, perhaps
23 It may provide relief
24 Threshed
25 Firm concern
26 Levying
27 Mast source
28 Under way
29 Has reciprocal influence
31 Morse vehicle
36 Shem's father, in the Douay Bible
40 Number openers
42 *"Au contraire"*
43 Alexander who ran for president
44 Ancient British people who revolted against the Romans
45 Abrupt dismissal
46 Photorealist Richard
48 It may be hooded
49 Bit beginner
51 Mil. unit

ANSWER, PAGE 248

50

ACROSS

1 Nasty biter
10 Nasty biter
15 Hinterland
16 *The Jade Mask* star
17 Erotic
18 Soap substitute
19 Shipping point for the Columbia Basin Project
20 Get clean, in a way
21 Roll remark
22 Molders
23 Avalon alternative
27 Aegean port
29 Kind of concerto
30 Miss California of 1969
34 Moving parts?
36 "I'm outta here"
37 Minimally
39 *Peut-___*
40 Word after public or territorial
41 Lets go
42 Crime preventers, perhaps
44 William the Silent's foe
47 Lab test result?
48 It fell to Sherman on Sept. 2, 1864
53 Cons
54 *The Horse in the Gray Flannel Suit* star
55 Crowd drawer
56 Castle execution
57 Umbrella plant, e.g.
58 Evening people

DOWN

1 Colliery carrier
2 Ozeki's specialty
3 Historian's concern
4 WBA heavyweight champ of 1979
5 Like partly melted snow
6 "The Fishin' Hole" composer Hagen
7 Brother of a sort
8 Soon-to-be-flat tires, perhaps
9 Bush went to it
10 Didn't just glimpse
11 Do-it-yourselfer's shopping mecca
12 Daniel Inouye's purview
13 Pass along
14 Part of Denver
22 Start of an interdiction
23 Time out?
24 End at
25 Being urgently sought, in a way
26 Preparing to be used again, perhaps
28 No nymphs
30 Court star from Novi Sad
31 One may have an ID
32 Grendel, for one
33 Some voters
35 "Hmmm ..."
38 Together
41 Kind of engine
42 Run up
43 Bass of pop
45 Treeless tract
46 Chemin de fer declaration
48 Employs Chisanbop
49 One of Marley's Wailers
50 Before before?
51 Grandpa Walton portrayer
52 Nasty biters

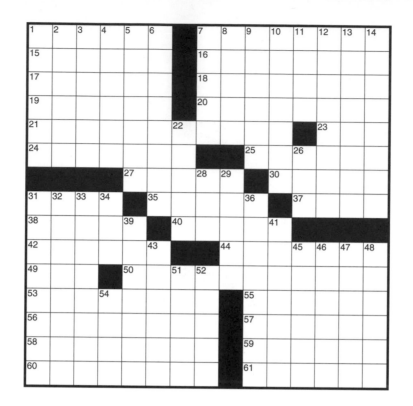

51

ACROSS
1 Wild
7 *I Kid You Not* autobiographer
15 Lacking reciprocity
16 Feminist Rich
17 Doing less damage?
18 Haole's home, often
19 Shapely computer game?
20 Pushed
21 Cheshire and others
23 It may require refinement
24 Delightful
25 John Lithgow's ___ *in the Bathtub*
27 Take in
30 It may cover your elbows
31 Patsies
35 Moon of Jupiter
37 No ornamental
38 College near Cleveland
40 Master
42 Does like a demagogue
44 You may not have room for it
49 Like some grins
50 Paul Muni's 1937 costar
53 Focus of some runners
55 Use one's imagination
56 With interruptions
57 Some sharks
58 Benjamin Britten opera
59 One of Mr. Drummond's adopted sons
60 Least ruffled
61 Just about

DOWN
1 What anodynes do
2 Toughen
3 Sunday school site, sometimes
4 Some decorations
5 Orense's region
6 Visor of a sort
7 Painter Wyeth
8 Catbert's creator
9 "Geez!"
10 Movement of an organism in response to a stimulus
11 Former Rhode Island senator
12 Soybean, vis-à-vis beef
13 *Taltos* novelist
14 Became ripe, perhaps
22 Chemical compounds
26 Provincial turndown
28 Caress clumsily
29 Kind of secret
31 High-quality toys, perhaps
32 Source of some nonfatal wounds
33 Remembers in church, in a way
34 Took advantage of a tête-à-tête
36 Part of CARE
39 Producer of some of dark colors
41 Friz Freleng's real first name
43 Split alternative
45 Earth tone
46 Fascinate
47 Relate differently
48 In
51 Desktop collection
52 Part of *le gouvernement*
54 Preweigh, in a way

ANSWER, PAGE 252

52

ACROSS

1 Pass in a hurry
6 "At least some progress was made"
15 Gay leader?
16 One holding a chair, perhaps
17 Rigel, e.g.
18 Buck up
19 Attach again, in a way
20 Shatner title word
21 He hit 61 in '61
22 Springs
24 Like some books
26 Bit of knight wear?
29 It serves Tel Aviv
30 Misled, in a way
31 *"Winnie ___ Pu"*
32 Supermarket stock
36 Oscar nominee for *The L-Shaped Room*

37 Connecticut senator
38 Enlist again
39 *2001* extra
41 *The Mambo Kings* director Glimcher
42 Proven reliable, in a way
47 Crusader's foe
49 Carol Burnett played her
50 Gambler's funds
51 Opposite of take: Scot.
54 Producer of some trucks
55 School principles
57 Cowboy, at times
58 Debated on the side of
59 Centipede producer
60 African carrier
61 *Bewitched* actor

DOWN

1 Refs
2 Extra page, perhaps
3 Entrée that sounds like a dessert
4 *Moravagine* novelist Cendrars
5 Half of a mime team
6 "Why should ___ you?"
7 Pointed antler branch
8 What Nixon said on *Laugh-In*
9 12 *meses*
10 Electioneer
11 She played Vicky in *American Pie*
12 Where Oprah was tried
13 Elton John's real first name

14 Supported, as a bridge
23 Pointed
25 Coming-out party?
27 Using as a springboard
28 Pertinent
32 Biggie on base
33 Granary gizmos
34 You may take aim at it
35 Let your feelings be known
40 Like some colors
43 Like a stuffed shirt
44 Harsh
45 Drugstore chain
46 Sugar
48 Astronomical discovery of 1801
52 Spears, to many teens
53 Weird: Var.
56 Letter lineup

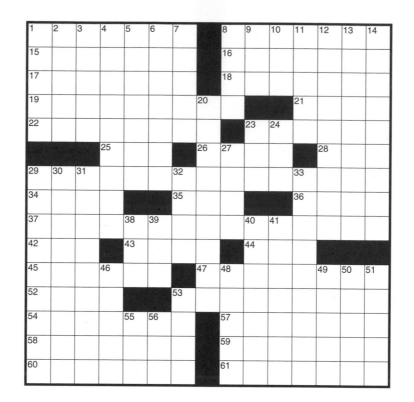

53

ACROSS

1 Some things are beyond it
8 Yet
15 Soon to be delivered, perhaps
16 In what other way
17 1984 Estevez film
18 Breathing obstructor, sometimes
19 No junk-food junkie, presumably
21 It's available in bars
22 Garment worker who matches pieces
23 Prefix with dynamic
25 Latin abbreviation meaning "of age" that is seen on old gravestones
26 Cliff and Clair's son, on TV
28 Bit of retaliation?
29 Minivan model
34 Clinton un-appointee Guinier
35 Dewey, e.g.: Abbr.
36 Reams
37 Car model
42 *Weekly World News* topic
43 Hooker?
44 Ceiling
45 Skinny?
47 *Ruddigore*, e.g.
52 It was created on Oct. 1, 1958
53 Left by mistake, say
54 Do over
57 Caber wielder, e.g.
58 Apply lead-in
59 No kiddie lit
60 Badges of authority
61 Attached, as a coat lining

DOWN

1 Una ___ (with the soft pedal depressed, in piano music)
2 ___ a Lonely Number (1972 Trish Van Devere movie)
3 Gloomy guses
4 Triassic fossil bird
5 Fan
6 Laugh at, say
7 First name of "Mr. Cub"
8 Comparative follower
9 Mortar tray
10 Krupp of hockey
11 It may be innate
12 Walked-on block
13 It borders on the Aegean
14 It has smooth skin and shallow eyes
20 Illustration chooser, perhaps
23 Hill, in Haifa
24 N.L. Central team
27 Web designer's expertise
29 Pleasant thing to be on
30 Ready for the doggy bag, maybe
31 Bill beneficiaries
32 You may see reactions in them
33 Headache, in Le Havre
38 Drama deg.
39 Make quiet, perhaps
40 1968 hit by the Turtles
41 Upper-atmosphere phenomenon
46 Day of *la semaine*
48 Tiara wearers
49 Bombastic
50 Bingham of *Baywatch*
51 Boutros-Ghali's successor
53 People who believe in spirits?
55 He directed Chow in *Crouching Tiger, Hidden Dragon*
56 Busy person's alleged workload

ANSWER, PAGE 256

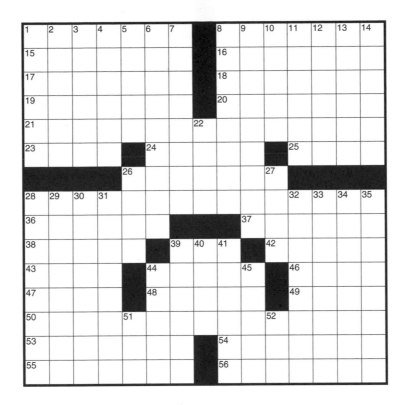

54

ACROSS

1 Like some smiles
8 Poiret pieces
15 Bob Seger or Barry Manilow song
16 Salivary gland
17 Feels like it
18 Rotate a limb, in a way
19 Formicary
20 Records over
21 They're not easily detected
23 He had a hit with "Java"
24 Widely used African language of commerce
25 It: Italian
26 Least seedy
28 It may be difficult to get through to
36 Like some statements
37 *The Building of the Ship* imperative
38 It may be passed from father to son
39 One may appear on a tree
42 See 44-Across
43 Vojvodina resident
44 With 42-Across, shapely dessert makers?
46 Pip
47 Singer of the #1 R&B hit "On&On"
48 Golden Triangle export
49 Abd-er-Rahman Khan, for example
50 Choice words
53 Circle
54 Aging agent
55 It has 120 seats in Israel
56 15-___ (easy field goals)

DOWN

1 Put in for another cycle, perhaps
2 1972 Billy Wilder comedy about Wendell Armbruster
3 Car hitting another car, often
4 Because
5 First name in park shooting
6 Out
7 Having a second part, perhaps
8 Notifies
9 Some elements
10 Loyalty
11 Don't charge for
12 Infantry campsites
13 Cops, at times
14 Midland's neighbor
22 Goalie Grant who won the 1988 Vezina Trophy
26 Look down
27 It may make pit stops
28 Reduces
29 Irrationality
30 Info in Picard's log
31 Roman legions had six
32 Broken
33 Make clear
34 Oil source
35 Safeguards
39 Cities of Cibola, say
40 Romanian soccer star Dumitrescu
41 Indistinct
44 *The Bone Collector* costar
45 Word in Oklahoma's motto
51 Word in MGM's motto
52 Spring time: Abbr.

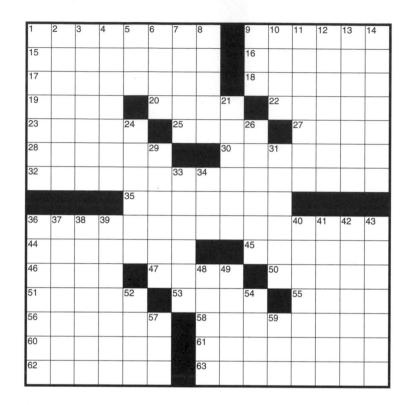

55

ACROSS

1 #1 hit of 1999
9 #1 hit of 1999
15 Having a sense of the beautiful
16 What you have when you're in the dark
17 Tony Montana, in the title of a 1983 film
18 She speaks Spanish
19 Dean's *Lois & Clark* costar
20 Enrapture
22 One with a CD, e.g.
23 Bluff deposit
25 Twist in a bar
27 Three-piece piece
28 Hardly blue
30 French motto starter
32 Zipping, in a way
35 Arnd Schmitt or Laura Flessel
36 Rap from 2Pac's *2Pacalypse Now*
44 McKennitt of folk
45 Medium setting?
46 Firm leader
47 They may be kept on you
50 Symbol of strength
51 Trucks with bulldog hood ornaments
53 *La Débâcle* novelist
55 Abbr. for the unlisted?
56 Propose
58 Friend in a private dining hall?
60 Bulldog, at times
61 Rainbow bird, e.g.
62 *The Wall* novelist
63 Mature female fish

DOWN

1 Close for comfort
2 Seminole Wars warrior
3 Eye
4 Wolf of literature
5 Court gesturer
6 Pippig and Hagen
7 What an arm curl strengthens, non-technically speaking
8 It may be stolen
9 TV debut of Oct. 11, 1975
10 Ostriches' extinct cousins
11 Scale spans
12 Rock bassist Nick
13 Locates on the dial
14 Cheer
21 City opposite Ciudad Acuña
24 Pull out
26 Misleads, in a way
29 Impurity intentionally added to a pure semiconductor
31 They're massive and relatively hot
33 City in Maricopa Co.
34 Word before board or box
36 Flaw
37 Pulitzer of *The Prize Pulitzer*
38 ___ Set
39 Amorous couple
40 Portrayer of one of the Keatons on *Family Ties*
41 Protective overlay
42 Kid, at times
43 Fans, at times
48 No-hitters?
49 Be unlike New York City?
52 Snick's partner
54 Floundering
57 Like some cells
59 Put in stitches

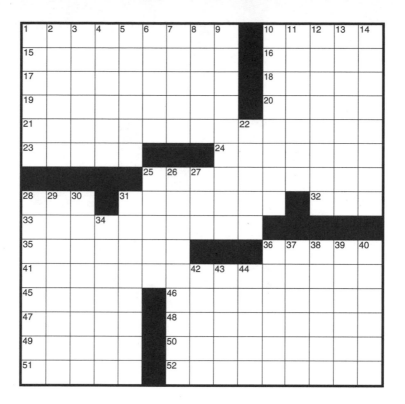

56

ACROSS
1 Kind of seal
10 Expectant one
15 1990 comedy with two sequels
16 Lizard kept as a pet
17 Ellipses, e.g.
18 Dried orchid tubers used as food
19 Patty Duke film that was Pacino's feature debut
20 Wine's "nose," e.g.
21 They show that you owe
23 They're painful to the touch
24 Like some crimes
25 Doctor
28 CIA's maritime counterpart
31 Performed several songs back-to-back, perhaps

32 Letters to the editor?: Abbr.
33 R and B
35 Poison
36 Columnist Alexander
41 Swift set it forth
45 "___ do"
46 It may be used by a star
47 About to go through the roof
48 They may be Maced
49 They're set for marriage
50 Piece of schlock
51 Slow sellers in summer
52 Capital of Saint Vincent and the Grenadines

DOWN
1 Sinks one's teeth into
2 *Lost Continent* star

3 Key with no sharps or flats
4 "___ Mucho" (#1 hit of 1944)
5 Start of a Kipling assertion
6 Buffalo Bill, e.g.
7 Gimlet and screwdriver, e.g.
8 Film-score composer Morricone
9 Army extra
10 Can escape if necessary
11 Hot
12 It has 24 legs and 8 heads
13 Weather
14 Fixes, as a collage
22 "That hurts!"

25 Ariadne's father
26 Raymond Massey's *East of Eden* role
27 Indian restaurant bread
28 Tethys's offspring
29 Involving no value judgments
30 Make a supplication
31 Rare, e.g.
34 Under
36 Atoms
37 Alert while driving, perhaps
38 Star: Prefix
39 Like Archie Bunker
40 Hannigan of *American Pie*
42 ___ di pollo (chicken breasts)
43 Like a ___ a trap
44 Jungle swinger

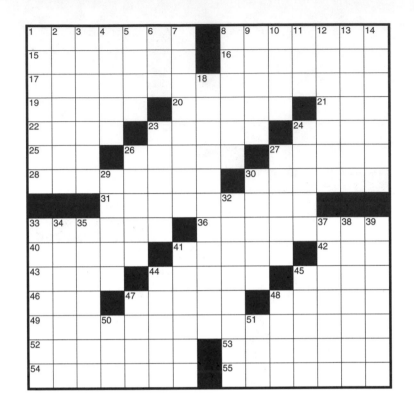

57

ACROSS

1 Thin linen fabric of fine close weave
8 Less limited
15 Spanish sherry
16 Beatitude
17 It represents an exchange, in part
19 El Greco's birthplace
20 Batman creator's family
21 Julie Brown's "'Cause ___ Blonde"
22 *That's a Plenty* trumpeter
23 Front five?
24 San Francisco's ___ Tower
25 Goose, in Genoa
26 Kind of shirt
27 Wet ride
28 Disastrous defeat
30 Made blank, in a way
31 Sought shelter
33 Kind of Italian?

36 They often feature fiddlers
40 Car starter?
41 CNN Washington Bureau Chief Frank
42 Cornet, e.g.
43 Some wings
44 Begins to appear
45 Fox's partner, on Fox
46 *Fists of Fury* director Lo ___
47 Playground retort
48 They may be performed in the service
49 Some officers
52 *The Ten Commandments* actress Taylor
53 It may appear after an article
54 Lay close
55 Range between the Elbe and Oder

DOWN

1 Siamese cuisine?
2 Land of "chromium steel" and "wire-spoke wheel," in song
3 Burrower with permanently closed eyelids
4 1980 American League MVP
5 Skip it
6 It's like -like
7 It may give you directions on the side
8 Starr with a report
9 Punjabi princess
10 Work
11 You can bank on it
12 Like some distinctions
13 Monk living in solitude, say
14 Evaluated anew
18 Kind of dip or soup
23 White gold, e.g.

24 Flamenco fireball
26 Cooking evidence?
27 Formula of belief
29 Napoleonic states
30 Levels
32 Zygotes
33 Oars
34 It may be timed
35 Wins the support of
37 The like
38 *The Stepford Wives* actress Newman
39 He lost the Republican nomination to Eisenhower
41 Felt, e.g.
44 Speak, in Soissons
45 *Cheers* waitress
47 Sentence structure?
48 Demond's television costar
50 Offensive time?
51 It's protected in South Africa

 ANSWER, PAGE 245

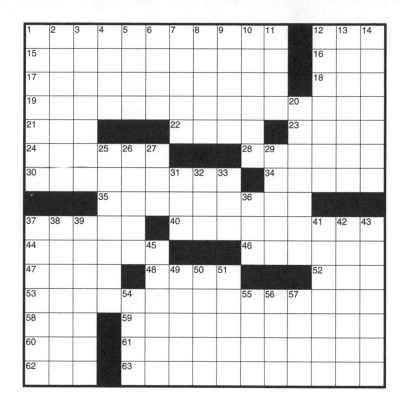

58

ACROSS

 1 Potassium or sodium
12 Really relax, slangily
15 Unquestionably gone
16 Figure skater Kyoko
17 Bitingly critical
18 Like some coughs
19 It made sustained migratory flights
21 Third of *nove*
22 Whilom
23 No celibate
24 Slips
28 Some poker hands
30 Posse quarry
34 *Alive* setting
35 He played Mr. Miyagi
37 With respect to
40 Old calling need
44 Wu-wei is a concept in it
46 *In the Meantime* author ___ Vanzant
47 One of the Ghostbusters
48 Short comings?
52 Vandal
53 1995 swashbuckler
58 Wild butter
59 Unable to escape, perhaps
60 It may be in a bed
61 Largish garment bag
62 Broke the tape, maybe
63 Enters the priesthood, e.g.

DOWN

 1 Avoided extinction, perhaps
 2 *Single and Single* novelist
 3 Some Hapsburgs
 4 Puts in
 5 Untimely?
 6 "The race ___!"
 7 Stray's problem
 8 It finishes
 9 They may be taken in buses
10 Aces
11 Napoleon defeated the Austrians here
12 Recorded, in a way
13 Traveling
14 Festivity
20 One of the Windwards
25 Name
26 Sign of joy, sometimes
27 Busts and such
29 TV actress Sagal
31 Marshall product
32 Play conclusion?
33 It might be struck in Spain
36 Palindromic reggae singer Kamoze
37 Had to retract a statement, perhaps
38 It first blooms at about age 40
39 Liveried servants, of sorts
41 Not slowly
42 Indy great
43 Some space probes
45 First name in homemaking
49 *The Fountainhead* protagonist
50 Important Indian
51 Hampshire homes
54 "Thomas the Tank Engine" character Sir Topham ___
55 "___ sorry"
56 Pathological projection
57 Put down

59

ACROSS

1 Go on and on
11 They may be exchanged in church
15 Wildly agitated
16 Lingering effect
17 "Big Cat Country" locale
18 Swamp thing
19 Soapstone, e.g.
20 They may be exchanged in a lab
21 Boston or Chicago, e.g.
22 Composite
24 Middle name of a U.S. Vice President
25 Celestial Seasonings selection
29 City in Böhmen famous for its beer
30 Johnson County Community College locale
33 X-rays, CT scans, etc.
37 Belmont and Preakness champion of 1953
38 San Jose community
41 Best Documentary of 1952
42 Emptied a shoe, maybe
43 Some cabinet members?
45 Style moderne
46 Send to Coventry
47 Congratulate oneself
51 Kind of meet
52 It doesn't carry passengers
55 *Soap* family name
56 *The Assignment* star
57 Court attention-getter
58 Exhortation for a panicky person

DOWN

1 Eddie who played third base for the Senators
2 Stage org. founded in 1935
3 It may be held by a secretary
4 Longtime McDonald's chief
5 *Liquide vital*
6 1979 disaster area: Abbr.
7 It's near Ann Arbor
8 Mississippi feeder
9 No good feeling
10 Greek island in the Aegean
11 Kevin Spacey's role in *The Usual Suspects*
12 Gobs
13 From what cause
14 Bloated
22 In any case
23 Camper's dwelling, perhaps
24 Pain-free place
25 Tonsorial challenge
26 1997 French Open winner Majoli
27 It may prevent a spike
28 "If I Had a Hammer" singer
29 Nixon received one
31 *seaQuest* ___
32 Glimpsing
34 Century-starting date
35 Comic cry
36 Indian title
38 Supplements
39 Room
40 Surrender possession
43 Parking structure?
44 Half a barrel organ?
46 Dispense with the lyrics, perhaps
47 Waiting to exhale?
48 Track component
49 Wife of Vladimir I
50 Children of the late 1960s, briefly
53 "Revolution 9" co-creator
54 O-S connection

ANSWER, PAGE 249

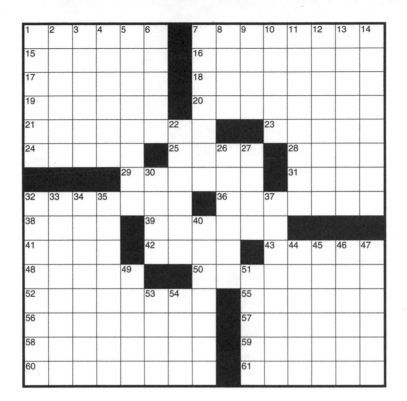

60

ACROSS

1 Darwin is served by it
7 He's encouraged to "sing us a song," in song
15 Lack of quiet
16 Robert De Niro played him
17 Kafelnikov lost to him in 2000
18 Develop anew
19 *As I See It* photographer
20 OK'd, with "to"
21 Lube
23 Runny refuse
24 Looming choices
25 Decides upon
28 You might say it when you get it
29 One to one, e.g.
31 Jungle array
32 You may have one for life
36 They're often rented
38 One way to direct a helm
39 Stick
41 Soft foods
42 French silk center
43 Ness foe
48 Cremona craftsman
50 Finnish relative
52 Inferior position, symbolically
55 Ill-fated highflier
56 Light
57 Lug
58 Some thinners
59 Blissful
60 Giants, maybe
61 Take exception to

DOWN

1 Soft and wet
2 Like some sweaters
3 Start of a Sarah F. Adams hymn title
4 Discoverer of New Zealand
5 Offer?
6 Tuna trapper
7 Fortification elevation
8 Features of *géographie*
9 Deck quartet
10 April and May
11 Directive during a checkup, perhaps
12 Joined securely
13 Boyle Heights resident, e.g.
14 Uncalled-for
22 Brat's place, perhaps
26 Megacorporations
27 Alone, in Amiens
30 First moonwalker's first name
32 One of a fairy-tale trio
33 North Carolina county whose seat is Graham
34 Opted for a different suitcase, perhaps
35 Diagnostic packages
37 Orson Scott Card novel
40 Dove, for one
44 Since way back when
45 It's east of Durrës
46 John's songwriting partner
47 One might put out a feeler
49 Playground retort
51 Flower of Rome
53 Frank's wife on *Laverne & Shirley*
54 Tiger, e.g., briefly

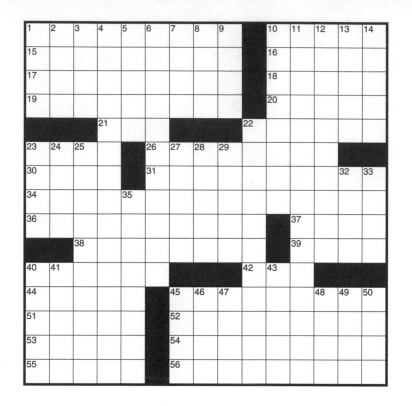

61

ACROSS

1 Exhibition areas
10 ___ de la Frontera, Spain
15 They may be mature
16 Fair, in Florence
17 Rush drummer
18 Resell for a big profit
19 Telescope parts
20 *Road* ___ (Bob Hope/ Bing Crosby movie)
21 Suffix of pasta names
22 Source of corruption
23 Defeater of Washington at Brandywine
26 Video game designer's concern
30 Blue-and-white team
31 Think successfully, perhaps

34 New Amsterdam was on it
36 Written in Java, say
37 Arthur's one-time rival
38 Bindlestiffs' bundles
39 Faithful follower?
40 Effervesces
42 Deck (out)
44 Capital of Pas-de-Calais
45 Computer program promoted while still in development
51 ___-Poo (role in *The Mikado*)
52 One walking, perhaps
53 Avian production
54 Kind of decimal
55 Diner in a 1981 film
56 They're in high positions

DOWN

1 Not cracked
2 Long of politics
3 Dog in a strip
4 He rode Ferdinand
5 Put in a new cage
6 Short-term relationships?
7 Edible South American tubers
8 Kind of technicality?
9 Streakers since 1968
10 Doesn't vote
11 Winning back as a friend, perhaps
12 Ike Turner's Mississippi birthplace
13 Noted puppet dragon
14 Bitterness, e.g.
22 They may have franchises
23 Beginning half

24 1937 Luise Rainer role
25 Damaged by the elements, in a way
27 Joe Buck's friend
28 Efficacy
29 Punishing?
32 Running back Curtis
33 Juice bar stock
35 Dark volcanic rock
40 Present presenter
41 Langoustine, e.g.
43 Black-and-white school, maybe
45 Sink or swim
46 Paul Bunyan, at times
47 Rap's Salt-N-___
48 Jordan is in it
49 Cost of living?
50 ___ per second (luminosity unit)

ANSWER, PAGE 253

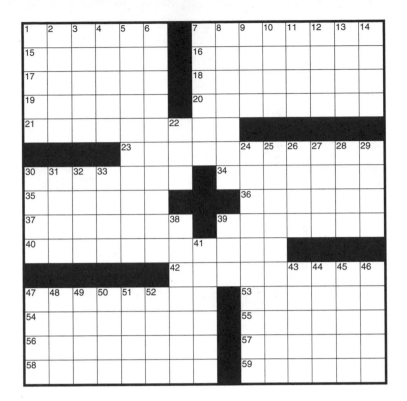

62

ACROSS

1 Olympic event
7 Olympic event
15 Setting of some symphonies
16 Paul McCrane's *ER* role
17 Brook
18 Ready for war, perhaps
19 Time out in Tijuana?
20 Foes
21 It's not too bright
23 Small Mexican jumper
30 Get through the cracks, perhaps
34 In suspense
35 One doing rounds, perhaps
36 Addis Ababa native
37 Rain forest youngsters
39 Unwise way to make a decision

40 Théâtre Italien premiere of 1843
42 Lacking identification, in a way
47 Callous
53 Weave new rattan into
54 "So?"
55 Part of a sundial that casts the shadow
56 Like some statues
57 Dazzling successes
58 Sophisticated people
59 *Walker, Texas Ranger* actress ___ J. Wilson

DOWN

1 Texas air force base
2 Opera ___ (oeuvre)
3 Flamingo, e.g.
4 Gino Vannelli's "___ Wanna Stop"
5 Where money is won

6 They may be found in trees
7 *Slappy and the Stinkers* star
8 Iteration intro
9 Kenyan president Daniel ___ Moi
10 Ed Sullivan's Gigio
11 Benefit package providers
12 See 51-Down
13 Dilly
14 Succumbs to boredom, perhaps
22 London loc.
24 Blows up again
25 Not currently playing, perhaps
26 Labor Dept. div.
27 Old Brazilian money
28 Scores
29 Compose e-mail, e.g.
30 What some people sing

31 Show on a large scale
32 Asteroid whose orbit crosses Earth's
33 Sea food?
38 Juice, in a way
39 Different ending
41 Nobel-winning Norwegian novelist
43 Where *enfants* are educated
44 Missouri town
45 Brief cybermessage
46 Slow-witted
47 Good mousers
48 Wedge in a crevice, perhaps
49 Convertible, e.g.
50 Anti-___ (airplane maintenance device)
51 With 12-Down, welcome sight for a tailgater
52 One of Tennessee's symbols

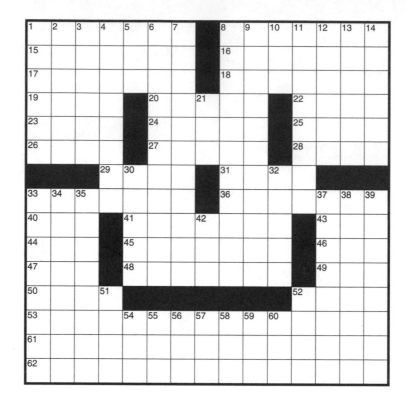

63

ACROSS

1 Was humbled
8 Mimic a wolf
15 State University of New York locale
16 2, for one
17 ___ Sea
18 Purify, in a way
19 Broke the law, in a way
20 Lighted stacks
22 One of Minnesota's many
23 Chulalongkorn's domain
24 Two, for one
25 Son of Judah
26 Topic preceder
27 Trooper's aid
28 Horse course?
29 An Osmond brother
31 Tots' time-outs
33 Urban legend
36 Sophie's choice, e.g.
40 Org. for bridge builders
41 Anastasia, e.g.
43 *The Talented Mr. Ripley* murder weapon
44 Letter run
45 Los Angeles Philharmonic director
46 2000 title role for Richard Gere
47 Sloth, for one
48 Movement direction
49 Unpleasant face covering
50 Unnamed coauthors: Abbr.
52 ___ Sea
53 Clark Clifford's predecessor
61 Fraternities may have them
62 They're rarely revealed

DOWN

1 He beat Medvedev in 1999
2 It falls on a strike
3 Win over
4 A goner
5 Doctrine
6 New value judgment
7 *The Alphabet Murders* star
8 Not likely to tax
9 Back-to-back Oscar winner in the 1930s
10 Sounds of hesitation
11 Free
12 Richards of *Jurassic Park*
13 Lecture
14 Dame Terry and others
21 Clear
30 Numerous, slangily
32 City near Dallas
33 It's not directly attached to the sternum
34 Ticket line?
35 Source of some drugs
37 Temper
38 Court of the court
39 Composition of some decorative lamps and vases
42 Hatchery supply
51 Daugavpils resident
52 Arabic for "commander"
54 Smits of the NBA
55 Initials of a patently famous man?
56 Slick 50 competitor
57 Sch. on the Charles
58 Calculator button
59 Certain orientation: Abbr.
60 Shell trajectory

ANSWER, PAGE 257

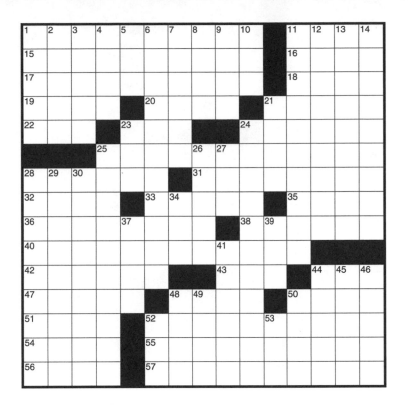

64

ACROSS

1 *Talley's Folly* Obie winner
11 1-Across was on it
15 1829 peace treaty site
16 Fulda feeder
17 Where you might get the shakes
18 One of the untouchables?
19 A model might model for it
20 Word command
21 Business in 2002 headlines
22 Stone of rock
23 Nod, perhaps
24 Prioritize, in a way
25 Diaphoretic drink
28 ___ Islands (supposed Fountain of Youth site)
31 Fathoming
32 *The Loneliness of the Long-Distance Runner* author Sillitoe
33 Fish catcher, perhaps
35 Vex
36 Very careful
38 Candle holder
40 Basis of election predictions, perhaps
42 Street competitors
43 Bert's twin
44 Fathomed
47 Eight-time Grand Prix winner
48 Ariel's love
50 Film runner?
51 Spread selection
52 Finding fault with
54 Holds down, in a way
55 With time pressure
56 It uses sevens through aces
57 Underpriced product, perhaps

DOWN

1 Some carvings
2 Member of Johnson's cabinet
3 How humor may be delivered
4 Like some predictions
5 It may be made or hit
6 Grilling group
7 They're made in hospitals
8 Barreled
9 Liz played her
10 One with a clutch
11 They may be seeded
12 Purpose of the Magi's journey
13 Arising from a member of another species
14 Film featuring an 18-year-old F-16 pilot
21 Decades, perhaps
23 Sure shelfmate
24 Black-and-white, maybe
25 Superlative qualifier
26 Lacing aid
27 Not to, maybe
28 Shell producers
29 Elvis Stojko's rival at Nagano
30 Lady of Spain, maybe
34 Word of welcome
37 Apollo's symbol
39 Blitzer's milieu
41 Allies
44 Cone, e.g.
45 Stag
46 Host, e.g.
48 Songwriter Rapee
49 Divests
50 ___ land
52 North, e.g.: Abbr.
53 Letter string

ANSWER, PAGE 242

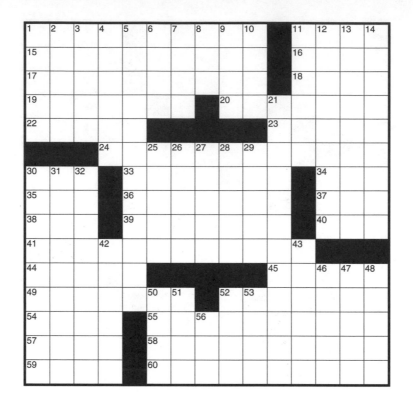

65

ACROSS

1 Blusters
11 Walk way?
15 Like movers' choices
16 Olecranon locale
17 Rambo, e.g.
18 Comment after a fall
19 1984 U.S. Open winner
20 Yet to happen
22 Contemporary of Helena
23 They may be joined
24 It may have flight info
30 Roberts of the diamond
33 Quit thinking about, perhaps
34 It might be struck in Mexico
35 "Kiss Kiss Kiss" singer

36 Most insecure?
37 Former Japanese premier
38 Unitel alternative
39 Information source
40 You may build on it
41 Tax write-off, perhaps
44 It's good for a few bucks
45 Senate member, e.g.
49 Some cavalrymen
52 Yeast enzyme
54 Peek follower
55 Place from which you might take a Tijuana taxi?
57 Dump on
58 Not calling it quits
59 Nipper
60 Workers in strike zones?

DOWN

1 Cause for alarm?
2 Nuts
3 Spohr's Opus 32, e.g.
4 Performed exceptionally well, in jazz lingo
5 Hardly stared
6 Wave producer
7 "Silent Night" penner
8 Driver's number
9 Wuhrer of *Sliders*
10 Alamance County college
11 Feedback producer, perhaps
12 Perfume ingredient
13 So that one may
14 Becomes fixed
21 Bypass
25 *A Confederacy of Dunces* novelist

26 They may be muonic
27 See 29-Down
28 One may be unlikely
29 With 27-Down, Los Lobos member
30 1996 Olympics shocker
31 One way to be romantic
32 Cause of some dermatitis
42 Part of AGI
43 Like a Mickey
46 Champion of dance
47 First woman member of Parliament
48 Some advertising signs
50 *Rent* actor
51 Pak of the links
52 Reason to mourn
53 Lady chapel locale
56 Dog surnamed Hoek

ANSWER, PAGE 244

66

ACROSS

1 Reformed Cistercian
9 Court decrees
15 In an unproductive way
16 One who tries to lose
17 Lipton product
18 Monster movie filmed in Tohoscope
19 Highest point
20 Aloft
21 Hardy heroine
22 Italian sonnet part
24 Doubled
25 "Footloose" singer
26 Mexican fruit cooler
28 "You ___ mouthful!"
33 Satellite, e.g.
34 Tim Matheson's role in *Animal House*
35 Fox, e.g.
38 Toolbox item
39 Russian city near the mouth of the Yenisei
45 Robes of ancient Rome
46 Highbrows
47 Smell, in Soissons
48 Maria Muldaur or Reba McEntire song
49 Drool
50 Macedonian port
51 Kind of *ristorante*
52 Some eastern Europeans
53 Odium
54 Hydrolyzing enzyme

DOWN

1 Round alternatives
2 Expelled
3 Like a melody
4 Yesterday, so to speak
5 Hoops team, e.g.
6 Postage stamp alternative
7 Removing with little effort
8 High-strung, perhaps
9 Allow
10 Amazon feeder, to natives
11 Change the completion date of, e.g.
12 Expert on the right?
13 Playwright McNally
14 Spanish envelope abbr.
23 Bygone title
25 Recipients of drug tests?
27 Tell's home
28 They may be effective across the board
29 Offerer of a "Magnifica" class
30 Hardly hip
31 Kennel volunteer, probably
32 From Hué, e.g.
36 Spoiled the effect of
37 Response to "What have you been up to lately?"
40 Fixed, as a basket
41 One working on the board, maybe
42 Thin layer
43 They may be high
44 Creatine ___
46 Fine, filmy gauze fabric
49 PTA concern

ANSWER, PAGE 246

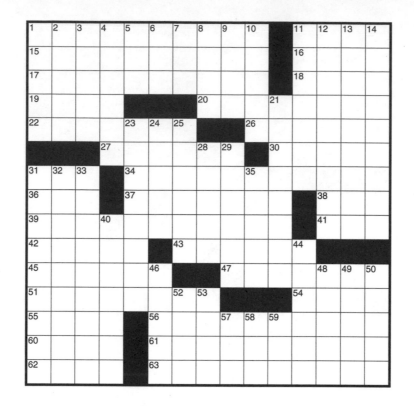

67

ACROSS

1 Bandit's master
11 Voom lead-in
15 Noble Sissle's *Shuffle Along* collaborator
16 1987 Pulitzer-winning critic
17 Person in Washington, e.g.
18 Occult character
19 One may undergo surgery
20 Mozart opera setting
22 Groovy?
26 Perfume compound
27 Risks arrest at a stadium
30 Shannon Miller's Missouri birthplace
31 Spanish "-ess"
34 Literal interpreter of the Bible, most likely
36 ___-eared
37 College figures
38 Cry of annoyance
39 Waters off Pusan
41 Kind of table
42 Quarterback Smith
43 Protests, perhaps
45 Little vise
47 Right-triangle ratios
51 Like some treatments
54 Word-processor command
55 Company associated with ding-dongs
56 Assassin, e.g.
60 He beat Nick at the 1988 British Open
61 John O'Hara best-seller, with *A*
62 "So ___ to you, Fuzzy-Wuzzy ...": Kipling
63 Seafood dish

DOWN

1 Wisecracks
2 Extravagant
3 Jordan, e.g.
4 Fertilizer ingredients
5 Haw lead-in
6 Snap targets, for short
7 *Last Exit to Brooklyn* director Edel
8 Ironclad gunboat builder
9 "Bounce Back" rapper ___-Lo
10 Land
11 Abut
12 20s on
13 It's not seriously wrong
14 Like the iris
21 Biblical psalm, sometimes
23 Hails
24 Biblical flora
25 Makes an officer, maybe
28 Prefix with focal or local
29 Brown-coated mustelids
31 *Past Imperfect* autobiographer
32 Sought safety
33 Boone tune
35 "... for whose dear love ___ and fall": Shakespeare
40 Big Apple bistro
44 Some speech sounds
46 Wing: Prefix
48 Running away, in tag
49 Lucky strike
50 Broadcast
52 Faulkner title words
53 Short puff pieces?
57 Fulfilled
58 Kin of -ian
59 Here-there linkup

ANSWER, PAGE 248

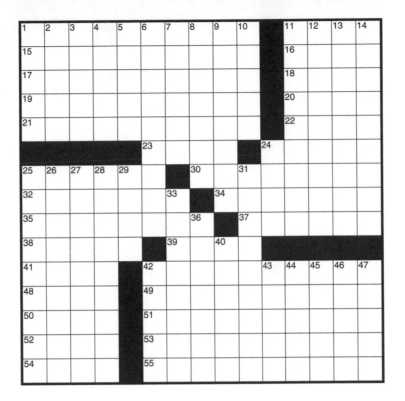

68

ACROSS

1 What a pricey product may have
11 Scandinavian tongue
15 World War II conference site
16 Pioneer in sign language
17 Eponymous museum founder of Fort Worth
18 Places for aeries, possibly
19 Counterpoint part
20 Guess beginner
21 Picks early, perhaps
22 It may fly
23 Yesterday, in Yucatán
24 Tanglefoot, e.g.
25 From Chianti
30 Fall apart
32 Unable to play, in a way
34 Cleared of trees
35 Viral disease of citruses
37 Their blades shorten blades
38 Neighbor of Togo and Burkina Faso
39 ___ thousand
41 Many Monopoly properties: Abbr.
42 Good lookers?
48 *Aliens* character
49 Most of the 1990s
50 Composer Khachaturian
51 Associated with two arm bones
52 Black: Italian
53 Viewed narrowly
54 Some punches
55 Observes

DOWN

1 Rogue
2 Fink, perhaps
3 "___ Mio"
4 Los ___, California
5 Letter openers?
6 Amusement parks
7 Discussion
8 Lured
9 Having no core
10 Some guardian spirits
11 Sentiment in a holiday tune
12 Drive specification?
13 Outermost limits
14 Nags
24 It has body parts
25 Star
26 Still attached
27 It may be salt-glazed
28 Present time
29 No short time
31 Member of the cashew family
33 Figure in a British defamation suit
36 Fabric of silk and cotton
40 Chorus section
42 Some bras
43 Truckler
44 Like some labels
45 They may be drawn from
46 Daughter of Zeus
47 Beauty spot?

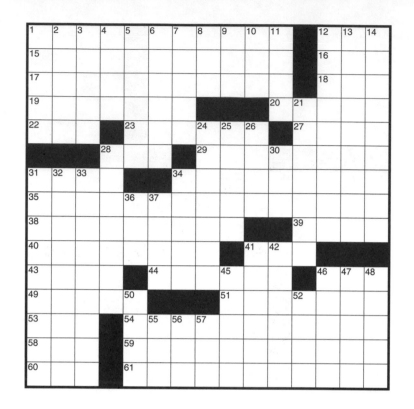

69

ACROSS

1 Scene of a 1958 coup that overthrew the monarchy
12 He upset TED
15 National coming-out day, maybe
16 Wild groomer
17 Like the Six-Day War
18 High rock pile
19 Harvard's ___ Library
20 Hockey players, at times
22 *The Ice Storm* director
23 Test
27 Molière play part
28 Song from Michael Jackson's *Thriller*
29 Number of copies printed
31 Holy Ark locale
34 Important iron ore
35 Jim Murray wrote for it
38 1986 Rock and Roll Hall of Fame inductee
39 More, to Browning
40 Homeless shelter of sorts
41 Burn up
43 Screen
44 False start?
46 Skirt
49 Between, in Brest
51 Scar descriptor
53 South Korean president after Chun
54 Seeds may be found in them
58 One way to go: Abbr.
59 Bari's body
60 JFK, e.g.
61 No altruists

DOWN

1 Donnybrook
2 Home on the range?
3 Treeless tract
4 Wife of Hercules
5 Far from boorish
6 Opposite of deny
7 Roma Downey's Ireland birthplace
8 Actress Lupino
9 *Where's Poppa?* actress Allen
10 Like some coasts: Abbr.
11 Ruling Windsor, for short
12 Blatant display of bigotry
13 Blazer and others
14 Breviloquence
21 Most of Spain, once
24 Small game fish of the California coast
25 Drove
26 Comeneci's collection
28 Appleseed, e.g.
30 Mounted
31 Used lavishly
32 Shot worth noting
33 Pink Floyd song
34 People may run in them
36 Bears are in it: Abbr.
37 Get a handle on
41 Cook up, so to speak
42 Place sharer
45 They serve as pivots in hand rotation
46 Bluing, e.g.
47 Net gain?
48 Flat-topped topography
50 Some guesses
52 Where you may brace yourself
55 Parabasis, e.g.
56 One of a bookmark collection
57 Personnel paring: Abbr.

ANSWER, PAGE 252

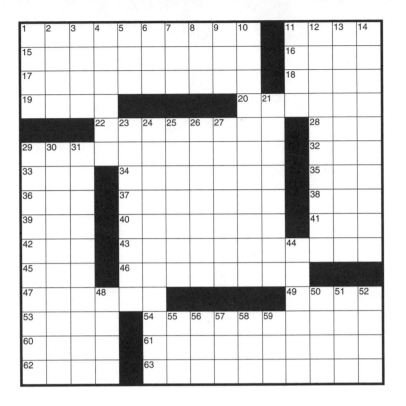

70

ACROSS

1 Be clueless
11 People doing book reviews?
15 Dentist's concern
16 Membership list
17 College stretch
18 ___-Altaic
19 Kind of column
20 Lion tormentor
22 *Kissinger: A Biography* author Walter
28 Fan alternatives, briefly
29 It may inspire passing thoughts
32 Hind foot?
33 Salonga of song
34 Energetic motion toward a point
35 Rene Auberjonois TV role
36 Org. with many schedules
37 One in a cheering crowd, perhaps
38 Pro ___
39 Alcott's ___ *Boys*
40 Hall-of-Fame basketball coach Don
41 La lead-in
42 It may cause you to see spots
43 James Caan/Mandy Patinkin movie of 1988 that led to a TV series
45 Ruth's 714: Abbr.
46 1994 sci-fi film starring Kurt Russell
47 60 ___ (typical bulb)
49 They're far from endangered
53 Bee's kin
54 Ravel's *Boléro* calls for one
60 ___ law
61 Architectural supporter
62 Turns black, maybe
63 Did in

DOWN

1 Hotel nickname
2 Take ___ at (challenge)
3 Wind-current catcher
4 Donizetti's *L'___ d'Amore*
5 Chevron wearer: Abbr.
6 Dinghy thingy
7 Producer of wall flowers?
8 More than slow down
9 Announcement to passengers
10 Three-time Formula One champion
11 Motley ___
12 Big name in relief provision?
13 Town in San Luis Obispo County
14 Professional pitcher, perhaps
21 Scorns, in a way
23 John Wayne war movie, with *The*
24 Sandstone impregnated with bitumens
25 Mistress of Pericles
26 Jalopy
27 Seasoning
29 *North* star
30 Electrostatic printing
31 Idles
44 Like a span of oxen
48 Poet Gallagher
50 Porto ___ (Benin's capital)
51 Not kosher
52 One lorded over?
55 Outlawry
56 Dakota shooting witness
57 Series finale?: Abbr.
58 Cartoonist Browne
59 Bitter, e.g.

ANSWER, PAGE 254

71

ACROSS
1 Backhanded
8 Company clothes hanger?
15 Star in Auriga
16 Big falls
17 Innumerable
18 Flower arrangements
19 Suit accessory
20 Pliable leather
21 Pig, perhaps
22 Like some numbers
24 Quaint
26 They take major orders
29 Surfing expenses?
30 Chosen by another name
35 Histocompatibility determiner: Abbr.
36 Tatami composition
37 Baskets
40 Scrutiny
46 You may be under one
47 Jack, queen, and king of hearts, e.g.
48 Potent ending
49 Dr. J was its MVP three times
51 Steals the scene from, perhaps
52 Oft-removed pair
54 Verses
55 Five Nations members
56 Photographer Model
57 Recuperation aid
58 Try to halt expansion, perhaps

DOWN
1 Shield constellation
2 Layer of sediment
3 Feinting foot stamps
4 First NBAer to score 20,000 points
5 Kindly
6 Cathy's dog in the comic strip "Cathy"
7 Lutheran thanksgiving?
8 Anent
9 They may be in balloons
10 Like flip-flops
11 Disqualifier, at times
12 One getting wet
13 Gunpowder, e.g.
14 Mah-jongg wind
23 Lower in status
25 Touched
27 Sarah Purcell series
28 Heading abbr.
30 Popeye's alternative
31 Cutting edge creator
32 Tapped anew
33 If not
34 Port named for William IV's consort
38 18th-century picaresque novel
39 Pacific coast behemoth
41 Most likely to be fed a line, maybe
42 Scabious relative
43 Whip up
44 Some musical groups
45 Promontories
48 Travel route
50 Right hand, briefly
53 Hillary, for one

Answer, Page 256

72

ACROSS

1 It leads to Panama
16 Anne Bradstreet setting
17 They may lead to weight problems
18 Some metabolic maladies
19 Blue or Cross
20 Knock over
21 Shook
25 Crank
30 The Magi visited him
31 Journalist Kupcinet
34 *For a Few Dollars More* director
35 "Them," perhaps
36 Tarbert turndown
37 Kurt's wife and favorite singer
38 President's concern
41 Exclusivity of a sort
42 Minuteman's place
46 Put on the books

47 First postdelivery words, often
51 Places for chalets, perhaps
54 Not planned
55 Book with only one chapter
56 String used in railroad construction
57 Medicinal plant of the parsley family
58 Caribbean Indians
59 Vending machine visitor, maybe

DOWN

1 War assets
2 Tower of London feature
3 Word on a Mexican stop sign
4 *D.O.A.*, say
5 It ends "In her tomb by the sounding sea"

6 Wolfed down
7 Like a pack mule
8 "Put ___ on it!"
9 Rapper Jones
10 *My Michael* author
11 Balance coordinator
12 River of southern Bulgaria and Turkey
13 Eric of *The Real World*
14 Plot, perhaps
15 Bairn, possibly
21 Shakes
22 Don't keep in
23 Steptoe surrounder
24 What you can say again?
26 Age
27 *Pêcheur d'Islande* novelist Pierre
28 Like some mathematical functions

29 One past 12
31 They're boundless
32 Palm switch
33 Isuzu sport-ute
39 Mamet play
40 *La Cautiva* poet Echeverría
42 Two-time South African prime minister
43 City east of Grand Rapids
44 Unit in a lambert's definition
45 Two hundred fifty-six dr.
47 Containing one of the halogens
48 Fast one
49 Like chestnuts
50 Tribe of Israel
52 Dog's pursuit, sometimes
53 Yemen's capital

ANSWER, PAGE 258

Hard-
to-Solve
Cryptograms

Introduction

A cryptogram is a fairly straightforward puzzle. Every letter gets changed to another letter of the alphabet; letter substitutions remain constant in any one puzzle but change from one puzzle to the next, and we decode the code.

The method might be simple, but these puzzles aren't easy. They're called "Hard-to-Solve Cryptograms" because their creators have painstakingly removed the easiest steps usually available to puzzle-solvers. Articles, conjunctions, and even prepositions have been eradicated whenever possible. Very few solutions have the rhythms of ordinary speech. And simple phrases, such as "the early bird gets the worm," may be transmogrified to something like: Early rising avian catches earthworm, appeasing hunger. Perhaps worms should snooze longer.

So how would you even begin to solve them? Well, one of the most popular methods for experienced solvers is to separate out the consonants and vowels. Letters that occur only once or twice are most likely consonants, as are letters that make most of their appearances at the beginnings and ends of words. Letters between two consonants are usually vowels. Once you've made a start on that process, start looking for words that begin with two consonants; the second letter is a good candidate for H, L, or R. If many words end with the same consonant, your best bets are D, S, or T. Three consonants at the end of a word might be –ght or –tch. And determined as they may be, puzzle-makers have trouble eliminating all prepositions. Though they may have sidestepped in or on, they probably had to use within, into, above, or atop to do so. Look for likely places and patterns for these and other longer prepositions.

Lest you despair, there are also hints for each puzzle. There may be a hint in each title—but keep your mind flexible here. Something entitled "High Spirits" might be about some elated people, but it more likely describes ghosts in the attic or a mountaintop salon. Under each cryptogram you're referred to three hints on how to decode three letters in the puzzle; those hints are listed on pages 86 and 87. Use these hints sparingly, lavishly, or not at all, as you please. But have fun, and never, never, never give up!

Hints

1 U → R	39 A → Y	77 C → G	115 K → X	153 E → I	191 C → T
2 A → H	40 L → G	78 F → H	116 N → R	154 X → I	192 I → W
3 P → S	41 P → I	79 C → O	117 K → P	155 V → Q	193 E → S
4 C → V	42 T → P	80 W → B	118 H → A	156 Y → P	194 X → T
5 G → F	43 Q → N	81 D → L	119 X → G	157 B → C	195 Q → A
6 B → Y	44 Z → W	82 G → E	120 J → M	158 S → V	196 T → I
7 X → Y	45 P → G	83 W → I	121 L → S	159 A → F	197 Q → P
8 D → E	46 T → A	84 X → P	122 K → S	160 R → Z	198 Y → Z
9 Y → C	47 M → T	85 B → T	123 D → T	161 K → G	199 A → P
10 C → W	48 Q → R	86 P → E	124 S → U	162 I → E	200 O → H
11 T → X	49 V → N	87 E → P	125 A → C	163 V → M	201 K → I
12 B → S	50 O → Y	88 Z → O	126 U → G	164 U → O	202 P → B
13 D → Q	51 E → Q	89 C → E	127 G → A	165 J → O	203 H → M
14 X → O	52 K → H	90 F → R	128 O → J	166 A → V	204 H → F
15 H → O	53 H → U	91 F → Y	129 I → F	167 Q → E	205 U → Q
16 U → E	54 W → S	92 D → U	130 Q → S	168 Z → A	206 P → U
17 J → U	55 O → I	93 F → C	131 M → Z	169 Y → N	207 P → F
18 D → W	56 N → D	94 L → O	132 Q → K	170 X → R	208 H → W
19 T → U	57 U → M	95 E → L	133 A → G	171 X → S	209 A → O
20 N → E	58 D → X	96 R → P	134 J → D	172 J → S	210 V → P
21 Y → E	59 D → Y	97 X → W	135 A → S	173 F → X	211 Q → U
22 W → U	60 A → E	98 I → X	136 C → Y	174 D → H	212 E → Y
23 T → R	61 T → O	99 D → N	137 P → M	175 O → E	213 J → F
24 F → E	62 I → L	100 R → S	138 P → T	176 U → D	214 T → M
25 E → K	63 J → E	101 W → Y	139 L → D	177 K → M	215 E → H
26 R → D	64 Y → V	102 L → E	140 S → N	178 W → O	216 G → Q
27 G → M	65 N → Y	103 X → V	141 V → S	179 C → R	217 V → E
28 L → T	66 C → H	104 D → O	142 P → A	180 L → U	218 I → T
29 Y → L	67 T → M	105 J → A	143 U → F	181 I → R	219 U → K
30 R → H	68 C → M	106 Q → B	144 P → W	182 Q → H	220 G → C
31 T → N	69 A → T	107 T → H	145 Z → I	183 M → F	221 U → N
32 K → Q	70 W → T	108 F → Y	146 I → N	184 O → D	222 L → I
33 G → P	71 O → P	109 Y → I	147 X → B	185 V → H	223 F → T
34 K → A	72 F → W	110 H → T	148 B → M	186 A → I	224 E → A
35 Z → Y	73 S → X	111 F → L	149 H → I	187 G → S	225 I → A
36 P → H	74 G → O	112 Z → N	150 S → E	188 B → H	226 F → S
37 M → O	75 Z → T	113 R → I	151 S → P	189 X → U	227 R → W
38 Y → O	76 Y → S	114 Y → M	152 M → B	190 U → H	228 S → F

Hints

229 Y → G	**267** R → N	**305** L → X	**343** M → S	**381** T → W	**419** L → A
230 I → S	**268** O → M	**306** U → S	**344** E → Z	**382** B → A	**420** J → G
231 D → S	**269** D → F	**307** P → N	**345** D → I	**383** U → V	**421** X → D
232 K → T	**270** T → E	**308** W → V	**346** A → N	**384** V → B	**422** V → F
233 K → Z	**271** A → W	**309** O → W	**347** Z → L	**385** Z → V	**423** K → C
234 Z → U	**272** G → U	**310** L → H	**348** E → D	**386** Y → X	**424** B → P
235 B → I	**273** L → N	**311** O → B	**349** Y → A	**387** I → O	**425** B → N
236 J → Y	**274** G → N	**312** T → J	**350** I → G	**388** M → N	**426** N → Q
237 R → B	**275** J → N	**313** L → R	**351** S → H	**389** V → C	**427** G → Y
238 G → X	**276** P → O	**314** W → D	**352** O → A	**390** R → E	**428** V → I
239 Q → M	**277** Q → L	**315** P → K	**353** A → M	**391** H → P	**429** X → M
240 B → O	**278** D → A	**316** M → Y	**354** R → O	**392** K → L	**430** W → K
241 H → C	**279** R → Q	**317** I → U	**355** X → S	**393** F → J	**431** R → A
242 M → K	**280** N → L	**318** H → Z	**356** E → C	**394** M → U	**432** U → W
243 A → L	**281** E → N	**319** J → W	**357** G → K	**395** X → L	**433** K → B
244 D → G	**282** H → R	**320** Q → G	**358** M → V	**396** Z → D	**434** J → L
245 J → H	**283** K → U	**321** N → I	**359** Q → W	**397** U → B	**435** C → S
246 O → N	**284** B → T	**322** S → Y	**360** T → B	**398** N → C	**436** J → I
247 M → H	**285** O → T	**323** H → D	**361** E → W	**399** U → Y	**437** G → D
248 E → R	**286** F → I	**324** C → A	**362** X → C	**400** D → V	**438** A → L
249 C → N	**287** S → M	**325** V → X	**363** J → R	**401** O → R	**439** H → S
250 L → C	**288** K → N	**326** C → Z	**364** L → F	**402** W → L	**440** P → C
251 O → Z	**289** U → L	**327** B → L	**365** N → O	**403** K → Y	**441** E → O
252 Z → G	**290** I → Y	**328** W → A	**366** F → O	**404** C → P	**442** W → H
253 S → L	**291** N → W	**329** V → O	**367** D → M	**405** T → G	**443** S → R
254 G → L	**292** B → E	**330** W → Z	**368** Z → E	**406** I → B	**444** J → D
255 R → U	**293** E → I	**331** Q → O	**369** Q → I	**407** S → T	**445** U → I
256 H → L	**294** M → C	**332** I → H	**370** O → G	**408** H → Q	**446** V → W
257 M → P	**295** K → P	**333** W → R	**371** R → J	**409** V → U	**447** O → U
258 S → G	**296** T → D	**334** E → G	**372** I → P	**410** L → J	**448** L → O
259 Z → M	**297** C → I	**335** F → N	**373** V → A	**411** B → U	**449** E → O
260 E → F	**298** G → T	**336** Z → S	**374** T → F	**412** I → C	**450** C → U
261 T → L	**299** T → C	**337** R → T	**375** J → B	**413** R → K	**451** W → N
262 N → G	**300** W → C	**338** I → Z	**376** S → K	**414** Z → H	**452** I → S
263 G → J	**301** I → K	**339** R → F	**377** U → X	**415** U → I	**453** F → A
264 O → L	**302** J → T	**340** R → L	**378** K → O	**416** A → Z	**454** H → G
265 N → S	**303** T → S	**341** Q → T	**379** N → T	**417** U → T	**455** E → H
266 M → R	**304** P → J	**342** N → H	**380** X → F	**418** K → F	**456** B → T

1 Spirited Spot

NHAIWRUGY BUAAUOW GOCUFD CHIRP BONEZ
GIRLDAY RUSTYNAIL ROWDP, OTDW, "YDVIUAO
WHNEURSLUFP."

Hints: 415, 438, 352

2 Wisecrack!

"LFFW TSWC QLWW CYED WLPLDCN TLDCW OLV
OSRDA." WS CP EDA VEAUS EAW WEN. CVRL,
JRC CYUW UDTQRALW CYL WYLQQW.

Hints: 54, 65, 277

3 Fanatical Gardeners?

PAN GHPQPH, KOZEHYNLNK PMH PAHCZQTK RNQLZ
QSH, MQZ MHLZAOGNK IR TQPOYNZ MAH
GNLXHLFNK LOPNZ PH AHTHL OP.

Hints: 15, 138, 336

4 National Security

VHCE EGZHSPJ GE JPVX GU IPEZQCGE PWPSRZHTP:
ZAHV ILGKPSZ HV VG VPSLPZ PTPE DGRLV ZLRFD
JGPVE'Z XEGO OAQZ AP'V JGHEC.

Hints: 141, 444, 59

5 Cracking Up

HURLS-STALE JOKE NJTAIN INRKE IJRZN
RLNW NJRTS, XYLN OXTF, INTAKE WOE.
UYZN OTG IQWTNI IQURLN.

Hints: 25, 178, 230

ANSWERS, PAGE 259

6 Making the Scene

WDJ IVTZ YTF JTAQZ IVHM; TWEDV CTFD SUE

SLAQO. ATOM ITGMZ AHOM IVDWMZ, SLM

STAQDG ITUF IGHLFVZ.

Hints: 372, 35, 47

7 What A Drag!

MK MW WOZS WDGW BVS UGWKEMIIK OSKBOW

DBWSI HMKQIGLK G KMPV OSGHMVP "PSBOPS

FGKDMVPWBV KUDISQQSH DSOS"?

Hints: 150, 240, 174

8 Oh, Neal!

HUNJYEUWHI NUQP HXNQM NUQIVSMIE HDHYFVF

NGVY-HJWOVGOSB QSFVYBYHFQHMV HMWIVMV:

MWV WVOPTHS JNTVMW.

Hints: 442, 365, 211

9 Any Antiques?

IJPWU IEPR IVDPEHVDR IDXG IJKWEPJHEPN

IXDRENP IJWHXDERK IVDPEKQRZ IJYXDEHR

IDRPWQ IAJH.

Hints: 129, 14, 307

10 Hoover Says ...

QCFSR CTP CF CAVERN XTTPRXRNXQAP

CNNTCZNXEF WET NDCN PAPVPFN EW EBT

REZXPNI JDXZD RPPSR BFPCTFPY VEFPI.

Hints: 174, 23, 441

11 Not a Square Deal

ZQQJHEADQ SEDBQZADIJQDA DVB NPVFJK
LPAUHPV FJK WDIX TXZO: SEZO SEJYIZPVY LEI
XZW ZV "RDB YXDLJ."

Hints: 145, 251, 278

12 Woody Allen Quote

X'L GMC Y AUDI EMMO ODXAUD ... MGTU X CDXUO
LYNXGE Y V-CVDG YGO JMVGO VW QWUZZXGE
YGCXOXQUQCYKZXQSLUGCYDXYGXQL.

Hints: 409, 274, 184

13 Senior Citizen's Complaint

JHQCKAIC T WQTHH CJGD J LCKQKIPJLCTN
XDXKPR, QCD VTHX LPKGTUDU YKFJUJRW TW KV
ZADWQTKYJEHD ZAJHTQR!

Hints: 54, 256, 429

14 Your Money or Your Life?

FZKOGM DLEBF ORWCE RXGBDKH IKM GR TLG
VLFRCE RXBCBRC KJRWG VWZTLZM ORZ
XKGBLCGV: VBDXHM KVQ GNLBZ JKCQ.

Hints: 298, 235, 84

15 Touchy

MQZCGL DCXOMN PCGI WMBCME HKQWN KHUMYFZ
FK DKGCYMIQT FAEQYRCTS AMQNZFWKTS
WKOSATMYRZ. WMZOGF: "W."

Hints: 333, 378, 2

16 Broken Skylight?

MOAD OD CELDQ FODBLF LC KYGMW SOBQLFD
SPDWPQQPD JPCH KELJYPOSM, "LGE HDJYLMHB
APEBHD OM DLF LKHD."

Hints: 142, 99, 341

17 Thank Goodness They Didn't!

EDLXQJSAL, ZBLGO STRUDEL STEJDOLBFUVL
XFVLEX, STFGXATB CADVTJTCADSTCJMSATVTYDSFV
XTRL.

Hints: 194, 102, 281

18 Wishbone of Contention?

LIEIPNTGNR ETXDB BGVWIPH YNCIM YTGIM
VFGVWIR YTNRVFGHI OGPF P-HFGTPH HNJGRE
"OI MX VFGVWIR TGEFPH."

Hints: 138, 309, 14

19 Change to Morgue?

DROGCEQRVPDOHQ ECBLM MLCMBCE GLAQ
RPHDOQCG RIUL HIB DVPKOMLM OQ SPIGM
VLECBL OQHLGA CAQLV ROB. JICEMCVF!

Hints: 341, 159, 254

20 A Cut Beneath Him?

KLENB FLGI YLEF-OBIICIFX OVNB RETB SLK PEN
OLECG VDWHFVHPCK PHCQ HN EXVDJ FVGVDJ
CHOD   RLOIF.

Hints: 188, 162, 309

21 Dressed to Kill

YEIJDXT CERKOTX VXQOKCEI BXKFR JETR, LKHOD
KOCTINOT KCOTLKCRJI JXKV ICKBX LHDCEZKHWX
VQCYKXD.

Hints: 79, 55, 392

22 That Big?

YJTCXCICW TGZWSCJW DGPPXRK RASJTCSRF
CPGTJWCPXR AWGUTCW URCKA RHSKC-XCKQR
AYGR: AJVR SURWSI RRR.

Hints: 390, 432, 324

23 Overgrown

KPG RXI AJJ BWGIWEZ JAM HGYMK UXI UGZYE
AEG NPGE PGM FXFXSUGM IYIIAAK UGFYSG
NYIGMSGTAE-KWVGB.

Hints: 93, 397, 209

24 LSD Trip?

ZCJDC AJGBW XNGMF JXFCG ZJGEC YCJBW
RJGFI. UBCJT ZNTCG SJVTF FJPCM MCDCT
QCCPM. BJYZC AUTCI.

Hints: 89, 315, 105

25 Gangway!

IZHBLXBZR, EBNCGDOO-EODJ, SDLFGZUW
DGEIJZFC RWZHSOCJ BNCG JDGF, SDOJ JVDGM,
RVBGC UGBMZRCOQ.

Hints: 134, 264, 278

          ANSWERS, PAGES 259 TO 260

26 Pants on Fire?

RKIPZMJEWO HZODJEI SVZYK SWODKP IZYWUK-RZPK
HZGUJM. HWUYJTK MVEOKY OKZUMD GKYUZAO ELI
SEVAKOYKUJHJMZYJEI.

Hints: 449, 146, 436

27 With Six You Get Egg Roll

AJDF QYSVIEXTR JX ISKNJ-FNBXJL UJRNVY MYKA
TYMX LYKT UYVRLBN, LYG ES DJX, OFEV RNVSTFK,
NFGSJKE XJQBNLEO.

Hints: 216, 38, 296

28 *His* Not Good?

IMKGBTWKGMV HJJMQ EHWFMN KGHGOM EHKW'G
ETK MHV. KAONZGCV SMNG ETK IHK OYNQ, AHVLMF
GEHG CS KCBM QCOWY NHFQ.

Hints: 455, 118, 375

29 Clerical Mishap

SEOQJ SQREM SEFZIAH SQICT SQOIM. SBREA
SQKIG SQBAELIT SIMJEGL-NZIJ SQGIHEMJ. SBHIZM
SEOBMQVIT SEMDQGLT.

Hints: 158, 115, 71

30 Someday, Maybe?

YDUJ DYZPRXK AHFPNIZ KRFAPHD: NYDFPMTJ
HKMYDNRZ, KLNYDHA UYXNRHK, YFURXA WRFHXZY
MRUWDPKH ZJWPMYF UHXL.

Hints: 354, 180, 57

31 Aerobic Exercise

GAHFTK WHMDDTK, DMKPAGXTL IZ ZTMKG CN
TJWCGYKT, RTDG PTQ HANT IZ TPTKRTDAE YGT
CN THICQ RKTMGT.

Hints: 359, 270, 406

32 Youthquake?

HKBFMSEV HSNA-KSXARK VWKEXA OW KOXP, NOJRT
OW EQ OI HBW XOWG HSEKQNRZ, IRZW PBT WKOQ
WS HBW HBKD.

Hints: 204, 55, 70

33 Fancy Service

LBSCE AYFG LRGK BQY YCSA; NDB JFEQQ VBSF
BRN, JLCEN NLQAYF DQKI: GLQBVIF, VICLQBN, GBU
KFCN WBL VYBDE CVN.

Hints: 369, 420, 240

34 Taking the Fifth

VWOX OX QJ YAMOJQAB JRFOXW XJVJU, ZLV Q
UAVQOJ FVVA YG VW QFCWQZV WQX ZJ YHOVVM
PAB VOH OV QCCQAX.

Hints: 55, 171, 275

35 Gesundheit!

STUCK GSEAUCSFZB BELCHY, E.G. GUMS SCB BE
OZOOZE SEZ AD WSE FIZ TUYF MLHZMD FU GUTZ
UPF DUPE CUYZ.

Hints: 248, 220, 71

ANSWERS, PAGE 260

36 Pay Attention Now!

GITXUFDL XWIGQM FJIQIJ WGUJIH CTVTHNTIFH,
BDWTCH WIQVW CWDQ EWVH ZWFBU FUQC, VJF
UTC WVM GSDD.

Hints: 196, 68, 81

37 Above Reproach?

KDHOHKHUZ HU UTZSONHVF ONYO MTB KYV
SYUHPM YCTHG ... QM GTHVF VTONHVF, UYMHVF
VTONHVF, YVG QSHVF VTONHVF.

Hints: 49, 149, 423

38 Nutcracker

LDPVXROQ LGDQ WPFVXK PDHOFW KCPLX WODGFL
KXVHFW PVC, CMXF QXPSK GFCH PDIK HR MXDH
YMGQX YMHQX MHOKX VQPSK.

Hints: 15, 247, 389

39 First, Learn to Walk

BJMTPWZDL WKDTZ AJMLW WUROVTP YJTSDB FRLW.
GJTI RIMOZ GJLDWRE JOBYKVU PBYTRWZVU
ZLVMYKA TDHZ UDTZMLB.

Hints: 6, 165, 45

40 After the Crash

OIQDN IQYUP-GVOM XQAVEPUW XAORNW, CHJXWM
RWEONI WYVUQJ IVGUZHMW, GQDRI ZMVDN EHOR
MHUW JHOIWR NAQUJC.

Hints: 386, 329, 417

41 To Each His/Her/Its Own

TRANSMOGRIFY GUSKTAM UINOGSEMY; DSOFOY
KXLGU AXGOFITRE; IXTTEAY CLOP BXEGUA; PA
YFXNT GNOV CXKVS.

Hints: 42, 337, 290

42 Temptation

GR NMWWTF-FECZFUJ ZBMJPFUC, ZBF GEJEJE, JXZ
ZBF EQQTF, BEC GFFJ HMWFTR BFTW ZX GF ZBF
DXUGMWWFJ DUAMZ.

Hints: 275, 224, 261

43 Good Advice

QM OB ZQMRDC QVHQBM RDVG OL, ICLLGDO ICDO
YPECAMRQRYDPM DI NCYOL YM EDPRYNADAM RD
CLERYRAGL.

Hints: 268, 129, 337

44 Proverbial Definition

FZYVUQIZ: GBYVZ, BXMG FZEMW, BRRL ABVZ ZEL
QISCXVL, QMCIWL BOX FILC, ACHL FBYSV RBS
PCSFG VBOISW LBMEVISG BSQZIX.

Hints: 197, 414, 240

45 The Spice of Life

EKRBVU, EKIJU OPEIVNLB JEISBLQ RIVU NLBWPOIE
CLPVFQ IVC BNGKL QISBLU OBRKQNPAEK
OBVJKONPBVQ.

Hints: 225, 95, 399

ANSWERS, PAGE 260

46 The Long Good Buy ...

W'A WG LTDIO IL YEWAWGTBWGH TWO ZIEECBWIG:
BUYS JUICER BTNY BUY UIAY JUIZZWGH GYBXION
ILL BUY TWO!

Hints: 190, 353, 364

47 Try T-F!

YALE LEGIT OMNI YLY KVUHHIF RUGBLVG KVMJCF
PVG WLVJX TLG EUTX OVGF GL YLY KVIFGULT GL
UTMCLAMGM.

Hints: 32, 156, 298

48 Anyone Disagree?

SMGWWG EG PGHKFHWAYHMX SJXCKZHCGE:
"MC MX QJC QGAGXXHWT CJ KQEGWXCHQE CYMQOX
MQ JWEGW CJ HWOKG HPJKC CYGF."

Hints: 171, 125, 333

49 Self-Defeating

FORGET INDIAN WOE MN AGCN MSXEGET HDUE LDSX
DUE FDSYN RD TNR XGH DB O XOR, FOXXL NZNXYDE
BDYHGWC XNZGEHY SY.

Hints: 337, 20, 405

50 Remembrance of Things Past

YIHNEU YEU YLHNX HNI GOYJSIHNEUC, VWKOUITE
SYKOJ GIYEVT, OKCXTE PHI KVT VITYZ XINVA, DYEX
CHZT, CVITYZ.

Hints: 389, 270, 259

51 Purple Prose?

CLUE TUMID RUMP SEXY, ZYBUD UXSG REBAD RMU
AULI TMZO CMETYO UMBT AMZBUT EYBR-QXYT FLAG.
PMJLY RBOD ALFWEYT ILOW.

Hints: 95, 339, 37

52 New Sounds

BXYGQDS EBV ZHFSHRSX RDS EBVYQDYHS,
QBRSHRZHC RDZE JKEZLBG ZHERMKJSHR ZH
RDS SZCDRSSH-OYMRZSE.

Hints: 193, 150, 325

53 Bacon and Eggs

XTZ GNEEDVRMNG GHWV GXCPHF. TBRA IXANCP BD
WBNF EFXDIPV SNLHZ OTHNCPNI, SNTKPNI EFDMKP.
OBDL WBC!

Hints: 357, 305, 92

54 #2 Didn't Try Harder?

GTNEM ANHMT LNAQG UKMQE KDEGM ANHMT:
KNEMI-QDCTM TNBEG GTNEM NK MTDEMI OUIG
HNEAUS ANHMT JBNMU.

Hints: 418, 47, 107

55 Not a Likely Trio

VTWUZASJR VTUPRPJUWS, VTFXQJKJR VTUPXQT,
VTPXVSA VIXJXZUWS VTJXPD VHQUZAS CXO VWUTZ
VTPUIXQB PQXFCLQ.

Hints: 409, 252, 445

56 Say Thaw?

EYE CAT QUIP IMATH HQU ECBVULYZ INOABHYZ
RQA QIE YOBADOYI? QU'E VYU IRISU IH OYNQH
RAOEUPYON YJ HQUPU RIB I EAN.

Hints: 348, 110, 227

57 Bon Appétit!

UXCOMZ HJPGV GNR XCDSZ HJFI, FTPEVKXO
VHJWNOMPX, DNHEFIKTP VSCDFWN. SNHUZ SCWU
OCEWV KWFEPRNH.

Hints: 131, 285, 219

58 Brunch Is Better

ANWHC FPKJ MBF JHWZX IHXZ DJKHX VKHGN, AJBC
DUBENO. BNJPAHGO WNX ZNBJX XZKRYHCW. IZNC
MPCN, GUHRA ABGE HCXP ANM.

Hints: 414, 382, 192

59 Process of Elimination

LMPNBU OJCIB JCQK AMPXT QRFGOOJB XGSB KC
YCNT RZGSW (DCFU DMAGFU). JBYK HWCP ZMQ
FGRI: LHQK E GPU V KMJBQ.

Hints: 79, 53, 434

60 Lightweight Division

CYWTFPCO CTYA, CIQCYWM CBZWT MWBWCZ UA
LFWZOCYWIW UHRRFWI, SFPEWM JO BJWI ZQWFT
JKO IFNW: DTWOCMC COM SCOCYC.

Hints: 324, 114, 230

61 Rainer Thought

NFRYT QNJWT: "RJKT MJHOFOWO FH WXFO, WXLW
WQJ OJRFWVSTO CNJWTMW LHS WJVMX LHS INTTW
TLMX JWXTN."

Hints: 70, 270, 359

62 Foursome

TWO-PAIR BILGE-TWYGE, UNTPAG-ZVNQR SIAX-BYL,
AVB-AYXG LBV-LYUGE, AGXL-BYQC OGT-UIQ
RVNZAG-RILG.

Hints: 438, 28, 82

63 Comforting Statistic

WYYGNPVHO BG BUL DWBVYWH, GJB GS LDLNA
BUGJIWHP QLGQCL RUG ILLZ WH LTGNYVIB, GHCA
SVDL WNL NLWCCA QGIILIILP.

Hints: 400, 228, 102

64 Hello and Goodbye

BHK DBFMVAVJNJ DFBXJFT QNNJFMN: "XENEMN
QHIQWN AEXJ DHJQNVFJ—EL ZBM MRJ QFFEXQH,
MRJ KJDQFMVFJ."

Hints: 63, 265, 409

65 Feathered Friend

YHER TEAAGT NYXAQUY DQTZQD EMOIAE, UXHPT
GHMONMOU, UZNT OHPPZI PF UZOIHXDZ. H VAEW
HOI YMT DAOZN HXZ TAAO GHXNZI.

Hints: 118, 170, 202

ANSWERS, PAGE 261

66 Not Good News

KEDXEH DGC, ERM, XOVRP PEHYRDH OZOXUDEW,
YUN EDW ZNXKEHXDAWN QEZ XMDH ZRXU KWOX
DYPU KWOX AWDXYNZX.

Hints: 295, 355, 441

67 Audience Participation

QAPFOBH ZYPALVXD UVL-DFBWJ SPYRD SOHWJVBZ
QUAXDEOB, TXFQPOYRVDH SOBUF LUAWT JVWT
EXUPRF.

Hints: 108, 300, 245

68 Dry-Clean Only

NDZE NP DIZ PZV N. ERSPNP KRDRFGS: "VRQIZX
QNFL VGBL QINBD MGB DIZ VGBLNPS KFRQQ. GPZ
IWPXBZX DVZPDA XGFFRBQ."

Hints: 368, 307, 446

69 Fundamental Identity

BCOD NSARCPCNSB AP DMIMHRMF VB BCOD
VOKNMD PZAQUMDP, CD RHQU ZSMDMCT. AL CZSMD
JCDFP, BCOD DMHD MLF AP BCO.

Hints: 447, 79, 351

70 Not Raphael

PDWPSHBPOERJ NIONPWE PUPOE NIBMHOPY SING
NIONPSE CHEF NIIGHOK APBI. BRSXZPP SPRAY:
"BRAIOOR ROA NFHJA."

Hints: 148, 387, 246

71 Animal Crackers

DANGER OR ILL: PGON POTZGNE GFD. UDFO
BLDATE ZAD. XSYS TDMXE BOYX. KWAQ PDZE
LXOUS. XGGUGN ZLGE MDMXLL.

Hints: 448, 294, 82

72 Out of Bed ... and Back

SPIDER COSMIC SU HZTT-TIUQJF PFSUJG
BZZBZZ JCSLA EKIC FIB MZCSUQ SBLCEBLJZ
HECON, AZAJOSUSUQ PEPPNR SUYZCN.

Hints: 234, 261, 302

73 Here, Kitty!

ULQLSFWL, QMRRAS XLFC WAZW PS ELFCUF
EAUFASZ PR SLQCU RPX RCEASC RCQLECU;
FAZCX, XPNDO KXPJC KPKMELX RPX QLECU.

Hints: 339, 95, 140

74 Etiquette Alfresco

GRACEFUL XQZ HU JUFKUE NAFJO QO YAGLAGJ AL
ORU RBYU ORQO ORUZ DACC ORUL TB YCQZ AL
ORU YBAJBL AKZ. –XAJJ XQLLUFJ

Hints: 186, 273, 16

75 Re R & B Rx?

ZR CA! FQ JW XC HU ZX HT KZ JL YI? FQ TH KZ PB
"FK"? WZ NZ! RB: "FX FK FQ DI KZ CB ... PA CB, YI
FQ ZM JQ FQ!" QZ PB FK.

Hints: 292, 380, 130

ANSWERS, PAGE 261

76 How Irresistible!

RAQUW (WLAG) REMR: PSLZL EZL PCU ZNGLR
AW PSL NWABLZRL: PSL GEC UT VZEBAPM, EWH
LBLZMFUHM GAOLR APEGAEW TUUH.

Hints: 100, 316, 451

77 Change in the Weather

IKU'D JUSOIKUJNG NR ROA XUEJARUIXUN JD
HKODJUM UKNOAX NR AXNKWJKNX JU
SRAAXUCROD, HKNKHWGDIJH TKGD.

Hints: 241, 379, 436

78 Joke Variation #173

JBL ZRFO EBIM NBGM SK KRDG KB EJRFQG R XHYX?
PBHU: BFG KB MEUGL SK SF RFN KJUGG KB
IUBKGEK XOMKRFNGUM.

Hints: 147, 82, 232

79 Keep Up the Good Work

NSMQRV MRVRIU, IECTB PSVN FQUVEMUCBR KVSGX
MSKRMQRV, RIMUCBEIQEDK PEVIM DGD-XVSXQRM
SVKUDEHUMESD.

Hints: 272, 84, 161

80 The Changing Sound

XKZLQCSL ZLF ZJQCSL DFPFXZL ZLF DQCSL LXA
DFFP DQCSLZ ZQ FXWF ZLF AJQCSLZ, MZ GXW
ZQCSL GLFP GF BQCPA MZ FVRZH.

Hints: 450, 258, 310

81 By Georges!

BEKPXERXNA HIZTIPNE IB HREZNJ BDJAP SN FDGG
JNYNE SRYN XDZN XI BDJDPS BRZIKP ITNER PDJHN
SN DP BIENYNE UDMNX.

Hints: 387, 431, 248

82 Worn Out?

XISW-KWLSQGPM PSOLYNQI GLIAPRM GNT-SRWI,
TWLVS, IHWRM ARTSI, VRQM ASQYLP VRWDI;
YNBSWI XQWRBSP.

Hints: 316, 230, 189

83 What? Me Worry?

IDKBP IXCDYNPBO MNQFAXU KSCPV KWCJ WKNJC
ANKI LPIUCTKS. YPCNJ XFWKVQCJ TCIKAP VQNWKS
KWQVA ANQFD.

Hints: 297, 134, 116

84 In a Lighter Vein

RCWNZTW GWK KZFFAMDR SA SUD UAKEHSWT
OZKS TWKS SZDKRWI: UHK EUIKHNHWM GWMSDR
W YTAAR NAZMS.

Hints: 26, 290, 407

85 Classic "Huh?"

IMV TKXIMTRB MVUQVIXNIN KDKXI IMV BXLMI, UXHV
TEU AMVBKNMXH, UXWLUERWJKSERI MXQ.
—TUEQ GKQVN GEFAV'N RBFNNVN

Hints: 374, 263, 108

ANSWERS, PAGE 262

86 Looking Before Leaping

WPUKCV FOTSDPVAG COTSAV NPVME
BOTJLGVYW-APSV YPNOA QKOYG AKWFVYPUQ
ZUMOYG, ZBCE DZY BEVKGZ-DOPUC.

Hints: 424, 193, 88

87 Process of Elimination

GNU ON BISTRO D IDYAT BODOSA: ODJA NQA GSZA
BTDF NW YDLFTA DQK IGMR DUDE DTT OGA RDLOB
OGDO KNQ'O TNNJ TMJA D IDYAT.

Hints: 285, 412, 261

88 But No Green Stamps

FOR ALKA SELTZER' FOYFBAFSZR LYZE
RKUZERALEZR: QZAAZE ILLO, IZNZE FOODADYZR,
VLNZE UEDTZR, BL DBODSZRADLB.

Hints: 69, 368, 94

89 Pure Kitsch

RZHWIO-OWXM YSXJQPAF, OPQRDWE VPQIWXJA,
VSEZRWQ YSRZ, RQPIAX OQDWA DWPNR JWBN
ZASRN-ZSXDNH CSNQRL RDAIQEZ.

Hints: 209, 83, 71

90 To Start the Day

UYBFWVJ FKR QKWFR UYRRV: "ABGRFWGRA W'ZR
DRTWRZRN IA GIVX IA AWS WGMBAAWDTR FKWVJA
DRPBCR DCRIEPIAF."

Hints: 205, 385, 135

91 Utopia

OR TONED USED ART HAY MAN TOLD COB, DOG MAN
TOLD CAME, ART BATE MAN TOLD NOG AM HOUR,
SIR'E O PANT MAN FOR.

Hints: 209, 352, 174

92 The Price of Progress

WNCMQG AQNCETM WKQLMF FKLMU TQMCHF TKQCU
ZNQ AKXWMGF. MKTI TEUFNWMQ GND KULMC
"AKAMQ NQ APKUFHT?" FDHTM.

Hints: 199, 48, 299

93 Good Scene

XSFTZ RSXV UPLGJPXCZPW ZUDQSECM SWMCXV.
WDYZ MCGFTZPU DJPU JSHUCXZ VUGKHPCZ RCYZW
ZTUG ECMK VUPCK.

Hints: 272, 1, 410

94 Rolaids May Not Be Enough

BATHES FOOT NEOIFOP QOUEC LUKKI PTING QUFB
ZOMFYJOE DYKKIEOZZI, RYZYHTI, HBOEGUTP,
KANNBUTU, ITC MACHO PIANO.

Hints: 233, 415, 175

95 Bad Stuff

QZBJGZUOJMC YZEOC, EPGA, ZUJB QZJV, AZQFZAC,
DNSGQGUZQFGVE, COUCOCQZ: AQGEE VZOJGVZN
TQGBSUOE.

Hints: 89, 285, 193

96 Or Maybe the Bronx Zoo

ISCRCXCB USC TWLC FJOM, GJBVDRJWM, JRV
QBDQWCM HWJO, JR JXDJBO GQLWV TC USC
TJWWHJBE QK GSQDGC.

Hints: 360, 402, 105

97 Who's Hue

PMH YAUACQ KCHHV, OHUUAX, BVG EUFH TBO EH
QOVAVOTQ ZAC DVHSWHCDHVYHG, YAXBCGUO, BVG
THUBVYMAUO, CHQWHYPDIHUO.

Hints: 382, 9, 179

98 Wrong Idea

GRQYMYXPNPWO, TMKPIMXPOU JGEX RWRPMQ GO
QMZYMLRMX QMNGOT, LEQMT, "YVPQ PQ OGY YVM
XMWK LMWOPOU GJ KWRGX TWH."

Hints: 237, 130, 74

99 Revenge Is Sweet

DMTF GCKVFREWOOMKR IEXWH OMTLZ KXMNV
JCDKZICTL. YCZZV KXOZ ZQXTXDXR XIJVE
UWOOWO. QECDH VKSCFZ TFKQU YXEJF.

Hints: 311, 261, 108

100 Riddle. (Are You Nuts?)

VD FTL PMJW HWJWA RVATAH VA TAW PMAI MAI
WVUPN VA NPW TNPWZ, OPMN IT FTL PMJW?
M IVDDWZWAEW TD M RVATA.

Hints: 61, 346, 96

101 Avoid Boredom

YCF YO ETF PKCV ABPBJKG UBFHFA YO KSXBHF EY
XKQSFXBJJBKCA: "CFXFG OYJJYM K DKCRY KHE
MBET K DKCRY KHE." –TFGDFGE DYVFG

Hints: 103, 371, 38

102 "Happy Days Are Here Again"?

OGNYZ RGWOGBBGR OGLV-GBZLZG CLOPGZ
CXUQZ RGWOGBB GIGY ZQTBG CTBZ FGLVTJB LYR
GYGOUGZXN OGLVZTOB.

Hints: 401, 82, 12

103 Dry Humor?

BSVRSJKQKIMTJ XSSJT, UHMPWQF OSLT XKVJMPMGZ.
JBSMV EGJBVKKX JKOSQT GVS SXEVKMLSVSL OMJB
"BMTT" GZL "BSGVTS."

Hints: 188, 150, 127

104 Trendy Taste

YTWGJFA GSAC CFJEHXAP JXYRYFJ, XJPBGGSBH
WJFJP YWBIR MJFWJNBG EBIARJX, PBZHI NYWKJXP.
LYTTBAW XAFBWS PBWS.

Hints: 351, 220, 235

105 Sly Dresser

UKCHPONI, FEMGKNEGNI PEICKG SCD UCOMNG
"YCCH VJOH" SCI HPOLP-KNMLHP WEUQNH, NDHIE
BOGN VPCJKGNIV, TNL TEMHV.

Hints: 79, 198, 58

 ANSWERS, PAGES 262 TO 263

106 Too Hard to Hold

OFIFODJ AOKWKVA DUOJQSP: MVKXQEU WODJGMZUD
FWMJVSQK. WUHKR ZMNVYU YRXKUDQMVXNR
QSJVGUX FDQXK HOKQPVU.

Hints: 72, 442, 232

107 For Driving After Dark

YGRMI KVUEMB JCPTFMB, VJPYA GYIS KBOPIIM
QBPCPYA, BMOWJ, "PN SGV TOY BMOW CZPJ, SGV
OBM VE CGG TIGJM."

Hints: 74, 41, 169

108 Oxymoron, or Censored Opinion?

"MG YIMSZ GMQOCZIH GMQOC YIMSZ, PKL GMIZ
GMQOCZIH GMQOC GMIZH, BOPC LV 'GIZZLVS
GMQOCZIH' GMQOC?" —QZVIQZ YPIUMK

Hints: 5, 320, 200

109 Driving Hard

QVA ENOTXGA GYRNGHE BTOQIL DGITGOA ENOSXY
DGVPPIQMQIL YUWQ SIES WUBQGI YEOQR.
EOTVPUO TINTOE.

Hints: 315, 389, 369

110 Good Answer

FBTKWBC FH KPTZZ HX FWCBB-IBTC-HPUZ:
"MX IBZFBCUTI LTZ LBUGBZUTI, LWTF MZ FHUTI?"
CBZNHGZB: "FHQHCCHL!"

Hints: 176, 290, 223

111 Relatively Speaking

OR JHSVYFBD CVEFGHRU? BCHIAUNFSFIN TDZHWUD
VWY MCVED JHOFER FU CVOD, HIG ZCYFUBOHU
TDZHWUD BCDR HYDI'B.

Hints: 118, 66, 95

112 Going Pop

MYNVI QMUVNYG YUQGB KEMW AMENH AGNW VUBI
XGVPF NUQOF, VZKQGN XUQF NMOU, VOMAC HGCJI
VZOUYWGN, QMRU QUJMKZPRV.

Hints: 271, 318, 239

113 Maturation

WE OIL USUALLY, AMROE'T ZNSGR NOT PSAYLTTLR
TMCL ANSDALLY ANMXTOYR USHL NXYRDLR
QSGGSYIT MY ALGLHSTSMY.

Hints: 69, 143, 169

114 Some Don't Need Any

QPHK SPEK-WMPKMK TPF AWMF QJTMJFM YJOMK
UBF PZ WHT: "DJK TPKM QJTM WMPKQ YMIUMVZ.
JF JZWMIQ, WM YBZ WPHI."

Hints: 442, 214, 335

115 "I Want to Go ...

... HFIE JK CL MNJJMO PQFRR RAFIE ND
EOFMFEOEBF, AFSFNN, SAOQO JAO
ABCBABCBDBEBDBEBFGBFF PK RSNCCNDP HL."

Hints: 321, 411, 33

116 Nonplussed

HILZMNRQXK, NSRTLMZHK, LMIEC RQTIMD AISGEKT
GMTKQXZS WTMFZHNKR. TOEAZRIMK KUNGRHD
ONZLSIKT NSSEXTMZAD.

Hints: 182, 429, 140

117 Who Kneads Dough?

KFJJTBUNPJLP'T YAMJIFD RPI MJXUFT ORATF OLNFT
TAUI UAO-KDLXFI ZPDZT. YAUVT UANFI ZRF KLF
DPZFT AY KFJJ'T PMJZT.

Hints: 394, 275, 24

118 Road Warrior

LBSVRL IHV LUSNL HL SNOGV GEGL KQABGV
LRTIJGV SO LRHRTSO NHCSO HMGHZ: "BHLL NTRM
IHQRTSO: ZVTXGV IMGNL RSKHIIS."

Hints: 82, 121, 424

119 Puzzling Persona?

FYEQBAXPI SEFHXPIAW, TPKBYXFNA GFETPUQKA
FEPBQXDKU IQNPUXEGK ZGKTUEPWS: "SNQDKAETG
SXGFQKNPB."

Hints: 287, 101, 307

120 Such Sweet Madness

PLO YIXOZPRNZTOT EGKBOXXKG EKJGOT XMGJE KZ
LNX QGKXXFKGT EJHHCO YZT FOZP QGYHM
XKCWNZS LNX FYBBCO.

Hints: 318, 87, 72

121 A Change for the Worst

ABDOMINAL TDOXARAYS IMTTMXVI NY DAOUN
ONNOTH EDWRA ONNAXCNWSP NY NUOZAUIA
XMRNWTYRYUAL CROWL TOUCAN.

Hints: 379, 299, 404

122 Slam Dunk?

XPNM KTCNG "PZX'T YPN XNKYPNA IB YPNAN?"
XEFY UPKVQNAFKEM TBEFFNG GAEMC ZM
DINTYEZMNA, ANBFENG, "AKEMEMJ."

Hints: 97, 36, 317

123 Word Queeries

EG WEIQVJVPVW FQVA CVIIO, LYV FV "QVJVPVW"
FQVA AVLU? EG WEIKYVVU FQVA KLZUEDZI, LYV FV,
EG GDDPQLYWO, "KYVVU"?

Hints: 217, 5, 72

124 Too Much Talk

QAA PEL NKGAZ'W Q WPQHL QVZ UQVI KS BW QGL
WPQHLEQVZW, CBP KBG DKARPRJRQVW PLAA BW
PELGL QGL WPRAA Q AKP KS EQUW.

Hints: 438, 138, 195

125 Another Word Queerie

"QUIRE": POX INUSE ZRQNRIOPEX TIEZ QIBCERYROV
DRKS IE BIES ASNNSEY TURQU QPO WS SOQEXCNSZ
WX RNY UIBIOXB?

Hints: 80, 248, 7

ANSWERS, PAGE 263

126 Premature Celebrating?

CNUILK XUZIG JKI DEEZIILIS TNS VNGFDEF, AOJ
PXU JNVG "SNNHU? RNO HOUJ AI ZDGGDEF! DJ'U
BKSDUJHXU IYI."

Hints: 345, 281, 162

127 Just Stringing Him Along

HRUO ATZN QLJB PBLGYO VROHZTLCY PTU XRCBFP,
BFDP: AGML FTX RCL GZAONL PRSQ HRZ WDCL
VTZBFYGO, RBFLZ GB ODNL.

Hints: 377, 3, 92

128 Vicious Circle

EWYWL PVEA TJVDJ GEW DHPW BVLMX. JGT VM VX
HE WQQ VM DJGDI-BSRR GB DJGRWMXWLGR, OSX
XJW LWMSRXVEQ DJVDIWE VME'X?

Hints: 320, 245, 281

129 Floral Profusion

QVLFUOQ CXQC PCCBUQ LOA TCN HUOA SDQYJQ
HYCDQXW, QLPK DUSK HCNX GQSLYW WSLFGQA
CO QLPK WUAQ.

Hints: 79, 167, 440

130 A Pox on You

BAGEL ROCKY BAOYVZ PEG OSOEKYN YLCONLIEKS.
EKNUVACOMVZ ENLIZ NUN, BOPEKS COYI GALEYEUK,
GEYUMAZY. CAVEAT!

Hints: 379, 293, 437

131 Words Are ...

... TZYVMPL, LIXTURL ZOUMPT, VMQ MB AVM AVS
NLYAVMLMZIS TZUEW ZOLA BM NUMT BY ABXMZ
ZOLA UM PIVTT EVTLT. —TZLUMDLEW

Hints: 75, 303, 388

132 Front-Yard Blight

PGMV AWHF BLG QOBVIL AWHPB: XOPQ XNZVBOI
ANZFOPRHV PHM HJBPJFTGW WGZN, NOYG
ANZFOPRHV VGYGP LJPCWGC BH HPG.

Hints: 141, 412, 310

133 Ham and Wry

MV. P. OXJSHTZ'P VHZRUA UB CIUXAXQO OXIXQO C
FUVKJXVHQZ BUT C SCA KHTBUTVCQFH: "VN AHCT
FRCK! OUUA XPQ'Z ZRH MUTA!"

Hints: 163, 3, 370

134 Moira/Mario?

CBCOACWP RFN VAUDFTAW FCFSVFXN FN KFJPVBOA
UFNOBXA PK UAVNPC NAAIBCS NPDP FXQNAXACO
PC MBCOAV AJACBCSN.

Hints: 249, 314, 276

135 Another Danger

QAEAUL QPGRAIY LVYAIL LT TPY ETYRF HIJ GTHA,
QTL SYTH MTHMU, MPL SYTH PQUISA, IZBQZ WTEAY
WRIQLU.

Hints: 152, 206, 43

136 Cut Up Those Credit Cards

"PIJCMGIX VZZKN RIW EXFWJ DZFM BCMRCBJGZW
ZT VMCIJCM JAGWVN." —SGXXGIP XCINJ ACIJ PZZW
GW EXFC AGVASIDN

Hints: 59, 88, 137

137 It Works!

VIRE FWP WHVFPVV, TWH TIV SHHN LHHM, IV VWP
VPNZPE UIFP APIU, "WHSP RF RV FNDP FWIF
WDOXPN RV FWP JPVF VPIVHOROX."

Hints: 141, 86, 15

138 Safari, So Good

ODRFMCBZK OBFXMAZWUC: HRPMOVYN ZVOBWZK
FRXC PBQD CBKXYNZO WOMCQ RV PORKX-PZE
DZBO ZNRKX CHBKM.

Hints: 401, 144, 168

139 Vintage Groaner

BAEEQ UEP ZAPPED: AM I LDZZACT ICP I LIEM
NUBOB I NDCO ICP I LIEM, YLIO PUDB I FUIOEUIP
NUKD OU? ICBYDZ: OLD PUNS.

Hints: 225, 310, 95

140 Tiptoe

UJFNVI NU EARFYNEU RQN PJCZI: "UJF FJ
MIYEOSAPEFI FXI VJYYNCJYR NU FXI XJAYR JG
YIMJRI NU FXI SJJFR JG ERVIURNJU."

Hints: 321, 100, 165

141 Fractiously Overtalking

WORDMANSHIP DIPMULEKFSO XMPSDBWOUIL
KANEMSOUIPJ JWRUMSDPYAI FARNSDBWKPJ
XMKYIWUSNPR.

Hints: 266, 62, 86

142 Historical Alternative

AKDH RINHE DJJIVIM O YDL MVNHS, O. XNHZDXH
VIKXNIM, "NJ LYNU NU LIO, N'XX LOSI ZDJJII. NJ
LYNU NU ZDJJII, N KOUU."

Hints: 213, 162, 117

143 In Hot Water

DAEMS NSBUS XEIITFEA JKW YPPY EKCQWV NQTATN
NTXMNWXMPCTIB; TVMPJ, DTIJ YWAKCTWI: CRW
UTIT MWWMY FWTA JTN VWCQ.

Hints: 322, 57, 178

144 See Spot Run

BARKED UNIBYDODO PANWP WISHING LIKED PGNKB
KB UKHIKY XUDNET, UDNRKBJ MIETPKN PWKOG
PGODNWC.

Hints: 289, 408, 430

145 Good Question

APTDKPSZ RIPYF OAXLPN XY OAF NIQFW KXJT:
"BD OABN BN OAF ITOBLPOF MPLF, JAG PWF OAFG
QTPGBYM BO PMPBY YFHO GFPW?"

Hints: 235, 319, 261

146 Takes On Perspective

"QRIGVQHA QSKWIGHIH QS RQWIKE UWPUPWEQPS
EP PSI'H RQHEGSKI TWPA EDI UWPMVIA."
–FWQEQSXH PT BPDS XGVHFPWEDC

Hints: 276, 439, 353

147 ... And All Through the Doghouse

KXCLH BXQ PES LJWFP HXOF GQXPBI OFMSEWFQA
EM ASFYU, BEPLFYOFC GYBEP MYS. ('SZYA CFPJFC
GFFM EQ LQFYAF NYAA.)

Hints: 157, 189, 44

148 No Foot Like ...

QAWGZXW RTLGYZ IFY ZWGULGQ UBWKK; QAWGZJW
KWLZ IFYC JLQFI IYWUF FLK TBZ ZTQK KTJY GYV
IALUEK.

Hints: 328, 120, 78

149 Torten, Too

QHTA KEQHGPI: FPM VNKTHMAFQ PTG KFPZ
VPLKEZT DZEGHJI DQPIHTJ VNKFZAE CZEX UEQCJPTJ
XEAPZM'V VHLMK.

Hints: 416, 52, 305

150 Heavy Misapprehension

UPQ VDPO LTF QPVCID QJDZIPFB IJB WRJUHDTU
LTF VDB GJBVB. VDB ZFPJDTF OXBD IJAP HUTQU
KVRZI JGTXD QIJRPB.

Hints: 428, 123, 105

151 Wild-Goose Chase

AWL XSN. IEH LED OR PIT OFT HAY PA DTP ITS GTP
LAD UR AN; HEP BAT! NIT NUB COG (RAP ART ASP
AS HOP), NA STY, NUL FES, IUL ROW.

Hints: 332, 139, 244

152 Cockeyed Optimist?

JFFUBA SNGYJ DK FIVOP, ANE JONKKJ OUBE CDDQ
JLVIYJ IO IB IBASF UBOD FILP—OPNJ, "FTFVE LSDQ
PIJ I JSUTFV SFIBUBA."

Hints: 172, 24, 225

153 Secretary Spread?

GLNOQ AYSBJ KEMVG HWZ UYEAJLVX UWYJQ ISBEI
ZWAFLVS. MVKWOSG AETQLCN HMCN CNMAJ
OPLSUWAJ LVNE LVTMN NBWQ.

Hints: 98, 251, 222

154 Watch Out!

PFU AREYOU PQS MUPKMR AJ GAVU Q DAMLGU:
AX HYK CKP PFU NMYRD XADKMU AR HYK OADFP
WU CAREFUL. —QRYRHOYKJ

Hints: 267, 195, 283

155 Quite a Responsibility!

"PW BQJ XEVSFJEAJ CV IJSXDXCE RJASXEJW, BQJ
WCAXPS XUKCIBPEAJ CV PIB XEAIJPWJW."
—PSRCFW QFNSJG

Hints: 142, 456, 79

156 Dropping Out

QX TQ! GE D ERQJOB XJM BUSSUHLAWE
ZOUTWUTN WXUM GQMW HQGGQT HXJOJHW O.
VXJW MXQLAB U BQ?

Hints: 331, 27, 401

157 Making Ends Meat

VLNJ, VLBCUKBC VLGWTHF VYWAN KBGS TKN
VHHI-CFKBZKBC QYWTKBH YBZ CHGN Y UKGGUH
VHTKBZ KB TKN ESFA.

Hints: 384, 201, 77

158 A Gem of a Puzzle

ZGKKJCVRJD XPCJJCGVF XPGKCJCGV WBWPGJZT
HEVFPGTF UPWFFCJD NCFQ BCJID CPCZWTHWVHW
EM VWN BWOCHGV EUGJT.

Hints: 233, 297, 434

159 Without a Seatbelt, Yet

XCOSW OIUJM MXC DTONNL VSCHQOQM NXCCV AXU
CQFULN SPWPQH UQ PQWPOQ CTCVXOQMN? ACTT,
MXOM'N O YPQC XUAWOX CAC WJC!

Hints: 271, 164, 47

160 Wrong Audience

TRLMQA TFJI SWZ PGV IJKZWFRS VRSK, BREGKZ
WIRJV DGKE FWSK HFWLGKZRMC. TXRSQ PGCCMQ
EGVCTP CPVGTE.

Hints: 25, 435, 299

161 It Happens

XYF QIYV XYF'MD KHJJAD-GSDJ VRDI XYF RDGM
"LIGB, ZMGZQAD, GIJ BYB" PDNYMD XYF SDW WY
WRD PMDGQNGLW WGPAD.

Hints: 424, 70, 127

162 Initial Insight

OUA "ECIIF" LWAEOCYB, OY LWYOA XUCOAUAJT, QJF
HA YWD "KCDEO CBOCQJOCYB YK EYQA OYOJIIF BAX
TAPAIYRQABO."

Hints: 285, 62, 108

163 Topless in Tampico

IKSMGQ, LKDVSA SQOXKBAVM KRQJX BQOX
QHKSATP-PTBBQL OQFRHTHQ, IJBTO XQ IKHN,
"V BQUTN FP GKX VS OKZZHQS, MVOMQ."

Hints: 331, 294, 34

164 Downhill From Here

GYHQIDE AWDSU IDEJKG ARUSSR ZJPS YJUZS ZDLR
RG VSU YGEJY VGAIDRJY. RVSH XGN VJPS RVS
IDEJKG D.E.M.

Hints: 356, 185, 29

165 Mess Hall

MVTMYY POB BEZMY ERL QILE YTUEEAGQW'Y ARITU
FEV OIW EZMK TOKKEL YLQTGY ONLMK YOIWCQTU
YJRRYUMW FS LUMKBEY.

Hints: 255, 441, 76

ANSWERS, PAGE 265

166 Saints Be Reprised?

VIZEEZAHT HEJDA XZNTZPZWJ KIWJ BDVIDWJDF
DLOTHPHJZNP BDMHBFZPM NXDBEDHTNIW KHEE
WHLNOSNPZWJ.

Hints: 344, 118, 145

167 Ay, Ay, Ay!

FDHBRHBR ZDPQC MLVXIP, URHBI, MRXVYR, FDHB
YTSDVPR. UTGY ORE, CYIFRHBRHBT ZIUT, ZVLP
ARUYC YRHI.

Hints: 431, 241, 188

168 Does It Hurt?

KZ YLZ YXX WVDXUJMLW YSI UYNSJZLW, YSI MDL
TYJZLNYX NW MDL MKS BXZWC YSI FXMMI YSI
FMSZW. —JCMLZYD

Hints: 349, 92, 313

169 Sweet Revenge

GCPJQ GIMJ TLIM; THKPWZ AHQ OPUAGZ VPXQ
LROM. YPMGAXHZ YHQA MOQIWG: JOPUAYLMQ
EALJO ELWPDO, CAL CLWT XLCJ DHVO.

Hints: 10, 94, 266

170 News From Lafayette

CRYPT GOT STALE CRBTO POLD PTHYJ KHJI ASRMB
MBGDAT VTFLR, KIHFD ARPOY QTFL DYPTB AIOYLB
TLSR NOUCT.

Hints: 304, 61, 125

171 Vocal Advice?

UP UT WILD OIHEGXH PR LIBF IAKLDEPIF EXQQHIT
BHRXF; UP JBD CI POI CITP LITERATI PR PIHIEORAI
TBHITEILTRAT.

Hints: 162, 415, 256

172 Beef Jerky

CRUNCHTAUTLY ONIX: OHJEAN XHLM MTEMJ JBLU
BI JMTLLN GHLM; JEVBY GHOGJ TVRL, UWEMJ
HLAHEMN EXHOG.

Hints: 53, 242, 65

173 The Rude Kingdom

QBWJBULWBVQLS QLJGU ASBY IPPSPMGKLS JLUF
APSSPEGVM UDV-GV EGQX EGSY ELJGQG, ILVR
IBNUL LVY DVMULKGPDC MVD.

Hints: 49, 92, 338

174 How Long Can It Last?

MW FINDABLA, FCMAE MGDEMH-JALKBN
MGDEMH-JALKBN LKOOAELDFP FQKIM
LKCCAA-NEDBRDBS LKITPA, SAMJ UIDMA QKEAN.

Hints: 250, 378, 268

175 Where's Smokey?

ICGUYCDD IXUCDZ IMUC IMTFZCUD IUCNHCQZYA
IXHQO IUMTFZCQCO IGHQG IYCCMQT IUXK
IYMJBCUMQT IYGKCD.

Hints: 129, 29, 231

Answers, Page 265

176 Needs to Be Resolved

ABCDEFG AHBIDJFGJ IKLIBE AFDMJ CDGFIDE MDC
IOFMIDGI IKHDIBCEIJ JFNFCD FD BPI NHBQPI
RHNFGFMIJ.

Hints: 324, 99, 159

177 Grid Lock

BICK ZAPS HOGI FLDK YOGI BAPD DIOM CEXI TOMB
SEDI. DINK FSOT: ULHI HOED GOBI PUID ZOYJ CSIP
AXIM SICK REBI.

Hints: 144, 99, 253

178 Revenge! (Maybe ...)

PRE YJA RLA WNO UCH. KLA WCO LIO FCO SFQ LJQ
LIA PCI UCO PKE BLE LON DNN WLK. UFE IFD RLP
SLO GLO DRF XLE HNO BLE FIN ALE.

Hints: 212, 3, 20

179 High-Strung?

MADLOB RETURN WHUZBY FYASB YUOSBX UJXBY
HARLMQ PUXON. PAVBRX DLOXAY ("HTOSZ XAVUZ")
ETLBXHZ HBJX OATYX.

Hints: 51, 376, 256

180 Nature

DAEF ODIVELUA ELYMP GR USBCZF PGCSBY HRC
JDLIV PEDA RH KBGSC. HRN KBGIQSP RUS YLUDGS,
EDUASP BG ODYZ ZLCO.

Hints: 354, 204, 222

181 Hit the Road, Jack

NKVRQLKUWC NULSFYKU NRDL NFMKCS NWQVS
TKLS NWCVKUWC NRFIKQZ NFIO TSRQ NKMKI
NUMRY NWXJRYRI KQLU NUJJO.

Hints: 280, 50, 358

182 Speed Demon

SGC SRQIL XGCEIBROLVK TCFR RCARSTCE
FBGDDTA, RQIBFGWTCE RFNIB SRFRBTLFL. HTDI
XBIGXL NTL OCFTSIVK ZGLLTCE.

Hints: 354, 269, 208

183 No Children, Please

WHIM YHJ EBJOKFDT EDCLGMO! YMDAO GXHC
AKJBIX EBALGM, UHEAOMJ OKMJIBFHJ, DAOB AXGID-
COB. JAPX.

Hints: 235, 363, 135

184 Petal Power

FLOWERS FLAIEQQM FILR ZPVJO YLPOH.
HQRAO MARSH XPUIO PTLDQALML SQUISH
VWAHOLTMWIDRD PTOMILY.

Hints: 367, 255, 419

185 Old Saw

FPR XEXYTJTGWA JXYZRCFRY PGZRH FG AXER FXS
IGCRL QL VGYBTCU WCHRY FPR FXQMR, QWF TC
FPR RCH PR UGF CXTMRH.

Hints: 390, 22, 323

186 Killer Cryptogram

MDR CODY DJKW BH WJKYBK LWYZJC. FZGDJZ
MDR KWH KJM, "BKAYAMDOAWNDRC KZYWKZWH!"
CDEZDHZ ZQCZ MZQQC, "YAWJ CAZ FQDLC!"

Hints: 363, 328, 2

187 Water Music

FATHER FENCEGUY WENCFTA HYWQH ALWQH GWQH,
OUUR RUDE GU GDCEGJ PCGCYA UY GDCEGJ
MCYGS, DMFLMCNCY LUPCA ZFYAG.

Hints: 106, 22, 118

188 Second-Hand News

LDX TIKJH PTKF PQKRA "MIAFNH UNYRM,"
MKWIH KQKJA, MTJDVH PQDPW UJDA PTRASIX
MDF, VKMPTIH JIHNQM.

Hints: 143, 47, 353

189 Recess

TSIVWQ-RVLR BNPXRNQ TSQM-QVLLNH TSILUN LMO
AWQ TSYNIVUNJ. TSLLUVIL, TSOZ QWZN, TSTVBJS
PUJW WAANQNH.

Hints: 312, 124, 40

190 Practical Example

UCRRLT ZLTZCITQTK EWYULYQWT CHECIQBCTOR
KCOR QTOCIINEOCM FACT RZALLU UNTZA DCUU
IQTKR.

Hints: 289, 64, 100

191 A Man of the Whole Cloth?

LYING ABOUT QBOUR QLTYG EBGA WAPOS ZBRAOT
WNBIRG, YLSR QNLTU MALNKI. GEP MPWR WNPZI
WRITUP MYINKSFLO KTBYGS.

Hints: 19, 2, 276

192 Unkindest Cut

MCETMCY HBEXPCM ROY LPRFCLSCRMC NDZCM
MCGMTECL SDDP XNRLLTX, XPROATOA STANCE
TOED PRINCE.

Hints: 36, 151, 133

193 Don't Call Us ...

EPVQFLLPW AKLKTPV BOQAOQQPB YFEPMSW
KEEWOGKLJ KMJPV PROLT GSVVOGSWSA IOJKP
CVOJJPL COJY AKSIP GVKRFL.

Hints: 353, 124, 220

194 Kernel From Triply Lost Bee

"QKINIEC"? "TINNIER"? FICUS "DINKIER"?
BRUCIA NRMHIHLO FIC US PHOLADFIA, UGH
PHOLAD PJSBBSO KS IRA'H.

Hints: 56, 225, 260

195 Soap Opera

YW KLEWZA, O.R. IHHKAL'R SERIAL CHAR HW
MBYWX; UHAR BEOWULF YW LYDAL. KHBXR IAEL COF
SELMBA, "Y'G SLYWCYW' YW VIA RAYWA ..."

Hints: 451, 313, 100

ANSWERS, PAGE 266

196 Leapfrog Accident?

WINDJA MNDFIPUJ BPJMUKA MUGDSKIHTP WGFIP
EKHJM COPT MOPA MUA FGWLQIHS GQMPU RGTA
SKIP XGNIM ENDS.

Hints: 367, 151, 47

197 Just a Coincidence

ZCA, D BITV GRC NTHHTICAG MDPAG YIO WYAG
IYHCA TI CYPGR, KFG RTV HYIZ ECTEWC RYSC ZTF
HCG IYHCO HTRYHHCO NRYIQ?

Hints: 203, 398, 30

198 Less Filling

RGNXTS GRGAZBAXZ VPU AXC ZBAJP QVAX GOPXT
OVAZVAY VP DBJQZA'P FGNX XABJYL ZBJYL PB
GIBVZ YBVAY VA PLX LBQX.

Hints: 138, 346, 396

199 No Stars in the Guide

VAINLY FLAG SAGO HOUR: CRAMBO, POET SELMA.
FTEN ZR XYRL: MYC ER PAU. (XRHVY FENO ZO SYAO
WLEI IAG SLEUMI OGNLE.)

Hints: 238, 186, 255

200 Getting It Together

HMCCJ, XKPYZG EKXG VNFDMOAHGH INKQYJ
VKTHME ONBBZG OKGPGH MLWKRGFDQANHZJ WJ
NHKUT NUKING HANDSOME LGDSAR.

Hints: 236, 4, 173

201 Jurisprudence?

SIMPSON SADMLRN, SXROHPJR CRTRMLR, WNOHOMH
YPLSAMCDSH, NIPMV ZPHMRLLRL, YOUR SADXHXAAY
EAYR AT HER ZEAFFRX.

Hints: 209, 170, 110

202 Careless

ANDREC GCPHLILGCDN PR Q FQN KQI QIMDZ,
"BLJN JIJQH, V. ZDIEQNWDI?" "P WCPRM RLW,"
CD QRIKDNDZ–QRZ ZPIQGGDQNDZ!

Hints: 163, 396, 8

203 Ordinary Politics

"SNYAWEFU LFMNYUWW" GWYNANNE? THAMFERN
CWBYANUG, FOWHTHEQ SWAAHZUN THAFAMNY.
AMYFMNQC SYNONEMA RFUFXHMC.

Hints: 178, 289, 136

204 Pleh!

FKNTWHVQHXO TECCSQ OPGFHZEOHPZ OZQWHQB
TWSXGBZPNQF FTQOXAXOWSSK APZ BKFSQYXO
FPSMQZF.

Hints: 253, 326, 386

205 Timeless Philosophy

OM DAVITEOY XIANXI DONKEY QAEYSM ARS,
"SCI TOW OPSIN SAVANNAH EM SCI SCENT TOW
AP SCI NIMS AP WARN KEPI."

Hints: 209, 116, 407

ANSWERS, PAGE 266

206 Mudslinging

EUROBONDS SHJOHDIC HER FAIB EDRIAFCNPBE
KZNBAR NZ YBHKB WHNYXHNBA, WHWU
CZNXDNYRNHCEDCI.

Hints: 80, 379, 249

207 Flown Home

SGFAUBY, YSMPLFX PIGEON FOWL ROXMBK
YNIXUPS PAX. PEMNBWGF AUK, RNMGYSL RIEA
IWLON IRKGELUMB, WFUBESOK.

Hints: 229, 351, 28

208 Monstrous!

"JOZLI" LISRV IGWEF "FCZLI." "TJAGW" FUJIOV
"VJKFL OILYF." "RMSY-VMNF" DWAFV AMHQIB IPZFL
"GMY" ISH IPWLF "YMISZ." XWQ KFIDXB!

Hints: 225, 178, 17

209 Consuming Passions

LETTUCES WPD ODPIUTA P.Y.E. SUYO GEZDIUOR
LBDX BRIR: RSCDX JELEIDTU, BREWLBRRYR,
SEWQGUTARIY, ETW TEZRS DIETARY.

Hints: 206, 390, 188

210 The Site of Blood

DEP UZIH UZHD IZCKNJD CZTWHANI TCNJIX TIP
DPCAIUZ. MEZI XNITHAIU V IZUTHAKZ, WETG
FTJUED MENFZ MTP HN VTIY.

Hints: 46, 186, 146

211 Ship Shape

BLECHY STARLET, YTPOTREM UEPW TQUSFCHZ
APHZRELARCPH OTRJPBZ HPFJ LZTB, DTOLZCHY
ZRLBTHRZ ICRJ FEN RFHYTHR.

Hints: 245, 276, 453

212 On-the-Job Training

QKTF FADV YKOY, "LJJWZKXX CKY AHTAXXABW
VGAVKGKWPJB LJG VJXPWPTY. P'U KXGAKUO ZAAB
ZJJAU KBU NKBRAU PB ALLPRO."

Hints: 165, 60, 395

213 Arrested Development

ZRWUNGUCA VZVQCKM VQNMMCF XR KAZFC
GNRMWRW VTWKS, VZBBCAXRL BANG ANKSD
GNZRMWXR KWUXR BCECA.

Hints: 267, 328, 27

214 A Turn for the Worse?

IRNJPAZ CFOKWJN-HNO FIERO KNYR UNEXOWLPHZ
HJNSK NCPRO WOUNE MONEY LOST DPFHX KNOXRP
HONDA.

Hints: 241, 401, 11

215 Still Going Strong

CARTOON LAD, WHITEJOY ATPR LRWHN RNZAP
FHTG GOHNL ZHEM, ERTPATIOL ZNRHYEHLPATU
LADPOOT-ZAP-CON-LOERTY ATXR.

Hints: 354, 186, 58

216 A Royal Pain in the Castle

VEEM DILLY LUTHOFLSK. BKL NIBS ALLU SKOS
BKL KOB BIAALMLC NEML SKOY KLM BKOML EA
FOC KLTM CORB.

Hints: 52, 441, 13

217 Even Score?

IXYTKG URLICMG ATMLXCI FROCK ULOGAZ,
MYSUPR MYZCYU, IXYLMKG CLUNG. MYRNIGAZ
FTEI ICREATED G.

Hints: 74, 233, 452

218 No More Tangles

BZURDBVHD ARUXHWVS KALJG QLAVN JBDC
NRWWSVN UABHEVG ESBZQBHK DAVGGVG: EXDG
CVA CRBA RHN CVA SLGGVG.

Hints: 56, 330, 187

219 Won't You Come In?

ACECGIKMIO QSMUCK MOAMGCU WKMEYGCOCU
WBD MOGF SIKBFK; HIQ FOBD CACOMOE GCIJQ
WFK CACOMOE FW LYIKIUCQ.

Hints: 166, 89, 334

220 The Fab Four

ABCADEF GH IADJKLHINGMF, OLKDIPQGMF,
CLDJEAMOHGMF, IHK RAJQJRL SGQQ TGHK ...
EOAL IDA HAUAD JPE JT EOAGD AQANAHE.

Hints: 225, 153, 60

221 Beach Party

MANHS RMHZ DUTLCOFPQ UFLYMJ, LONG
GTSEOFD CUZ CMPQZ STRAND OEH; QTHJ,
QIEYRZ GTODY-AMYF PINCH PNEIJ AES.

Hints: 132, 10, 160

222 No Sweat!

RKX CUCXHAVC, KWC TFJQ RCTTKB PKLLCN OAV
ECEKXQ, PMEICN DK HKWHTMVAKWV, FWN TCD OAV
AEFLAWFDAKW XMW BATN.

Hints: 378, 451, 170

223 A Campaign Promise You Can Believe

XCIG LATIN MCI JQZAM MCQGV CI'N NB QJ IFIPMIN
KLHBZ BJ GIX HBZT, XQFFQLK RSPTFIH ZIWFQIN,
"Q'N NIKLGN L ZIPBSGM."

Hints: 56, 177, 111

224 Un-Funny Bone

STU BWIXTES TSOTILSX EI BCLFB ES
ZITBACK-UHMTR ZCEEI, PITHYB WFFTI HIQ.
(SEO CHWXALSX HPEWO AWQTIWB BLOWHOLES.)

Hints: 140, 119, 441

225 Vow of Poverty?

ZYX WYVUTUSRQ SWPYW QSRTON NS MSZLYWN
QKSIYQAJZ. TWSRK HSVPYP RKSZ HJUVUZT NS
NRWZ KWSKOYN.

Hints: 379, 255, 112

226 Brush With Fame

MYXPRAM OMGYL ROKKU OIGWYLE BOIROGYLU
JAYFLOSWU YZ BOAR-JOMC ZLPKMW SOAKGPL.
(AG'E COUP'E WILLOW, EPILOG!)

Hints: 442, 313, 186

227 Mercury Left Behind

FYI WHY JHPF FWHQ, ZPFYI, JHPF AYIGQ; ZY WHY
SYHY PI YWHXS. XSLQ KYLIE QP, ZSP EYXQ XP
CHLAY PGH QWXGHI XPCWM?

Hints: 146, 21, 282

228 Two on the Aisle

IBRJ FPRATE BVPT SCHTEI SCEITH MVBJE BRIG
SHTCIE. OHVBTP MRPH (FRIED ESPRIT) ESPTCA
STICHE. SPRTEI PLTA ATFPRE.

Hints: 151, 270, 218

229 Be Careful How You Play

XI BIXNYQ WORXHIX LKA LYKQRXP HQISCOY!
RX WIOOYPY, KERN AI ESWL OISN ESARW, LY
ALISON LKDY JQKWHRWYN AKTY AKU.

Hints: 310, 387, 135

230 Surprise!

ITSG THEGXHZTSA QSEIYGT VOZI AVOZEIWKQRT.
TOUIZAEGST YSOTHRKN JTH ITKF QJWXAI QHUSN
WQR UXN.

Hints: 126, 443, 65

231 Pyramidal Wisdom

CLEO FIGS PTAH VCIGEP RIXYSTVA QSLTKV. HIPLF
XLDA YTELO OSIX USINK STRA, ULSEAF. LEVI NISHC
HSFTKQ: YIEAKHL.

Hints: 91, 110, 387

232 Sheltered Life

SHOTGUN, KZWTPYRN GRAZE RGX
MZUGNL-TWIN-NGH NHRSLIHUE. NHMGLE BZRG YN
PHJGR LZ HWW YR LGRLN, HRK TZUTZYNGN.

Hints: 82, 118, 265

233 Alphabet Oops!

XYZ? PYXWDTDZXPZOW KANSNTH YWLGSWOOWD
USZARG AO RATIO KW GINDO END YZOANYZS
XHGSWMAUG ZGGNUAZOANY.

Hints: 433, 365, 285

234 Distinctive Quantifications

XABCYABCZABCFEUDAL CZ ZCHOP-GWELOX RWOA
CR BEZCK. XARYAKUZPSSUQSA CZ BAOLCKUS SCRA
WG ASADAR ZPSSUQSAZ.

Hints: 148, 297, 336

235 How Dry We Are ... NOT!

FOUR RACY (PIGS FCJO, MPFD HCMY, IGCX SYIC)
ECAD DZAP GCWY, RYPA CNGD. REDS QPWL CMRY
LYMF, NHCW, DBCR, HECK EYWD FOWL.

Hints: 206, 8, 38

236 She Got Her Stars Crossed

MELVIN QCPA JPCPYIPUN UCPLNY QMBXGS FJNT
FPAMT QVTEY BTQVXNE GMD CNGBCT CMGJNC GJMT
GCBN XPLN.

Hints: 245, 31, 276

237 Sole Men

LIRQVJIE FQ FG JGMUWEV ZRGFEQJIP JGARPJO
QVJWI SIWOFP ZJFU XRRDJO HY LP QVJ XVWY
ZRGD FGO SWEV SIWFI.

Hints: 453, 156, 341

238 Personal Worst

BNMBNPONZ WMZFOL NZPIGHGF RJZGRA KGNHLP
NF UA ANBKLPIJTNZ. NXLGH NIXMR FNLG, PIT
PINTO PINT NINA WJPLKNPLG.

Hints: 67, 192, 3

239 Thankless Job

NGIIEAC GNXAI XGDEYAU DIAAC YTFEYG. NREFA
MEIAJTX UDIWOOFAU DRIGWOR SITXYRAU, MAFEXA
SGWXCU CGNX FTCCAI.

Hints: 30, 370, 181

240 Here in Dupli-City

NRGCPXOKW DRNQD BOUGH IRAQI QKA SPURS
APHOWK BQHX ARNMGPKX NRCOPUH. GQKE CQWPH
CPU GOKMXP YOC BURG GQNJOKPH.

Hints: 301, 73, 27

241 To Shrink Canvas

XY ZB QDJLQQXYV PQDKZ, X HFFMDP HXMD K
CDSDD KYP CODY K NXVNKZ. ZB SUBJOXKCQXUC
ELPVDP X NKU ELUC CNF CDYCU.

Hints: 8, 291, 154

242 Crime and Punishment

AUGER: RFNWXASU HNDREQ ZAOSHVB DRLAUQ
OLG. HFAWSY: OPEN DRY SUBTLE–SCALP IRE FAIL.
XSERFL? AYUSN.

Hints: 386, 221, 128

243 Inelastic Demand

YNWJSIN IQN QSUQ OLWI LK BSESAU, RN OXAALI
QXEN KXSBNY IL ALISON QLR SI WISBB CNTXSAW
WL JLJDBXC.

Hints: 94, 227, 20

244 Monkey Business

XPUUPB XTLUDRBHWW XPBGWICRNLPB WEEPING
NTIWRNWBWS SWGDLNW LUDIPCWS PIORBLHRNLPB
PE QORBSRB DRNIPKG.

Hints: 362, 57, 318

245 Danse Macabre

JUDY "NZTYL WZTYL" HZRWZOYM EUCY GKFYMDUTYM
IUF DXRY AXDN HZVVXK. NY WGD NXO JYVD VZZD XK
... IGD LZG TKZA DNY MYOD.

Hints: 342, 88, 422

ANSWERS, PAGE 268

246 Warm, Not Cool

CRYPT CZYPW CUYSNWNPTK, CRTMQK CSWMT,
CRUTNQ CZNCURJ, CWCNPKQ CVVSCNKNPW
CPXNTPQ CVVCSTR CSQNKQNXCRRJ.

Hints: 324, 340, 210

247 Can You Dig It?

DVP LOUAKNKXFJU EOOLFVX KZJFYFDV KA XVOFJJ
JLOTFQOVJ FV UCO ZDUCAKKQ QBJU CDGO AKTEJ
FV CFJ CODY.

Hints: 66, 286, 119

248 Ironic, Isn't It?

UHDCFBRZEBH QJHDH: QJESHJSIT ETESAHA
FIDM-ETERBHA GSERD—RZZHAREBHFN ZRQKCIBHQ
UNBLEMISHED BLHISHZ.

Hints: 259, 113, 130

249 What a Cluck!

LRVYESPOM LKBMSVGQP KFQUPYHVB VDPBQOT
YBGALRKFC APHORTVBE. QHBKYEPF CVRMIKFYS
FPBDVGQRX QNGOTEPM.

Hints: 426, 86, 381

250 Practice Makes Imperfect

PTBAVM SETUEMKM APKHU IVES KYTK BARTOK EM
KAA HTML PAO TBTKHVOM TUX KAA XEPPEWVJK PAO
SOAPHMMEAUTJM.

Hints: 232, 207, 421

251 Coined Phrase

FEJKDQDFEXYQ TED ZXKJXAX VEBCUX JQ
JCXAJGBZKX EBAX QXKHDS EBH GD HXBK
TJGE AXCHJCU SBVEJCXQ.

Hints: 130, 104, 215

252 Bankruptcy Blues

ACH, ORBIRKRE, HEKYE DSEGH TCZRKRYCSA
CPRHYH—NQBSTNRTC. FGHY CPEURKC FEKGEBA
DBCTRY DEBT HYEYCUCKYH.

Hints: 39, 393, 288

253 Down and Out?

CUZXMBFKHLNJOW CMBYK DWUSCJK (COZBXK
ZCSRHNYK) ZLNDEK ANJKLUXVBM KHCUYLOXSB.
YHBMXAKCZOW, AEBAR ZLNSABM.

Hints: 264, 101, 324

254 Where There Is No Vision ...

XE MUT YGER AB MUT IYXER, X THOTSM MUT
AET-TQTR ZGE LACYR IT IJGERTR GD G LXMSU
GER ICJETR GM MUT DMGNT.

Hints: 154, 270, 209

255 Look on the Bright Side

CBMYFKHIZBW UMC FBBOKCH SAZSUBZYKFZ
UKFYBMWF FKHC, XSCFPEZF SAZKUKFZ, DIS
AYBFXYKQBF YSFB-XSESYBW HEMFFBF.

Hints: 226, 201, 249

ANSWERS, PAGE 268

256 Last Words

JMQVK JACK VEC ZMJ ECBCEECQ JM VX QCDCVXCQ
FTJ VX CWCDJEMCZDCIAVWMNEVIARDVWWK
DAVWWCZNCQ.

Hints: 302, 403, 373

257 Solid Proof

OMPEDFGRSPTE EQPSW WAGTWC WSODTHVIDS
EORGE, AFGSGDE RPRGMDFGRSPTE UGDWVSG
WAGING, GDMF QGTWDHPTDI.

Hints: 271, 82, 193

258 Frank Query

TED EDGRDL LNVWEPD KR JL BIG IRK ARMY EZL
JRYK RUKLD YRWA PD VETXEMLY RU KLD EDA CODY
PD VETXEMLY RU LPMIK?

Hints: 99, 427, 354

259 No A for Effort!

RYPMA EGPI KMVRUPC ULYEG BRAG CVLSGO TOP
FLYK, KATRYSO MVTX, AVLSG MRPETLKA, KVLT DRUX.
CRYPT SLUMPC ALDK.

Hints: 257, 86, 69

260 Say It With Flowers

JOVXGPGBJ VXJJK FKKJ'P TFLJ FLLJKBP TWHJTE
ZTWIFT SWXVXJB JTJQFKBTE RGPATFEJR WK
DFCWQFKE LCGZZWKGJI.

Hints: 155, 250, 288

261 No-Win Situation

MONEYBILKSB ORLBENL KE QJKEBDX-INDY FREA
RVVJHEB CKZIB LKZIBSHDDX RLZHN MIN VREEJB
RSSJLY R VINVA-CRBN!

Hints: 201, 343, 389

262 Hang Up His Picture

WORK UDK DM HOJAIKLIJ HDKURULIKLSF JIMNUIU
LD NUI ULNT MRKTIJ, HSORYRKB, "LDD YNHE
RKLIJMIJIKHI."

Hints: 183, 241, 306

263 Black Thumb

YENBOIL YV XK PVJCATNEIYC SOS IVY PANT YPAX.
LGVH—YPAK ENN HOYPAGAS HPAI ECBAS YV CYEGY
TEKOIL GAIY.

Hints: 224, 55, 36

264 Crime Doesn't Pay

PTR YQLNR TBZRL PB ZKHG BC PTR FSPG IBVWRVX'
MHXRMHKK PRHU MQP IHX WRZP BC PTR MRCFT DBV
VRDQXSCN PB XPRHK MHXRX.

Hints: 240, 152, 392

265 Doctor's Orders

MHCHISOUISUO, KLAAHOBG DUBBHA URUG
ALISON FEESDH QFLIK, BHEC KSNO KUGSON,
"JUDY KQFICBG. KSC. KCUG."

Hints: 122, 191, 262

 ANSWERS, PAGE 269

266 Take a Bow

MYJYRZRZ MDYXAZXVW MZYRZCCZSN
MVDQNDSYRXV; MVDBYMC MZXUZRVCC MDNSMAVW
MZIIZXYAN MTEXUZRJ.

Hints: 257, 145, 435

267 Double Stops?

MJLAM SOY DBLQCZEJL FSGJ XAZJOZCSQ TJLIJL
CO ARRCOI. OJD UATXSOV DCQQ TSHJ
LJXLAYBUZCGJ ALISON.

Hints: 246, 209, 350

268 Murder Ahoy!

WCKUZ EXBLCYKP VORP DXBE EHPUXON HICKSON
CYPKA DPBNZ UAKQHT, EXOY WHYO QHNRAO
UHCFXP UCARNKP.

Hints: 361, 169, 138

269 White Background

ABCDEF GDBCH GDIJKBEB LMNBKMJLIE AHAHIHOOD
PFDCL EQDDMR. LKIBALHM SHLEJIB RIHNDBKECT
HNUKDLENLE.

Hints: 345, 199, 240

270 Mission Accomplished?

RXPZQPLW BCXWT VNHKBCWNMGD SNCG SMGPZPMN
FCNQD FPBT VCLOJLBPCLMZ DHLBMU KNJDJLBD
OJUMBPCXD CRDBMVZJD.

Hints: 72, 85, 377

271 The King's English

FAURE ERSCVFM IB SPOZZOPROBE' LAOBFV,
ERBSRBS "AIUF ZF VFBMFPAD" OBM "DIG OPFB'V
OBDVCRBS HGV O CIGBM MIS."

Hints: 438, 383, 425

272 Transmission Problem

YES HEAR FLIP YUNPO SEJBN PUNK QNTBROS
ECHOS TMS TBVOJ MSODBNLP TEQO BJOE:
"EAA JBTFP YNTPBJOSOJ."

Hints: 243, 413, 443

273 Bad Signs

NOW BCNOWE DOC ALISON OWE FCIZS QWLH UCZ
UDWLEKZS GIZKUOWQ OKB XF DLUOKZS OKU OLZQU
DKNO UCLG.

Hints: 200, 18, 306

274 Sellers' Market

FVLMI FVKMLQIJA QWJXKLOX EXVIK KIJWLV MFVU
SLY, BALOUK EOHJQ BEFWL KVLOUFVS OAJXVZ
MOVIELAWFUL.

Hints: 189, 102, 286

275 User-Unfriendly

AMWYLDBJG BELOP WGBAFOC WPYJF AWYLDBJG
EGYHO QFCMDYLK WOLDPMH XYHO. WBPO FPBIHOA:
JDYWNT NOTIBMPC.

Hints: 300, 353, 172

276 Double Fun

FRREUNFDEW UINNDH ITTAU RBCQQG
JNKKWT-EHTK LCDDTLU LTEWWG UCAAWT,
UCJJTL-URBFFW FPPNRNEW UCHHTUOU.

Hints: 306, 454, 366

277 Spin Doctor Needed

SRO JESHG ANDREAMST TEAK TRRURSA MSQAN
MVYSQ DRKYDT KGRDFA. NIRH VLAN GRMDS NY
TRMG OENI DRUDRAART "ZRRGESQA."

Hints: 390, 135, 296

278 Portapuppies

JACK VZR WGZMM WZBBLCM JLXA BAQMQ QDMZM,
VZR HCX WZBBQDMZM, FZHM XAQX EZBF RD EZG
CQMV XGQKMDZGX.

Hints: 2, 194, 327

279 He Blew the Answer

"OURQSOCUT, QUIM CLAM CTPAR MCPD EURZ
PC DUST RIVC MCUX?" "URED JUST FARSCIM:
CHU CU CHU CU CHU CHU."

Hints: 164, 191, 59

280 The Hole Truth

UCKUFE OHMYUAE PIHEYARI: "LQIHF KUDRE AR
RHDNHPTEI LUKH; IC-QV LDLQIBO!" FINAL SUREIFL,
"AL OPHOBPIF WARTY-YHRBIF?"

Hints: 186, 121, 90

281 Beg Canto

OSEBCOH HANKIE OCLCEIZZA, HAKNSE OCE
SWUSMMSKUS, UIRMP OSEDIET HITS OIORMCE
CEACH DIE BAH CLAP CRPASKUS?

Hints: 71, 324, 439

282 Alpine Hurdle

ALISON LISAW ST FNZTJSXX LXQXNO MND ST
DJA ZQB NC NDJAW LISAWL QTF ZQL URLD QT
NELDQPXA QXARDSQT.

Hints: 60, 195, 365

283 British Uprising

JKHPJKOQQ MOLCLY IPNKOAORONU NZ
IPLINBORONU-LUYOUW BLURLUJLB XB "NUL PHQL
HI CORK CKOJK CL BKNHQY UNR IHR."

Hints: 372, 337, 10

284 Incredible!

MONKEYS GUTSYAMI TOUMB HYKK NT IXACTS
YVME NKOAC BEKT YV IYL DEVMBI, PTM YVQYMTI
MHE-PTOU IXNIAUYGMYEVI.

Hints: 441, 109, 392

285 Crime and Punishment?

KBDOXGEH GQDOK JUTV TED SDUKTE GK ZOXXDQ
SXOHGOUGKV. KBDOXGEH JUTV VOEW GK FETPE
OK UDKDOUZM.

Hints: 122, 454, 163

286 Some Things Never Change

OQGIBDSQ EJDCQJ PKYC OGMQ OGI HKS
XFPZFYDSV CODY GXCKGB FSQ: "QYXGZQI
BQFZGJI NQBDQMQI YZFCCQI."

Hints: 200, 76, 167

287 The Ides of April

COWKR BYIB SKIBY IRS BILKZ INK VKNBIOR, AK
ZYDPJS GK KLBNKQKJF CNIBKUPJ BYIB DRJF DRK
OZ IR IRRPIJ KWKRB!

Hints: 267, 85, 104

288 Oxy

OXLIKEXFARMXGUY PEUKUGH PXEZI XLK CUZR
HGUHGVAY RGUC RKVGERKCV AYVR AKUP IUAK
UKI MUERYKUXG.

Hints: 415, 454, 232

289 Oh, Just What I've Always Wanted!

REAL CLIMAX RUGBY: SODA SLIML, ADIO
BLYKUMU, ELZAGBAI EAU, FORR FNEAIN, YOABA
YNCFIAIN—SEOY XLDMT SUGM RELCUGWN.

Hints: 415, 95, 151

290 Christmas Angel

EFIMPTOQTBPI-OTNRU UGQZ GPQM WQM VPTQUWFK
VXFGP, VBTNIO ZPI JNT VUNBGFOWB. TPXNYQG JTNX
VBQOP PIBQFGPM JNTKP.

Hints: 141, 86, 429

291 Four-Star Service

UQCL QL MKCBUWXNQXL JBZVW: "ZJV YWXZZVLQLC
BY KLEVPRVXP RQZJ SWVXUKPV QU ZJV GBD BY ZJV
FJXHDVPHXQE."

Hints: 217, 369, 77

292 She's Calm Now

NKRGUV ECRGUL XFURGUHLOT RGDXXUV RGDFLW
CX OKRGCF (LURGKOD VDKRGKFKW), RGKEPOT
DERGKFKHZ LFDHRGKOKLT.

Hints: 279, 380, 201

293 "Mirror, Mirror on the Wall ..."

"TBLDIZ DT B TEIL EC OYBTT, PNZIZDR AZNEYUZIT
UE OZRZIBYYQ UDTGEJZI ZJZIQAEUQ'T CBGZ AXL
LNZDI EPR." —F. TPDCL

Hints: 303, 370, 393

294 Ho! Ho! Ho!

UANYOU, ENAAK ZGCYU, ISKTANVRU: UNIS
UCWNYMCL OCYG NVOCKDKVEDL YPNUGU ISNIRDKVE
ISKDMYGV GBGYLFSGYG.

Hints: 201, 334, 353

295 Late in the Day

ONE MASTER TYSASHOM ICYHUPHL: "ZXHE YWTOO
WHE CHRNE SI DTYS CNR YXTLIZY, NS WHTEY SXH
YAE NY TCIAS SI YHS."

Hints: 407, 264, 76

ANSWERS, PAGE 270

296 Cereal-Killer

SENSUA-LISM, DOLLA-RTYM, MAZW-LYURLAYOR
JSWWIZ-SH MZZF-RAHZR TYUZQ-LYSWZM
SIFTS-JAWR. FEZWZZU-SDZE IYUD-PSLZM.

Hints: 250, 186, 368

297 Good Deeds

PCXOK (PUZINQZCV, MZIV MCZSO) SUKR WUKR,
PXR UIZGBOK (GOQ AUIV ZDO., EUI UGO) GOR
WUKR (KLGSO CZGNON UG WUKR UEROG).

Hints: 164, 175, 337

298 Limn Eric

CDIVCAG RAXY HUCB ZAYCDZ: "NTD TDGXDZ
SZHZAYCDZ FUG RXKEB XR DXHZ NTD FZTA YG
NXTH, GZH BTG HX YZ 'GXV PZAYCD'?"

Hints: 114, 99, 297

299 Come and Get It!

UNYRP EKPORUKPY IYOU SHGL UA ZAKRF VRW
SYGHKFY UNYJ GAKZQ OAU CHJ ZAKRF EAP RU SJ
UNY UNRPUYYOUN.

Hints: 325, 308, 347

300 Liszt-en Up!

CRYPTOGLAUX NUQSATZXLYP HJTQUX HZASJUCTPLO
ZGTHYAXQ OAK TCAZU. HJTRXLPY XUJLMGP
EGLYNUZQ HLTKA EGLB.

Hints: 391, 209, 361

Cunning Mind-Bending Puzzles

Introduction

Welcome to *Cunning Mind-Bending Puzzles*. This section presents a cross-section of puzzle types of varying degrees of difficulty. Puzzles of this sort are now being used in schools and business seminars to develop critical-thinking skills. The puzzles selected here offer both the challenge and the fun of using your mental prowess to find solutions. Some are clever and subtle; some are wily and provocative. Sometimes you will have to "think outside the box," and sometimes, as it were, inside the box. Find a hidden phrase or title; come up with the missing number in a series; unscramble words, and decode messages. . . . this is a gold mine of challenges that will tease and tantalize you. (Don't worry, though—there are no trick questions, nor are there any questions that require any advanced knowledge of any subject.)

These puzzles are just as much fun to solve in groups as they are to solve by yourself, so don't be afraid to ask for help. They are also presented in random order, so feel free to skip around. Now get in there and mix it up!

1

Using only four numerals and any mathematical symbols you choose, can you produce an equation that will yield the number 300?

2

Suppose all counting numbers were arranged in columns as shown below. Under what letter would the number 100 appear?

A	B	C	D	E	F	G
1	2	3	4	5	6	7
8	9	10	11	12	13	14
15	16	17	–	–	–	–

3

Nancy and Audrey set out to cover a certain distance by foot. Nancy walks half the distance and runs half the distance, but Audrey walks half the time and runs half the time. Nancy and Audrey walk and run at the same rate. Who will reach the destination first (or will it be a tie)?

4

The following seven numbers share a unique property. What is it?

1961   6889   6119   8008   8118   6699   6009

5

Find the hidden phrase or title.

6

In the puzzle below, the numbers in the second row are determined by the relationships of the numbers in the first row. Likewise, the numbers in the third row are determined by the relationships of the numbers in the second row. Can you determine the relationships and find the missing number?

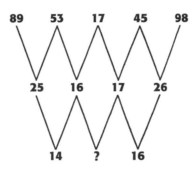

7

A mathematician's will stated that his wife should get one-third of his estate, his son one-fifth, his older daughter one-sixth, and his younger daughter $9,000. Who received more, his older daughter or his younger daughter?

8

What single-digit number should go in the box with the question mark?

6	5	9	2	7
1	4	3	5	?
8	0	2	8	1

9

In a store that sells clocks, I notice that most of them show different times. A grandfather clock reads 2:15, an alarm clock reads 2:35, a digital clock reads 2:00, and the store clock reads 2:23. The store clerk says that a clock in the corner has just been set correctly. It reads 2:17. What is the average number of minutes, fast or slow, that these five clocks are off?

10

Find the missing number in the following series:

$$\frac{2}{3} \quad \frac{7}{12} \quad \frac{1}{2} \quad \frac{5}{12} \quad \frac{1}{3} \quad \frac{1}{4} \quad \frac{1}{6} \quad \frac{1}{12}?$$

11

Find the hidden phrase or title.

Cheaper by the dozen

12

While reading a newspaper you notice that four pages of one section are missing. One of the missing pages is page 5. The back page of this section is page 24. What are the other three missing pages?

6 20 19

13

Suppose *a*, *b*, and *c* represent three positive whole numbers.
If $a + b = 13$, $b + c = 22$, and $a + c = 19$, what is the value of *c*?

ANSWERS, PAGE 273

14

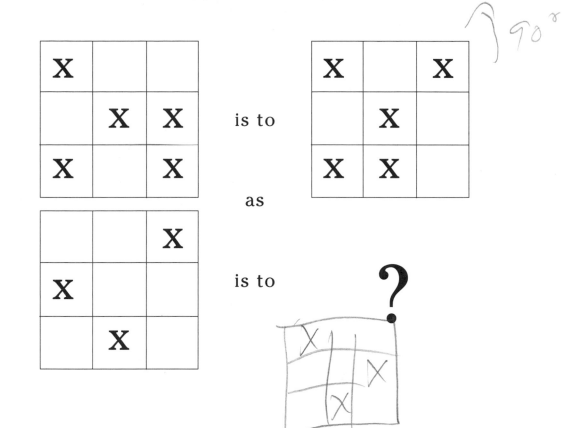

15

Below is a "trickle-down" word game. Change one letter and one letter only on each line to arrive at the word on the last line:

MOVE

more

mare

mark

BARK

16

Sarah is older than Julie and Maggie. Maggie is older than Paula. Ann is younger than Julie, but older than Paula. Ann is younger than Maggie. Sarah is younger than Liz. Who is the second oldest woman in this group?

17

What is the missing number in the following series?

13 7 18 10 5 ? 9 1 12 6

18

Find the hidden phrase or title.

Broken
promise

19

How many triangles of any size are in the figure below?

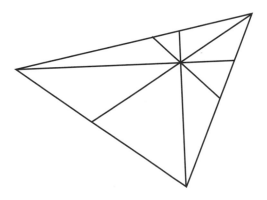

20

Which is larger: 2^{73} or $2^{70} + 2^3$?

ANSWERS, PAGE 274

21

Find the hidden phrase or title.

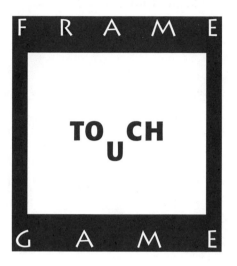

22

Which of the following is the smallest?

a. $\dfrac{\sqrt{10}}{10}$ **b.** $\dfrac{1}{10}$ **c.** $\sqrt{10}$ **d.** $\dfrac{1}{\sqrt{10}}$ **e.** $\dfrac{1}{10\sqrt{10}}$

23

Find the hidden phrase or title.

ANSWERS, PAGE 274

24

There are four colored pencils—two blue, one green, and one yellow. If you took two pencils from a drawer and you knew that one was blue, what would be the likelihood that the other pencil was also blue?

25

Unscramble this word:

KISDTYCRA

26

A certain blend of grass seed is made by mixing brand A ($8 a pound) with brand B ($5 a pound). If the blend is worth $6 a pound, how many pounds of brand A are needed to make 50 pounds of the blend?

27

Find the hidden phrase or title.

28

If you wrote down all the numbers from 1 to 100, how many times would you write the number 3?

3, 13, 23, 30, 31, 32, 33, 34, 35, 36, 37, 38, 39, 43, 53, 63, 73, 83, 93

ANSWERS, PAGE 275

29

Each of the following three words can have another three-letter word added to its beginning to form new words. Can you find at least one three-letter word to make this happen?

Ear

Less

Anger

30

What is $^3/_4$ of $^1/_2$ of 4^2 minus $^1/_2$ of that result?

31

Below are six discs stacked on a peg. The object is to reassemble the discs, one by one, in the same order on another peg, using the smallest number of moves. No larger disc can be placed on a smaller disc. How many moves will it take?

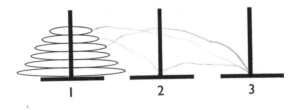

32

From the word "service," see if you can create 15 new words.

33

Below is a list of numbers with accompanying codes. Can you decipher the code and determine the number on the last line?

Number	Code Number
589	521
724	386
1346	9764
?	485

34

Which is greater, a single discount of 12 percent or two successive discounts of 6 percent—or are they the same?

35

Find the hidden phrase or title.

36

Here's a fun and challenging puzzle for those who remember their algebra. Evaluate the following:

$$\frac{x+y}{x^2+y^2} \times \frac{x}{x-y} \div \frac{(x+y)^2}{x^4-y^4} - x$$

37

Below is a sentence based on moving the letters of the alphabet in a consistent manner. See if you can crack the code and come up with the right answer.

BRX DUH D JHQLXV.

ANSWERS, PAGE 276

38

The geometric figure below can be divided with one straight line into two parts that will fit together to make a perfect square. Draw that line by connecting two of the numbers.

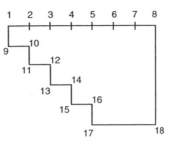

39

The number six is considered a "perfect" number because its factors add up exactly to the number itself (3 + 2 + 1 = 6). What is the next perfect number?

40

Find the hidden phrase or title.

41

Some pibs are dals.
All dals are zons.
Some zons are rews.
Some rews are dals.
Therefore, some pibs are definitely rews.
Is the above conclusion true or false?

42

Which is larger: one-third times one-third of a dozen dozen,
or one-third dozen halved and cubed?

43

The *Genesee Flyer* leaves the station at 60 miles per hour. After three hours, the *Seneca Streamer* leaves the same station at 75 miles per hour, moving in the same direction on an adjacent track. Both trains depart the station at milepost 0. At what milepost will the *Streamer* draw even with the *Flyer*?

44

A cyclist can ride four different routes from East Klopper to Wickly. There are eight different routes from Wickly to Ganzoon. From Ganzoon to Poscatool, there are three different routes. How many different combinations of routes from East Klopper to Poscatool can the cyclist take? (Do not consider going directly from East Klopper to Poscatool: all routes pass through Wickly, Ganzoon, and Poscatool.)

45

The ratio of $^3/_7$ to $^4/_9$ is which of the following:

a. $\dfrac{8}{9}$

b. $\dfrac{35}{36}$

c. $\dfrac{3}{4}$

d. $\dfrac{27}{28}$

e. 1 to 1

ANSWERS, PAGE 277

46

Find the hidden phrase or title.

making up for lost time

47

Kelsey has flipped a penny 17 times in a row, and every time it has landed on heads. What are the chances that the next throw will land on heads?

48

Can you place a symbol between the two numbers below to create a number greater than 4, but less than 5?

4 5

49

Below is a teeter-totter with a 5-pound weight placed 10 feet from the fulcrum and a 6-pound weight placed 5 feet from the fulcrum. On the right side of the fulcrum is a 16-pound weight that needs to be placed in order to balance the weights on the left side. How many feet from the fulcrum should the 16-pound weight be placed?

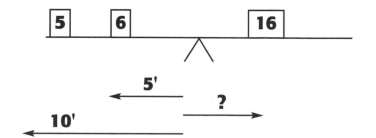

50

The following puzzle is one of analytical reasoning. See if you can determine the relationships between the figures and the words to find solutions to the two unknowns.

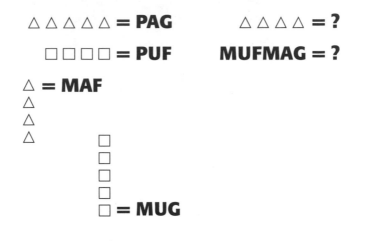

51

Find the hidden phrase or title.

52

Given the initial letters of the missing words, complete this sentence.

It is 212 D F at which W B.

   ANSWERS, PAGE 278

53

Find the missing letter in the following series:

2 T 4 F 8 E 16 S 32 T 64 ?

54

See if you can match each word in the left column with its meaning in the right column:

1. Unctuous	a. Study of the universe
2. Riparian	b. Relating to the bank of a lake or river
3. Porcine	c. An interlacing network, as of blood vessels
4. Plexus	d. An upright post
5. Platitude	e. Fertilize
6. Cosmology	f. Briskness
7. Concatenation	g. Relating to swine
8. Alacrity	h. A series connected by links
9. Fecundate	i. A trite remark
10. Newel	j. Oily

55

A box of chocolates can be divided equally among 3, 6, or 11 people. What is the smallest number of chocolates the box can contain?

56

Which figure does not belong with the other four figures?

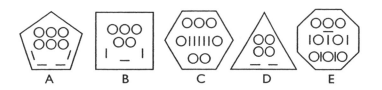

57

I recently returned from a trip. Today is Friday. I returned four days before the day after the day before tomorrow. On what day did I return?

58

Find the hidden phrase or title.

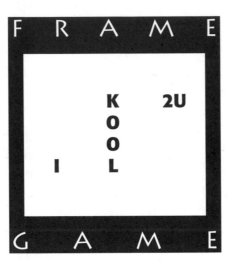

59

A microscopic slide has 7,500 bacteria dying at a rate of 150 per hour. Another slide has 4,500 bacteria increasing at a rate of 50 per hour. In how many hours will the bacterial count on both slides be the same?

60

A man told his friend, "Four years from now
I'll be twice as old as I was fourteen years ago."
How old is the man?

61

Which figure does not belong with the others, and why?

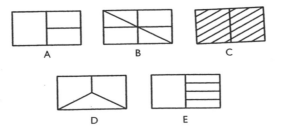

ANSWERS, PAGES 278 TO 279

62

Find the hidden phrase or title.

63

The probability of drawing the Ace of Spades from a deck of 52 playing cards is 1 in 52. What is the probability of drawing the Ace, King, and Queen of Spades on three consecutive draws?

64

Sometimes things that are mathematically or scientifically true seem impossible. You may think this is one of them. Can you guess what a cubic yard of water weights?

17 pounds
170 pounds
1,700 pounds
500 pounds
98.8 pounds

65

If a team wins 60 percent of its games in the first third of a season, what percentage of the remaining games must it win to finish the season having won 80 percent of the games?

66

Given the initial letters of the missing words, complete the following sentence.

There are 50 S in the U S F.

67

If $\frac{1}{2}$ of 24 were 8, what would $\frac{1}{3}$ of 18 be?

68

In this "trickle down" puzzle, you must change one letter of each succeeding word, starting at the top, to arrive at the word at the bottom. There may be more than one way to solve this—use your creativity!

P A R T

———

———

———

W I N E

69

Find the hidden phrase or title.

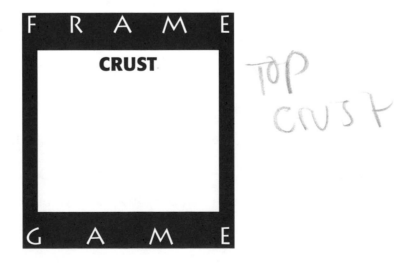

70

Solve this puzzle without using a pencil or calculator:

$$1 \times 1 = 1$$
$$11 \times 11 = 121$$
$$111 \times 111 = 12{,}321$$
$$1{,}111 \times 1{,}111 = ?$$

71

Find the hidden phrase or title.

72

There are six murks in a bop, eight bops in a farg, and three fargs in a yump. What is the number of murks in a yump divided by the number of bops in a yump?

73

What is the missing number in the triangle on the right?

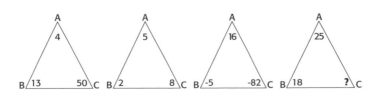

74

If the volume of a cube is 729 cubic feet, how many cubic yards is it?

75

If three pears and four oranges cost $.39 and four pears and three oranges cost $.38, how much does one pear cost?

76

What is the missing number in this grid?

15	81	168
23	111	?
5	27	56

77

If I quadrupled one-fifth of a fraction and multiplied it by that fraction, I would get one-fifth. What is the original fraction? (*Hint:* There are two answers.)

78

A six-piece band has agreed that the entire band will be paid $1,225 per gig. But the leader of the band is paid twice as much as each of the other five musicians. How much does the leader earn each gig?

79

Find the hidden phrase or title.

Double play

ANSWERS, PAGES 280 TO 281

80

What's the missing number next to the letter "E"?

P7   H4   O6   N6   E?

81

Find the hidden phrase or title.

82

In a foreign language, *fol birta klar* means "shine red apples." *Pirt klar farn* means "big red bicycles," and *obirts fol pirt* means "shine bicycles often." How would you say "big apples" in this language?

83

Find three consecutive numbers such that the sum of the first number and the third number is 124.

84

If $16_a = 20$ and $36_a = 32$, what does 26_a equal?

85

Find the hidden phrase or title.

86

What nine-letter word is written in the square below? You may start at any letter and go in any direction, but don't go back over any letter.

T E M

R C O

I G E

87

Can you position four squares of equal size in such a way that you end up with five squares of equal size?

88

At a reception, one-fourth of the guests departed at a certain time. Later, two-fifths of the remaining guests departed. Even later, three-fourths of those guests departed. If nine people were left, how many were originally at the party?

ANSWERS, PAGE 282

89

Find the hidden phrase or title.

90

In spelling out numbers, you don't often find the letter "a." Quickly now, what is the first number, counting upward from zero, in which this letter appears?

91

Find the hidden phrase or title.

92

With five fair tosses of a penny, what is the probability of its landing on heads five times in a row? (*Hint:* Remember, the tosses constitute a sequence of events.)

93

What physical characteristics do the following capital letters share in common?

A H I M O T U V W X Y

94

What comes next in the following series?

240   120   40   10   2   ?

95

A triangle has sides of *X*, *Y*, and *Z*. Which of the following statements is true?

1. *X–Y* is always equal to 2.
2. *Y–X* is always less than *Z*.
3. *Z–X* is always greater than *Y*.
4. *X* + *Y* is always greater than *Z* + *Y*.
5. No correct answer is given.

96

Find the hidden phrase or title.

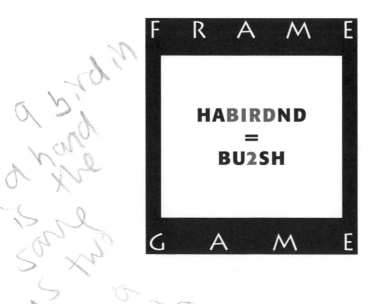

a bird in a hand is the same as two in a bush

ANSWERS, PAGE 283

97

Given four points in space and connecting three points at a time to determine a plane (extending to infinity), what is the maximum number of lines that will result from all intersections?

98

What is the missing number in the circle below?

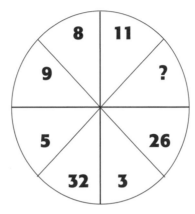

99

When purchased together, a pair of binoculars and the case cost $100. If the binoculars cost $90 more than the case, how much does the case cost? Give yourself about 15 seconds to solve this.

100

A cube measuring four inches on each side is painted blue all over and is then sliced into one-inch cubes. How many of the smaller cubes are blue on three sides?

101

In this "trickle-down" puzzle, start at the top and change one letter to each succeeding word to arrive at the word at the bottom.

FAST

MIND

102

A clock strikes six in five seconds. How long will it take to strike eleven?

103

Find the hidden phrase or title.

104

Sammy Johnson has two sisters, but the Johnson girls have no brother. How can this be?

105

Decipher this cryptogram:

T'M QPFASQ RS TD LATOPMSOLATP.
—G. N. KTSOMY

106

Given the initial letters of the missing words, complete this sentence.

There are 9 I in a B G.

107

What three-letter word can be placed in front of each of the following words to make four new words?

MAN
HOUSE
CAP
AM

108

Find the hidden phrase or title.

109

Imagine we were to adopt a new number system based on 13 instead of 10. Show a way in which the first 13 numbers might be written.

110

How many squares of any size are in the figure below? Be careful; there may be more than you think!

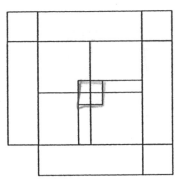

111

Electric current is measured in amps, resistance is measured in ohms, and power is measured in watts. What is frequency measured in?

112

Find the hidden phrase or title.

ANSWERS, PAGE 284

113

Unscramble the following word:

LAMPANETRYARI

114

How would you write 944 in Roman numerals?

115

What is the missing letter in the last circle?

116

If 2,048 people entered a statewide singles tennis tournament, how many total matches would be played, including the championship match?

117

Decipher this cryptogram phrase:

SEO LXABXGS JW EMLLGQOBB.

118

What four-letter word can be placed in front of each of the following words to form new words?

LINE
PHONE
WATERS

119

Find the hidden phrase or title.

120

The numbers in each box below have a relationship in common.
Can you identify that relationship and find the missing number?

2, 11	4, 67	5, 128	3, ?

121

If you have a two-in-five chance of winning something, what are your odds?

122

How many triangles can you find in this diagram?

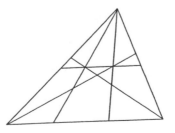

ANSWERS, PAGES 285

123

Find the hidden phrase or title.

124

Complete the following analogy:

B-sharp is to C as Bach is to ?

Cryptic Crosswords

Introduction

A cryptic crossword differs from the conventional variety mostly in the nature of its clues. In a conventional crossword, a clue is a more or less straightforward definition of the answer. A cryptic clue, on the other hand, is a kind of riddle in two parts. One end of the clue is a definition. The other end is a bit of wordplay that leads to the same answer in a more roundabout way. The solver must discover which end is which and where the dividing line falls. The definition and the wordplay can appear in either order—but are never mixed.

There are many kinds of cryptic clues. Each kind has its own indicators that tip you off to what type of wordplay is involved, and the number in parentheses at the end of a clue tells you the number of letters in the answer. Once you hit upon the answer, it fits the clue like a key in a lock, and every word in the clue is accounted for.

For example, a clue for THRONE might include the definition "big chair" as well as the wordplay hint that throne is an anagram of the word HORNET. It would be a little too obvious if the clue said "Big chair that's an anagram of hornet," so the clue-writer chooses a more subtle word or phrase suggesting a mix of letters. The clue for THRONE might read: *Big chair bothered hornet (6)*. The word "bothered" suggests that the adjacent word, "hornet," has been tampered with in some way. "Big chair" defines the answer. The clue could also have been phrased: *Hornet flying around big chair (6)*. Here, "flying around" suggests that the letters of "hornet" are moving about.

There are eight basic types of wordplay. Here are tips for spotting and solving each one.

1 ANAGRAM The clues for THRONE above are two examples. Here is another: *Reach up at tangled skydiving apparatus (9)*. "Tangled" indicates that a rearrangement of the adjacent words, "reach up at," will provide the answer, PARACHUTE, which is defined in the latter part of the clue as "skydiving apparatus." An anagram clue always contains a word or phrase (like "confused," "weird," or "badly formed") that suggests mixing, strangeness, or poor condition. The anagram indicator is always immediately adjacent to the letters to be scrambled, and those letters will be given explicitly. If a clue contains a word or set of words with the same number of letters as the answer, and these letters are located next to an anagram signal, try anagramming the given letters.

2 HIDDEN WORD *Plumes in knife at her side (8)* This clue indicates that a word meaning "plumes" is found inside "knife at her side." The answer is FEATHERS. In a hidden word clue, the answer is spelled out in correct order in the clue; no rearranging of letters is required. Even so, these clues can be tricky. *Aha! Green pens match (5)*, for example, tells you that the phrase "aha green" "pens" in a word meaning "match." The answer is AGREE. The clue-writer has made "pens" look like a noun meaning writing implements, when actually it must be read as a verb meaning "holds."

3 REVERSAL *Returned beer of kings (5)* A word meaning beer, written backward, will yield the answer, a word meaning "of kings": REGAL. In some down clues, the indicator may suggest that a word be written upward. For example, the answer to *Ambush split up (5)* is TRAP ("ambush"), which is PART ("split") written upward. In reversal clues the indicator is always beside the definition of the word being reversed, not the definition of the answer. Words or phrases like "backward," "in retreat," "heading west," or, in down clues, "rising," and "northward," may signal a reversal.

4 HOMOPHONE *Hot dog topping gathered for the audience (7)* "Hot dog topping" is MUSTARD, which sounds like "mustered" (or "gathered") to an audience, i.e., to hearers. Sometimes homophone clues are punny, as in: *Fast remedy for gray hair, it is said (4)*. A "fast" is an extreme example of a DIET, which sounds the same as "dye it," or "remedy for gray hair." Any word or phrase that suggests hearing or saying the answer word (such as "hear," "listen to," or "from a reporter") can signal a homophone.

5 TWO MEANINGS *Metal guide (4)* This clue gives two meanings for LEAD. (The word "lead" has two different pronunciations, too, although this is not necessary in a clue with two meanings.) Clues of this type often involve puns, as in: *Ahead of time, like a nobleman? (5)* The answer is EARLY (or

EARL-Y). The question mark at the end of the clue, as in regular crosswords, suggests that a verbal prank is being played, and that the solver should watch out. Clues with two meanings can often be identified by their brevity.

6 DELETION *First off most uncompromising mountain (7)* "Most uncompromising" is SEVER-EST. If you take the first letter off, as the clue suggests, you get the answer, EVEREST. Sometimes the deletion is made at the end of a word, as in: *Almost climb onto wild pig (4)*. By almost taking the word BOARD ("climb onto"), you get the answer, BOAR. Deletions can be made in the middle of words, too. Indicators for deletions are words like "beheaded," "heartless," and "endless."

7 CONTAINER *Kid keeps near this evening (7)* Here, the word TOT ("kid") goes around (or "keeps," in a figurative sense) NIGH ("near"), giving TONIGHT ("this evening"). A container clue may also be expressed in the opposite way—as one word inside another, as in: *Points out lion in tropical islands (9)*. By putting the word CAT ("lion") inside INDIES ("tropical islands"), you get INDICATES ("points out"). Words and phrases like "outside," "around," and "holding"—or "inside," "wearing," and "surrounded by"—indicate containers.

8 CHARADE *Anti-abortionist ate spread (11)* As in the game charades, a charade clue breaks the answer into pieces and clues them individually. An "anti-abortionist" is a PRO-LIFER, the word ATE is given directly, and together they spell PROLIFERATE, which is defined as "spread." The words making up a charade are always etymologically unrelated to the answer. Thus, "bookworm" would never be broken into "book" + "worm," since those two words are related in meaning to the whole.

COMBINATIONS Not all cryptic clues involve only one type of wordplay, as do the examples above. Sometimes a clue will involve a combination of two or more wordplay types, such as an anagram inside a reversal, or a container as part of a charade. For example: *Someone beyond criticism raced wildly in boat (6,3)*. The answer here is SACRED COW ("someone beyond criticism"). It is made by inserting an anagram of RACED (which is signaled by "wildly") into SCOW ("boat").

SURPRISES These eight devices, and combinations thereof, account for nearly every kind of word-play you will encounter in cryptic crosswords. However, occasionally a novel kind of clue appears, such as: *Eight botch theft after ignoring the odds (5)*. The answer, OCTET, is a group of eight, and can be gotten by ignoring the odd letters of "bOtCh ThEfT." The key to solving unusual clues like this, as with all other types, is to follow the literal instructions.

BITS AND PIECES When a clue-writer breaks an answer word into parts to describe it in the word-play part of the clue, it may not break neatly into smaller words. Individual letters or groups of letters may be left over. The clue-writer must also define these, of course, and will sometimes do so in play-ful ways. For instance, "the capital of Japan" may turn out be the letter J, and "the end of September" could be R. Abbreviations may be used, if they are common. Thus: "eastern" = E, "grand" = G (as in money), "right" and "left" = R and L (respectively), "Pennsylvania" = PA, "love" = O (from the tennis score), "fifty" = L (Roman numeral), and "chlorine" = CL (in the periodic table). And the word "article" in a clue could mean any of the grammatical articles A, AN, or THE.

Here's a charade clue that contains several bits and pieces: *Nearly ace final in school months ahead of time (6)*. On playing cards an "ace" is the letter A, the "final in school" is L, "months" equals MOS (a standard abbreviation), and these all go ahead of T (a scientific abbreviation for "time") to get the answer, ALMOST ("nearly"). (Relax: this is only a demonstration clue; few real ones would include this many abbreviations.)

& LIT. (AND LITERALLY SO) In almost every clue, the definition and the wordplay are separated by an indicator word, but once in a great while the two parts of a clue completely overlap. For example: *Author perhaps penning the foremost of essays! (7)*. The answer, THOREAU, is an ana-gram of AUTHOR (signaled by the word "per-haps") going around, or penning, E ("the foremost of essays"). Read the clue once in full and it pro-vides the wordplay on the answer. Read it again in full and it defines the answer. The exclamation point at the end is the traditional sign of an "& lit." clue—a hint to the solver of the clue's special nature: self-referential wordplay.

PRACTICE PUZZLE 1

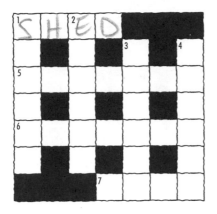

ACROSS

1 Get rid of gardener's building (4) *two meanings*
5 Heavy sword gashed girl (7) *charade*
6 Shorten grid Abe reconstructed (7) *anagram*
7 Hits friends back (4) *reversal*

DOWN

1 Also, CIA leader holds party (6) *hidden word*
2 Records tenants after introduction (6) *deletion*
3 In audition, manage composer (6) *homophone*
4 Dozing Lee is eaten by snake (6) *container*

ANSWERS

ACROSS

1 SHED means both "get rid of" and "gardener's building"
5 CUTLASS ("heavy sword") is made up of CUT ("gashed") and LASS ("girl")
6 ABRIDGE ("shorten") is a reconstructed version of GRID ABE
7 SLAP ("hit") is PALS ("friends") backward

DOWN

1 SOCIAL ("party") is held by "alSO CIA Leader"
2 ENTERS ("records") is RENTERS ("tenants") after its introduction (first letter)
3 HANDEL ("composer") sounds like HANDLE ("manage"), as suggested by the indicator "in audition"
4 ASLEEP ("dozing") is LEE eaten by ASP ("snake")

PRACTICE PUZZLE 2

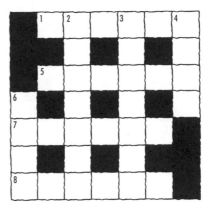

ACROSS

1 Endlessly talk about Olympic event (6) *deletion*
5 Stop energetic carrying game at start of season (6) *hidden*
7 Suddenly attacks water plants (6) *two meanings*
8 Sell bicycle, we hear (6) *homophone*

DOWN

2 Thrust poems I'd written (7) *anagram*
3 Hide once owned by Coolidge (7) *container*
4 Thus on the subject of tender (4) *charade*
6 Ambush split up (4) *reversal*

ANSWERS

ACROSS

1 DISCUS ("Olympic event") is DISCUSS ("talk about") without its last letter, as suggested by the indicator "endlessly"
5 OPENER is "game at the start of a season" and stOP ENERgetic is carrying it
7 RUSHES means both "suddenly attacks" and "water plants"
8 PEDDLE ("sell") sounds like PEDAL ("bicycle")

DOWN

2 IMPOSED ("thrust") is a rewritten (anagrammed) version of POEMS I'D
3 CONCEAL ("hide") is ONCE inside CAL ("Coolidge")
4 SORE ("tender") is SO ("thus") + RE ("on the subject of")
6 TRAP ("ambush") is PART ("split") written up

ACROSS

1 Clever bow (4)
4 Reportedly lost in fog (4)
7 Kind of wheel allowed in highway (8)
8 A bit of elbow room in Paradise (4)
10 Gertrude's mug (5)
11 Rock star of no importance (5)
12 Breaks first ground (5)
13 $100 in new deli for a hero (2,3)
15 Almost make muffin material (4)
16 Most intimate hint about Nabokov's origin (8)
17 More than one big head goes rolling (4)
18 Peg capturing Harry's heart in "A Place to Hang Your Hat" (4)

DOWN

1 Olympian in hardware store (4)
2 TV show host shot *Long Riders* (3,7)
3 Hint: stay with pool equipment (3,5)
4 My carrying scarf down is thought-provoking (5)
5 Drunken pirates set for a racy dance (10)
6 Wrong volleyball gear brought up for court game (6)
9 Sailor at a distance embraced by prophet (8)
11 Delight in debut of performance: *Rent* (6)
12 Calls for a gymnastic event (5)
14 A stake in *Volcano* making a comeback (4)

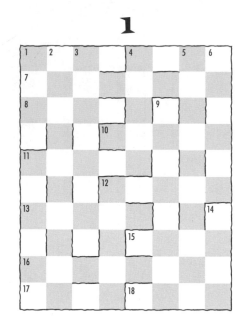

ACROSS

1 Dagger lit from behind in fight (8)
8 American writer beginning to memorize sonnet (4)
9 Remain undecided following unsatisfactory tip (5)
10 Chances are a newspaper offers special delivery? (8)
12 Small and smooth (4)
14 Love to chatter about green light (4)
15 Pose as college grad, turning in place (8)
17 Wagon holds a small weight (5)
18 Ruined Sol Hurok's finale (4)
19 Broadcasting antihero in a new presentation (2,3,3)

DOWN

1 Wall covering crops is raised by company (6)
2 Announced brownish-gray drink (4)
3 Like negligee worn by one in France—utter foolishness (6)
4 Rent, to procure paintings (4,5)
5 Selena's music turned up on a plane (6)
6 Sign submarine captain up (4)
7 Examine word heard in church that's first part of the Bible (9)
11 Redesigned rinks around university where winter athletes can be found (3,3)
12 Single absorbing article: "Cold Comfort" (6)
13 Arrest involves one loser (6)
15 Indifferent operator after call for assistance (2-2)
16 Hack it up, holding chopping tool (4)

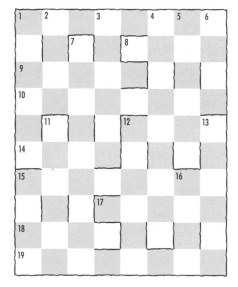

ANSWERS, PAGES 286 & 288

ACROSS

1 Hit wristband? (4)
4 Sketched Nancy, the detective (4)
8 "A pathologist works here," doctors state (7)
9 Mark a black beetle (6)
10 Okay, fathers valued fur (8)
12 Claim Armstrong returned (4)
14 Bother removing two middle pieces from brainteaser (4)
16 Relishes travels without kids? (8)
17 Collects $1,000 plus tips (6)
18 Essentially, he invested in a pie (2,5)
19 Reports city prosecutor before tax cut (4)
20 Liberal arts leader (4)

DOWN

1 California politicians brought up spooky character? (6)
2 Spelunker's tool hit hard in airplane trip (10)
3 Modern Persian well off, if in France (5)
5 Teacher drops TV antenna (6,4)
6 Assemble men holding a sign (6)
7 Reportedly contemplated walk through deep water (4)
11 Sleep in busiest airport (6)
13 Criminal snares former Egyptian leader (6)
15 In strike, laborers initially make foolish remarks (5)
16 Principal had consuming energy (4)

3

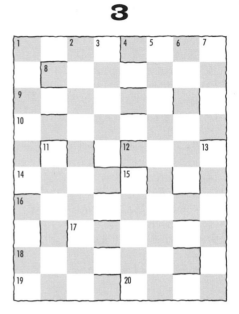

ACROSS

1 Put down prosecutor's animals (6)
7 Patriots displaying rebellion (4)
8 Finish off skimpy cheese selection (4)
9 Nary a soul empty after lunchtime (2,3)
11 Horse in South Dakota covered with spangles (8)
12 Shoot wolf from behind (4)
15 You sometimes have to tie it up and beat it soundly? (4)
16 Callous hustler's maneuvers (8)
18 Suggestions tossed aside (5)
19 Rent drop (4)
20 Intent woman acquires ring (4)
21 Rocky's decline in work (6)

DOWN

1 Property is converted into wealth (10)
2 Maiden trimmed on both sides with right hand (4)
3 Mark has given up, almost (3,5)
4 Simmering a bit of bear grease (5)
5 Restaurant patron with zero cash (6)
6 Teases Stallone for no reason (10)
10 Order John to be at work (2,3,3)
13 *The Incredible Hulk's* Ferrigno turned red—it's more flashy (6)
14 Cut *Moonstruck* actress in audition (5)
17 Barking animal shut up (4)

4

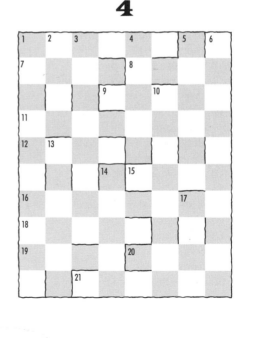

ACROSS

1 Game birds kick up a fuss (6)
7 Something thorny in a plot came up (4)
8 Stooge spoils retreat (4)
9 Test fish, holding fork? (3,3)
10 Aircraft in battle distort route (8)
12 Flavoring article is eatery's first (5)
13 Almost stupid as a French novelist (5)
14 Austrian composer butchers plays (8)
16 Number in Spanish article divisible by two (6)
17 Magritte's partial awareness (4)
18 In the sound, look for wharf (4)
19 A place to drive around while relaxed (2,4)

DOWN

1 Get big, menacing sound before the finale (4)
2 Bond is in for upcoming novel (5,1,4)
3 Pair of students splitting round, fat bird (7)
4 Fashion steps over a fence for the audience (5)
5 Before ram, leap fences? (10)
6 Changes in staler bananas (6)
11 Country song about guys (7)
12 State positively, "Lock one up" (6)
13 Two singers wrapping five in comforter (5)
15 Wear out an important part of a car (4)

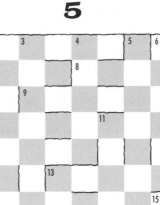

ACROSS

1 Sandwich shop lied freely (4)
4 Back rests extend between supports (4)
9 Because of two-piano composition, start to object (3,2)
10 Shared skewer holding piece of lamb (5)
11 Huge lasso returned after pair of cowboys left (8)
13 Sore wound, sort of pink (4)
14 Auditor's cry cut short (4)
16 A sort of dancing light ahead of army officer (8)
18 Thick liquid stuff contains energy (5)
19 Contests populations (5)
20 Pavarotti's three kilometer journey (4)
21 East End developed garden (4)

DOWN

1 Embarrassment from Disco Dancing shirt (10)
2 Sexpot stripped Montreal player (4)
3 I do it foolishly! (5)
5 Staff for each boy Len raised (9)
6 Relaxed in consulate, as expected (2,4)
7 Ladies vote against botched sign (10)
8 A weapon has low fee (9)
12 Seize headless doll inside automobile (6)
15 Five Gaelic poems (5)
17 Message from Rome: Beware collapse (4)

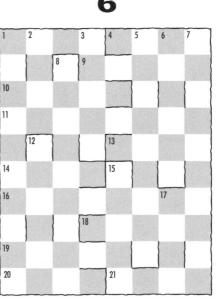

ANSWERS, PAGES 294 & 296

ACROSS

1 Iranian dialect is normal, see? (6)

7 Honestly crazy, in secret (2,3,3)

8 CompuServe member! (4)

9 Move prison (4)

10 Creed of Christianity is 75% niceness (6)

11 Get atop cedar's first branch (5)

15 Almost pay friend of John Paul II (5)

16 Ornaments bother nurses (6)

17 Weakens vital fluids (4)

18 Guy's partner at a big party (4)

19 Little devil wanders around, becomes a better person (8)

20 Gully near Roy Orbison's property (6)

DOWN

1 1/16 of a pound added after bit of price jump (6)

2 Photographer as a lens-mad drunk (5,5)

3 Hour taken by a ninny, someone short (6)

4 High regard is insufficient for Ms. Lauder (5)

5 Yell back, after second-rate actress Hamilton: "It doesn't lead to much" (5,5)

6 String instrument untruthful person heard (4)

12 Sound of a gunshot over Oregon city in the northeast (6)

13 Somewhere in Texas, a Pole's going nuts (2,4)

14 Father's opposite seen in Pennsylvania (5)

16 A murder or theft, for example (2,2)

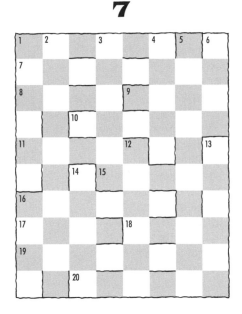

7

ACROSS

1 Few beets ruined hearty meal (4,4)

7 Eight islands created by terrorist group (7)

8 Battle instigator once again put the heat on (4,4)

9 Money from Italy left retirement plan (4)

11 Stains backgammon pieces (5)

13 Boyfriend describes unknown poet (5)

18 Ask accommodating Republican for a big piece of ice (4)

19 Jackie is born on ground (8)

20 White noise spoiled piano pieces? (7)

21 Senator accepts suit color (3,5)

DOWN

1 Archer went ahead and participated in a sport (6)

2 Computer message held back by parliament (1-4)

3 Mistaken about a piece of jewelry (7)

4 Discussed unique Asian city (5)

5 Build interior of the rectory (5)

6 In recession, attract orphan (4)

10 Anticipate cost, including smeltery materials (7)

12 Employ song in dances (4,2)

14 Muddy abode! (5)

15 Skinny opening in grocery item (5)

16 Expert's excellent speech (5)

17 Greek god is concerned with shaved head (4)

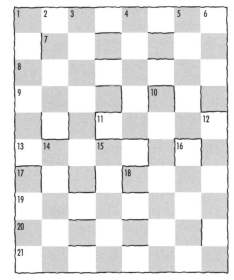

8

ACROSS

1 One who composed an icy mass (4)
4 Stratagem for receding hairline? (4)
7 Nothing changes egg producers (7)
8 Play the role of a very short dam builder (6)
9 A laborer, strangely, living in a tree (8)
11 Check for drops of water falling in your ear (4)
14 Carried away rat that's eaten bit of poison (4)
15 The salty crackers under the table (8)
16 You ultimately hit one woman with a fat lip? (6)
17 By mistake, spilled oil in Libyan port (7)
18 Record is set in Washington (4)
19 Bet a Sicilian hothead turned back (4)

DOWN

1 Actor in swamp pictures (6)
2 Summit break after evening (7)
3 Antenna with its bare bar bent (6,4)
4 Militia raiment includes crown (5)
5 Accelerate joy with spiritual vision (10)
6 Eddy's put in stitches? (4)
10 Stop behind a Spanish paving (7)
12 Pen musical note "E" in "Bad Lie" (6)
13 Movie about an outbreak of fear (5)
15 Begged for leather endlessly (4)

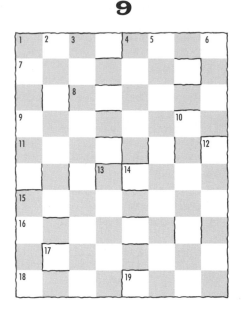

ACROSS

1 European soldier's head is found next to bed (4)
4 Hear story end (4)
7 Name-drop in a sneaky way—sorry (6,2)
8 Clip end off Hibernian flower (4)
10 Curious temperature repulsed ear-biter (5)
11 In part, ruling out jargon (5)
12 *Home Improvement* star dropped behind the leader (5)
13 With assistance, have a dog? (5)
15 Move 20th letter in title (4)
16 Once again, pick up back rest (8)
17 Cut list crookedly (4)
18 Pale and, at first, bashful (4)

DOWN

1 Barbecue rod points upward (4)
2 Her acclaim confused Hoagy (10)
3 Gave directions to one tired stranger (8)
4 Also taking in Kentucky city (5)
5 Mischievous bears on top of drain (10)
6 Pressure Oilers' center soon (4,2)
9 Singles out one distress call coming about after midnight (8)
11 Threatens decreases (6)
12 Dealer truly keeps listening (5)
14 Fancy celebration started late (4)

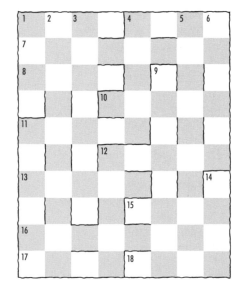

ANSWERS, PAGES 302 & 304

ACROSS

1 Pick each fresh garbanzo bean (5,3)

8 Sidekick's much improved (4)

9 Remove front of thin missile (5)

10 Visit eccentric outside family circle (4,2,2)

12 Cried, covering piece of paper with moisture (4)

14 Fly-catching amphibian pulled with the tongue (4)

15 Mixed up in covert scheme (8)

17 Stacked pastrami at first deli counter (5)

18 Return of "morning head" (4)

19 Previous state lies between "full" and "empty" (8)

DOWN

1 Chap almost rented ski lodge (6)

2 Leading man in *The Rock* (4)

3 Type of college dorm keeps well prepared (6)

4 Price that you'll pay for calling in bellhop fluctuates (5,4)

5 Old World countries featured in Amateur Open (6)

6 Preacher's saying bad name (4)

7 Battle Roosevelt, Simpson, and Sadat (6,3)

11 Hurt Yogi's pal (3-3)

12 Electrical cables twist around one (6)

13 "Color laundry in Tide," I said (3-3)

15 Part of sleeve scratches after being trimmed (4)

16 Speaker's conceited manner (4)

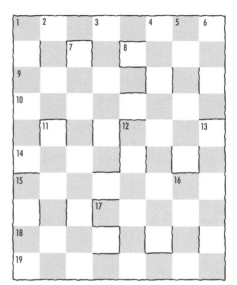

11

ACROSS

1 Reportedly prepared a gift, lost in thought (4)

4 Returned some computers in swindle (4)

8 Visionary hero completely holding back clumsy fellow (7)

9 Outlaw grabbing money machine—he wears a mask (6)

10 Later on, I ordered Chinese, perhaps (8)

12 Speech defect is found in vinyl record (4)

14 Mother pig's litters (4)

16 The way in which to catch wild goose: pen (8)

17 Amid decay, study rat, for example (6)

18 Democrat absorbed by new insignificant payment (3,4)

19 Game show accommodates network (4)

20 Introduction to Seattle Mariner bigwig (4)

DOWN

1 Popular miniseries containing second-rate mechanical workers (6)

2 Phrase for upcoming bit of sun: "soak it up" (3,2,5)

3 Strings holding back of alarm clocks (5)

5 Provisional government's leader enters mainland (10)

6 A kid relaxed (2,4)

7 Singer Tormé hosts a banquet (4)

11 Knitted sock also coming up in quilt-making session (6)

13 Russian czar obtains tungsten alloy (6)

15 Turns over plants to the audience (5)

16 Damage high limb (4)

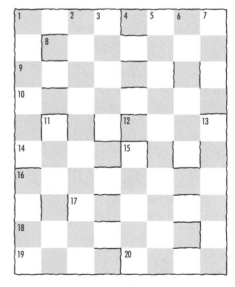

12

ACROSS

1 Chinese vessel (old boat) turned back for European city (6)
7 Call for a place to spar (4)
8 Rate chief ot police "excellent" (4)
9 Delay for a parking space (5)
11 Name girl changed in Zola novel (8)
12 The Red Sea's middle: abounding endlessly (4)
15 Tree back of grove is burning (4)
16 Most abrasive stoolie nabs CIA agents (8)
18 Flower for a grave unfinished (5)
19 Star amid piano variations (4)
20 Said, "Post, man" (4)
21 Turning around, observe Seinfeld's neighbor (6)

DOWN

1 Something to pay for $1,000 carpet chore (10)
2 Frost poem read aloud (4)
3 Hottest inert gas transmuted (8)
4 For starters, our poor teacher is clonked in the eye (5)
5 Sweet and clear, I let loose (6)
6 One leading beauty, if heard (10)
10 1862 battle against uprising naval officer (8)
13 Think about a boy (6)
14 Stick with small fruit (5)
17 Only part of a pump (4)

13

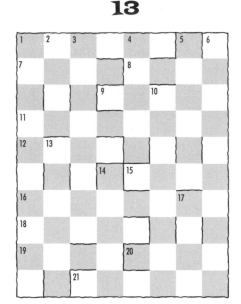

ACROSS

1 Server follows sports team off (6)
7 Copy mid-sixties triumph (4)
8 Staff crushed part of a nutmeg shell (4)
9 Certain films upset Madras (6)
10 Father buries artists (8)
12 Fountain brought revitalization, in part (5)
13 Start being strange (5)
14 Prompt one-liner that is about tank (8)
16 Cavity packer (6)
17 Reportedly spots cooper's tool (4)
18 Thought aide silly (4)
19 Rate donkeys satisfactory (6)

DOWN

1 Over 8/13 of the alphabet (4)
2 Curses rapiers having damage (10)
3 Neatest ditties for the fiddler (7)
4 A pad attached to one violin (5)
5 Shortages leave a lasting effect on urban areas (10)
6 Not as much applied instruction (6)
11 Grenade tossed—get ready (2,5)
12 Female-chaser perfectly describes TV host (6)
13 Hear computer info is lousy for teenagers (5)
15 Letters fill counter (4)

14

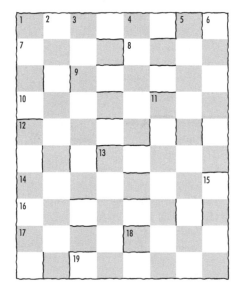

ANSWERS, PAGES 310 & 312

ACROSS

1 Minor struggle with head of department (4)

4 Information is somewhat backward (4)

9 I am passing East Lake Drive (5)

10 Peter Rabbit's creator loses head for frisky character (5)

11 The cutting sixties protester is tough (8)

13 Los Angeles loves Asian country (4)

14 You and I shall rise to the surface (4)

16 Type of fracture beginning to hurt Delta, for one (8)

18 Ocean tossed light boat (5)

19 "What ho!" said entertaining Musketeer (5)

20 Small child becomes attached to empty handbag (4)

21 Theater award for New York (4)

DOWN

1 White part of Swiss cheese with warm bread (5,5)

2 Heard Mommy's sister chip in (4)

3 Tries to slim down legislatures (5)

5 Copying boxing ring that's attractive (9)

6 Spoiled brat is last to admit mistake (6)

7 Actor friend's mark before the final in sociology (4,6)

8 Sailor gripped by meager illumination from the night sky (9)

12 Slowly securing a rough shelter (4-2)

15 Bachelor at most recent party (5)

17 Either way you look at it, it's lunchtime (4)

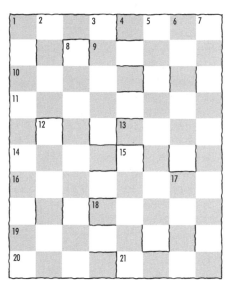

ACROSS

1 A Highlander's neckwear (6)

7 In retrospect, specify limits for astronaut (8)

8 Embrace English giant (4)

9 At hearing, rotate duty (4)

10 Herded deer the wrong way in anger (6)

11 Region around northern battlefield (5)

15 South Carolina provided one genre of movies (3-2)

16 Print a novel up to a point (2,4)

17 Stare at operator with broken leg (4)

18 Ring finished with friend's gem (4)

19 Difficult medium for painting in volume (8)

20 Santa's Teddy bears sampled (6)

DOWN

1 A study involving high school for artists (6)

2 Encouraging member of the Beatles amid scorn (8,2)

3 Most of the globe, as once shaped (6)

4 Hazy upper atmosphere around Missouri (5)

5 Teamster boss keeping everyone with me in shrine for sports heroes (4,2,4)

6 King, before getting married, called joint (4)

12 Review of Oscars is over (6)

13 Advertised speaker's physique (6)

14 Leave Spanish drunk (5)

16 It holds nothing over a very small amount (4)

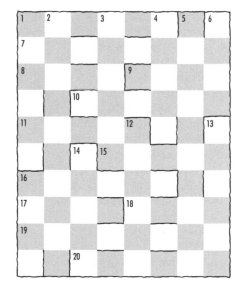

ACROSS

1 Served very hot meals for animals, including sheep (8)

7 Gad—following little rascal makes you better (7)

8 Astronauts resort to stick with no end (8)

9 Cover up what's tanned (4)

11 Playwright said to be in the red with unpaid bills (5)

13 Beats 500 Jamaican exports (5)

18 Method in Alamo defense (4)

19 Plot in a lady's novel (4,4)

20 Contrary in the matter of metrical writing (7)

21 People fighting a translation of *Le Roi d'Ys* (8)

DOWN

1 Angled, if turned and dropped (6)

2 Fat lip I had briefly (5)

3 Flip took a doctors' group to court for film in 1984 (7)

4 Reportedly raised bakery item (5)

5 Still on time for contest (5)

6 Study the start of the Depression (4)

10 Silly people embracing no Italians (7)

12 Tired general nabbed by agent (6)

14 Where cowboys perform in ragged ring (5)

15 Imitated Demi Moore's debut the wrong way (5)

16 Summer snake (5)

17 Ruins creator of Milky Way (4)

17

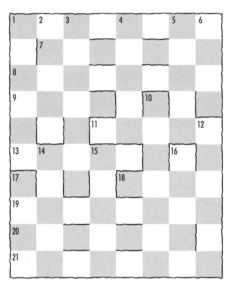

ACROSS

1 Sort of test lesson after commencement (4)

4 Entranced rodent holding piece of popcorn (4)

7 Businesses for tennis equipment (7)

8 Reported someone leaving city in England (6)

9 Elected officials capturing Darth and Storm Troopers, perhaps (8)

11 Male surrounded by ten federal agents (1-3)

14 Blade cut front end off of outcropping (4)

15 Ah, tinier bugs flying around (2,3,3)

16 Reject must eat doughnut with egg (4,2)

17 Syrup initially tried with nutty cereal (7)

18 Playwright understood about front of house (4)

19 Islands in Florida's legends (4)

DOWN

1 Circles newspaper announcements describing Russia's premier (6)

2 Unusual Armani suits finally worn for 1988 movie (4,3)

3 Carrey's detective happening to be in car (3,7)

4 First off, produces clarinets and oboes (5)

5 The number of guests at 10:00 hoedown (10)

6 Criticizes abstract arts (4)

10 Tractor-trailer rides on idly, without swaying (7)

12 Greek god discovered in another mess (6)

13 Cast is finished, we hear (5)

15 Egyptian goddess lives twice (4)

18

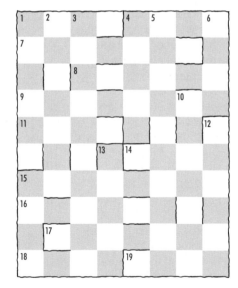

ANSWERS, PAGES 317 & 286

ACROSS

1 Remove duplicate letters from access cards (4)
4 Record *d* = 100 (4)
7 Leave senior holding identical fabric (8)
8 Some bemused birds from Oz (4)
10 Farewell broadcasts started late (5)
11 Tyne consumes one every twenty-four hours (5)
12 Reporter's reserve troop (5)
13 Bad grade in a large exam (5)
15 Heard dog so long (4)
16 What's inside pleases (8)
17 Stops, not starting repairs (4)
18 Cross heart at hearing (4)

DOWN

1 Declined a dropout's degree (4)
2 Parallel porno scam I arranged (10)
3 Adjusting tenure is greedy (8)
4 Marvelous letters at front and back of diary? (5)
5 Mediocre doctor doesn't care (6-4)
6 Defoe character changed course (6)
9 Headache initially miffed Arthur's mom (8)
11 Mar six piano keys? (6)
12 Trapped by bears, lieutenant stops (5)
14 Bewildered head of sales in car dealership (4)

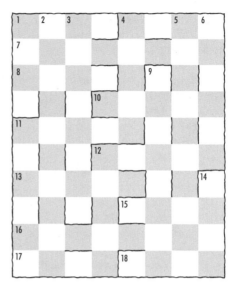

19

ACROSS

1 Wise person keeps pace with modern era (5,3)
8 Attempt is crazy, in retrospect (4)
9 Maria Shriver's featuring songs (5)
10 Turned back *Love Story* author at border for rifles (8)
12 Thin one fitting into small, large, and medium (4)
14 Lunch interrupted by start of stage direction (4)
15 Retracted broadcasts about slender island nation (3,5)
17 Peruvian native amid fire (5)
18 Some deer sleep soundly? (4)
19 Captured Ardennes after struggle (8)

DOWN

1 Principal put page into old hat (6)
2 According to one fairy (4)
3 Talk about the French ski lodge (6)
4 A game kids play with spear, concisely (2,1,6)
5 Yielded silver brought up at ore deposit (4,2)
6 Before shot, energy declines (4)
7 Misfortunes to go in cycles for *Oliver Twist* character (4,5)
11 She has country concerts coming up, not hip-hop (6)
12 Part of anthem penned by Miss Tanzania (6)
13 A demon wildly wailed (6)
15 Team expressed sorrow audibly (4)
16 Mistakenly take shrewish Shakespearean role (4)

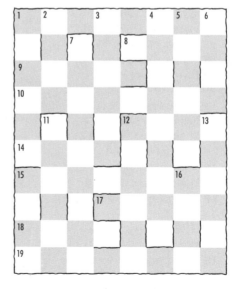

20

ACROSS

1 Our group shot Friday on *Dragnet* (4)

4 Confusion about crooner's last throat problem? (4)

8 Brother holding competition with farmworker (7)

9 Said overcast occasion is best (5-1)

10 Soak two large nuts (8)

12 Recognize Swiss hero (4)

14 Missouri shortstop's sign of inactivity? (4)

16 Obscure quote about wet blanket retracted (8)

17 "Yes," I pronounced repeatedly (3,3)

18 Number of uniform written in pen (7)

19 Essay about a cafeteria need (4)

20 Observed in an odd way, the germs swarm (4)

DOWN

1 Home for a Native American rug with a bit of mildew (6)

2 European city is into punk rock (10)

3 Commanded northern region of Germany (5)

5 Land in area Lestat exploits (4,6)

6 Flier's cheer about carnival site (6)

7 Ringer leaving heartlessly (4)

11 Someone with a club about to strike back (6)

13 Cracked my clue in school (6)

15 Starts from scratch, picturing each night that's passed (5)

16 Point of changing seat (4)

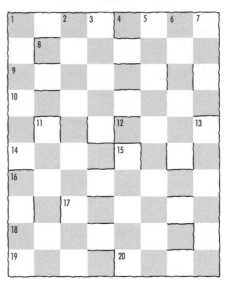

ACROSS

1 Suggest past chief of police is covered with acne (6)

7 Confused Oakland athletes eat endlessly (4)

8 I empty out a letter (4)

9 Forthcoming Paton novel (2,3)

11 Counter brought attention to cakes and pies (8)

12 Fighter pilot brought round hospital for pain (4)

15 Retro video-game system loses its freshness (4)

16 Blows up generals in a riot (8)

18 Bald stranger has one spontaneous comment (2,3)

19 Steals from Mr. Lowe and Mr. Reiner (4)

20 Legendary ship's freight not opened (4)

21 Large German city in decline (6)

DOWN

1 Animals face wet ears (5,5)

2 Tropical spot is left empty (4)

3 Military building employed in *WarGames* shallowly (8)

4 Tells stories about northern routes (5)

5 Susan takes time at sculpture (6)

6 Group discussion cast aspersions (3,7)

10 Fires one of those shipworkers (8)

13 Type of complex, rare bird (6)

14 I say, "Demolish and build" (5)

17 Acclaimed genius maintains advantage (4)

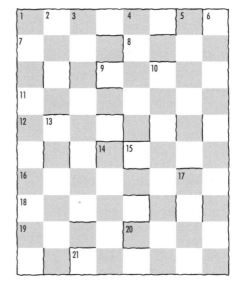

ANSWERS, PAGES 292 & 294

ACROSS

1 Jeer rudely in front of court outcast (6)
7 Farm team put five more into oven? (4)
8 Concerned with most of Ernie's back (2,2)
9 Lunatic did in sitter behind closed doors (6)
10 Dishonor carried by FBI agent grew bigger and bigger (8)
12 Head of company on screen (5)
13 Vitality or taste (5)
14 They're there already, holding light (8)
16 Sticker: "Container holds fresh pie" (6)
17 Naysayer employed by Banting (4)
18 Reportedly study clarinet piece (4)
19 Fancy marble, dull base (6)

DOWN

1 Demonstration after the first summit (4)
2 Taking advantage of Arafat's group in leaving (10)
3 Have O.J. free before end of month–God (7)
4 Cried, tossed apple drink (5)
5 Mooch bananas for dear Lee (10)
6 Provide splitter (6)
11 I write in red, not green (7)
12 Minos, for one, spilled nectar (6)
13 Rotten pea is brown (5)
15 Boy and Spanish woman (4)

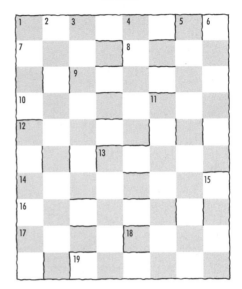

23

ACROSS

1 Father accepts Republican support (4)
4 Snakes that are venomous as afterthought (4)
9 Former vice-president again accepts $1,000 (5)
10 Color lines getting exploited (5)
11 In time, Giant running back is essential (8)
13 Sound from west wing (4)
14 Look for Indian worshiper at hearing (4)
16 Suffers humiliation at investing money in trust (4,4)
18 Middle Eastern native in small German car (5)
19 One that hurts an inhabitant of a Midwestern state (5)
20 Writer Ferber's *East and Westward* (4)
21 Distinctive flavor of brown sugar at heart (4)

DOWN

1 Resist a pie prepared in bakeshop (10)
2 Downpour destroyed Iran (4)
3 Quiet times for congressional workers (5)
5 Upcoming hits containing an instrument in the percussion family (5,4)
6 Audibly sells bikes (6)
7 Engrossing big-band music takes permit (10)
8 Barhopping changed from then to now (2,3,4)
12 *Poseidon Adventure's* debut taken in by upset leaders of Venice (3,3)
15 Insufficient time to follow up examination (5)
17 Ball and racket for Thor's father (4)

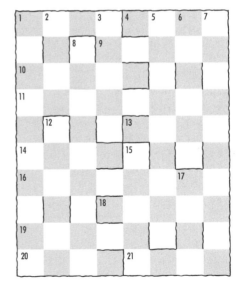

24

ACROSS

1 Stint with chief of police after theatrical hanging (6)
7 Jerk interrupting jazz buff's rap (8)
8 Run into a Hindu hero (4)
9 Some constellations scatter? (4)
10 Total for a large oaf (3-3)
11 Have room for 1,000 in entrance of mine? (5)
15 Pull up to a bar at center of small country (5)
16 Naughty fellows hearing where congregations may be seated (6)
17 Start off breezy race (4)
18 Specific item in the debut of *Top Hat* (4)
19 Promise, being careful about wild talk (8)
20 Cryptic teaser for an occasion in spring (6)

DOWN

1 Southern elite riot (6)
2 Taking no chances when consuming Shalala's wine (10)
3 CIA lit out for a crooked character? (6)
4 Flower groups in the audience (5)
5 College graduates swallowed slander (10)
6 Almost express a bit of sports info (4)
12 Sat up after article with Greek letters (6)
13 One suffering right after 1955 Borgnine movie (6)
14 Doctor cared for inner circle (5)
16 Solution the two of us pronounced for a New Zealander (4)

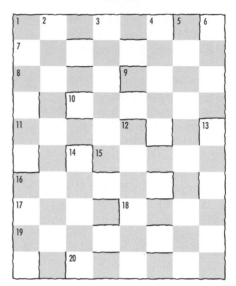

25

ACROSS

1 Bats scare our guest at a party? (8)
7 Part of sitcom: "Itt" shows neglect (4)
9 Ghost's noise by the mostly evil cemetery (4,4)
10 Fester's face: real weird and beastly (5)
11 Blood-colored—that is, when turned down (5)
14 Swamp Thing spat audibly (5)
15 Fat Pugsley's heart initially torn out (5)
17 Brain with bugs seen in it (8)
18 Bad times for vampires heard in confusion (4)
19 Cut-off hand's back in sod we disturbed (8)

DOWN

1 *Addams Family* prop we found in a sort of salad (6)
2 Morticia's wildly passionate (9)
3 Embraced by Fester, I scream (4)
4 Haunted house for you and me and her (5)
5 Ghost tears up the "Thing" (6)
6 Lurch's part auditioned? (4)
8 Picture with allure could make Gomez rail (9)
12 Witches making CD with trancelike singing? (6)
13 Pugsley's head, under ground, cut off (6)
14 Cooked guts with old relish (5)
15 Wednesday holds back thrill (4)
16 Intend being wicked? (4)

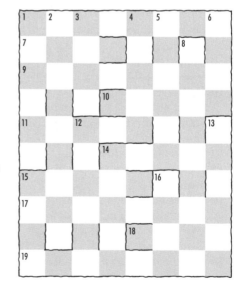

26

ACROSS

1 Star skiers at rocks (8)
7 Problem acquiring a piece of Intel computer company (7)
8 Criminal finally caught by choppers on call-in TV show (8)
9 Interrupt passage from church altar (4)
11 Emitted a low tone in conversation (5)
13 Winchester's last seen in Col. Potter's camp, in Swamp (5)
18 Rotten apple turned pitch black (4)
19 Write a book based on *Free Love* 'zine (8)
20 Judge: "No place for sinners" (7)
21 Write label on U.S. government building (8)

DOWN

1 "Traveling Man" the song (6)
2 Hares destroyed crop (5)
3 Planter's tools fix trellis (7)
4 Relationship of air to ground (5)
5 Push borne by pushover (5)
6 Family dog's face is friendly (4)
10 Flying in air, flying in air (7)
12 Express love for Dorothy before much time (4,2)
14 Quote a mortgage separately (5)
15 He appears in TV film (5)
16 Arizona secured by knockout round buzzer? (5)
17 Cut tailor's items up (4)

27

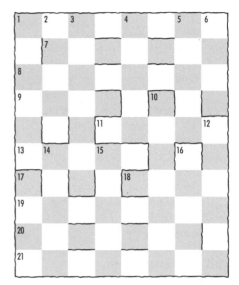

ACROSS

1 Cards lying in front of a cesspool (4)
4 A great number float (4)
7 Angry worker trapped in arena (7)
8 Asian residents deposit $1,000 in banks (6)
9 Musicians flying starship (8)
11 Always the First Lady, right? (4)
14 First of critics covering talk (4)
15 Bury established business (8)
16 Craving engineering T-shirt (6)
17 More annoying nobleman has hit the slopes (7)
18 First off, picked nylons (4)
19 Measure someone in pain, say (4)

DOWN

1 More cunning sort of hunter (6)
2 Travelers cut short party hosted by actor James (7)
3 Suits each Tuesday displayed in doorways (10)
4 Strict doctor with identification (5)
5 Held by Danes: the ticket number? (10)
6 Throw to shortstop (4)
10 Awkwardly rotates kitchen appliance (7)
12 Pair of athletes wear out clothing (6)
13 Inherently blue (3,2)
15 Desire a vermouth before church (4)

28

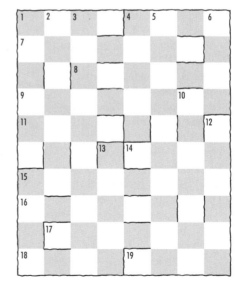

ACROSS

1 Help suppressing conservative's biting sarcasm (4)

4 Help suppressing bachelor's sounds of sorrow (4)

7 Farmworker ran first in competition against champion (8)

8 Finishes remodeling dens (4)

10 Plots to seize a necklace (5)

11 Tropical location is rented (5)

12 Father took command, showed fear (5)

13 Doctor taking in a bit of money from the Middle East (5)

15 Reportedly get rid of loafer (4)

16 Surprisingly good news occurs (4,4)

17 Wild party, peculiarly gory (4)

18 Was triumphant at start of trade convention (4)

DOWN

1 War god right in the middle of rising ocean (4)

2 Republicanism in organization including a group of stars (5,5)

3 Stylish party at end of Mardi Gras is marked by lethargy (8)

4 Covering Haggard novel and Spielberg movie (5)

5 Actress Fonda to hold title to city in Barbados (10)

6 Drunk and therefore exploited (6)

9 Outcry from hobo roughly grabbing confederate (8)

11 Characters from Spain dig orange color (6)

12 Dupe holy man, turning in wages (5)

14 Small amount of money conveyed to an auditor (4)

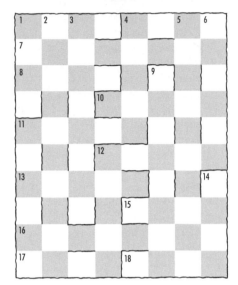

29

ACROSS

1 Cuba liberation grips island (4)

4 Includes woodworking tool in discussion (4)

8 Founder catches insect and bird (7)

9 Lacking a goal, Rodman collapses (6)

10 Poor elected official joins mature repartee (8)

12 Tennis player shelled kidney-shaped nut (4)

14 Small amount of water seen in hydroplane (4)

16 Let's elaborate about hot place where sweethearts go (4,4)

17 Show coach Lombardi after game's end (6)

18 Heavily attacked arts retrospective associated with government agent (7)

19 Pitch sots out (4)

20 Discover cable-sports award (4)

DOWN

1 Sarcastic bachelor rebuffed Ms. Winger (6)

2 Off-road vehicles on curve chasing left and right (4,6)

3 Nation in relief after recession (5)

5 Syrians block a location near Sudan's capital (10)

6 Henry boards filthy sailboat (6)

7 Type of gin that's dull on the tongue (4)

11 Cave design got rot (6)

13 Uncovered furnace at club's restaurant (6)

15 Excellent informer turned over switchblade (5)

16 Final thing a cobbler needs (4)

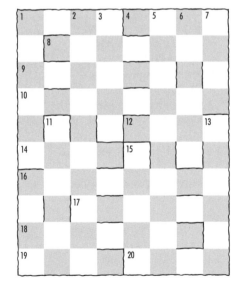

30

ANSWERS, PAGES 308 & 310

ACROSS

1 For sport, the founder of *The New Yorker* wears ornamental braid (8)

8 Compassion of mine and a bit of yours (4)

9 Island drink at middle of day (5)

10 Jumped out of the water bed, having come to (8)

12 Annoy everyone after beginning to gargle (4)

14 A female tennis great (4)

15 Pair of animals—that is, large and small dogs (8)

17 Not ready for loony tunes (5)

18 Indian's unending faith (4)

19 Musical instrument crushed by red oak (8)

DOWN

1 Prosecutor pursues innocent Greek character (6)

2 A container not entirely shut (4)

3 Model T tore around a turn (6)

4 Head of state takes a toke east of Sri Lanka (9)

5 Hard peg taken in underhanded (6)

6 Said I'd looked (4)

7 Author drunkenly lay around vent (4,5)

11 Try for the wrath of a serpent? (6)

12 Run around circle with Yank in Mexico (6)

13 Salted nuts didn't get stale (6)

15 Belt is something worn in Oxford? (4)

16 Beheaded certain king (4)

31

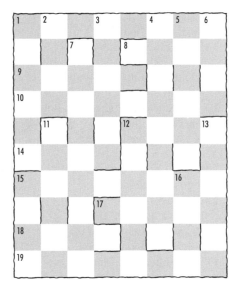

ACROSS

1 Where to get marble game (6)

7 In the Sound, brings in vessels (4)

8 Fascinated by Ford car with front trimmed (4)

9 Classical poet is a big hit (5)

11 Lacking optimism, famous Argentine general retreats (8)

12 Seabird's change of course, you might say (4)

15 Awful native offers bone (4)

16 Relatives captivated by ladies' shoes and fall fare (8)

18 Slightly tilts menus (5)

19 Held back by zookeeper's fencing material? (4)

20 Bill, possibly, takes time for a party (4)

21 Well-loved Communist goes after trouble (6)

DOWN

1 Upend quilt Dotty made five times (10)

2 With shaved head, get rid of desire (4)

3 A complainer slams wordplay (8)

4 One among degenerates causing disturbances (5)

5 Spielberg's playing fast and loose with events (6)

6 Woody's going around California, as predicted (10)

10 Fashion-industry worker/ gold-digger takes ill (8)

13 Prepares jokes, succeeding easily at first (6)

14 Chose vandalized depot (5)

17 Mention collar is turned up (4)

32

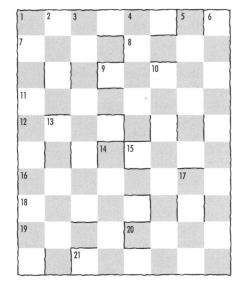

ACROSS

1 Grill in rose garden soaked up sun (6)
7 Make engravings and the like with bit of heat (4)
8 Then Pacino heads west in Asian nation (4)
9 Floats high above Scotland's capital (6)
10 Family taking shelter with one Iranian leader (8)
12 Carolina senator acts as director (5)
13 Lived like a lecher, turning decadent at last (5)
14 Bullfighter's cheer about holding audition (8)
16 A river vessel carries a Mideastern leader (6)
17 Lives near the French resort in the tropics (4)
18 Spotted tying up loose ends (4)
19 Bow in front of Arkansas disk jockey (6)

DOWN

1 Bill or Arthur beginning to kneel (4)
2 Matthew or Stewart hiding under least favorable conditions (2,3,5)
3 One engaged in study of the sun around church (7)
4 Santa's workers left stocking December 24th and 31st (5)
5 Blue stream enters bend (10)
6 Help guitar player after opening (6)
11 Deceit: a mixed drink (4,3)
12 Returning to put in locks—it's a bunch of nonsense (3,3)
13 Table supplied with more food from the South (5)
15 Attorney General upset one Republican (4)

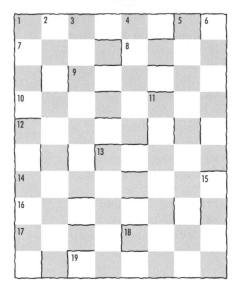

33

ACROSS

1 Made some music in Los Angeles (4)
4 Town of 1,000 engulfed in receding ocean (4)
9 Home of smeared adobe (5)
10 Area for true movie's debut (5)
11 Blazes out of control in Fresno (8)
13 Bit a Mr. Selleck (4)
14 Smog finally consumed something golden in San Francisco? (4)
16 Dealing with giant rocks after first half of tremor (8)
18 Fly around western edge of Nevada with a detective device (5)
19 "It's the actress Shearer, or I'm a loony" (5)
20 Stats for Dodger pitchers' ages (4)
21 Mister T grabs a returning streetcar (4)

DOWN

1 Spanish call me after it's back in season (10)
2 So it is in Sacramento (4)
3 E.g., L.A.'s wild storms (5)
5 Tsunami, on shattering big hills (9)
6 Hollywood director cut the top off California tree (2,4)
7 Shaky, as some grim earthquake record (10)
8 After California party, wind up in an eatery (9)
12 Bay feature with high shady spot (6)
15 Little kids flipped, eating California's last weasel (5)
17 Snooze at a wine-making valley (4)

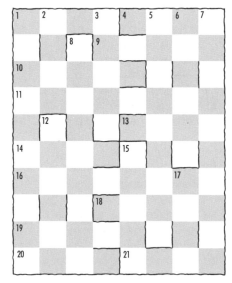

34

ANSWERS, PAGES 316 & 318

ACROSS

1 Young socialite swallowed argument (6)

7 Urchin wandered around in better health (8)

8 Touch horn when backing up (4)

9 Hobbyist's set of parts finally became flying toy (4)

10 He leaves the Peruvian container (3,3)

11 Older berry-producing shrub (5)

15 Appeal one way or the other (5)

16 Silver medalist Stojko, following onset of pulled groin? (6)

17 Burden (ours) (4)

18 Almost snarl, "Don't be so infantile" (4)

19 Near miss troubled discussion groups (8)

20 Overlooking offering from tribes, ideally (6)

DOWN

1 Baby's garment settled after riding up? (6)

2 Encouraged ancient spreading plant (10)

3 More pretentious pleasure-seeker blows his top? (6)

4 Toss out some of the victors (5)

5 Desecrator's destruction was the fastest (3,1,6)

6 Need rocky garden (4)

12 At hearing, drops rules (6)

13 Examine foreheads, say (6)

14 Sounds like fruit dropping straight to the ground (5)

16 Emily, stop dancing (4)

35

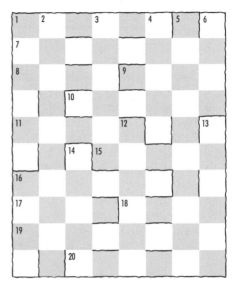

ACROSS

1 Prepare dry place for electronic device (2,6)

7 Beaten 0 to 1, following unsatisfactory touchdown (7)

8 U.S. car—I mean, convertible (8)

9 Walter Mitty's middle name (4)

11 Portion of *Q&A* getting edited out (5)

13 Share Spanish literature (5)

18 Inheritor edges away from the IRS (4)

19 Cruise or use the oars, in the future (8)

20 Fixed a man's head wound up (7)

21 Sentimental about handle—it opens the door (5,3)

DOWN

1 Traces lost shipping containers (6)

2 Deer flanking west side of mountain peaks (5)

3 Composed lie, pure and simple (7)

4 It's rolled in gold for so long (5)

5 On Tuesday, stick up decree (5)

6 Broadway show's opening (4)

10 Broke Ed's plastic model (2,5)

12 Speaking in pig Latin, damage throat (6)

14 Hop over hole's plug (5)

15 Jeremy is embracing Ron (5)

16 Part of computer disk in fluid died (5)

17 State bridges out ahead (4)

36

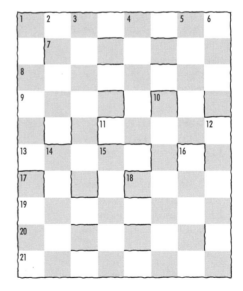

37

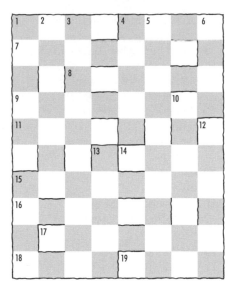

ACROSS

1 Obstruct English noblewoman (4)
4 Eat too much, stomach gets large (4)
7 Impersonate ardent hosts carousing (2,1,4)
8 Cardinal, corralling worker, spoke wildly (6)
9 Paternal pilot has change of heart (8)
11 Returned light metal/uranium component (4)
14 Truck tailing one Russian tyrant (4)
15 Getting in touch with everyone in band (8)
16 Navy prepared a drama (6)
17 Churchill gains a lot of weight (7)
18 Reversed position at start of televised trial (4)
19 Fire excellent staff (4)

DOWN

1 Nitwit eats up before you and me (6)
2 Slow to play and chip in, in poker (7)
3 British writer mixed drinks around morning (6,4)
4 Albee's finale appropriated by fellow playwright (5)
5 Baltic nation hosts Republican and one uplifted at Verdi opera (2,8)
6 Neat yard–it is coming up (4)
10 Pressures slender boy (5,2)
12 Translated "gene" in "generator" (6)
13 Insufficient study on front of *Time* (5)
15 Ecstatic, performed hip-hop music for the audience (4)

38

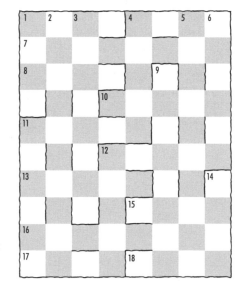

ACROSS

1 Cut some of Schiaparelli's material (4)
4 True, Dior's original article is "pop" (4)
7 Fashion leader: "No flower" (8)
8 Shirt's front label: "For men only" (4)
10 Great space for a guy sporting a tux (5)
11 Force front of dress to tear (5)
12 Sister acquires Armani's first two garments (5)
13 Wearer of a robe and a conical hat in magazine *Us* (5)
15 Part of London very hot on Coco's last piece (4)
16 Dotty remodels less often (8)
17 Hem covered by polished gems (4)
18 Menswear item with "vee" established (4)

DOWN

1 Reported poet's work for a fashion photographer (4)
2 De la Renta moved around town and changed back and forth (10)
3 Measurements of jewelry framing each damsel's face (8)
4 Tailor nears a place to get snagged? (5)
5 Drunken model–she is in ruins (10)
6 Sleeve is worn by a swashbuckling Frenchman (6)
9 Quartet in fabricated moose fur (8)
11 End of Ms. Moore's blouse, at the back (6)
12 Leather was convincing to an audience (5)
14 Categorize Blass's last scrap (4)

ANSWERS, PAGES 290 & 292

ACROSS

1 Actor died in awful bit part (4,4)
8 Understood pronunciation of a Greek letter (4)
9 Seat us next to that woman (5)
10 Once again make part of a harness with long slit (8)
12 Edges away from writer's pony (4)
14 Mr. Young heard sound of relief (4)
15 Doctor catches one of the fish (8)
17 Shabby jazz musician left Kentucky (5)
18 Make an alteration by beginning to press fiber (4)
19 Long and arduous part of anybody's séance (8)

DOWN

1 Obscure nonsense: passages from reviews (6)
2 Flower got bigger (4)
3 Star of *Mrs. Brown* gets back of hair wet (6)
4 Meet in brief before court (9)
5 Maverick sent in Summer Olympics competition (6)
6 Make fun of true intellect (4)
7 Slender, sticky whatchamacallit (9)
11 Felt sorry for chief of police I got even with (6)
12 GI's car runs illegal imports from Cuba (6)
13 Embargo includes any plant from India (6)
15 At first, sale offered half off for part of New York (4)
16 Great resistance to a vegetable (4)

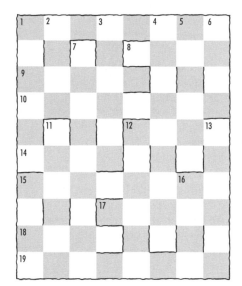

39

ACROSS

1 Are thuccethful in thchool? Way to go (4)
4 Mountain climber's challenge upset pals (4)
8 Count CD Laura damaged (7)
9 Letters from so boisterous a musician (6)
10 Hardly celebrating day's beginning, we hear (8)
12 Rotate chin a short distance (4)
14 Shame about Ursula's front tooth (4)
16 Submissive, like a prayer worthy of confirmation? (8)
17 Request a r-ring (6)
18 Severely reduced spending adopted by Yale after reorganization (7)
19 Immediately, ten invested in volleyball equipment (4)
20 Small top didn't stay in place (4)

DOWN

1 Reminder: dance with Barnum (6)
2 Philosopher wears Texas outfits not given to a single woman (10)
3 Hot light causing anxiety (5)
5 Ellen built new Lloyd's of London ringer (6,4)
6 Physics Nobelist set parameters for one hundred thousand dollars (6)
7 In Paris, blood provided evidence (4)
11 Abrasive stuff turned up on computer attachments (6)
13 Was tipping followed closely? (6)
15 Music-store purchases a pet's chewed up (5)
16 Alda is being held by Jessica Lange (4)

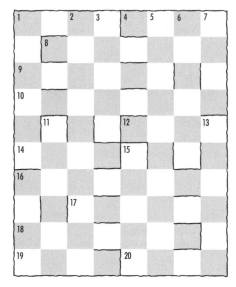

40

ACROSS

1 Gear part put in reverse with skill in kid's vehicle (2-4)
7 John, in Welsh church's center, facing the wrong way (4)
8 British school memo is returned (4)
9 Train station had drinks counter (5)
11 Careless California police in band (8)
12 Half of Uranus is on the far side of a certain atmosphere (4)
15 Same odd plateau (4)
16 Spoken about stone overturned in site of shootout (2,6)
18 United Nations backing drunk up to a point? (5)
19 Arranged lone Christmas tune (4)
20 It's heard for every sound of contentment (4)
21 Auto with favorite floor mat (6)

DOWN

1 Outwits nature gods with morphing (4,6)
2 Love actor Kilmer's shape (4)
3 Small weight of gem turning up in cat's eye flaw (8)
4 Rushes and recites for the audience (5)
5 Hikes South in heavy footwear (6)
6 Vermont healer tries keeping vigilant (2,3,5)
10 Pages holding outline for glass alternative (5,3)
13 Remove one's tie? Not after well-built guy goes topless (6)
14 Cry on unveiling petroleum found in Virginia (5)
17 Race around bit of land (4)

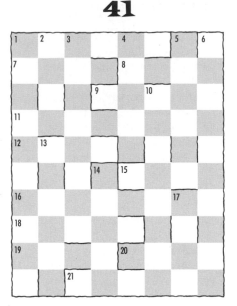

41

ACROSS

1 Spanish corn and asparagus pieces (6)
7 French article about one new profession (4)
8 Someone coming into money among the Irish (4)
9 Valley houses English king after Queen Anne (6)
10 Maria ran off with an Italian sauce (8)
12 Leaders of Sweden and Norway are in a trap (5)
13 Cheer for the Spanish at movie's end (5)
14 Hard, rough climate around Finland's heart (8)
16 Before game of chance, leader of Belgium is drunk (6)
17 Different trains at Estonia's capital (4)
18 Travel stops popular with Poles (4)
19 Rebellion in United Nations and others (6)

DOWN

1 Problem of numbers engulfing Portugal's last ghetto (4)
2 Playwright's country valley circled by Italian river (10)
3 Reestablish a scion with English vessel (7)
4 Reportedly brownish French river (5)
5 Russian plane shares in people's movements (10)
6 Oil country of Europe by the sound (6)
11 A couple from Basel isolated seafood (7)
12 Bachelor in Rome's prepared grave (6)
13 Dined in English school at hearing (5)
15 Fee upset Scot (4)

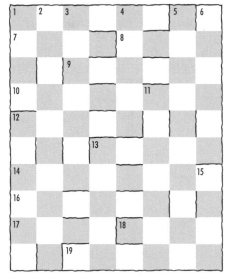

42

ANSWERS, PAGES 298 & 300

ACROSS

1 Pass new taxes (4)
4 Club with hot tub (4)
9 Subway crossed half of road (5)
10 Moral concept grasped by the thickheaded (5)
11 Plays containing ten scenes (8)
13 Dog owner's command beginning to enrage Spot (4)
14 Overtimes following last of scheduled periods (4)
16 Drive fast to fill lifeless battery (8)
18 Nation's poor are O.K. (5)
19 Fourth segment of Super Bowl rocks joint (5)
20 *I Love Lucy* actor's bad side (4)
21 Move up fifty-one feet (4)

DOWN

1 Left desk cluttered and confused (10)
2 Bug one naysayer (4)
3 Upturned lips on Kyle's face— it's a smile, sort of (5)
5 Perfume dispensers adjust to arm size (9)
6 Try to keep lunch arrangement (6)
7 Use recipe to stuff hot pot's contents? (10)
8 Saucy food ruined Rob's shirt (5,4)
12 Porter catches up with husband and wife (6)
15 Lower Subaru's front hood (5)
17 Page from simple affidavit (4)

43

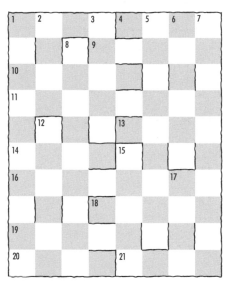

ACROSS

1 Celebrity is against church formality (6)
7 Desert rider arrived with lascivious look (8)
8 Help Lincoln at source of trouble (4)
9 Take out sticky fruit (4)
10 Used abrasives sadden converts (6)
11 In Mexico, Peter roped bucks (5)
15 District Attorney describes hit play (5)
16 Female grad corrected manual (6)
17 U.S. president not finishing lively dance (4)
18 Pavlova put article forward and backward (4)
19 Having time, existentialist finally took five-year trip (4,4)
20 Listen to pleasant type of rock (6)

DOWN

1 Rogue sampling from Italian shrimp dish (6)
2 Call to Beth to change dining room linen (10)
3 Delay bothered trader (6)
4 Manages finals in English, Science, Algebra, and Economics (5)
5 Concludes Ted turned up with furs (10)
6 Brought up loaf for the audience (4)
12 Speak publicly about felon's last fine (6)
13 A shaggy creature's found under rightmost of Greek boats (6)
14 Pair of guards fall behind prison camp (5)
16 A&P's east alcove (4)

44

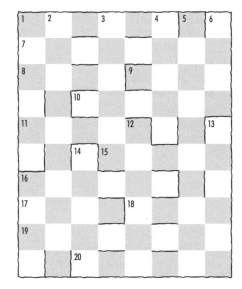

ACROSS

1 Sort of flavoring in company's cold desserts (8)
7 Lab gear broken in high-school course (7)
8 One keyboard instrument turned up as part of set (2,1,5)
9 Wild hogs–oh, my! (4)
11 Unlike Mom to lose face (5)
13 Assistant keeping head of state away from everyone else (5)
18 End of censoring relieved network (4)
19 Characters stuffing screech owl–in essence, this bunch is in a mess (4,4)
20 In the middle of Missouri, gripped by dread (7)
21 Kinda bad to throw a party on making a comeback (3,2,3)

DOWN

1 Stain a British sports car–it's returned (6)
2 In truth, a noisy Asian capital (5)
3 Lace–it's exotic part of underwear (7)
4 Top TV medical drama involved in wager (5)
5 Conservative breaking actual treaty (5)
6 Fools in health clubs doing flip (4)
10 Love or like *Moonstruck* star? (7)
12 Mouse or rat's lair in decay (6)
14 Jerk with South Carolina medical-insurance plan (5)
15 Far end of field has swallows (5)
16 Palomino originally obsessed with spotted horse (5)
17 Scrutinize small fire (4)

45

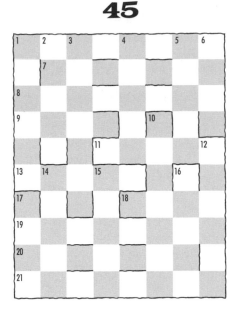

ACROSS

1 Steal chicken's head bone (4)
4 Some quiet children make an impression (4)
7 Annoyed bears in front of snow coaster (7)
8 Article tied for a prince (6)
9 Call headgear back for a NASA flier? (8)
11 Nail a horse's equipment (4)
14 "Kay," formerly called "Bender" (4)
15 Vermin having to be in French dens (8)
16 Egg dish and bagel I objectively permitted (6)
17 Here's a gift (7)
18 Mafia leaders play the role of two Poles (4)
19 Lost a $100 bill, reportedly (4)

DOWN

1 Pure thrill's beginning in hunt (6)
2 Sheep call in storm (7)
3 An actress I cast and a man taking a bow? (5,5)
4 Bush with the Spanish rose turned up (5)
5 *Main Street* sadly ends (10)
6 Cut a bit of white in chicken (4)
10 Solvent with top-grade tint (7)
12 Coin stuck firmly inside veggie (6)
13 Earl's drunk in a French town (5)
15 Stick around a street (4)

46

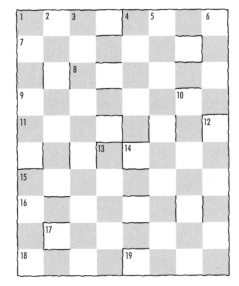

ANSWERS, PAGES 306 & 308

47

ACROSS
1 Gray, like the outside of hosiery (4)
4 Suckers returned as an afterthought (4)
7 Made a guarantee covering spring that's no longer fresh (8)
8 Marsupial after removing the middle nut from a tree (4)
10 Show up in Paris early (5)
11 A ring! (5)
12 Greek warmonger captures west end of Athenian neighborhoods (5)
13 Correct a grand conclusion (5)
15 Group of people did imitations of a rooster (4)
16 Unpleasant person accepted by rational author of detective stories (8)
17 They say I will land in the water (4)
18 Chooses zero points (4)

DOWN
1 Requests pack animal to carry king (4)
2 Upon reflection, foams at the mouth about Western star Gibson's violent movies (5-2-3)
3 Hang around old play that's stayed in the theatres (8)
4 Dismissing the odd characters, I saw his role twist and turn (5)
5 Drop in now with public-relations expert (5,5)
6 Fortunetellers adopting no expressions of contempt (6)
9 Dangerous building divider, if installed upside down (8)
11 Tennis player retracting one's story (6)
12 Irritate topless joint (5)
14 On The Love Boat, Lauren beheaded farm animals (4)

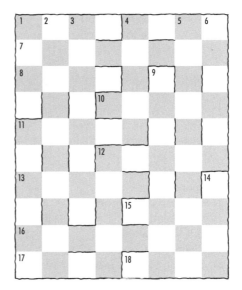

48

ACROSS
1 Even Judge Ito is consumed by evil (8)
8 Award not returned before the Fourth of July (4)
9 Sap finally cleaned shower (5)
10 Called breaking-and-entering act "crazy" (8)
12 Automaker's cry overheard (4)
14 Royal family member's article for the Voice (4)
15 Swift, for one, posed with flower shirt (8)
17 Farm division lacks leadership (5)
18 A problem for teens: crack injected with nitrogen (4)
19 Grand Beach is behind you (8)

DOWN
1 Enlightened one's pal had reformed (6)
2 Measure marathoner after the event, say? (4)
3 In Scandinavia, Teutons fly a plane (6)
4 "Shape" describes a hoedown partner in dance formation (5,4)
5 Finish corn and make love? (6)
6 Eddy newly made batik (4)
7 Professor's aide ran into alternative director (9)
11 Take up weird chants (6)
12 Gives up on fights (6)
13 Club he'd washed (6)
15 Showed deep disgust for gaiter (4)
16 Study sulfur and tin (4)

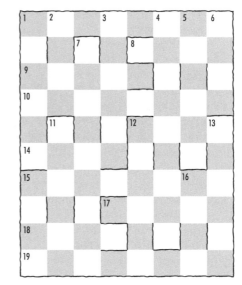

ACROSS

1 Going back depressed a soldier who ran away (4)
4 Run into swarm heading the other direction (4)
8 Managing stocks from a kingdom (6,2)
9 Shift end of proton right away (6)
11 Walk dogs, perhaps the wrong way (4)
12 Dealer returned rare paintings (6)
14 Grin about one figure of speech (6)
16 Music maker edges away from tramps (4)
19 Bid for an auction lot (diamonds)—forget it (2,4)
20 Backing National League player in lower Egyptian city (4,4)
21 Underworld river branches, reportedly (4)
22 Ocean's flow bound by sound (4)

DOWN

1 A military cop's sound equipment (4)
2 Bow in the middle of droll rallying slogan (3,3)
3 Held command, keeping popular with rules (5)
5 Selfish act from end of movie got cut (3,4)
6 Changed gears, keeping advantage (4)
7 Heard couple settle bill for rug? (6)
10 Stonework Madonna holding son (7)
12 Crowds love entering retro game (6)
13 Quiet Celt originally wearing tartan (6)
15 Center field ultimately shrouded in fog (5)
17 Excessively upset after bit of beef Wellington (4)
18 Give up place in a tournament, reportedly (4)

49

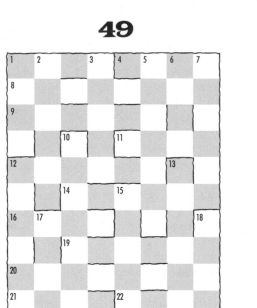

ACROSS

1 Pines sheltering evil Greek (8)
6 More disreputable crackpot is heard (7)
8 Story's end read aloud (4)
9 Blacken a plantation's name (4)
11 Way of locating boy with a rat's face (5)
12 After hug, pace and talk pompously (5)
14 Sondheim's ultimate song?! (5)
16 Boone: "Not any boomerangs available" (2,3)
18 Cruel-sounding manner (4)
19 After the start, follow the course of run (4)
20 New corsets for ushers (7)
21 Surprise: Morrison's sitting in tree (8)

DOWN

1 A street party in Rome's park (9)
2 Sound of precipitation heard (4)
3 Edits novel that is in Latin (2,3)
4 Sparser tipper (6)
5 Car tire fixed, or not fixed? (7)
7 Moroccan town swamp has landscaping tool buried in it (9)
10 Many a pal seems sad about working (7)
13 Swear for group back in AT&T (6)
15 Blacksmith's clothing article worn by expert (5)
17 Indian garb of inferior quality announced (4)

50

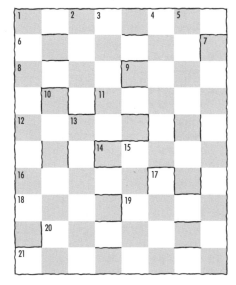

ANSWERS, PAGES 314 & 316

ACROSS

1 Beat up smug faces (4)
4 Pig's home receives a visit (4)
7 Run-down houses not close? (4)
8 Overheard that guy's song (4)
9 Indicated crooked dealings (8)
12 Big snake moving on Canada (8)
13 Mystery author's vacation including times away from home (3,5)
18 Encounter lame horse (4,4)
19 Firmly drawn letter in Greek and English (4)
20 Remove the skin from piece of puffer fish (4)
21 Donations from heartless graduates (4)
22 Detects sound after opening sound detectors (4)

DOWN

1 Coffee contains celebrated condiment (7)
2 Overturned negative vote in university fraternity (5)
3 Basketball player tossed coins (5)
4 O'Neal's house audited (4)
5 Pain reliever uplifted forlorn time (7)
6 Admen pitching remedy (5)
10 Largest two mothers bearing eleven (7)
11 Guards unhinged portals (7)
14 Peer gripped by some qualms (5)
15 Broken petri dish (5)
16 Say outright (5)
17 Chooses balmy spot (4)

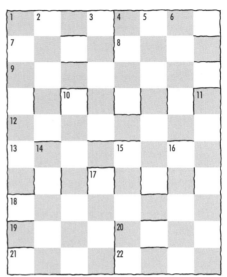

51

ACROSS

1 Recordings featuring first-class rascals (4)
4 Confine group of sheep lacking leader (4)
7 Creature destroyed Manila (6)
8 Ascertained horse blankets used the wrong way (4,4)
9 Head of mathematics cut back test (4)
11 Relieve running back, even covered with grime (7)
13 Attack a sailor by the sound (7)
17 Tale following Pavlova's first bend in a ballet (4)
19 Impetuous people laugh at the commercials (8)
20 Drink that's brewed an excess of time after introduction (6)
21 Guinness Stout, cold (4)
22 Cutting through cake entirely (4)

DOWN

1 Showed up right before a shooter (6)
2 A German agreement by war hero (4)
3 Art movement platform filling block (7)
4 Hungarian composer's record listened to (5)
5 Chisel bit of rock in grotto (5)
6 Swiss artist's modeling material, reportedly (4)
10 Congress worker gets bad loot (7)
12 Murders stranger on ides (4,2)
14 Wind beginning to stir body of water (5)
15 Temporary head of hospital interrupting a medico (2,3)
16 The person that is at a stop (4)
18 Unemployed doctor lied (4)

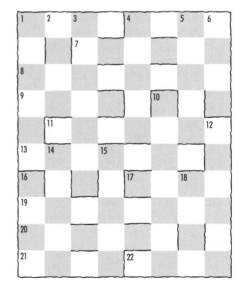

52

ACROSS

1 Muslim wrapping outside of engine (8)
7 Car's out of control in curves (4)
9 Wild horses heard in city borough (5)
10 Spanish gent interrupts independent Brit (8)
11 Said, "Ick a waxy flower" (5)
13 Starts with pencil fillers (5)
15 Bordering on a mad goat's activity (8)
17 Walked audibly with stick (5)
18 Writer's imitation of a person in conversation (4)
19 Cryptic setter in participation (8)

DOWN

1 Check large antelope in plateau region (9)
2 Thoreau's last writing reached a higher level (6)
3 Give and take with Bee and Mayberry's sheriff (5)
4 European country acquires the man's sports business (9)
5 Long for sea chest's contents (4)
6 Study nothing in an Irish province (9)
8 Oddest pair of saints carrying compass (9)
12 Dialects surrounding love poetry by Pound (6)
14 Celebrity catches one domestic flight (5)
16 Head for back of alehouse in Prohibition (4)

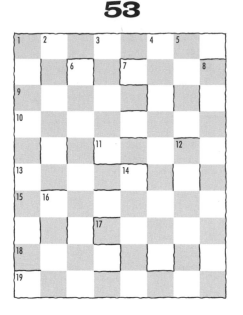

53

ACROSS

1 *Sunset Boulevard* star leading grand farewell performance (4,4)
7 Willa Cather heroine changed a nation (7)
8 AT&T desires foreign diplomats (8)
9 Poorly sewn material for rags? (4)
11 Tiles specially designed for tropical locale (5)
13 Belgian village among cypresses (5)
18 Look noble (4)
19 Threaten to wrap up incense (8)
20 Pasta luncheon's ending with lots (7)
21 Emphasized sweets must be sent back (8)

DOWN

1 Overheard sailors' tune in cabin (6)
2 First of women swallowed red liquid (5)
3 An annoying person leads to North Sea port (7)
4 Hosiery boxes (5)
5 Relative's error in winning (5)
6 Show disgust initially grabbing snake (4)
10 Claims supporter is breaking orders from the bar? (7)
12 Escalating garbage free for burning (6)
14 Wine to drink up (5)
15 Bill wearing First Lady's slip (5)
16 Birds inside these eggs seen from behind (5)
17 Nearly crowded rooms (4)

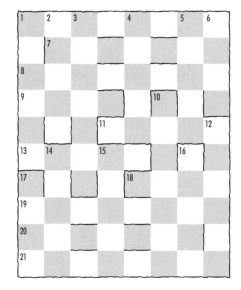

54

ANSWERS, PAGES 289 & 291

ACROSS

1 False god destroyed a lab (4)
4 Recalled delay at a party (4)
7 Second-rate judge makes a case for South American city (8)
8 Preminger having it both ways? (4)
10 Cash fare that's hard to stomach (5)
11 St-strange play (5)
12 True sports stuff, say (5)
13 Bank hosts a kind of race (5)
15 Leather mask (4)
16 Find 500 is 100 extra (8)
17 Return in the chopper (4)
18 Put down wrench, as told (4)

DOWN

1 So I initially back up nonfiction works (4)
2 Opposite the *Titanic*, swimming (10)
3 Nevertheless fear tall drunk (5,3)
4 Newlywed suite is under $1,000 (5)
5 Angular measurements singled out for a change (10)
6 A nouveau riche bigot on TV (6)
9 Healing parish priest with I.V. inserted (8)
11 Dorset eccentric took steps (6)
12 Some citizens accosted an Italian anarchist (5)
14 Each time rather saucy (4)

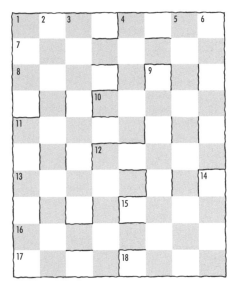

55

ACROSS

1 Private lives lead to deviating (8)
8 Pop fusses about (4)
9 Measures tail of sleeping sheep (5)
10 Roughest traitor catches secret agents (8)
12 Fall in love when embraced by Doctor Page (4)
14 Use a towel on outside of a cart (4)
15 Pieces of stage scenery broken apart by Feds (8)
17 Tie a guy from Fife (5)
18 Breaking out new cane (4)
19 Be good with private novice (8)

DOWN

1 Handle for a girl riding horses around (6)
2 Valuable fluids right in ocean (4)
3 Left hint in an unimpressive way (6)
4 In sort of daze, cheer for open-mindedness (9)
5 Nary a faction backed a guy with bright ideas (6)
6 Mad dog at the front and at the back (4)
7 Rubbing Houston the wrong way, sang about soldier (9)
11 Country cooking fat in your ear (6)
12 Kills deer wrong (4,2)
13 Harry and Dotty Peters (6)
15 Wild guess: nuts turned up (4)
16 Big book, in my opinion (4)

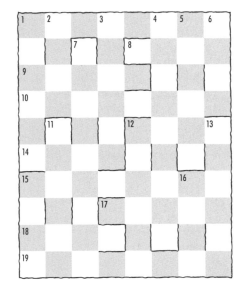

56

ACROSS

1 Collide with second-rate referee (4)
4 One knight returning flower (4)
8 Inquire about Ms. Garr's star (8)
9 Suddenly grew feverish in the midst of feast (4,2)
11 Reportedly failed to see film (4)
12 Piece of cheap fabric—it adds color (6)
14 Prior or parish leader (6)
16 Soldiers capturing a base (4)
19 Toadies beginning to sweat in Mideast nation (3-3)
20 A shop tool opening in its entirety (2,1,5)
21 Analyze time and place the wrong way (4)
22 Overheard pop star doing nothing (4)

DOWN

1 Hit front of ball with wood (4)
2 Addicts getting high—they'll put you in your place (6)
3 Take right away from attractive minor (5)
5 Viciously criticize Rhode Island horse (3,4)
6 Goddess lives and breathes? (4)
7 Winter athlete's wild streak (6)
10 Tropical fruits dad raised, for example (7)
12 Approach company with steaks (4,2)
13 We put in vote for American general (6)
15 Fish dish from southern United States and Hawaii (5)
17 Different part of channel selector (4)
18 Place for bouncing babies born south of Kentucky's capital (4)

57

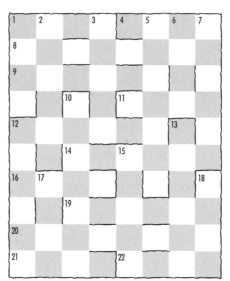

ACROSS

1 Head of state caught in financial need (8)
6 Rustle head of cattle and most of an enclosure with western moose (7)
8 Entertain a great number (4)
9 Pure foreign country (4)
11 Order displayed in histrionics (5)
12 Duplicate igniter (5)
14 Baby's smile shows cavity (5)
16 Skater Lipinski clutching one crown (5)
18 Playwright edges away from vocalist (4)
19 Sound spoils stringed instrument (4)
20 Racetrack figure pitching spitter (7)
21 SAT score upset philosophical guy (8)

DOWN

1 A chemist reviewed carbon structural diagram (9)
2 In the mouth, certain breads swell up (4)
3 Opposed to college prank (5)
4 Pilfer no toys, oddly enough (6)
5 Most frightful alien captures Cleveland Indians (7)
7 Peddlers stuck out clogs belonging to that woman (9)
10 Rain dances not freaking out Met (3,4)
13 Sad time before Havana uprising (6)
15 Thick piece of wood over a light wood (5)
17 Hit bottom (4)

58

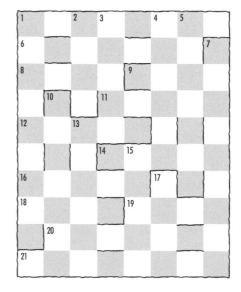

ANSWERS, PAGES 297 & 299

ACROSS

1 Nice fashion (4)
4 U-shaped pipe piece split from behind (4)
7 Path stretched out, we hear (4)
8 Healthy supply of water (4)
9 Never said I'm parking within the law (8)
12 Huge musician's booking some funny business (8)
13 Contrarily, he has slob criticize inscription (8)
18 Breaks Fashion Issue hat (8)
19 Dorothy's companion for true love (4)
20 U.S. uncle describes $100 swindle (4)
21 Plan designation for a low-budget film, then rewind (4)
22 Is canning stew the wrong way (4)

DOWN

1 Famous transvestite finally took trail (7)
2 I am landing on two feet (5)
3 Reportedly gave out a letter? (5)
4 Identical cord is cut short (4)
5 Concert article needs editing (7)
6 Out—I bail out (5)
10 Rattle a movable barrier surrounding it (7)
11 Divisions one's put in school manuscript (7)
14 Former monk (5)
15 Drive out first of Oldsmobiles covered with corrosion (5)
16 Greek god accepts each song of praise (5)
17 Last of campers haul pack (4)

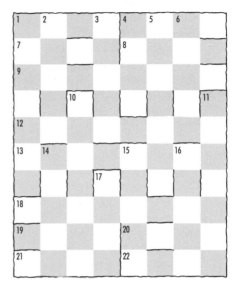

59

ACROSS

1 Object to nonsense embraced by annoying person (7)
8 Pilot holds right amount of land (4)
9 Monsters seen in progression (5)
10 Prophet confines a distant traveler in a boat (8)
12 Sailor is turning ankles (5)
13 Colorado company with a hot beverage (5)
15 Leading lady's featured in *Exploitation* (8)
17 Source of gold ring: actor Sal (5)
18 Obligation on America (4)
19 Distinctive writer's pen tip (7)

DOWN

1 District attorney writing before court is out of order (10)
2 Rookie's first period fury (4)
3 Felon's taking the fort (5)
4 Rat eating Indian food and running around (9)
5 Most accurate advice ultimately kept in confidence (6)
6 Confirming famous drummer at university, amid sound of a drum (7,3)
7 Expand fight surrounding Western spread (6,3)
11 United Nations captured by chief naval officers (6)
14 Lear clumsily grabbing one character in Shakespeare play (5)
16 Basketball team sent all over (4)

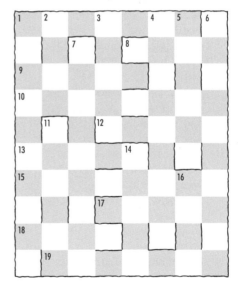

60

ACROSS

1 In Aesop, a story ended (4)
4 Nabokov novel with male gardener? (4)
7 Dependable essay about American president's end (6)
8 Kid grabbing Swiss girl in Russian novel (3,5)
9 The lady's hug is for the story's main man (4)
11 Playwright includes love advice (7)
13 Author of *Nine Stories* dropping a pitcher (7)
17 Shot most of play (4)
19 Hear a Mayan author pens an Indian epic (8)
20 English spar with wit (6)
21 Places in Tess altered (4)
22 Alabama author's dregs (4)

DOWN

1 Passages containing Ovid's first deep feeling (6)
2 Long article on revolutionary (4)
3 Hormone editors abused (7)
4 Poet in a university study (5)
5 Reconcile French style in English poet Housman (5)
6 Fictitious tale in my author's heart (4)
10 Except for the first letter, able to read word again (7)
12 *A Couple of Rounds* (guy's book) (6)
14 After the debut, delight with Rent (5)
15 Approaches end of narration with listeners (5)
16 *Iliad* god strips topless (4)
18 Italian poet losing the first bet (4)

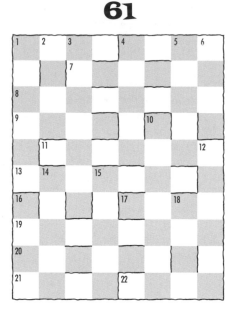

61

ACROSS

1 Dr. Seuss book put antelope's heart into insect's body (3,5)
7 Endlessly stupid studies (4)
9 Priest heard animal in the Andes (5)
10 Ignore Civil War general holding claw (3,5)
11 Certain shelters beginning to change a capital of Bolivia (5)
13 Harder to find area mostly surrounded by railroad (5)
15 Newspaper column discussed wild-animal refuge of a sort (4,4)
17 Rested, I would lead in the past (5)
18 Irritate arm without fail (4)
19 Female churchgoers chopped elm? No way (8)

DOWN

1 It's tough to accomplish radical revolution by going backward (4,5)
2 That guy Leonard goes over a U.S. capital (6)
3 Deli masterpiece contains some beans (5)
4 Flipped over pay TV that could be taken back (9)
5 Author unknown in the near future (4)
6 End-of-game comeback from one side (9)
8 Deny tales swirling about 1970s rock band (6,3)
12 Steak I braise on the outside, wrapped in bread (3,3)
14 Kind of broadcast advertisement in South American city (5)
16 Between introduction and conclusion, sent up Charles Lamb (4)

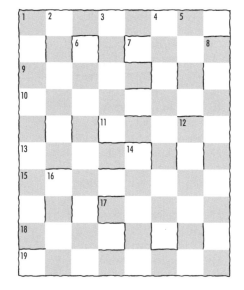

62

ANSWERS, PAGES 305 & 307

ACROSS

1 Knight eating bit of trail mix (4)
4 Drains hot tubs the wrong way (4)
7 Left school girl in European nation (8)
8 Authentic country dance called (4)
10 Movie actor shows gratitude after premiere (5)
11 Those folks' true successor (5)
12 Piece of veal covered with dull-colored sauce (5)
13 Returning work by English poet (5)
15 Sounds like primary part of a horse (4)
16 Incorporated Egyptian god as one (2,6)
17 In the sound: appropriate places for yachts (4)
18 Cash in one's chips at end of pot—it's a losing proposition (4)

DOWN

1 Nimble secret agent catches Republican (4)
2 Be obedient to one of the Kennedys in east (3,3,4)
3 Writer traveling via liner (3,5)
4 Boosted spaghetti-sauce brand's sweetener (5)
5 Upstart holding king and ace at end of game in upscale address (4,6)
6 Maudlin drunk in small gym (6)
9 No fair! A's going wild after game? (2,6)
11 "The South" is part of a doctoral student's work (6)
12 German invaders captured high school (5)
14 Take it easy in Empire State (4)

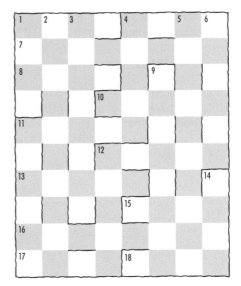

63

ACROSS

1 Next rude digit has stuck out (8)
7 Angle from old boat house in the sound (7)
8 I do taxes, Dotty gets rusty (8)
9 Finely cut 500 diamonds (4)
11 English diarist spies on hearing (5)
13 A Latin's into South American and Cuban music (5)
18 Knight's wild rice (4)
19 Note penned by a wise old Greek forebear (8)
20 FDR's idea of uncovered fish, reportedly (3,4)
21 Next real screwball is outside (8)

DOWN

1 Beaten Sox due for departure (6)
2 "Kiss a cross" is a Cartesian line (1-4)
3 Play a prank on the Parisian drip (7)
4 Customs of speech in American era (5)
5 Magritte after starting *My Foe* (5)
6 Post all but the first of poems by Kay (4)
10 Trade jabs with bronzed Greek (7)
12 Carla's sick of holy rites (6)
14 English queen, by addition (5)
15 Filed a claim against English Leather (5)
16 String loop held by TV handyman (5)
17 Decline of Hollywood's Duke pronounced (4)

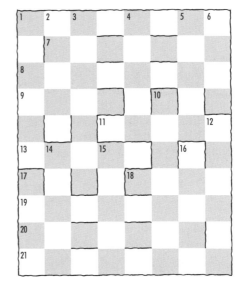

64

ACROSS

1 Eats birds (8)
8 Take a picture–camera sweeps from right to left (4)
9 Reportedly plotted political corruption (5)
10 Never do a jumping attempt (8)
12 Penny drove to my hearing (4)
14 Touches labels in a store (4)
15 Smith or Jones going around one foreign country (8)
17 Got started, for example, in the middle of Prohibition (5)
18 Cheers for Lech Walesa and others, after introduction (4)
19 Study record of teeth (8)

DOWN

1 Most Solomonic messages teach, in part (6)
2 Counsel North after battle (4)
3 Certain convicts shot rifles (6)
4 Circle part of church with anger, normally (2,7)
5 Vehicles from Washington go north and south (6)
6 Don't close extra box (4)
7 Color level in time for the new year (4,5)
11 In a manner of speaking, mishandle trinket (6)
12 Film is anemic, poorly produced (6)
13 Small high-schoolers club (6)
15 Wearing foot protection, put front end of hoe into dirt (4)
16 Massachusetts-to-Illinois delivery (4)

65

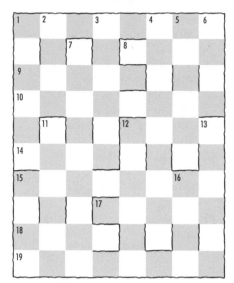

ACROSS

1 At hearing, take pictures (4)
4 Platonic letters Mrs. Kennedy read aloud (4)
8 Curse a famous conductor with North American retrospective (8)
9 Peeping Tom cut out last half of trip to Europe (6)
11 Risk by a kind of blocker (4)
12 Resident in fleabag has tourists horrified (6)
14 Not well employed? (6)
16 Enormous pole in tank (4)
19 Edges away from spangled horse (6)
20 Huge loss in fuel (8)
21 Lioness slaughtered seal (4)
22 Fastener controls pressure (4)

DOWN

1 Don't use Second Avenue (4)
2 One hug could be sufficient (6)
3 Retract leases on a monument (5)
5 Skeptic present at involuntary movement (7)
6 Part of concomitant drop (4)
7 Mother sadly returned greeting (6)
10 Carves "XXX" on city trains (7)
12 Commercial comes with sexual-immorality warning (6)
13 Sports venues write up more reasonable article (6)
15 Bugs printed with hot pink (5)
17 Army truant reported a barrier (4)
18 Assist that fellow with old record (4)

66

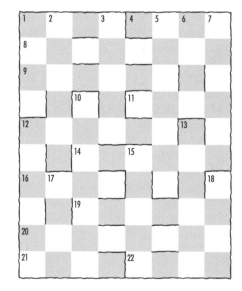

ANSWERS, PAGES 313 & 315

ACROSS

1 Caveman-era scholar has attitude (5,3)
6 Accept a welcome with love (5,2)
8 *Cabaret* actress involved in theatricalization (4)
9 Little guy in open convertible (4)
11 Occupation rated poorly (5)
12 Get rid of all competition for Daniel? (5)
14 Pares bananas with harpoon (5)
16 *Jumping Rope*—a stage show (5)
18 Intelligent questions from the speaker (4)
19 Long needled tree (4)
20 They hold 250 amperes (1-6)
21 Yokel pursuing objective: "Be very thorough" (2,3,3)

DOWN

1 Cook allows bad dish for the first course (5,4)
2 Grainy food for zoo's inhabitant (4)
3 Playing a note—wow (5)
4 Relaxed with a guy (2,4)
5 Nothing unusual in cheerful greeting (4,3)
7 Gravely, I approach egg container? (2,7)
10 Film about crooked policemen stirred cops' ire (7)
13 While climbing, a peasant swallows cold soda (6)
15 A parish's leader embraced by friend of the church (5)
17 Crashed Milo's fancy car (4)

67

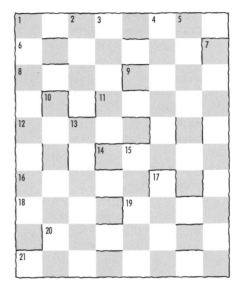

ACROSS

1 Start to catch pitches and bounders (4)
4 Among the ears, give rise to sounds in the cornfield (4)
7 Cuckoo tail touched the ground (4)
8 A wild owl is inexplicably missing (4)
9 Beads surrounding Emily's fragrant plant (8)
12 A titled woman carries plot in Eliot book (4,4)
13 Overindulge movie dog wearing fancy dress (2,2,4)
18 Hordes backing an expert on milk (8)
19 I'm in surprisingly revealing skirt (4)
20 New York player has left tuna sandwich (4)
21 War god offers ship in myth (4)
22 Reportedly use some sheep (4)

DOWN

1 Worry about old horse's slaughter (7)
2 In hearing, permitted to be heard (5)
3 Stop lying about a source of power (5)
4 Visited California, then Maine (4)
5 Familiar with a crushed wafer containing bit of onion (5,2)
6 Term conveying "large planet" (5)
10 Catch hosts skinny dipping? (7)
11 Renters catch up with workers (7)
14 Mid-October rain ruined radio station sign (2,3)
15 Occasion, say, for cooking herb (5)
16 Where's first healthy sea creature? (5)
17 Group beginning to tour carnival city (4)

68

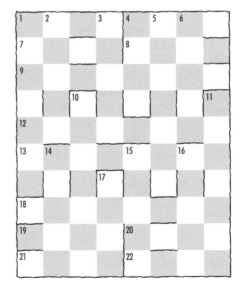

ACROSS

1 Heard top cartoonist (4)
4 Republicans turned against old Kelly creation (4)
7 Caricature is done for inventor (6)
8 Sly pair of strips, completely united (8)
9 Note no-good foe of Flash Gordon (4)
11 Dessert with a crust splattered Dagwood's face (7)
13 Garfield, for one, with guerrilla's traps (7)
17 For starters, Oliphant was Englishman, not Welshman (4)
19 Dilbert's funny bits (8)
20 Ultimately, Calvin loves spinning stories (6)
21 Annie's original hitch dazzled (4)
22 Brenda's unfinished headline (4)

DOWN

1 Spacy cartoon about society (6)
2 "B.C." character I opposed (4)
3 Strip upset an alien (7)
4 Conduct of Id's leader in conspiracy (5)
5 Run Stimpy's pal over in "Dead Duck" (5)
6 Individuals in "Doonesbury" (4)
10 Groening mostly pens sheep for actress (3,4)
12 Dennis's first sneer: dumb and dumber (6)
14 Couple from "Archie" fight with weapon (5)
15 Baby bear editor magnified greatly (5)
16 Millay somewhat irritated Nast (4)
18 Something for kitty turned up in "Hot Spot" (4)

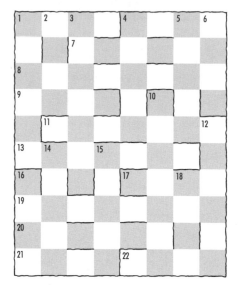

ACROSS

1 Dogs accepting few restrictions (7)
8 I'm thrilled revolver's left unfinished (4)
9 They crush *Lawrence of Arabia* (the novel) (5)
10 Film industry worker has turned in small container (8)
12 Relative mentioned city burned by the Saracens (5)
13 Zodiac sign changes after the first (5)
15 It's used as a lubricant, since oil is no good (8)
17 Mom's adorning a kind of jar (5)
18 If not eels, bats (4)
19 Admires Italian family at German spa (7)

DOWN

1 Wearing swords, children initially played hooky (3,7)
2 Pasture always stores fertilizer (4)
3 Have friends finish in Paris holding it (3,2)
4 House of York emblem otherwise contrived (5,4)
5 Choose part of this electromagnet (6)
6 Republican dislikes draws (10)
7 In need of cash, writes about Frasier's brother (9)
11 Newlywed holds left part of harness (6)
14 Balance plate (5)
16 Standard Agatha Christie mystery (4)

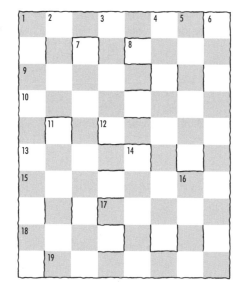

ANSWERS, PAGES 287 & 289

ACROSS

1 Reclusive author, 51, harbored by birth-control advocate (8)

7 Put a heavy burden on one cab (4)

9 Body of water tossed canoe (5)

10 Spare altimeter shows actual duration (4,4)

11 The whole world's lacking good places to put earrings (5)

13 Fortuneteller has finally hosted religious feast (5)

15 Regan's sister oiled car sloppily (8)

17 Interior designer's head is in fog (5)

18 Danger—rook is in front of king (4)

19 Cheers Hans' son, a radical (8)

DOWN

1 Mark lies about places to unload a Maserati, for example (6,3)

2 Upwardly mobile Decca and EMI at first give in (6)

3 Finally getting rid of the beginning and ending entirely (2,3)

4 Most of profit split by vulgar Italian patriot (9)

5 Former morning test (4)

6 Cut first part of the speech "Ritual Symbolic Wear in Tribal Life" (9)

8 See a stick beat hockey player's equipment (3,6)

12 Sheila could become a man (6)

14 Rule check is heard (5)

16 State "What's this!" keeping interest (4)

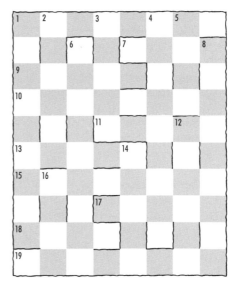

71

ACROSS

1 Irish figure with broken arm going into shock (8)

7 From behind, saw an item of furniture (7)

8 Really cooked his toast (2,4,2)

9 Greek bigwig in canal turned left (4)

11 Phantom member of Golden Horde (5)

13 Grave marker of sculpted steel (5)

18 Group of hunters want bird (4)

19 Ballroom dancing produced by Disney animation (8)

20 It's seen on the road, like parking brake (7)

21 Like the end of a pipe commercial in 3-D (8)

DOWN

1 Collars of small, medium, and large clothes beginning to expand (6)

2 Splashes water on dancing shoes (5)

3 Adjusts tetanus shot (7)

4 Charo's playing something from *The Metamorphosis* (5)

5 Inquires after cold kegs (5)

6 Said, "Forget it, understand?" (4)

10 Crazy old Whig is enthusiastic (3-4)

12 Petty dictator helps to make suffocating odor (3,3)

14 Some of the foolhardy refuse (5)

15 Move like a snake after shedding? It's limber (5)

16 Poet from long ago: A.D. ten, roughly (5)

17 TV show about police strike (4)

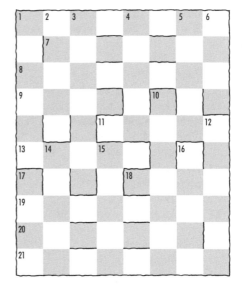

72

ACROSS

1 Stop New York team's comeback (4)
4 Essential grape juice (4)
7 Once, moms cooked soup (8)
8 Support first-rate opera (4)
10 Candy coins (5)
11 Sound of cash register (5)
12 Kung-fu master gets into fight extremely fast (5)
13 Combat zones (not including northern regions) (5)
15 Returned brooches and clip (4)
16 Fancy prison song (8)
17 Key passage read aloud (4)
18 Starts to leer, eying Grable's shapely gams (4)

DOWN

1 Examine source of suspicious fire (4)
2 Improperly test oilier items for cosmetic purposes (10)
3 Risk final outrage (8)
4 Married love life in French film (5)
5 A little school making a difference (10)
6 Make fun of Tuesday's service (3,3)
9 Feelers Anne put out after wager (8)
11 Shellfish involved in girls' camp illness (6)
12 Piece of cake included in price of ticket for comedy show (5)
14 Chooses foreign post (4)

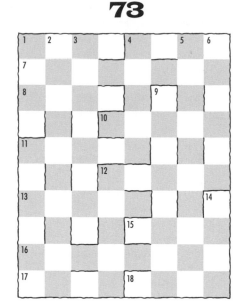

73

ACROSS

1 Agitate and lobby for folk-rocker (3,5)
8 Green stuff in cement (4)
9 Doctor fit badly, in a general sense (5)
10 *Playboy* feature took in female in the first place (8)
12 Gang leaders of Chicago recently ended warfare (4)
14 Winter vehicle with small electronic display (4)
15 Backed down, following future husband around capital of Nebraska (8)
17 Saint joins first woman and man (5)
18 Sounds like breads are affected by yeast (4)
19 Composer finally patronizes non-kosher butcher (8)

DOWN

1 Shifts pet birds, missing one (6)
2 Chief of operations on boat raised a vegetable (4)
3 Guard is fed up over result (6)
4 So I circle rotten types of chewy candy (9)
5 Charm a small Greek character? (6)
6 Require massage from the speaker (4)
7 Playful, unruly set, I think (9)
11 Endlessly clip and cut in medical facility (6)
12 Worker in taxi is a Harvard student (6)
13 Most far-ranging drama initially captured by actress Dianne (6)
15 Chop back piece off of earliest trees (4)
16 Veer unpredictably at any time (4)

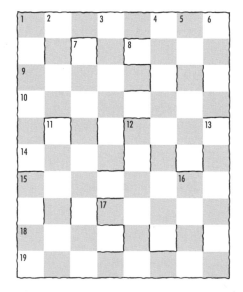

74

ANSWERS, PAGES 295 & 297

75

ACROSS

1 In maid's buggy (4)
4 Piece of glass hurt, by the sound of it (4)
8 Southern woman brought in red rose (8)
9 Dull sort of photograph on the front of large toy company (6)
11 Easily bruised items? For example, skinned nose (4)
12 Strange fellow fixed locks behind dam (6)
14 Boomer hearing church's rules (6)
16 Newspaper publisher Adolph taking away liter of water for the Scotch? (4)
19 Toted a novel so far (2,4)
20 Pastor embraced by devout prior (8)
21 Nimble closing of doors by snoop (4)
22 Teases Rhode Island with nonsense (4)

DOWN

1 Mary cracks up host (4)
2 Thin male ready to participate (6)
3 Don't encourage half of laundry soaps (5)
5 Galleon at sea vanished (3,4)
6 Somewhat insane Roman! (4)
7 Inventor flipped tag in bouquet (6)
10 Temperature taken by wealthier seismologist (7)
12 My error with rings (6)
13 High button almost turned up Jacuzzi (3,3)
15 The very bottom drain is ruined (5)
17 Fishmonger's offering crab (4)
18 James Stewart hides soldier's meal (4)

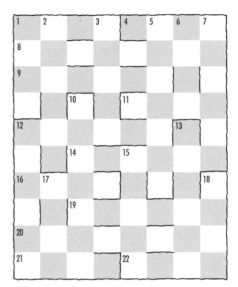

76

ACROSS

1 Quarterfinals and semifinals start to produce mass eliminations (8)
6 In a turnaround, Rome accepts representative ruler (7)
8 On the way back, encounter throng (4)
9 Skip French literature (4)
11 Cardinal that is coming back down (5)
12 Deserves Masters after commencement (5)
14 Chased anyone smuggling one kind of car (5)
16 Sunshade? Guest loses it (5)
18 Devours ham and steak, beginning with the second (4)
19 Love the French bagel spread (4)
20 Impolite to interrupt cross Canadian prime minister (7)
21 Where Jordan is hiding in one area's thicket (4,4)

DOWN

1 Retiring vice-president fit into Pete's main annoyances (3,6)
2 Big galoot is on top of unknown summit (4)
3 It's an Arab country, you guys (5)
4 Old sports federation went out of business (6)
5 Burned an author of feminist literature (7)
7 Extend circle confined to porter's kin (6,3)
10 Shine changed airdate (7)
13 They support public speaking, dancing, or arts (6)
15 Diminish the beginning and ending of earlier poem (5)
17 Discussed escape from pest (4)

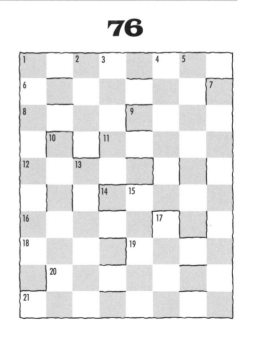

ACROSS

1 Grouchy person right in front of a truck (4)
4 Bit of sampling in hip-hop music—it can be grating (4)
7 The woman's ring champion (4)
8 Returned note to choir singer (4)
9 Russian flying group returning to the front in bunches (8)
12 Tourist hat's orange in the middle.... Really? (2,4,2)
13 Fancy collar clutched by tense movie director (8)
18 French painter's spouse maintaining spunky quality (8)
19 Commercial cue starting late for two singers (1,3)
20 Rial is foreign coin (4)
21 Reportedly chains bobcat (4)
22 When turned, spigots made sputtering sounds (4)

DOWN

1 Money for the needy raised cheer in urban area (7)
2 Rushes Cincinnati ballplayers, getting error (5)
3 The two of them eating nothing in diner area (5)
4 Float a lot (4)
5 Left foremost of sluggers in shrine for the best players (3-4)
6 Puts away last of equipment in plants (5)
10 Immobilizing weapon acutely hurt United Nations (4,3)
11 Hates to put in another order—it's an uncomfortable position to be in (3,4)
14 Prepared singer Helen for the audience (5)
15 Knocks down swords (5)
16 Extreme part of adult rating (5)
17 Prehistoric beast in Italy three times (1,3)

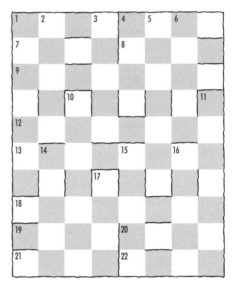

ACROSS

1 Crazy joke on Manhattan's center (4)
4 Overheard crowd for Mets or Knicks (4)
7 A survey operator for a Harlem theater (6)
8 Trash line in Grand Central Station (5,3)
9 The lady's taste of Broadway seasoning (4)
11 Sneer at bum closest by (7)
13 They light some Madison Square Garden events (7)
17 Spring at back of Brooklyn bridge (4)
19 Amiable drunk naps late (8)
20 Beaten Giants getting their fill? (6)
21 School in Village, to neighbors (4)
22 Look for waterfront area in the sound (4)

DOWN

1 New York City acquired deli meat (6)
2 Changed Shea Stadium's name (4)
3 Tabloid turned up heartless rents for little rooms (7)
4 Someone pulling for skyscraper (5)
5 Grads renovated a slum (5)
6 Spot Mr. Wolfe around Carnegie's rear (4)
10 Look at part of the *Times* for leak (7)
12 Person camping in Staten terminal (6)
14 Key for an apartment (1,4)
15 Gab about Apple's first line of stores (5)
16 Ape's loose somewhere in St. Patrick's Cathedral (4)
18 Something staked in urban tenements (4)

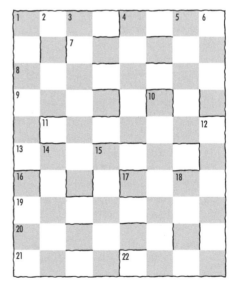

Answers, Pages 303 & 305

ACROSS

1 Distributes convertible test cars (8)
7 Egg on vandals "updating" Manet's originals (4)
9 Homer expert corrected "oar" in article (5)
10 Licks counters rudely (8)
11 Confidence of degenerate after start of trial (5)
13 Allows borrowing of unopened mixes (5)
15 Private Idaho houses so overdue (8)
17 Company describes cardinal rule (5)
18 Base still in use in recession (4)
19 Drops bad scene penned by dentist (8)

DOWN

1 Border of steel ain't flexible (5,4)
2 Rough classes audited (6)
3 Fish move quickly around mid-January (5)
4 Caveat due: better quit (9)
5 In speech, regrets trick (4)
6 Odds of recovering wild sprig soon (9)
8 Fraternal society has raised point: these animals are extinct (9)
12 Planted, granted, in ears (6)
14 Officer employed by Miss Argentina (5)
16 Store menial lets go of head of lettuce (4)

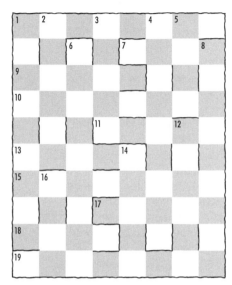

79

ACROSS

1 Support rain check (8)
7 Need about twenty-four sheets (7)
8 Discover unusual marital breakups (8)
9 Look, clothing line is announced (4)
11 Quick: length in imperial units (5)
13 Pull together a church service (5)
18 Snakes pass out (4)
19 Insults among peers? (8)
20 Run small R.V. (7)
21 Soften, as paints (8)

DOWN

1 Thrash reeds in front of a body of water (3,3)
2 Indians don't begin set of ballgames (5)
3 Divers always interrupting Mineo (7)
4 Country right north of Russian river (5)
5 Name of a woman included among their enemies (5)
6 One's unopened street hangout (4)
10 Hockey player Mark not as tidy (7)
12 Alberto's session features pitches (6)
14 Chop up candies for the audience (5)
15 Drop pair of slippers on baseball official (5)
16 Show a rope that's tangled (5)
17 Reportedly didn't see Niagara Falls feature (4)

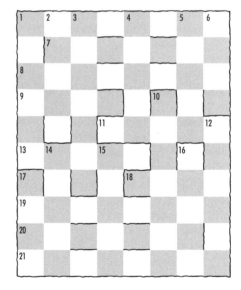

80

ACROSS

1 Fashion magazine with Spanish and French articles (4)
4 Robe from past time making a comeback (4)
7 Tip for sweetheart having jeans trimmed (4,4)
8 Spotted nightgown's front cut (4)
10 Female with shiny fabric in brilliant color (5)
11 Providers of down, e.g., see changes (5)
12 Penny isn't for cosmetics (5)
13 Decor for the neck of a Glaswegian, perhaps (5)
15 Coat tailored for an old Roman (4)
16 Style I pleated with a showy crest (8)
17 Endless rush for a cowboy accessory (4)
18 Yield some nice designs (4)

DOWN

1 Model's agency includes Schiaparelli (4)
2 Large diapers he fashioned with guidance (10)
3 British author and architect dressed in fine material (8)
4 Sheer fabric almost worked (5)
5 Developed great denim in a haphazard way (10)
6 Spilled tears about red collar (6)
9 I'm back in woolly coat with plastic (8)
11 Understands Republican is wearing pants (6)
12 Ring's held by each photographer's subject (5)
14 Announced cut in style (4)

81

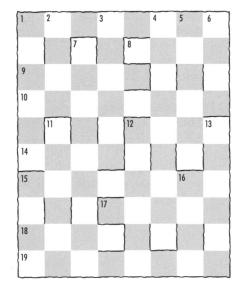

ACROSS

1 Discover yours truly invested in money-saving item (4,4)
8 Low number that's raised to a power (4)
9 See you later in Buffalo hangout (5)
10 Elderly women carry out bets (8)
12 Passing border is proper (4)
14 Listener beginning to perceive Wild West gunfighter (4)
15 Jazz musician has put together gossip (8)
17 Hit man is in place (5)
18 Pronouncedly nasty appearance (4)
19 Norm cuts vegetables (8)

DOWN

1 Calder sculpted rocker (6)
2 Love endlessly dull city in Scandinavia (4)
3 Note somewhat stymies harpsichordist (1,5)
4 Suffering grips Australian city that's not dense at all (5-4)
5 Old man's title is "god" (6)
6 Overheard wildebeest's information (4)
7 Allow sports car user near one end of the stream (9)
11 First off, author Sheehy had raised flower (6)
12 Map can elaborate video game (3-3)
13 Mel's circling back to overnight accommodations (6)
15 Leader of military enters top bivouac (4)
16 Over tip of Africa, toward capital of Portugal (4)

82

ANSWERS, PAGES 311 & 313

ACROSS

1 Stalk New York ballplayers from behind (4)
4 Running back swallowed bit of French cheese (4)
8 Singer appearing in Pretoria mostly (4,4)
9 A public-opinion survey by love god (6)
11 Put an asterisk next to start of sales pitch (4)
12 Clumsy rube in Asian country (6)
14 Animation pioneer's urges I'd held back (6)
16 Average individual's ice-cream-parlor order (4)
19 Basic maneuver at nine (6)
20 Succeed with humor about a beer barrel (4,4)
21 Different part of Israel settled (4)
22 With its sound, fly annoyed (4)

DOWN

1 Spaniard's first name for men only (4)
2 Drunks destroyed poster (6)
3 Fellow on the outskirts of Illinois city known for opera (5)
5 Gushing dwarf keeps it up (7)
6 On the way up, received a loose gown (4)
7 Like something used by a waiter in error (6)
10 Rising sun enveloping good-hearted bores (7)
12 Turned into bird's bill target, reportedly (6)
13 Rubbish by flower garden upset fellow with bills to pay (6)
15 Family members penning grand melodies (5)
17 Ring with friend's birthstone (4)
18 Surrender nut to an auditor (4)

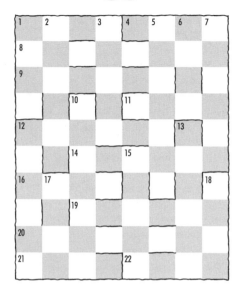

83

ACROSS

1 Detroit players develop new grids (3,5)
6 Endless hassle ultimately with rental buggy (7)
8 Note two postal abbreviations that begin with M (4)
9 Rainbow fish is free of fourth fishing line (4)
11 Tender translation of runes (5)
12 Be in charge of sound check (5)
14 Some ephemera were less polished (5)
16 Finer sort of room in back (5)
18 Attract minor returns (4)
19 Eucalyptus tree frames a place in the Marianas (4)
20 Baltic country slipping into sea (7)
21 He said, "No high sticking" (8)

DOWN

1 Artist Bertrand goes wild about medium (9)
2 Almost relinquish Patrick's costar in *Ghost* (4)
3 Bananas grown incorrectly (5)
4 Thin nose on the front missile (6)
5 Explains lip cosmetics (7)
7 Guy at the helm tenses arm awkwardly (9)
10 No longer working, like a car with new wheels? (7)
13 One way to pay Peruvians heading for home (2,4)
15 Rival of Corinth ready to enter wars after the first (5)
17 Actor Paul flipped over number one (4)

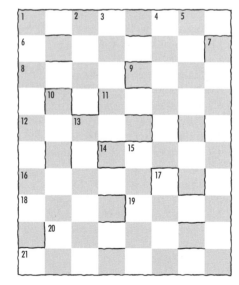

84

ACROSS

1 Little Richard embraces Clapton (4)
4 Restaurant lost face (4)
7 Jay North amid group of stars (4)
8 Speaker's poem was short (4)
9 California city's supply caught in cyclone (8)
12 Former partner's opening one no-trump: a sign of power (8)
13 Coal pile tossed into set of steam pipes? (8)
18 Famous economist has turned to political speeches (8)
19 Charge, bearing ram's head on the house (4)
20 Crackers cool off (4)
21 For the audience, screen Jekyll's counterpart (4)
22 Envisioned 7 minus 5 (4)

DOWN

1 Sampling of gumbo eaten by drunk Creole painter (2,5)
2 Unbend twisted axle beneath end of car (5)
3 Huge bird clipped building (5)
4 Fish with a tail (4)
5 Familiar with enemy, retreating after a battle (5,2)
6 Criminal put half of loot in swamp (5)
10 Spread out, and led a spy astray (7)
11 Squashes relative (7)
14 A really animated cartoonist (5)
15 Rock solid statues (5)
16 Heard harmony in composition (5)
17 Ken Kesey has this oddly positioned joint (4)

85

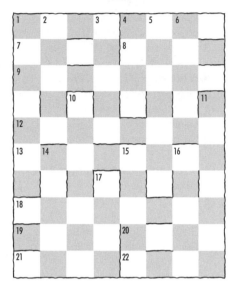

ACROSS

1 Illicit sellers of piano seats (7)
8 Charge pounds sterling (that makes sense) (4)
9 Silver and gold at a market (5)
10 Cause error in general price (8)
12 Hoarder of money lives in Maine, back of Dumpster (5)
13 Sign for new raise (5)
15 Little guy takes in little money, in principle (8)
17 Check with an oilman for capital (5)
18 Star stock finally dropped (4)
19 Nutty bread tax pocketed by senator (7)

DOWN

1 Stealing IRS mail, Pa wrongly keeps $1,000 (10)
2 After the first, rally in yen (4)
3 Hopper with bit of money for female group (5)
4 Showing new vigor, bum earns penny (9)
5 Group established within firm (6)
6 At one trial, loose change (10)
7 Bullish study, if returned before depression (9)
11 Roman broker's first routine with us (6)
14 Little southern shopping center (5)
16 Numbers on the front of each bill (4)

86

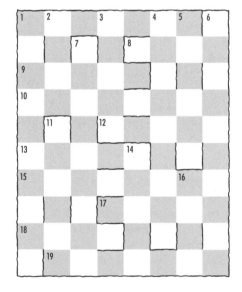

ANSWERS, PAGES 319 & 287

ACROSS

1 Win card game holding ace (4)
4 Tool cabinet (4)
7 Caught Daniel after a struggle (6)
8 Like a battery member of the 1968 Detroit Tigers (2,6)
9 Give a detailed account of opening of the building addition (4)
11 Brass hat manipulated both GIs (3,4)
13 Doomed one is trapped in out-of-control Ford (4,3)
17 A short taxi passenger from a distance (4)
19 Stamp soft East German coin (8)
20 Model earned charm (6)
21 Stitched four needlepoints? (4)
22 Pale actress initially coy (4)

DOWN

1 Chopped up for children (1-5)
2 Practiced island hikes (4)
3 Sign language on the job cut off idea (7)
4 Satisfies female with troubles (5)
5 Gave hug slowly (5)
6 Paradise found in Odense, Denmark (4)
10 Drivers sounded horns (7)
12 Jailer cut heart out of large bird (6)
14 Region behind egg layer (5)
15 Had seconds of Belgian waffles at Georgetown University (5)
16 Records decapitated gorillas (4)
18 Sly part of the foot (4)

87

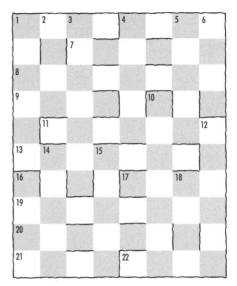

ACROSS

1 Board describes third-rate physicist (6)
7 Lasso deer, snaring Prancer's head (4)
8 Melville novel: Ring Low (4)
9 Riding pig in commercial (6)
10 Blow up English school, interrupting appointment (8)
12 One immersed in troubles for so long (5)
13 Position opens for unskilled workers (5)
14 Engineer drove bus to get sounds added to films (8)
16 Keep Mom in check (6)
17 Old tragedy, in part (4)
18 Cheese manufactured the wrong way (4)
19 Rodent eats piece of Stilton for dessert (6)

DOWN

1 Carelessly drop spur (4)
2 Playwright ran over Eve and Georgia (4,2,4)
3 Pronounced craving for rock (7)
4 Nocturnal critters with stings going around circle (5)
5 Hamlet character in favor of metal underwear (10)
6 Computer devices for Missouri Democrats (6)
11 Leap in like swarms (7)
12 Not knowing right from wrong in morning exam (6)
13 Arp uplifted party in Spanish museum (5)
15 A number in addition announced (4)

88

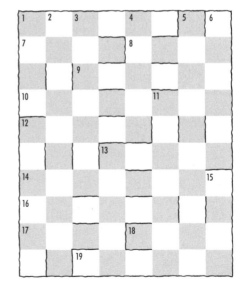

ACROSS

1 Spring-loaded item's smartest shot? (8)

7 French writer finished *Rent*, making a comeback (7)

8 Worked for scale outdoors (8)

9 Foot soldier swapped prize (4)

11 Quick to eat excellent meal (5)

13 Operated church and farm (5)

18 High point of Mimic for adults only (4)

19 Defenses are almost fully developed (8)

20 Slender model Kate's back in lounge (7)

21 Confront terrible cup of tea (4,2,2)

DOWN

1 Slight bit of malicious intent (6)

2 Freely laid new west part of boardwalk (2,3)

3 Fight with any pop singer (7)

4 *Superman* actor regarding sunset (5)

5 Footwear blows in a boxer's face? (5)

6 Overheard abolitionary novelist's stuff (4)

10 Frantically inhale referee's energy source? (3,4)

12 Groom x-ed out wedding ensemble (6)

14 Matriarch shows *Places in the Heart* (5)

15 Pursue leader of hoodlums in police investigation (5)

16 Robbed, losing tip of fool's cap (5)

17 Physical fitness maintains back of leg (4)

89

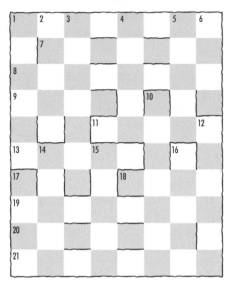

ACROSS

1 Some stereo components exist as an afterthought (4)

4 Bounce out, rounding second (4)

7 Zorro's specialty not starting as my specialty? (8)

8 Small bills get nose out of joint (4)

10 Composer missing train to get pancakes (5)

11 First of kids contributed to December's ornaments (5)

12 Imperious lad gets around Secret Service (5)

13 Suspicious of counterculture figure, by the sound of it (5)

15 Corner odd characters in Turgenev (4)

16 Jack enters dance at bughouse next door (8)

17 Knight retreats, with king in danger (4)

18 Laos is foreign, too (4)

DOWN

1 Baritone's asset, perhaps, turned up missing (4)

2 Baroque composer met no Baroque composer (10)

3 Cleric is one who feels pain sooner? (8)

4 Precious stones from leader of our friends (5)

5 Coarse nastiness about a French composer (5-5)

6 Epitomize piece of advice, if I heard correctly? (6)

9 Musician's bridging alerts nimble running back (8)

11 Clam roll ad is unusual (6)

12 Bankrupt crooked baker (5)

14 One form of vote! (4)

90

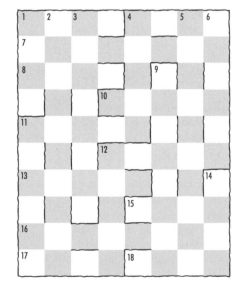

ANSWERS, PAGES 293 & 295

ACROSS

1 Cites crazy forester (6,2)

8 Swedish car sounds like a sheep when backing up (4)

9 Democrat leading Perot? That's rubbish (5)

10 Partly ignores us and eyes TV actress (5,3)

12 Reportedly drop match in time (4)

14 Critic's topic: star in a remake (4)

15 Lacking shoes, a sports official gets into heavy footwear (8)

17 A male cat's smallest parts (5)

18 What you pay after opening cereal (4)

19 Collecting royalty in the middle of downpour (6,2)

DOWN

1 Engineer erased map feature (3,3)

2 Pale brown section of piecrust (4)

3 Head of editorial revised Sassy articles (6)

4 New Jersey peninsula experienced quakes, trapping actor Garcia (5,4)

5 Prof's aide gave gift (6)

6 Comply with boyfriend, in pig Latin (4)

7 Be neglectful in storage room, missing first shelf (4,5)

11 Spy organization has organized certain cases (6)

12 Mollify head of state again and again (6)

13 Interrupts play with tunics (4,2)

15 Vocal "I'm cold"–you might hear it from a Scotsman (4)

16 Native of Muscat is missing a science magazine (4)

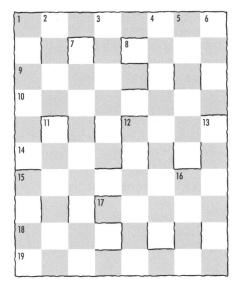

91

ACROSS

1 Rogue finally canceled con game (4)

4 Transported in colorful paper to the auditor (4)

7 Zero talk about victory for Holyfield (4)

8 Burden on you and me (4)

9 Examine succeeding Asian river trade (8)

12 Curse song about a certain note (8)

13 Despot gets around North Dakota hazard (4,4)

18 Ram and horse getting depressed (4,4)

19 Drag Arsenio by the ear (4)

20 One of Pop's partners gives a bad review to retrospective (4)

21 That man's having true successes (4)

22 Smears liberal arts (4)

DOWN

1 Quickly read question: "What might a bank robber wear?" (3,4)

2 Author's works soon going past copyright (5)

3 Generalissimo unthinkingly conceals horse (5)

4 Kind of wine came into existence (4)

5 Jerk is south of a N. European city (7)

6 Uriah's leadoff in proper Jewish festival (5)

10 Desire to leave pale tipster (4,3)

11 Notice friend returned computers (7)

14 Mr. Stevenson fiddled with a dial (5)

15 Pest takes in South Bend (5)

16 Pronouncedly change wedding location (5)

17 Birds head away from birds (4)

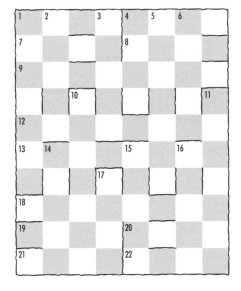

92

ACROSS

1 Story favorite: her faceless god (5,3)
6 Anthology keeps one better prepared (7)
8 Magazine carrying fiction back in Missouri (4)
9 Wager with drama's central Greek character (4)
11 Novelist with time to lean back (5)
12 Tolstoy's first hasty pulp fiction? (5)
14 *Twelfth Night* character married, accompanied by song (5)
16 A Southern writer is a Quaker? (5)
18 Story of heartless jungle cat (4)
19 Morrison's unfinished drink (4)
20 Book van fixed up for a writer (7)
21 Painter fabricated one verse (8)

DOWN

1 Lying trollop turns up in writing (9)
2 Beckett's last, with a no-good flavor (4)
3 In *Aliens*, Diana does manuscript work (5)
4 Nobleman wraps up *The French Stripper* (6)
5 Goddess in trim sea novel (7)
7 A railroad in indigenous story (9)
10 Crane is playing a certain angle (3,4)
13 Look for article in new paper (6)
15 Sheridan is absorbing to Chekhov (5)
17 Something funny about John Updike (4)

93

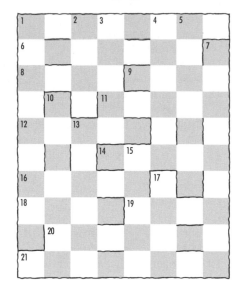

ACROSS

1 Former U.S. Open winner hangs around 1,000 members of a fraternal group (4)
4 Absorbed front of residential apartment (4)
8 Finally swim next to a trimmer shark (3-5)
9 Painter of *The Scream* takes in one German city (6)
11 Listen to swell field worker (4)
12 Avenge ruined European city (6)
14 Stage is partly jade green (6)
16 Almost rub out periods (4)
19 Chat freely at *Rent* (6)
20 "Fashion Closeout"? Go wild! (3,5)
21 Common Market includes unknown administrator (4)
22 Votes against any shifts before Sunday (4)

DOWN

1 Yours truly returned my award (4)
2 Praised Monet after the opening day (6)
3 Notice harbors in river (5)
5 Two articles on paintings, basically (2,5)
6 Contemporary look (4)
7 Thugs initially rob small item (6)
10 Slowly beginning to accept northern Italian poet (7)
12 Broadcast Travolta musical where some Europeans live (6)
13 Somewhere, synagogue is home to unorthodox beliefs (6)
15 Good British school board (3,2)
17 Pronouncedly regret fattening mixture (4)
18 Greek god beheaded horses (4)

94

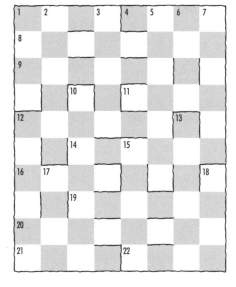

ANSWERS, PAGES 301 & 303

ACROSS

1 In Madrid, like a bridge? (7)
8 Figure without delay in a hospital (4)
9 A deli counter was in bad shape (5)
10 Fuel is not refined in spring (5,3)
12 Orchestra conductor's two notes (5)
13 Search globe for jazz band (5)
15 Enhancing the appearance of character ending season in *Loving* (8)
17 Underage gold digger gets a hearing (5)
18 Always head off high body temperature (4)
19 Stuck supplement on the outside of this place (7)

DOWN

1 Dazed person resolved gripping step with heel (5,5)
2 Two people beginning to play song (4)
3 Requires massages, so it's said (5)
4 Carol lies about ugly beast walking (9)
5 What nuns wear helps to make church a bit solemn (6)
6 Old city on the Volga getting tasteless premiere of radio commercial (10)
7 Federation keeps oaf bewildered (9)
11 Leave prima donna lady who exposed herself (6)
14 French resort supports band that's assured of success (2,3)
16 Letter is not excellent (4)

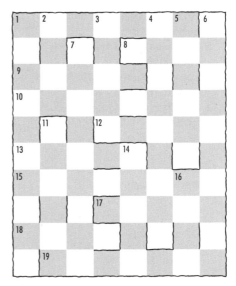

95

ACROSS

1 Barroom features dances with noisy shoes (4)
4 Ridiculous mid-fifties craze is back (4)
7 Heavenly light or penetrating glow (6)
8 Gold adds interest to financial support (8)
9 Face away from marble entranceway (4)
11 Unfavorable jingle? (7)
13 Soundly advise administration (7)
17 In gym class, train soccer great (4)
19 Wonderful editor of *Mad* (2,3,3)
20 Separate selection from Denis Leary (6)
21 Simple space station broadcast (4)
22 Whirl headless stuffed animal (4)

DOWN

1 Unfortunate bit of testimony brought up cigar (6)
2 Ocean's color amid seaquake (4)
3 Late breaking updates (4,3)
4 Verdi lost enthusiasm (5)
5 Rubs fingerboard ridges (5)
6 Indication of disapproval surrounding a job (4)
10 Instructed French cheese agent (7)
12 Might mix green with touch of yellow (6)
14 Location of Emerald City character's sunblock? (5)
15 Honker taking interstate creates disturbance (5)
16 I matched up article (4)
18 Transfer data disk kept by youngster (4)

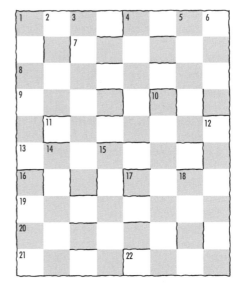

96

ACROSS

1 Arm of the Arctic Ocean re-created with ease (5,3)
7 Copper's broadcast on the radio (4)
9 Like warships buried in sudden avalanches (5)
10 Foreign wanderer approached (4,4)
11 Because stuffing is incendiary (5)
13 Sicken pitcher in the middle of pitch (5)
15 Out acquiring cravat for ruby wedding anniversary (8)
17 I repaired torn part of book (5)
18 Need jet after takeoff? (4)
19 Inviting farmer to keep piece of land (8)

DOWN

1 Incredible cuckoo flew round (9)
2 Sweepstakes winner sounds gruff (6)
3 Unbends what's bent (5)
4 Tiger seen wandering African plain (9)
5 New Age musician in African country losing capital (4)
6 Charge too much for plastic cover: $1 per (9)
8 Determine source of restlessness in *The Scream* (6,3)
12 Fruit cup and club sandwiches Tuesday (6)
14 Is located on both sides of northern borders (5)
16 Love partner's birthstone (4)

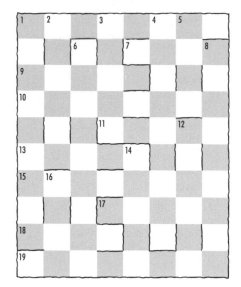

97

ACROSS

1 Armani's cracked basins (7)
8 Article that in Italy is long (4)
9 Practice dragging part of a dress (5)
10 Model can't pose for Acme (8)
12 Some wearers of fur are in high school (5)
13 Country boy's back in exotic sari (5)
15 Taking a fall, with rear of skirt shredding (8)
17 Spanish ring being worn with something silver (5)
18 Footwear stuff (4)
19 In finish, Erté changed and came in (7)

DOWN

1 Compare, and stay with a very thin sort of figure (10)
2 Light quality of a topless Ashley (4)
3 Flower on front of hood from Dublin (5)
4 A $100 fabric, one on a pleated item (9)
5 The woman's clothing in shows with radiance (6)
6 Green-sided shifts fashioned anew (10)
7 Study about a fashion hub's outfit (9)
11 Try Mel's new bloomer? (6)
14 Seedy item covered in cheap pleats (5)
16 See jacket when reversed (4)

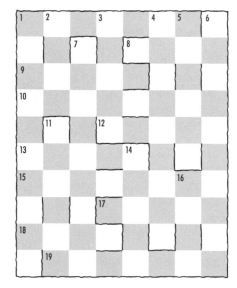

98

ANSWERS, PAGES 309 & 311

ACROSS

1 Luncheon meat surveys returned (4)

4 Discussed food later, in Italy (4)

7 Lack of productivity as diner's getting organized (8)

8 Table wine left on a boat (4)

10 Section of antipasto restaurant where you can buy food (5)

11 Cut piece of cheese with sharp part of knife (5)

12 Seven bananas—there's nothing odd about them (5)

13 Dance's popcorn treats (5)

15 Pervasive smell behind the first Pizza City? (4)

16 Plan on rice, as in a stew (8)

17 In quiche, added some lettuce (4)

18 Reportedly picks up food, like a chicken breast? (4)

DOWN

1 Weakens maple extracts? (4)

2 Skip lying about oven's origin (10)

3 Barker opened up some liquor (8)

4 Some dough not used in the common era (1-4)

5 Giant of good eating drops façade (10)

6 Rosie's chewed up willow twigs (6)

9 Note tenants put out second helping (4,4)

11 Wine originally at a party—it flows (6)

12 Excellent light meal for a big cat? (5)

14 Lobby while eating doughnut somewhere in Asia (4)

99

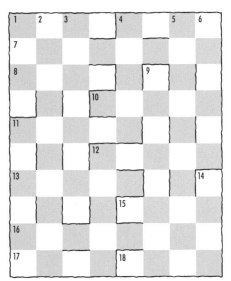

ACROSS

1 Breezes heading west around slender island (3,5)

7 Impair Florida city's comeback, for the most part (4)

9 Small bird that hurt the French teacher's head (5)

10 Further modify register at fair (8)

11 Wise guy has initially ridiculed army officer's nickname (5)

13 Farm seen in outer Anchorage (5)

15 Fleeing methanol liquid (2,3,3)

17 TV carpenter maintains large country estate (5)

18 Brother beginning to moan about kindergarten (4)

19 Ate crackers teen digs (8)

DOWN

1 Matador enters very minute area where supplies are kept (9)

2 Bananas now are Ivanhoe's love (6)

3 English city shows the way, they say (5)

4 Center of attention at university rally, of course (9)

5 Teases children (4)

6 Parading lively dance around Mom's sister (9)

8 I objectively designate assistant traffic officer (5,4)

12 Leave "the greatest" English soccer player (6)

14 Estate recipients head away from the tax agency (5)

16 Nobody shortened lunch hour (4)

100

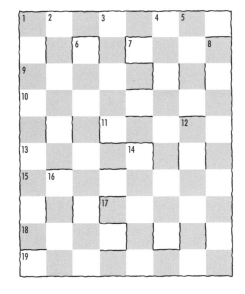

Answers

Answers: Cranium-Crushing Crosswords

1

```
D E A R A B B Y ■ A D V I C E
A Q U A B L U E ■ S E A N A D
M U T I L A T E ■ S A L A R Y
E A R N E S T ■ F U T U R E S
S L Y E S T ■ H A R H A R ■
■ ■ S T E F A N E D B E R G
A M C ■ D E U M ■ A L A I N
H A U L S ■ E T A ■ Y E R B A
A U R I C ■ L E I A ■ S S W
B I T T H E B U L L E T ■
■ F A R R A R ■ F R U M P S
W I L F O R D ■ L O A N O U T
I D O I D O ■ R U N S I N T O
P O O R E R ■ A B S E N T I A
E L D E R S ■ P E E R G Y N T
```

37

```
A P P L E J A C K S ■ E G G O
C L A Y M A T I O N ■ A N I L
C A T S C R A D L E ■ T O R A
U N T I E S ■ ■ A S I M O V
S E I N E ■ T A C K I N E S S
A L P S ■ B O L L I N G ■ ■
B O A ■ R E P L E N I S H E R
L A G ■ E A R T A G S ■ A X E
E D E N P R A I R I E ■ S I C
■ B E S T M E N ■ P I S H
N O N C A R E E R ■ S A N T A
A V A N T I ■ ■ D O R M E R
R E V E ■ G L A C I A T I N G
C R E W ■ H I L L P R I N C E
S A S S ■ T A K E S S I D E S
```

19

```
C L O W N S ■ A V I A R I E S
H E A R Y E ■ B A R N A C L E
A S F A R A S I C A N T E L L
■ ■ P O S T D A T E S ■
O I L ■ A R E T E S ■ A D O
U N I O N L A B E L ■ C M O N
T O M P E T T Y ■ Y V O N N E
C R I E S ■ A T M ■ A R E A S
O D E N S E ■ H I S S E S A T
L E S S ■ T O E T H E L I N E
D R T ■ S O U R E R ■ C A P
■ ■ C E N T U R I E S ■
M E M O R I A L S E R V I C E
A C E R B A T E ■ K I E R A N
C O N D O N E S ■ S E N A T E
```

55

```
N O S C R U B S ■ S M O O T H
E S T H E T I C ■ N O C L U E
S C A R F A C E ■ L A T I N A
T E R I ■ S E N D ■ S A V E R
L O E S S ■ P E E L ■ V E S T
E L A T E D ■ L I B E R T E
D A T A C O M P R E S S I O N
■ ■ E P E E I S T ■ ■
B R E N D A S G O T A B A B Y
L O R E E N A ■ O R A C L E
E X E C ■ T A B S ■ S T E E L
M A C K S ■ Z O L A ■ E T A L
I N T E N D ■ M E S S M A T E
S N O R E R ■ B E E E A T E R
H E R S E Y ■ S P A W N E R S
```

10

F	A	C	E	F	A	C	T	S	■	P	A	W	E	D
S	M	A	L	L	B	O	R	E	■	L	E	H	A	R
T	O	P	L	O	A	D	E	R	■	A	R	I	S	E
A	R	R	E	S	T	I	N	G	■	N	O	T	E	S
R	E	I	N	S	E	R	T	I	O	N	■	E	D	S
■	■	E	S	E	■	■	N	E	W	B	I	E	■	■
S	C	R	O	D	■	C	O	M	E	D	I	A	N	S
M	A	U	L	■	S	T	R	I	A	■	R	S	T	U
O	M	N	I	B	U	S	E	S	■	S	Y	S	O	P
K	E	N	N	E	L	■	■	S	L	O	■	■	■	■
E	R	E	■	D	U	A	N	E	A	L	L	M	A	N
D	A	R	T	H	■	B	O	L	I	V	I	A	N	O
O	S	S	I	E	■	H	O	L	D	I	N	G	I	N
U	H	U	R	A	■	O	N	I	O	N	D	O	M	E
T	Y	P	E	D	■	R	E	E	N	G	A	G	E	S

46

J	A	M	E	S	C	A	A	N	■	W	A	I	L	S
I	N	A	D	V	A	N	C	E	■	A	G	N	A	T
H	O	R	S	E	R	A	C	E	■	D	I	T	T	O
A	L	I	E	N	A	T	E	S	■	S	T	E	E	N
D	E	A	L	■	■	O	D	O	R	■	A	R	M	E
■	■	■	■	H	E	L	E	N	O	F	T	R	O	Y
S	W	A	H	I	L	I	S	■	T	R	O	U	V	E
L	I	B	E	R	I	A	■	H	A	I	R	P	I	N
A	L	L	S	E	T	■	D	E	T	E	S	T	E	D
C	L	A	I	R	E	D	A	N	E	S	■	■	■	■
K	I	T	T	■	S	U	M	S	■	■	M	A	N	E
N	A	I	A	D	■	P	A	L	I	S	A	D	E	D
E	M	O	T	E	■	I	G	O	T	A	N	A	M	E
S	I	N	E	W	■	N	E	W	S	W	O	M	E	N
S	I	S	S	Y	■	G	R	E	Y	A	R	E	A	S

28

A	L	L	N	I	G	H	T	E	R	■	P	L	U	G
S	E	A	A	N	E	M	O	N	E	■	R	O	T	O
S	E	T	S	F	O	O	T	O	N	■	E	V	I	L
I	R	I	S	E	■	S	O	L	E	■	S	E	L	F
S	A	N	E	S	T	■	■	S	E	I	S	M	I	C
I	T	A	R	T	A	S	S	■	■	L	E	E	Z	A
■	■	■	S	N	O	W	B	O	A	R	D	E	R	■
A	M	A	H	■	G	U	A	R	D	■	S	O	R	T
N	O	T	A	N	O	P	T	I	O	N	■	■	■	■
T	U	T	T	I	■	■	H	E	R	E	G	O	E	S
I	N	A	S	N	A	P	■	S	W	I	R	L	Y	■
A	T	I	T	■	B	O	I	L	■	G	R	A	M	M
R	I	N	A	■	R	O	S	E	T	A	T	T	O	O
A	D	E	N	■	A	N	N	S	O	T	H	E	R	N
B	A	R	D	■	M	A	T	T	R	E	S	S	E	S

64

J	U	D	D	H	I	R	S	C	H	■	T	A	X	I
A	D	R	I	A	N	O	P	L	E	■	E	D	E	R
D	A	I	R	Y	Q	U	E	E	N	■	N	O	N	O
E	L	L	E	■	U	N	D	O	■	E	N	R	O	N
S	L	Y	■	B	I	D	■	■	T	R	I	A	G	E
■	■	■	S	A	S	S	A	F	R	A	S	T	E	A
B	I	M	I	N	I	■	G	R	A	S	P	I	N	G
A	L	A	N	■	T	A	L	O	N	■	R	O	I	L
K	I	D	G	L	O	V	E	■	S	C	O	N	C	E
E	A	R	L	Y	R	E	T	U	R	N	S	■	■	■
S	K	I	E	R	S	■	■	N	A	N	■	S	A	W
H	U	L	M	E	■	E	R	I	C	■	L	O	L	A
O	L	E	O	■	C	R	I	T	I	C	A	L	O	F
P	I	N	S	■	O	N	D	E	A	D	L	I	N	E
S	K	A	T	■	L	O	S	S	L	E	A	D	E	R

2

38

20

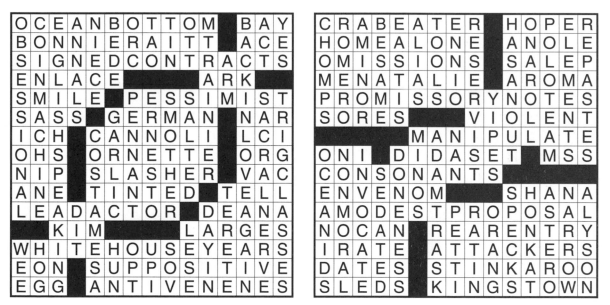

56

11

```
G E E Z L O U I S E ■ A L T E
A N N O Y A N C E S ■ N E A P
M S C O T T P E C K ■ T O R I
B I O M E ■ L A T I ■ I S T S
O L D E ■ A U X ■ M A H A L O
L E E R I N G ■ B O G E Y E D
■ ■ ■ N I G E R ■ A R E T E
L A T I S S I M U S D O R S I
E L E N I ■ N I T T I ■ ■ ■
S L E D D O G ■ E A R N E S T
G E N I E S ■ E F T ■ O N T O
I L I A ■ C I A O ■ A S S A Y
R U D I ■ A T T R A C T I V E
L I O N ■ R A M C H A R G E R
S A L K ■ S T E E L B A N D S
```

47

```
L A R A C R O F T ■ J O L I E
A L E X H A L E Y ■ I L O N A
I C E L A N D E R ■ M I N T S
R O L E S ■ S L O B ■ V E R E
S A S S E D ■ I S R A E L I S
■ ■ ■ ■ A W L ■ A T T I C ■
M I S T R I A L ■ K O R E A N
A N T H E R S ■ C E L E S T E
R A R E L Y ■ D E P L E T E D
■ M I M I C ■ E N A ■ ■ ■
C O V E T O U S ■ D A B B E D
O R E S ■ W R E N ■ C A R L O
D A F O E ■ G R E A T S E A L
A T O N E ■ E V A P O R A T E
S A R G E ■ S E R E N A D E D
```

29

```
P H A N T A S M A L ■ S H U I
O U T E R S P A C E ■ T A R N
P R I V A T E J E T ■ A S I T
P O L I C E C A R S ■ R A G E
A N T L E R ■ ■ B R I T T E N
■ ■ ■ Y S E R ■ O S W A L D
M E A T ■ ■ B E L L E I S L E
U P P E R C A S E L E T T E R
S H O S H O N E S ■ H E R S
L E S T E R ■ T H A N ■ ■
I M I T A T E ■ G E T M A D
M E T A ■ A C C E L E R A T E
E R I K ■ Z O O M E D I N O N
R A V E ■ A N I M A T E D L Y
A L E R ■ R O L E M O D E L S
```

65

```
B L O W S S M O K E ■ G A I T
L O C A T I O N A L ■ U L N A
A C T I O N H E R O ■ I M O K
Z O E L L E R ■ I N S T O R E
E S T E E ■ ■ ■ H A N D S
■ ■ D A T A R E C O R D E R
B I P ■ G O T O V E R ■ O R O
O N O ■ L O O S E S T ■ I T O
M C I ■ A L M A N A C ■ L O T
B U S I N E S S T R I P ■
B R O N C ■ ■ ■ R O M A N
L A N C E R S ■ L A C T A S E
A B O O ■ A E R O P U E R T O
S L A M ■ P R E S S I N G O N
T Y K E ■ P I N S E T T E R S
```

3

```
S T R A I T O F G E O R G I A
T R A N S I T I O N P O I N T
L I T T L E T E N N E S S E E
O B E S E ■ O R E I D A ■ ■ ■
■ ■ ■ M I C A S ■ ■ A N A ■
I N T E R V I E W ■ R A C E S
S E R G E I ■ R O B E S T E S
A B I G A I L ■ L E E T I D E
A U T O D I A L ■ A V A I L S
C L O N E ■ T A N N E R I E S
S A N ■ ■ A R T O O ■ ■ ■ ■
■ ■ ■ I T R I E D ■ R O S S I
T U R N S O N E S B A C K O N
O N E M O M E N T I N T I M E
S A L E S A S S O C I A T E S
```

39

```
G Q M A G A Z I N E ■ P S S T
O U T R A G E O U S ■ T A L E
E A S I N G I N T O ■ B Y E S
S R I ■ G I S ■ C O S E T
A R N O ■ E T H A N H A W K E
P E A R L S ■ A W E A T H E R
E L I T E ■ S U N V I S O R S
■ ■ ■ B A I L E E S ■ ■ ■
R E S T A R T E D ■ E N G L E
E X T O R T E R ■ A S T R A L
P H O T O E S S A Y ■ H A D A
L U K A N ■ ■ R E D ■ N A T
A M I S ■ J A M E S R A N D I
C E N T ■ I N I T I A T I O N
E D G E ■ F A B E R G E E G G
```

21

```
J A M E S W H A L E ■ S A L T
U N A N C H O R E D ■ C L A W
D I D T H E S A M E ■ Y O K E
I T E R A T E ■ ■ L A T H E R
C A P E R S ■ J E W S H A R P
A L L A Y ■ B U G E Y E ■ ■
B O A T ■ C A R R I E D O F F
L O N ■ B U S I E S T ■ C L I
E S S A Y T E S T S ■ ■ P E A R
■ ■ B E A S T S ■ F R A M E
O V E R A C T S ■ L E O N I S
L A M A R R ■ ■ R E M N A N T
E N I D ■ O I L E M B A R G O
A C R E ■ S T O P M O T I O N
N E S S ■ S E T S A T E A S E
```

57

```
C A M B R I C ■ B R O A D E R
A M O R O S O ■ R A P T U R E
T E L E P H O N E N U M B E R
C R E T E ■ K A N E S ■ I M A
H I R T ■ A B C D E ■ C O I T
O C A ■ A L O H A ■ C H U T E
W A T E R L O O ■ E R A S E D
■ ■ ■ T O O K C O V E R ■ ■
C R E A M Y ■ H O E D O W N S
R E N T A ■ S E S N O ■ H A T
E L L S ■ P E E P S ■ D A N A
W E I ■ C A N S O ■ R I T E S
M A S T E R S E R G E A N T S
E S T E L L E ■ E N D N O T E
N E S T L E D ■ S U D E T E N
```

12

```
R J R N A B I S C O ■ O R E O
H A S A L O C K O N ■ R E A P
O C T I L L I O N S ■ N A T E
S O U L ■ D E A F ■ R A R I N
■ ■ ■ M E R L E ■ A M E N S
S H O F A R ■ R E V E N G E
L A V A S ■ A G R A I N D I A
A V E C ■ S L O A N ■ T E N S
V E R I D I C A L ■ S A R T O
E N G L I S H ■ ■ M O L S O N
T O L E R ■ E M M E T ■ ■ ■
R I A N T ■ M O A T ■ I R A N
A D Z E ■ H I T C H A R I D E
D E E S ■ A S T R O N O M E R
E A D S ■ S T O O D O N E N D
```

48

```
F L E A P I T S ■ N O R U S H
T E N Y A R D S ■ O P E N T O
P A I N L E S S ■ N A B B E D
I N G R I D ■ ■ O G L A L A S
N E M A N ■ J A N E ■ G A R ■
G R A N D P A R E N T S D A Y
■ ■ ■ D R E N C H E R ■ E T A
A B S ■ O N S H O R E ■ D E W
R A M ■ M A T E R I E L ■ ■
T R A V E L E R S C H E C K S
■ S R I ■ C E D E ■ O S H E A
A C T E D O N ■ H U S A Y N
B E E F E D ■ I N A S E N S E
I N S O L E ■ F E R E N G I S
T E T R A S ■ I D I S S E N T
```

30

```
J A C O B U S ■ P R E T E E N
E L E M E N T ■ R E V E L R Y
M A D E I R A ■ A M I A B L E
I N A N G E R ■ M A L L R A T
M I R I E S T ■ S I D E I N ■
A S S I S T E D ■ N O O D G E
■ ■ E D O S ■ E N G E L
F R I E N D O F A F R I E N D
E A G L E ■ N O V A ■ ■ ■
U S N E W S ■ R E S C U E R S
■ B I G C A T ■ S T A N L E E
N O T A O N E ■ T E R M I T E
I R O N M E N ■ I N M A T E S
T A R T E S T ■ M E E K E S T
A S S E R T S ■ E R N E S T O
```

66

```
T R A P P I S T ■ A R R E T S
B A R R E N L Y ■ D I E T E R
O N I O N D I P ■ M O T H R A
N O O N T I D E ■ I N A I R ■
E U S T A C I A ■ T E R C E T
S T O O D I N ■ L O G G I N S
■ ■ ■ A G U A F R E S C A
S A I D A ■ O R B ■ O T T E R
A L G O N Q U I A N ■ ■ ■
W I N G N U T ■ N O R I L S K
S T O L A E ■ L I T E R A T I
■ A R O M E ■ I M A W O M A N
S L A V E R ■ S A L O N I K A
C I N E S E ■ S L O V E N E S
H A T R E D ■ E S T E R A S E
```

4

```
D I S T A F F █ P A L O M A R
E S T E L L A █ O L I V I N E
A S A T E A M █ T A B U L A E
T H R E E M I L E I S L A N D
H E S S █ █ L E M █ █ E N D S
█ █ █ K A Y A K E D █ █ █
S T O R A G E D I S E A S E S
R E T I R E M E N T P L A N S
S E A S O N E D V E T E R A N
█ █ █ L A R G I S H █ █ █
S P A N █ G A L █ O S O S
C A S T O N E S L O T W I T H
R U L E S O N █ A T H L E T E
E L A S T I C █ G R I E V E D
W I N T E R Y █ E A S T E R S
```

40

```
J A C K I E C H A N █ S W I T
A L O N G S H O R E █ L A N E
N I X O N T A P E S █ A S T A
E C O T O U R I S M █ T H O R
S E N T R A █ █ T I T T E R S
█ █ E R I Q █ T I E D T O
S H A M █ Y O U T H G R O U P
T O L E S █ T I A █ E N U R E
A S S A I L A N T S █ S T E N
S T A N Z A █ T E A L █ █
H I T T E R S █ █ M E G A N S
A L I A █ D E A D P A R R O T
W E A L █ O C C U R R E D T O
A T N O █ I C E D A N C E R S
Y O S T █ L O D E S T O N E S
```

22

```
A R M E N I A C O L O M B I A
C A U L I F L O W E R E A R S
A S S O C I A T E D E G R E E
S T I P E █ █ █ G E E N A
T A K E S P O T S H O T S A T
█ █ █ T H R E W I N █ █
C R O P █ O R E O S █ S C A R
R E V E █ N I N O S █ A L L A
A P E R █ I N A N E █ T O M S
P A N S █ E G G E R █ A S A P
G Y R O █ S H E D S █ R E M I
A M E N S █ A D O █ M O R A N
M E A N E S T █ V A L U A T E
E N D E M I C █ E V I N C E S
S T Y L I S H █ R A I D E R S
```

58

```
A L K A L I M E T A L █ V E G
D E A D A S A D O D O █ I N A
A C I D T O N G U E D █ D R Y
P A S S E N G E R P I G E O N
T R E █ █ E R S T █ R O U E
E R R A T A █ █ S K E E T S
D E S P E R A D O █ A N D E S
█ █ P A T M O R I T A █ █
A S F O R █ P H O N E D I A L
T A O I S M █ █ I Y A N L A
E G O N █ A R R S █ █ H U N
C U T T H R O A T I S L A N D
R A M █ A T A N I M P A S S E
O R E █ T H R E E S U I T E R
W O N █ T A K E S O R D E R S
```

13

M	A	G	N	E	T	I	C	E	Q	U	A	T	O	R
A	H	E	A	D	O	F	O	N	E	S	T	I	M	E
M	O	N	E	Y	L	A	U	N	D	E	R	E	R	S
E	Y	E	S	■	D	I	N	E	■	E	D	I	T	■
■	■	■	H	A	L	T	■	O	L	E	■	■	■	■
P	A	S	S	E	■	E	L	S	E	■	V	I	A	■
A	L	I	E	N	A	B	D	U	C	T	I	O	N	S
R	O	M	A	N	C	E	C	L	A	S	S	I	C	S
E	M	O	T	I	O	N	A	L	R	E	S	C	U	E
D	A	N	■	N	A	T	L	■	■	A	Y	E	R	S
■	■	A	G	T	■	O	A	S	T	■	■	■	■	■
A	C	E	R	■	I	R	M	A	■	L	O	M	A	■
T	E	L	E	V	I	S	I	O	N	R	O	L	E	S
I	L	L	M	A	N	N	E	R	E	D	N	E	S	S
P	L	A	Y	S	I	T	S	T	R	A	I	G	H	T

49

S	T	A	R	G	A	Z	E	R	S	■	A	B	B	E
C	A	M	E	O	R	O	L	E	S	■	C	A	L	X
I	M	U	S	T	A	D	M	I	T	■	C	H	I	C
F	A	C	T	O	R	I	E	S	■	T	E	R	N	I
I	R	K	S	■	A	A	R	■	M	O	N	A	D	S
■	■	■	■	F	T	C	■	N	A	P	T	I	M	E
A	B	O	I	L	■	S	T	E	P	S	O	N	I	T
S	E	N	N	A	■	I	R	T	■	E	R	I	C	A
S	E	T	T	I	N	G	U	P	■	E	S	S	E	X
E	C	H	E	L	O	N	■	R	I	D	■	■	■	■
S	H	E	R	E	E	■	N	O	N	■	L	I	C	E
S	T	R	A	D	■	S	O	F	T	T	A	C	O	S
I	R	O	C	■	R	E	T	I	R	E	M	E	N	T
N	E	A	T	■	E	A	S	T	O	R	A	N	G	E
G	E	D	S	■	G	L	O	S	S	A	R	I	E	S

31

H	O	B	A	R	T	A	U	S	T	R	A	L	I	A
U	P	A	R	O	U	N	D	T	H	E	B	E	N	D
N	E	U	R	O	B	I	O	L	O	G	I	C	A	L
C	R	E	E	D	A	L	■	U	R	I	D	I	N	E
H	A	R	T	S	■	I	N	C	■	S	E	D	E	R
■	■	■	■	A	N	A	I	S	■	■	■	■	■	■
H	Y	D	R	O	G	E	N	A	T	E	D	O	I	L
E	U	R	O	P	E	■	■	■	I	D	E	A	T	E
E	L	E	C	T	R	I	C	B	L	A	N	K	E	T
■	■	■	■	S	N	O	U	T	■	■	■	■	■	■
H	A	B	I	T	■	A	D	S	■	A	C	A	S	T
A	N	A	D	E	M	S	■	H	I	B	A	C	H	I
W	E	L	L	R	E	P	R	E	S	E	N	T	E	D
E	S	S	E	N	T	I	A	L	N	A	T	U	R	E
S	T	A	R	S	A	N	D	S	T	R	I	P	E	S

67

J	O	N	N	Y	Q	U	E	S	T	■	V	A	V	A
E	U	B	I	E	B	L	A	K	E	■	E	D	E	R
S	T	A	T	E	S	I	D	E	R	■	R	U	N	E
T	R	E	E	■	■	S	E	R	A	G	L	I	O	■
S	E	R	R	A	T	E	■	■	A	C	E	T	A	L
■	■	■	S	C	A	L	P	S	■	R	O	L	L	A
I	T	A	■	C	R	E	A	T	I	O	N	I	S	T
L	O	P	■	L	E	C	T	O	R	S	■	F	I	E
K	O	R	E	A	S	T	R	A	I	T	■	E	N	D
A	K	I	L	I	■	S	I	T	S	I	N	■	■	■
C	C	L	A	M	P	■	S	E	C	A	N	T	S	■
H	O	L	I	S	T	I	C	■	■	S	O	R	T	■
A	V	O	N	■	E	L	I	M	I	N	A	T	O	R
S	E	V	E	■	R	A	G	E	T	O	L	I	V	E
E	R	E	S	■	O	Y	S	T	E	R	S	T	E	W

5

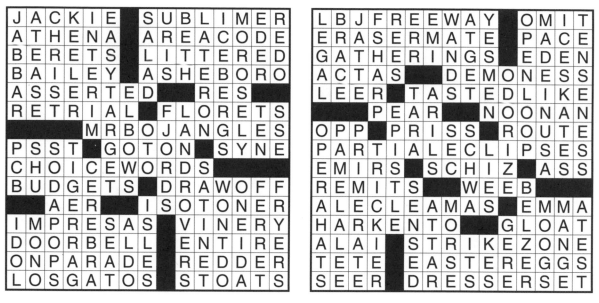

```
J A C K I E   S U B L I M E R
A T H E N A   A R E A C O D E
B E R E T S   L I T T E R E D
B A I L E Y   A S H E B O R O
A S S E R T E D     R E S
R E T R I A L   F L O R E T S
        M R B O J A N G L E S
P S S T   G O T O N   S Y N E
C H O I C E W O R D S
B U D G E T S   D R A W O F F
    A E R   I S O T O N E R
I M P R E S A S   V I N E R Y
D O O R B E L L   E N T I R E
O N P A R A D E   R E D D E R
L O S G A T O S   S T O A T S
```

41

```
L B J F R E E W A Y   O M I T
E R A S E R M A T E   P A C E
G A T H E R I N G S   E D E N
A C T A S   D E M O N E S S
L E E R   T A S T E D L I K E
      P E A R   N O O N A N
O P P   P R I S S   R O U T E
P A R T I A L E C L I P S E S
E M I R S   S C H I Z   A S S
R E M I T S   W E E B
A L E C L E A M A S   E M M A
H A R K E N T O   G L O A T
A L A I   S T R I K E Z O N E
T E T E   E A S T E R E G G S
S E E R   D R E S S E R S E T
```

23

```
D A R K R U M   B U I L T I N
C H I N E S E L A N G U A G E
I M M U N E R E S P O N S E S
V E S T E D I N T E R E S T S
          G U T T E R
A S L E E P       S T A T E D
U P I S     S C H O O L A G E
D O N T A S K D O N T T E L L
R I D E S H A R E   O B I E
A L Y S S A     M A S O N S
        R E B B E S
M O S T A P P R E C I A T E D
I N C O M E P E R C A P I T A
L E A V E N I N G A G E N T S
L A D A N S E   S N O R T E D
```

59

```
Y A C K E T Y Y A K   V O W S
O N A R A M P A G E   E C H O
S T L O U I S Z O O   R E E D
T A L C   I O N S   B A N D
        A L L O Y   N A N C E
M I N T T E A     P I L S E N
O V E R L A N D P A R K
P A T I E N T S E R V I C E S
      N A T I V E D A N C E R
A L V I S O   K O N T I K I
D E A L T   C H I N A
D E C O   S H U N   B R A G
S W A P   C A R G O P L A N E
T A T E   A I D A N Q U I N N
O Y E Z   T R Y T O R E L A X
```

249

14

50

32

68

6

```
L U N A T I C ■ S I L E N T P
A R A B I C A ■ I S A D O R A
R E G U L A R ■ G R I D D E D
S Y S T E M S A N A L Y S T S
■ ■ ■ D E E P S E A ■ ■ ■
A V I S ■ A R I L ■ A R E A
M A N H A T T A N I S L A N D
A N G O L A ■ ■ T I E D T O
S C O T T I S H T E R R I E R
S E T S ■ L E I S ■ T O R N
■ ■ ■ S C I T E C H ■ ■ ■
T I M E C O N S T R A I N T S
A C E T O N E ■ S U N B O W S
C O R O N E R ■ E D G E S I N
O N E N E S S ■ S E S T E T S
```

42

```
A T A R I ■ A R K S ■ T B A R
L A M A R ■ W E I L ■ H O S E
B R U N O M A G L I ■ O I S E
S T R I C T R U L E ■ U S E D
■ ■ ■ ■ A D L E R ■ S E T S
H I N G E ■ C A R ■ T A I ■
A S I U N D E R S T A N D I T
A N N I V E R S A R Y D A T E
G O O N E B E T T E R T H A N
■ F E R ■ M R E ■ A H O L D
M P A A ■ N O E L S ■ ■ ■
E A R P ■ A N N L A N D E R S
A L I I ■ D I G I T A L I S E
D E N G ■ J E T T ■ B I O T A
E R A S ■ A S H E ■ S I N U S
```

24

```
F R A N K L I N ■ E L L E R Y
L I S A L I S A ■ M A U M E E
A G I T A T E S ■ O B S E S S
W A T E R T R A P ■ S T R U M
■ ■ ■ E E L E R ■ S I R ■
R A T T E R ■ C S A ■ A L F A
I D I O T ■ B O E R ■ F L A T
C A M P A I G N T A C T I C S
A M E S ■ D I G A ■ L E V E E
N A P E ■ E R E ■ T E R E S A
■ N I L ■ A L S A B ■ ■ ■
A D E L E ■ S T R I P M A L L
R E C E S S ■ I N L E A G U E
A V E R S E ■ O I L S T O N E
L E S S O N ■ N E S T E G G S
```

60

```
Q A N T A S ■ P I A N O M A N
U N E A S E ■ A L C A P O N E
A G A S S I ■ R E E M E R G E
G O R M A N ■ A S S E N T E D
G R E A S E U P ■ S W I L L
Y A R N S ■ S E T S ■ I S E E
■ ■ ■ I N A T I E ■ D E N S
P A R T N E R ■ T U X E D O S
A L E E ■ I M P A L E ■ ■ ■
P A P S ■ L Y O N ■ N I T T I
A M A T I ■ E S T O N I A N
B A C K S E A T ■ I C A R U S
E N K I N D L E ■ B I G A P E
A C E T O N E S ■ E D E N I C
R E D S T A R S ■ R E S E N T
```

15

```
A L L T H A T J A Z Z ■ S P A
M A Y A A N G E L O U ■ A L T
E V E L K N I E V E L ■ N U T
B E L L E ■ F R A ■ U S A G E
A S L E E P ■ ■ R U L I N G S
■ ■ S M O G S ■ T A R G E T
F I S T ■ U N M E T N E E D S
A R T ■ F R U I T E D ■ L I T
D O U B L E S T A R ■ B O N O
E N D E A R ■ E L E G Y ■ ■
D O L T I S H ■ ■ D E L P H I
A X I A L ■ Y M A ■ R I L E D
W I E ■ I M P O R T U N A T E
A D S ■ N O N O N A N E T T E
Y E T ■ G O O D O L D D A Y S
```

51

```
S A V A G E ■ J A C K P A A R
O N E W A Y ■ A D R I E N N E
O N S A L E ■ M A I N L A N D
T E T R I S ■ I M P E L L E D
H A R D C H E E S E S ■ O R E
E L Y S I A N ■ ■ S I N G I N
■ ■ ■ A D O P T ■ S A U C E
S A P S ■ E L A R A ■ W E E D
H I R A M ■ S W A M I ■ ■ ■
O R A T E S ■ ■ D E S S E R T
W R Y ■ L U I S E R A I N E R
D I S T A N C E ■ I D E A T E
O F F A N D O N ■ C O N M E N
G L O R I A N A ■ A R N O L D
S E R E N E S T ■ N E A R L Y
```

33

```
A T L A N T A ■ T B I L I S I
D A Y C A R E ■ R A M A D A N
S P E E D E R ■ I N S U L I N
■ ■ D E M O N ■ S E R E N E
E T C ■ R O B E S ■ R E S T S
L I L T ■ R A T T A I L ■ ■
I B E A M ■ C A R R O T T O P
A I R P O R T S E C U R I T Y
N A K E D N E S S ■ S E D E R
■ ■ D E A R E S T ■ E E R O
O M A R R ■ S T L E O ■ S O S
S A B I N E ■ S O A K S ■ ■
C R A V A T S ■ A S A T E A M
A L B E R T O ■ D E P A L M A
R O A S T E D ■ S T I N K E R
```

69

```
B A G H D A D I R A Q ■ H S T
R E L E A S E D A T E ■ A P E
A R A B I S R A E L I ■ T O R
W I D E N E R ■ ■ I C E R S
L E E ■ T R Y O U T ■ A C T E
■ ■ P Y T ■ P R E S S R U N
S H U L ■ M A G N E T I T E
L O S A N G E L E S T I M E S
A L A N F R E E D ■ L E S S
T E N T C I T Y ■ I R E ■ ■
H I D E ■ P S E U D O ■ R I M
E N T R E ■ L E O N I N E
R O H ■ T O U R N A M E N T S
E N E ■ A D R I A T I C S E A
D E M ■ S E L F S E E K E R S
```

7

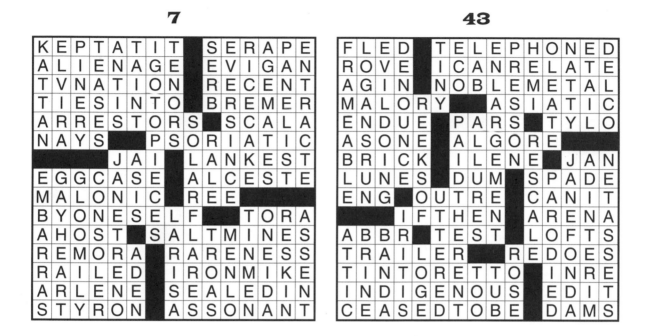

```
K E P T A T I T ■ S E R A P E
A L I E N A G E ■ E V I G A N
T V N A T I O N ■ R E C E N T
T I E S I N T O ■ B R E M E R
A R R E S T O R S ■ S C A L A
N A Y S ■ ■ P S O R I A T I C
■ ■ ■ J A I ■ L A N K E S T
E G G C A S E ■ A L C E S T E
M A L O N I C ■ R E E ■ ■
B Y O N E S E L F ■ ■ T O R A
A H O S T ■ S A L T M I N E S
R E M O R A ■ R A R E N E S S
R A I L E D ■ I R O N M I K E
A R L E N E ■ S E A L E D I N
S T Y R O N ■ A S S O N A N T
```

43

```
F L E D ■ T E L E P H O N E D
R O V E ■ I C A N R E L A T E
A G I N ■ N O B L E M E T A L
M A L O R Y ■ ■ A S I A T I C
E N D U E ■ P A R S ■ T Y L O
A S O N E ■ A L G O R E ■ ■
B R I C K ■ I L E N E ■ J A N
L U N E S ■ D U M ■ S P A D E
E N G ■ O U T R E ■ C A N I T
■ ■ I F T H E N ■ A R E N A
A B B R ■ T E S T ■ L O F T S
T R A I L E R ■ ■ R E D O E S
T I N T O R E T T O ■ I N R E
I N D I G E N O U S ■ E D I T
C E A S E D T O B E ■ D A M S
```

25

```
D V D P L A Y E R S ■ T O R T
A E R I A L V I E W ■ A N E W
T R A N S F E R E E ■ R I C O
E D I T H ■ S E L E C T O R S
R E N O I R ■ ■ P R E N U P
■ ■ S N O O T S ■ O S S I E
G P M ■ G O P H E R S T A T E
R A O ■ O T T A W A S ■ L E D
O L D B U S I N E S S ■ T D S
S M E L T ■ C A R P E D ■ ■
S P R E A D ■ ■ S C O P E D
T I N E T E S T S ■ T O R I O
O L I D ■ W H A T D I D I D O
N O S E ■ A U T O L O A D E R
S T E R ■ R E S P O N D E R S
```

61

```
S H O W R O O M S ■ A R C O S
A U D I E N C E S ■ B E L L A
N E I L P E A R T ■ S C A L P
E Y E L E N S E S ■ T O R I O
■ ■ ■ I N I ■ C A N K E R
H O W E ■ G R A P H I C S ■
E L I S ■ H A V E A N I D E A
M A N H A T T A N I S L A N D
I N D O N E S I A N ■ I L I E
■ ■ B E D R O L L S ■ N E S S
S P U M E S ■ ■ T O G ■
A R R A S ■ V A P O R W A R E
N A N K I ■ E X E R C I S E R
T W E E T ■ R E P E A T I N G
A N D R E ■ B R A S S H A T S
```

16

```
S T A T ■ K I R O V ■ J O V I
C A M E R A T U B E ■ O X E N
A P P E A R E D I N ■ B A R S
R A I N F O R E S T ■ S L O P
A N N E ■ ■ ■ D I A N A
B I G R I G S ■ O M I T T E D
■ C A N A D A G E E S E
S T R E E T A D D R E S S E S
T H E R M O P O L I S ■
R E G R E S S ■ Y O T E A M O
A S I A N ■ ■ M V I I
P I O N ■ D O L L A R B I L L
P E N T ■ O N E I D A L A K E
E G A L ■ P E N T A M E T E R
R E L Y ■ E S S A Y ■ M E D S
```

52

```
Z I P B Y ■ I T S A S T A R T
E N O L A ■ L I O N T A M E R
B S T A R ■ E N C O U R A G E
R E P I N ■ T E K ■ M A R I S
A R I S E S ■ I N P R I N T
S T E E L P L A T E ■ E L A L
■ L I E D T O ■ I L L E
B A G S ■ C A R O N ■ D O D D
R E U P ■ A P E M A N ■
A R N E ■ T I M E T E S T E D
S A R A C E N ■ E U N I C E
S T A K E ■ G I E ■ T O N K A
H O N O R C O D E ■ R O P E R
A R G U E D F O R ■ A T A R I
T S E T S E F L Y ■ L Y N D E
```

34

```
S T R A W S ■ P A T S A J A K
C H A L E T ■ A L E U R O N E
R E D F I R ■ L A N D M I N E
A R I ■ N O N A M E ■ A N O N
P E A C E M O V E M E N T ■
■ S T O R A G E D E V I C E S
S M O G ■ R A N I ■ O N A
T O R ■ M A G ■ S T L ■ M C I
O R G ■ O P U S ■ A M A D
P E R C A P I T A B A S I S ■
■ I D B E D E L I G H T E D
S C L C ■ T A T T E R ■ T M I
F I L A M E N T ■ R E M E E T
P R E S E N C E ■ C E M E N T
D E S E R T E D ■ E D I S T O
```

70

```
H A V E N O I D E A ■ C P A S
O R A L C A V I T Y ■ R O T A
J U N I O R Y E A R ■ U R A L
O N E S ■ ■ T S E T S E
■ I S A A C S O N ■ A C S
E X P R E S S L A N E ■ P A W
L E A ■ A P P U L S E ■ O D O
I R S ■ C H A N T E R ■ T E M
J O S ■ H A S K I N S ■ T R A
A G E ■ A L I E N N A T I O N
H R S ■ S T A R G A T E ■
W A T T E R ■ ■ A N T S
O P I E ■ O B O E D A M O R E
O H M S ■ C A N T I L E V E R
D Y E S ■ K N O C K E D O F F
```

8

```
C A S A G R A N D E   C E D E
L I P R E A D E R S   R E U S
I D I D N T D O I T   U K E S
M E T E S       N O P E A C E
E D E N   J A C K S A L M O N
    C H A C H I   S T O U T
P L A Y A C T I N G   Y U R I
H O B   Y O U N G E R   S S A
I N N S   B A N A N A P E E L
L E O I V   L E G U M E
G E R M I C I D E S   T A P E
R A M I R E Z       A I R E S
A G A L   L I T M U S T E S T
M L L E   I N S I S T E N C E
M E S S   E G O B O O S T E R
```

44

```
I T S A F A C T   S T I F F S
N E A T I D E A   T H A L I A
D E V O N R E X   R E G A R D
U B A N G I       E A R N E D
C O N C E A L S   A T E A S E
E X T E R N A L   K E E G A N
          K O R E A   A L E
A L P   P R E W A R M   N E D
S O U   R O S E S
S U L L E N   S A M S C L U B
O B L I G E   T E A L E O N I
O R I E N T     D A S S I N
N O N F A T   P L A Y S T A G
A C T O N E   Y E M E N I T E
S K O R T S   M I S R A T E S
```

26

```
C R A B   M E W   M A R C H E
L A L O   U R E   A G O R A S
A D A B   L I S   R E V I V E
M I S M A T C H   L I E B E
U A K A R I   A M E N   B A A
P L A Y E D A L O N G W I T H
        T I L L I E   A N I S
C O R R E S P O N D I N G T O
O B O E   C A V E I N
P R A C T I C E S E S S I O N
S O D   A P A R   T E A T R O
    T W I R L   C O R T L A N D
S H A N T I   O B I   A L A D
H E Y M A N   M I C   M I T E
A R S E N E   E T H   I C E D
```

62

```
R O W I N G   B I A T H L O N
E M A J O R   D R R O M A N O
E N D U R E   W E A P O N E D
S I E S T A   O P P O S E R S
E A R T H T O N E
      K A N G A R O O R A T
L E A K O U T   T E N S E L Y
E X T E R N     E T H I O P
A P E L E T S   I N H A S T E
D O N P A S Q U A L E
          U N L A B E L E D
O S S I F I E D   R E C A N E
W H O C A R E S   G N O M O N
L I F E S I Z E   E C L A T S
S M A R T S E T   S H E R E E
```

17

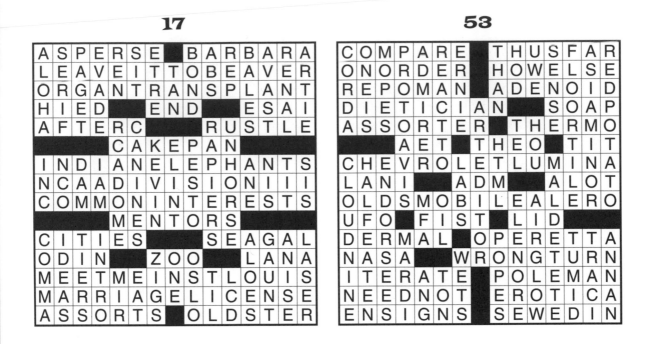

```
A S P E R S E ■ B A R B A R A
L E A V E I T T O B E A V E R
O R G A N T R A N S P L A N T
H I E D ■ ■ E N D ■ ■ E S A I
A F T E R C ■ ■ R U S T L E
■ ■ C A K E P A N ■ ■ ■
I N D I A N E L E P H A N T S
N C A A D I V I S I O N I I I
C O M M O N I N T E R E S T S
■ ■ ■ M E N T O R S ■ ■ ■
C I T I E S ■ ■ S E A G A L
O D I N ■ ■ Z O O ■ L A N A
M E E T M E I N S T L O U I S
M A R R I A G E L I C E N S E
A S S O R T S ■ O L D S T E R
```

53

```
C O M P A R E ■ T H U S F A R
O N O R D E R ■ H O W E L S E
R E P O M A N ■ A D E N O I D
D I E T I C I A N ■ S O A P
A S S O R T E R ■ T H E R M O
■ ■ A E T ■ T H E O ■ T I T
C H E V R O L E T L U M I N A
L A N I ■ ■ A D M ■ A L O T
O L D S M O B I L E A L E R O
U F O ■ F I S T ■ L I D ■
D E R M A L ■ O P E R E T T A
N A S A ■ ■ W R O N G T U R N
I T E R A T E ■ P O L E M A N
N E E D N O T ■ E R O T I C A
E N S I G N S ■ S E W E D I N
```

35

```
S Q U E E Z E B O X ■ J E S S
P A P A Y A T R E E ■ O M E N
O N S T E R O I D S ■ A I R E
O D E S S A N S ■ ■ A N N E E
F A T A H ■ K A R L B E N Z
■ ■ T O T O ■ M E L A N G E
D O T ■ T H R E E P I E C E S
I N R E ■ E A R L E ■ Z E T A
S T E A M E N G I N E ■ S I T
C H A R I N G ■ A T N O ■
R E T A R D E D ■ G R A P E
E R I C A ■ ■ I M A L O S E R
D I S H ■ W A V E R U N N E R
I S E E ■ A D A M A N D E V E
T E S S ■ R E S O L D E R E D
```

71

```
S L A P P E D ■ I D B A D G E
C A P E L L A ■ N I A G A R A
U M P T E E N ■ R A C E M E S
T I E T A C K ■ E L K ■ P E T
U N L I S T E D ■ O L D E N ■
M A S T E R S E R G E A N T S
■ ■ ■ A C C E S S F E E S
K O R E A ■ H L A ■ S T R A W
F I E L D G O A L S ■ ■ ■
C L O S E I N S P E C T I O N
■ S P E L L ■ S E Q U E N C E
A T E ■ A B A ■ O U T A C T S
T O N S I L S ■ P O E S I E S
O N E I D A S ■ L I S E T T E
B E D R E S T ■ E A T L E S S
```

9

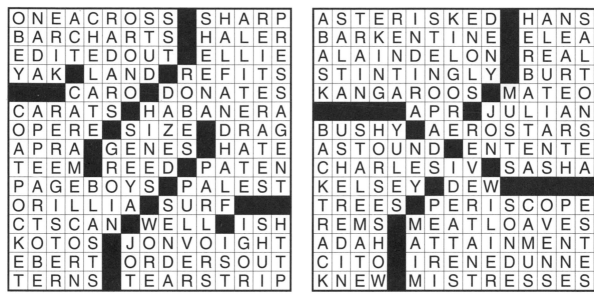

O	N	E	A	C	R	O	S	S	■	S	H	A	R	P
B	A	R	C	H	A	R	T	S	■	H	A	L	E	R
E	D	I	T	E	D	O	U	T	■	E	L	L	I	E
Y	A	K	■	L	A	N	D	■	R	E	F	I	T	S
■	■	C	A	R	O	■	D	O	N	A	T	E	S	■
C	A	R	A	T	S	■	H	A	B	A	N	E	R	A
O	P	E	R	E	■	S	I	Z	E	■	D	R	A	G
A	P	R	A	■	G	E	N	E	S	■	H	A	T	E
T	E	E	M	■	R	E	E	D	■	P	A	T	E	N
P	A	G	E	B	O	Y	S	■	P	A	L	E	S	T
O	R	I	L	L	I	A	■	S	U	R	F	■	■	■
C	T	S	C	A	N	■	W	E	L	L	■	I	S	H
K	O	T	O	S	■	J	O	N	V	O	I	G	H	T
E	B	E	R	T	■	O	R	D	E	R	S	O	U	T
T	E	R	N	S	■	T	E	A	R	S	T	R	I	P

45

A	S	T	E	R	I	S	K	E	D	■	H	A	N	S
B	A	R	K	E	N	T	I	N	E	■	E	L	E	A
A	L	A	I	N	D	E	L	O	N	■	R	E	A	L
S	T	I	N	T	I	N	G	L	Y	■	B	U	R	T
K	A	N	G	A	R	O	O	S	■	M	A	T	E	O
■	■	■	■	A	P	R	■	J	U	L	I	A	N	■
B	U	S	H	Y	■	A	E	R	O	S	T	A	R	S
A	S	T	O	U	N	D	■	E	N	T	E	N	T	E
C	H	A	R	L	E	S	I	V	■	S	A	S	H	A
K	E	L	S	E	Y	■	D	E	W	■	■	■	■	■
T	R	E	E	S	■	P	E	R	I	S	C	O	P	E
R	E	M	S	■	M	E	A	T	L	O	A	V	E	S
A	D	A	H	■	A	T	T	A	I	N	M	E	N	T
C	I	T	O	■	I	R	E	N	E	D	U	N	N	E
K	N	E	W	■	M	I	S	T	R	E	S	S	E	S

27

I	M	A	L	L	F	O	R	I	T	■	D	O	C	S
M	A	R	I	A	E	L	E	N	A	■	I	N	R	E
P	R	E	S	S	A	G	E	N	T	■	S	C	A	M
A	L	O	P	■	R	A	F	S	A	N	J	A	N	I
C	E	L	E	B	S	■	■	R	O	O	M	S	■	■
T	E	A	R	Y	■	E	C	T	■	L	I	E	T	O
■	■	D	A	D	O	O	R	O	N	R	O	N	■	■
C	L	E	M	E	N	S	B	R	E	N	T	A	N	O
M	I	N	I	S	T	E	R	I	N	G	■	■	■	■
V	A	L	L	I	■	L	A	C	■	E	B	O	L	A
■	B	I	L	G	E	■	B	R	I	B	E	S	■	■
A	L	V	I	N	A	I	L	E	Y	■	S	L	A	P
D	E	E	M	■	S	T	E	A	L	A	B	A	S	E
U	T	N	E	■	E	A	S	T	O	F	E	D	E	N
B	O	S	S	■	S	W	E	A	T	B	E	A	D	S

63

A	T	E	D	I	R	T	■	U	L	U	L	A	T	E
G	E	N	E	S	E	O	■	N	U	M	E	R	A	L
A	N	D	A	M	A	N	■	D	I	S	T	I	L	L
S	P	E	D	■	P	Y	R	E	S	■	L	A	K	E
S	I	A	M	■	P	R	I	M	E	■	O	N	A	N
I	N	R	E	■	R	A	D	A	R	■	O	A	T	S
■	■	■	A	L	A	N	■	N	A	P	S	■	■	■
F	A	C	T	O	I	D	■	D	I	L	E	M	M	A
A	D	A	■	T	S	A	R	I	N	A	■	O	A	R
L	M	N	■	S	A	L	O	N	E	N	■	D	R	T
S	I	N	■	A	L	L	E	G	R	O	■	E	G	G
E	T	A	L	■	■	■	■	■	■	■	A	R	A	L
R	O	B	E	R	T	S	M	C	N	A	M	A	R	A
I	N	I	T	I	A	T	I	O	N	R	I	T	E	S
B	E	S	T	K	E	P	T	S	E	C	R	E	T	S

18

```
H I G H H A T ■ R E G A T T A
A G R E E T O ■ A N O T H E R
Z I E G F E L D F O L L I E S
A V N E T ■ L A T ■ D A N T E
R E A L ■ A R M E D ■ S K I N
D U D ■ F L O O D E D ■ U M A
S P A C E M A N ■ C O M P E L
■ ■ ■ D E A D W R O N G ■ ■ ■
M O D E L A ■ A E R O S T A R
I V E ■ S T A Y O U T ■ I D E
N E T H ■ A L A R M ■ R E D D
D R E A R ■ I N D ■ L U B E D
S U N R I S E S E R E N A D E
E S T E F A N ■ R E V E R T E
T E E M E R S ■ S C I S S O R
```

54

```
R A D I A N T ■ A R T D E C O
E V E N N O W ■ P A R O T I D
W A N T S T O ■ P R O N A T E
A N T H E A P ■ R E T A P E S
S T E A L T H F I G H T E R S
H I R T ■ H A U S A ■ E S S A
■ ■ ■ ■ ■ P O S H E S T ■ ■ ■
C U S T O M E R S E R V I C E
U N T R U E ■ ■ S A I L O N
T R A I T ■ S I B ■ M O L D S
S E R B ■ J E L L O ■ L U L U
B A D U ■ O P I U M ■ A M I R
A S A N A L T E R N A T I V E
C O T E R I E ■ R I P E N E R
K N E S S E T ■ Y A R D E R S
```

36

```
T I M E P A S T ■ S T R I C T
A T A L A N T A ■ O H E N R Y
P A T E R N A L ■ D E N T E R
O L I V E O I L ■ A D O R E E
N O N E N T R Y ■ S A T U P ■
■ ■ ■ T A C H S ■ N A D I A
M I E N ■ T A O T E C H I N G
A N Y O N E S ■ O N E O N T A
T H E M O D E R N S ■ E G O S
H A L E N ■ S E E N A ■ ■
■ B I A L Y ■ S M A R T E N S
P I N N A E ■ P A R M E L I A
A T E S T S ■ A S I A T I C S
B E R N I E ■ C O N N O T E S
A R S O N S ■ E N G I N E R Y
```

72

```
A M A N A P L A N A C A N A L
C O L O N I A L A M E R I C A
E A T I N G D I S O R D E R S
S T O R A G E D I S E A S E S
■ ■ ■ ■ ■ B E N ■ R O B ■ ■ ■
J O L T E D ■ ■ ■ Z E A L O T
A M A H L ■ ■ I R V ■ L E O N E
R I V A L ■ N A E ■ L O T T E
S T A T E O F T H E U N I O N
■ ■ ■ ■ E L I T I S M ■ ■ ■
S I L O ■ E N A C T ■ I T S A
M O U N T A I N R E S O R T S
U N M E A N T ■ O B A D I A H
T I E L I N E ■ S A N I C L E
S A N B L A S ■ S N A C K E R
```

Answers: Hard-to-Solve Cryptograms

1 Columnist William Safire found wacky sunbelt nightclub named, ahem, "Tequila Mockingbird."

2 "Eggs cost less than seventy cents per pound." So TV and radio ads say. True, but this includes the shells.

3 The potato, discovered two thousand years ago, was worshiped by natives who performed rites to honor it.

4 Sign noticed on desk of Pentagon executive: This project is so secret even yours truly doesn't know what he's doing.

5 Blind-drunk hack thrust stick shift into third, went awry, struck oak. Left arm sports splint.

6 New play had wacky plot; angel made big bucks. Cast party cost plenty, but backer paid proudly.

7 Is it true that one Catskills resort hotel displays a sign reading "George Washington schlepped here"?

8 Apocryphal opus about opulently awarded over-achieving undergraduate athlete: *The Heisman Cometh.*

9 Fancy fine furniture from fascinating foreign factories furnished favorite French flat.

10 Banks are an almost irresistible attraction for that element of our society which seeks unearned money.

11 Irregular quadrilateral and convex polygon vex math whiz: quiz questions put him in "bad shape."

12 I'm not a very good driver ... once I tried making a U-turn and wound up spelling antidisestablishmentarianism.

13 Although I still have a photographic memory, the film provided nowadays is of questionable quality!

14 Crafty medic found optimal way to get second opinion about surgery for patients: simply ask their bank.

15 Easily piqued film review board objects to policeman thwacking headstrong roughnecks. Result: "R."

16 Sign in front window of plush midtown Manhattan café proclaims, "Our enclosed garden is now open."

17 Nietzsche, Freud combine considerable talent, coauthor philosophicopsychological tome.

18 Vegetarian group pickets famed fried chicken franchise with T-shirts saying "we do chicken rights."

19 Philanthropist named Deadman left hospital huge sum provided it would rename itself after him. Quandary!

20 Youth rode four-wheelers with much joy but would invariably balk at using riding lawn mower.

21 Bushmen outline perilous veldt hunt, claim lionskin loincloths help solve camouflage problem.

22 Himalayan mountain cobbler estimated Abominable Snowman wears extra-large shoe: size twenty EEE.

23 She put off dieting for years but began one when her cucumber tattoos became watermelon-sized.

24 Leave March first after large beach party. Ocean liner jaunt takes seven weeks. Cable money.

25 Humongous, coverall-clad, bankrupt archduke stumbled over dark, bald dwarf, swore profusely.

26 Mendacious fashion plate pushed nature-made fabric. Furtive closet search betrays own polyesterification.

27 Five gourmands in multi-ethnic bistro wolf down cold borscht, coq au vin, pear strudel, tequila nightcap.

28 Westminster Abbey Handel statue hasn't his ear. Sculptor felt his was ugly, carved that of some young lady.

29 Vapid vicar vaguely views viper. Vocal vixen violates verdant-hued vineyard. Voyeur vaporizes varmints.

30 Army rations delight soldier: garlicky escargot, sugared mangoes, almond polenta comprise typical menu.

31 Silver platter, tarnished by years of exposure, gets new life by energetic use of elbow grease.

32 Frabjous folk-rocker struck it rich, lived it up in fat city fourplex, next had trip to fat farm.

33 Roman pleb rubs oil lamp; two genii come out, grant triple wish: brioche, chariot, box seat for clown act.

34 This is an ordinary nglish sntnc, but a crtain lttr of th alphabt has bn omittd vry tim it appars.

35 Among carbonated drinks, R.C. Cola and Dr Pepper are by far the most likely to come out your nose.

36 Brightly garbed torero abhors miniskirts, claims arena male fans watch them, not him and bull.

37 Criticism is something that you can easily avoid ... by doing nothing, saying nothing, and being nothing.

38 Graceful girl dances around stage during second act, then leaps into arms of hero while whole house claps.

39 Youngster spent hours scaling monkey bars. Fond adult foresaw Olympic gymnastic triumph next century.

40 Using sixty-four kilobyte kludge, hacker debugs exotic software, finds wrong baud rate caused glitch.

41 Pterodactyls chomped hyracoids; koalas munch eucalypti; Yuppies gnaw quiche; we slurp crab gumbo.

42 By Middle-Eastern thinkers, the banana, not the apple, has been widely held to be the forbidden fruit.

43 As my pastor always told me, freedom from incrustations of grime is contiguous to rectitude.

44 Chutzpah: Youth, only child, offs both his parents, pleads own case, begs court for mercy toward solitary orphan.

45 Lemony, leafy cilantro flavors many tropical drinks and other savory comestible confections.

46 I'm in favor of eliminating air pollution: they should take the Home Shopping Network off the air!

47 Prof often gave pop quizzes without qualms but could not find guts to pop question to inamorata.

48 Pierre de Beaumarchais postulated: "It is not necessary to understand things in order to argue about them."

49 Hating people can be like burning down your own house to get rid of a rat, Harry Emerson Fosdick reminds us.

50 Around and about our playgrounds, children gaily prance, listen for ice cream truck, want some, scream.

51 Girl drops from blue, wears ruby flats for trip down golden road toward leaf-hued city. Movie fans tickled pink.

52 Adolphe Sax invented the saxophone, patenting this musical instrument in the eighteen-forties.

53 Old kibbutznik kept kosher. Lazy goyish au pair brought mixed fleishig, milchig brunch. Faux pas!

54 Short month comes after first month: forty-eight hours short of thirty days normal month quota.

55 Unsightly unicyclist, unworldly unicorn, uncouth ufologist unlock upright box using unciform crowbar.

56 Did you hear about the dyslexic agnostic who had insomnia? He'd lie awake at night wondering if there was a dog.

57 Klutzy chefs fix lumpy chow, oversalt schnitzel, microwave spumoni. Picky punk turns anorexic.

58 Begin your day right with fruit juice, bran flakes. Aerobics get heart thumping. When done, climb back into bed.

59 Jinxed bloke lost zingy Scrabble game to foxy champ (word wizard). Left upon his rack: just V and Q tiles.

60 American army, ashamed after defeat by Vietnamese bullies, picked on foes their own size: Grenada and Panama.

61 Rilke wrote: "Love consists in this, that two solitudes protect and touch and greet each other."

62 Sky-clad water-skier, muscle-bound half-wit, low-life two-timer, left-wing yes-man double-date.

63 According to the Vatican, out of every thousand people who seek an exorcist, only five are really possessed.

64 Old Portuguese proverb asserts: "Visits always give pleasure—if not the arrival, the departure."

65 Hawk swoops through museum window, grabs painting, gets nabbed by gendarme. A fowl and his Monet are soon parted.

66 Poison ivy, oak, sumac contain urushiol, the oil responsible for skin rash plus itch plus blisters.

67 Buoyant groupies lip-synch words watching bluesman, keyboardist wanly pluck hick melody.

68 Item in the new I. Magnin catalog: "Washed silk work shirt for the working class. One hundred twenty dollars."

69 Your philosophy is revealed by your bumper stickers, or lack thereof. In other words, your rear end is you.

70 Experimental concept event combines rock concert with cooking demo. Marquee reads: "Madonna and Child."

71 Unrest at zoo: Bear badgers emu. Puma hounds gnu. Kiwi ducks hawk. Lynx bugs okapi. Keeper goes cuckoo.

72 Icebox raider in full-length chintz muumuu trips over hem during impromptu foray, sustaining coccyx injury.

73 Samantha, Muffin rate high on latest listing of names for feline females; Tiger, Rocky prove popular for males.

74 Children may be served first at picnics in the hope that they will then go play in the poison ivy. —Miss Manners

75 Oh my! Is an FM DJ of DC to ax LP? Is CD to be "it"? No go! He: "If it is up to me ... by me, LP is OK as is!" So be it.

76 Simon (Neil) says: There are two rules in the universe: the law of gravity, and everybody likes Italian food.

77 Man's inhumanity to our environment is causing nature to retaliate in horrendous, cataclysmic ways.

78 How many cops does it take to change a bulb? Four: one to screw it in and three to protect bystanders.

79 Mother Teresa, Sibyl form charitable group together, establishing first nun-prophet organization.

80 Although the trough beneath the bough had been bought to ease the drought, it was tough when we found it empty.

81 Frustrated composer of *Carmen* finds he will never have time to finish famous opera since he is forever Bizet.

82 User-friendly lexicons display dog-ears, grime, stray pages, many pencil marks; covers unravel.

83 Space shipwreck brought alien amid Mardi Gras festival. Weird humanoid visage normal among group.

84 Dracula was summoned to the hospital just last Tuesday: his physician wanted a blood count.

85 The faithful hermetists await the light, ripe for chelaship, ringroundabout him. —from James Joyce's *Ulysses*

86 Minute backfield tackle views pachyderm-like rival guard lumbering onward, opts for pseudo-faint.

87 How to sculpt a camel statue: take one huge slab of marble and chip away all the parts that don't look like a camel.

88 Ads tout grocers' advantages over superstores: better food, fewer additives, lower prices, no indigestion.

89 Shrimp-pink bungalow, plastic flamingo, fuchsia bush, salmon patio tiles give house-hunter queasy stomach.

90 Quoting the White Queen: "Sometimes I've believed as many as six impossible things before breakfast."

91 An earth with one dog for each lap, hay for each loft, one poet for each ray of dawn, isn't a bore for man.

92 Modern produce market takes credit cards for payment. Each customer now asked "paper or plastic?" twice.

93 Night wind rejuvenates tropical island. Soft laughter over vibrant drumbeat wafts thru calm dream.

94 Hungry teen creates weird pizza snack with leftover mozzarella, bologna, gherkins, zucchini, and fudge sauce.

95 Radioactive waste, smog, acid rain, garbage, fluorocarbons, etcetera: gross national products.

96 Whenever the Blue Jays, Cardinals, and Orioles play, an aviary could be the ballpark of choice.

97 The colors green, yellow, and blue may be synonyms for inexperienced, cowardly, and melancholy, respectively.

98 Obstetrician, delivering four babies on September second, mused, "This is not the real meaning of Labor Day."

99 Wily moneygrubbing fraud bilks naive townsfolk. Posse nabs scalawag after hubbub. Crowd enjoys lynch party.

100 If you have seven piñons in one hand and eight in the other, what do you have? A difference of a piñon.

101 One of the many similar pieces of advice to vaudevillians: "Never follow a banjo act with a banjo act." —Herbert Boyer

102 Recent depressed real-estate market might depress even those most zealous and energetic Realtors.

103 Herpetologist meets, quickly weds mortician. Their bathroom towels are embroidered with "hiss" and "hearse."

104 Upscale chef flavored arugula, radicchio salad using balsamic vinegar, Dijon mustard. Yuppies relish dish.

105 Clothier, bandleader Harold Fox coined "zoot suit" for thigh-length jacket, extra wide shoulders, peg pants.

106 Awkward bathtub reading: outsize hardcover whodunit. Hefty volume mysteriously induces wrist fatigue.

107 Novel bumper sticker, using only Braille writing, reads, "If you can read this, you are up too close."

108 "If crime fighters fight crime, and fire fighters fight fires, what do 'freedom fighters' fight?" –George Carlin

109 Icy thruway asphalt during January throws jackknifing semi onto median strip. Trucker unhurt.

110 Teacher to class of three-year-olds: "If yesterday was Wednesday, what is today?" Response: "Tomorrow!"

111 My favorite holidays? Thanksgiving because our whole family is home, and Christmas because they aren't.

112 Artsy maestri remix blah waltz with sexy disco tempo, submit demo tape, spawn zingy superhit, make megabucks.

113 By age fifteen, today's child has witnessed some thirteen thousand five hundred killings on television.

114 Said bald-headed man when someone poked fun at him: "God made some heads perfect. On others, He put hair."

115 "... back to my little grass shack in Kealakekua, Hawaii, where the humuhumunukunukuapuaa go swimming by."

116 Logarithms, integrals, group theory confuse freshman verbalist. Educators swiftly diagnose innumeracy.

117 Pennsylvania's founder had uncles whose wives sold low-priced tarts. Folks loved the pie rates of Penn's aunts.

118 Sports car slows as owner eyes bumper sticker on station wagon ahead: "Pass with caution: Driver chews tobacco."

119 Chortling mockingly, unethical scoundrel contrived grandiose pseudonym: "Marvelous miscreant."

120 The absentminded professor poured syrup on his crossword puzzle and went crazy solving his waffle.

121 Exhausted chameleon succumbs to heart attack while attempting to traverse multicolored plaid carpet.

122 When asked "How's the weather up there?" Wilt Chamberlain spilled drink on questioner, replied, "Raining."

123 If disheveled when messy, are we "heveled" when neat? If discreet when cautious, are we, if foolhardy, "creet"?

124 All the world's a stage and many of us are stagehands, but our politicians tell us there are still a lot of hams.

125 "Choir": Any other dictionary word comprising five or more letters which can be encrypted by its homonym?

126 Joseph asked the innkeeper for lodging, but was told "Rooms? You must be kidding! It's Christmas Eve."

127 Foxy girl kept steady boyfriend six months, thus: gave him one argyle sock for June birthday, other at Yule.

128 Never mind which one came first. How is it an egg is chock-full of cholesterol, but the resulting chicken isn't?

129 Examine Oreo cookie and you find twelve flowers, each with four petals stamped on each side.

130 Medic warns measly kid against scratching. Intolerably itchy tot, making rash decision, disobeys. Relief!

131 ... strange, elusive things, and no man may permanently stick them on pins or mount them in glass cases. —Steinbeck

132 News from the kitsch front: pink plastic flamingos now outnumber real, live flamingos seven hundred to one.

133 Wm. S. Gilbert's method of avoiding giving a compliment for a bad performance: "My dear chap! Good isn't the word!"

134 Nintendo has replaced anagrams as favorite pastime of person seeking solo amusement on winter evenings.

135 Newest nuclear threat to our world may come, not from bombs, but from unsafe, aging power plants.

136 "Material goods can blunt your perception of greater things." —William Least Heat Moon in *Blue Highways*

137 Said the hostess, who was poor cook, as she served late meal, "Hope it is true that hunger is the best seasoning."

138 Rhodesian ridgebacks: powerful African dogs with singular crest of wrong-way hair along spine.

139 Silly old riddle: if a herring and a half costs a cent and a half, what does a boatload come to? Answer: the dock.

140 Notice in Austrian ski lodge: "Not to perambulate the corridors in the hours of repose in the boots of ascension."

141 Inscrutable clergywoman preachingly outwrangled disgraceful mustachioed profligates.

142 Upon being offered a hot drink, A. Lincoln replied, "If this is tea, I'll take coffee. If this is coffee, I pass."

143 Flaky pygmy cannibal duo sees author Philip pickpocketing; irked, find solution: two mini kooks boil dip Roth.

144 Novice launderer soaks kumquat juice stain in liquid bleach, leaving fuchsia skirt streaky.

145 Halfback Duane Thomas on the Super Bowl: "If this is the ultimate game, why are they playing it again next year?"

146 "Idealism increases in direct proportion to one's distance from the problem." —writings of John Galsworthy

147 Pudgy cur not given yule brunch leftovers of steak, congealed bacon fat. ('Twas denied beef or grease mass.)

148 Grandpa joined the dancing class; Grandma said they might teach his old dogs some new tricks.

149 Linz holiday: eat schnitzel and hear saxhorn prodigy playing scherzo from Wolfgang Mozart's Sixth.

150 New item for weight watchers has plankton for its basis. Its creator must have known zilch about whales.

151 Old Mrs. Hub dug in the ice box to get her pet dog an os; but woe! She saw zip (not one ort or bit), so Rex, sad cur, had nil.

152 Seeing lumps of earth, guy stuffs tiny wood scraps at an angle into each—thus, "every clod has a sliver leaning."

153 Ditzy clerk found jam blocking balky Xerox machine. Unfazed copyist just stuck zwieback into input tray.

154 The income tax return is like a girdle: if you put the wrong figure in you might be pinched. —Anonymous

155 "As the influence of religion declines, the social importance of art increases." –Aldous Huxley

156 Oh no! My k yboard has difficulty printing this most common charact r. What should I do?

157 Busy, bungling butcher backs into his beef-grinding machine and gets a little behind in his work.

158 Dazzlingly brilliant Brazilian emeralds contrast prettily with milky iridescence of New Mexican opals.

159 Heard about the classy pregnant sheep who enjoys riding on Indian elephants? Well, that's a fine howdah ewe due!

160 Comedy club wag hit bungalow town, joking about pink lawn flamingoes. Crowd hissed kitsch shtick.

161 You know you're middle-aged when you hear "snap, crackle, and pop" before you get to the breakfast table.

162 The "silly" question, to quote Whitehead, may be our "first intimation of some totally new development."

163 Pancho, waxing nostalgic about lost orangey-yellow sombrero, pules to pard, "I loved my hat in saffron, Cisco."

164 Olympic skier Picabo Street gave large gift to her local hospital. They now have the Picabo I.C.U.

165 Excess jam moves out into schoolkid's lunch box and over carrot sticks after sandwich squushed by thermos.

166 Quizzical Aztec violinist just requested explanation regarding overzealous jazz saxophonist.

167 Muchacha gulps frijol, nacho, fajita, much tequila. Next day, stomachache gone, girl wants taco.

168 We are all sculptors and painters, and our material is our own flesh and blood and bones. –Thoreau

169 Twins turn four; family has eighty kids over. Birthday bash result: neighbors phone police, who wolf down cake.

170 Banjo duo rocks bayou juke joint with crazy zydeco polka, while Cajun folk enjoy chunky okra gumbo.

171 It is very helpful to read encrypted puzzles aloud; it may be the best response to telephone salespersons.

172 Bodybuilding myth: muscly hunk kicks sand at skinny punk; scrag pumps iron, decks unlucky chump.

173 Temperamental tapir fled zoological park following run-in with wild wapiti, zany zebra and ungracious gnu.

174 TV audience, after thirty-second commercial about coffee-drinking couple, gets quite bored.

175 Fearless forest fire fighters frequently found frightened fauna fleeing from flickering flames.

176 Frantic forensics expert finds ancient DNA evidence exonerates simian in Rue Morgue homicides.

177 Deft bowl game punt came down near five yard line. Next play: huge gain made when back flew over left side.

178 Shy kid had pet bug. Lad put ant out for air and sun but sly jay ate wee pal. Boy now has fat cat who may get jay one day.

179 Novice squash player broke racket after losing match. Modest victor ("lucky today") quietly left court.

180 Ugly duckling limps to nearby stream for quick slug of water. Fox watches one minute, lunges at dumb bird.

181 Licentious lothario left lavish lunch with luscious leading lady when livid lover lumbered into lobby.

182 Man moves dangerously into oncoming traffic, overtaking other motorists. Wife dreads his untimely passing.

183 Come for birthday banquet! Feast upon shrimp bisque, lobster thermidor, Asti Spumanti. RSVP.

184 Bashful barefoot beau picks daisy. Yours truly gives inamorata lovely chrysanthemum instead.

185 The avaricious carpenter hoped to save tax money by working under the table, but in the end he got nailed.

186 You spot orca in arctic waters. Before you can cry, "ichthyophagous cetacean!" someone else yells, "thar she blows!"

187 Island inventor unveils Aruba scuba tuba, good down to twenty meters or twenty hertz, whichever comes first.

188 Boy hears chap claim "tempus fugit," takes alarm, throws clock from chimney top, watches result.

189 Junior-high teacher jury-rigged jungle gym for juveniles. Juggling, jump rope, jujitsu also offered.

190 Lesson concerning Pavlovian experiments gets interrupted when school lunch bell rings.

191 Alert Hindu finds fault with phony Vishnu priest, lays fraud charge. Two cops prove pseudo clergyman guilty.

192 Retired butcher and Shakespeare lover rewrites Pooh classic, changing Piglet into Hamlet.

193 Personnel manager dismissed hopeful applicant after eying curriculum vitae written with mauve crayon.

194 "Khadafy"? "Qaddafi"? Maybe "Gadhafi"? Libyan dictator may be strongman, but strong speller he ain't.

195 In France, U.S. hoofer's washer goes on blink; does laundry in river. Folks hear guy warble, "I'm wringin' in the Seine ..."

196 Clumsy tumblers destroy trampoline cable joist when they try backflip after zany pole vault jump.

197 Yes, I know the commonest first and last names on earth, but how many people have you met named Mohammed Chang?

198 Bakery abandoned its new donut line after finding it couldn't make enough dough to avoid going in the hole.

199 Bistro prix fixe menu: quiche, veal farci. Plat du jour: coq au vin. (Jumbo pâté de foie gras six francs extra.)

200 Savvy, fickle wife juxtaposes quirky jigsaw puzzle pieces ambidextrously by using unique southpaw method.

201 Cynical counsel, creative defense, blatant misconduct, lying witnesses, make courtroom home of the whopper.

202 French philosopher in a bar was asked, "Your usual, M. Descartes?" "I think not," he answered—and disappeared!

203 "Personal waterloo" foreseen? Distance yourself, avoiding possible disaster. Strategy prevents calamity.

204 Sympathetic puzzle constructor created palindromes specifically for dyslexic solvers.

205 As comedian George Carlin points out, "The day after tomorrow is the third day of the rest of your life."

206 Dyspeptic campaign ads urge disgruntled voters to heave bathwater, baby notwithstanding.

207 Hulking, ghostly saucer left beyond grayish sky. Scornful kid, brought back after abduction, flinched.

208 "Ultra" ranks above "extra." "Jumbo" equals "super large." "King-size" comes midway after "big" and afore "giant." How peachy!

209 Cannibal duo touring U.S.A. list favorite chow here: elbow macaroni, headcheese, ladyfingers, and navel oranges.

210 Shy gent gets nervous reaction around any syringe. When donating B negative, chap laughs whole way to bank.

211 During lecture, geometry prof explains construction methods Noah used, bemusing students with ark tangent.

212 Jack Kemp says, "Football was excellent preparation for politics. I'd already been booed and hanged in effigy."

213 Unabomber suspect spotted in crude Montana shack, suffering from Rocky Mountain cabin fever.

214 Wealthy formula-car owner made bankruptcy claim after urban grand prix stock market crash.

215 Pioneer Six, launched into solar orbit many years back, continues broadcasting sixteen-bit-per-second info.

216 Poor Queen Elizabeth. She must feel that she has suffered more than her share of bad heir days.

217 Schizo maestro directs waltz melody, rhumba rhythm, scherzo tempo. Rhapsody wins standing O.

218 Impatient Rapunzel grows bored with dazzled princes climbing tresses: cuts her hair and her losses.

219 Vegetarian spider invited frightened fly into parlor; was only evening teams for evening of charades.

220 Experts in aerodynamics, hydraulics, pyrotechnics, and geology will find ... they are never out of their element.

221 Among zany shipwreck heptad, prof figures why wacky gizmos run; kind, klutzy first-mate clown could mug.

222 For exercise, one lazy fellow jogged his memory, jumped to conclusions, and let his imagination run wild.

223 When asked the first thing he'd do if elected mayor of New York, William Buckley replied, "I'd demand a recount."

224 New surgeon entering OR slips on freshly-waxed floor, breaks upper arm. (Not laughing about humerus situation.)

225 New religious order sought to convert spokesman. Group folded upon failing to turn prophet.

226 Comedic actor Danny authors laudatory biography of laid-back French painter. (It's Kaye's *Hurrah, Seurat!*)

227 Men are from Mars, women, from Venus; we are here on Earth. This being so, who gets to drive our Saturn today?

228 Twin brides wore palest pastel gowns with pleats. Flower girl (bitsy sprite) spread petals. Priest rued debris.

229 No wonder Clinton has hearing trouble! In college, amid so much loud music, he should have practiced safe sax.

230 Hero encounters archfoe with switchblade. Eightscore friendly men help ambush angry bad guy.

231 Half your diet should comprise grains. Today make pilaf from brown rice, barley. Also worth trying: polenta.

232 Campers, dolphins enjoy new forest-plus-sea sanctuary. Safety zone is haven to all in tents, and porpoises.

233 DNA? Undergraduate biology newsletter claims it might be short for National Dyslexics Association.

234 Hemidemisemiquaver is sixty-fourth note in music. Hendecasyllable is metrical line of eleven syllables.

235 Daft trio (ugly diva, nude wino, glib yogi) hire ecru limo, tour isle. They jump into pond, swim, exit, whiz home damp.

236 Advice from horoscope proves faulty when woman finds unfiled tax return rather than true love.

237 Brothers at an English monastery enjoyed their Friday meal cooked up by the chip monk and fish friar.

238 Caucasian pundit answered lonely hearts ad by yachtswoman. After awful date, SWM swami swam away posthaste.

239 Worried owner notices treed calico. While fireman struggles through branches, feline bounds down ladder.

240 Competing local firms Kodak and Xerox design fast document copiers. Many pages per minute zip from machines.

241 In my recurring dream, I looked like a tepee and then a wigwam. My psychiatrist judged I was just two tents.

242 Intro: Olympian cyborg hijacks Boeing jet. Climax: jury box answer—adieu for life. Parole? Ixnay.

243 Despite the high cost of living, we cannot have failed to notice how it still remains so popular.

244 Common chimpanzee conservation efforts threatened despite improved organization of Ugandan patrols.

245 Late "Hokey Pokey" composer gave undertaker bad time with coffin. He put his left foot in ... but you know the rest.

246 Alone among aborigines, Aleuts argue, albeit amiably, against appraising ancient apparel artistically.

247 Any petrologist keeping obsidian or gneiss specimens in the bathroom must have rocks in his head.

248 Penultimate scene: scarecrow awarded long-awaited brain—immediately misquotes Pythagorean theorem.

249 Blockhead birdhouse inspector oversaw crumbling metalwork. Stricken goldfinch nervously squawked.

250 Famous pianists often quip that Mozart is too easy for amateurs and too difficult for professionals.

251 Philosophers who believe change is inevitable have seldom had to deal with vending machines.

252 Yes, Virginia, Santa Claus definitely exists—worldwide. Just examine January credit card statements.

253 Ambidextrously adept gymnast (albeit bankrupt) bought customized trampoline. Predictably, check bounced.

254 In the land of the blind, I expect the one-eyed man would be branded as a witch and burned at the stake.

255 Nearsighted man seeking optometrist misreads sign, consults optimist, who prescribes rose-colored glasses.

256 Today they are not referred to as deceased but as electroencephalographically challenged.

257 Icosahedrons sport twenty triangular sides, whereas dodecahedrons feature twelve, each pentagonal.

258 Can anyone explain to me why hot dogs are most often sold in packages of ten and buns in packages of eight?

259 Inept chef spoiled lunch with doughy rye buns, stringy pork, tough piecrust, sour milk. Diner gulped Tums.

260 Exquisite Queen Anne's lace accents lovely floral bouquet elegantly displayed on mahogany chiffonier.

261 Spendthrift partner in jointly-held bank account might rightfully argue she cannot afford a check-mate!

262 Vain son of carpenter consistently refuses to use stud finder, claiming, "Too much interference."

263 Talking to my houseplants did not help them grow—they all withered when asked to start paying rent.

264 The judge hoped to play on the city workers' baseball team but was kept on the bench for refusing to steal bases.

265 Veterinarian, suddenly called away during office hours, left sign saying, "Back shortly. Sit. Stay."

266 Paganini practiced pianissimo performance; perhaps pickiness prompted pizzicato plucking.

267 Xerox and Wurlitzer have potential merger in offing. New company will make reproductive organs.

268 Juicy whodunit kept show watcher aquiver until story climax, when Jane Marple caught culprit.

269 Polish viola virtuoso encounters paparazzi while skiing. European maestro graciously acquiesces.

270 Building tough cryptograms from familiar words with conventional syntax presents vexatious obstacles.

271 Elvis sighted on grammarians' planet, singing "Love Me Tenderly" and "You Aren't Anything but a Hound Dog."

272 Car Talk guys chose radio show moniker after NPR nixed previous name idea: "All Dings Considered."

273 The mother who caught her young deaf son swearing punished him by washing his hands with soap.

274 Inept Inspector Clouseau hunts stolen pink gem, wreaks havoc while sneaking around pantherlike.

275 Macintosh owner chomped crisp McIntosh while updating central file. Core problem: sticky keyboard.

276 Occasional skiing keeps chubby middle-aged runners really supple, summer-school official suggests.

277 New vinyl Streisand disc deepens angst among record clerks. They must learn to deal with repressed "Feelings."

278 When you cross collies with Lhasa apsos, you get collapsos, dogs that fold up for easy transport.

279 "Conductor, does this train stay long at your next stop?" "Only four minutes: two to two to two two."

280 Oxford tabloid headline: "Spear found in Naugahyde sofa; ex-PM suspect!" Regis wonders, "Is Thatcher vinyl-lancer?"

281 Perhaps Signor Pavarotti, singer par excellence, could perform some popular arias for his avid audience?

282 Eskimo skier in downhill slalom got in the way of other skiers and was just an obstacle Aleutian.

283 Churchill viewed prohibition of preposition-ending sentences as "one rule up with which we should not put."

284 Tabloid predicts earth will be sucked into black hole in six months, yet invites two-year subscriptions.

285 Stealing ideas from one person is called plagiarism. Stealing from many is known as research.

286 Headline writer must have had fun composing this actual one: "Escaped leopard believed spotted."

287 Given that death and taxes are certain, we should be extremely grateful that only one is an annual event!

288 Boustrophedonic writing works out like gnignahc enil etanretla hcae htiw siht its direction.

289 Flea market finds: puce parka, ecru dashiki, lavender lei, buff bolero, suede sombrero—plus tacky pink flamingo.

290 Kindergarten-group play lead had seraphic smile, strong yen for spotlight. Removal from stage entailed force.

291 Sign in Yugoslavian hotel: "The flattening of underwear with pleasure is the job of the chambermaid."

292 Piqued coquet frequently quaffed quarts of liquor (tequila daiquiris), quickly acquiring tranquility.

293 "Satire is a sort of glass, wherein beholders do generally discover everybody's face but their own." —J. Swift

294 Smurfs, Gummi Bears, Chipmunks: such Saturday fare unfailingly rouses chuckling children everywhere.

295 Lin Yutang astutely observed: "When small men begin to cast big shadows, it means the sun is about to set."

296 Armani-clad, Gucci-shod, diet-conscious battle-ax deep-sixes honey-coated Alpha-Bits. Preteen-ager long-faced.

297 Blues (Boardwalk, Park Place) cost most, but oranges (New York Ave., for one) net most (since landed on most often).

298 Inquiry from this ermine: "Can anyone determine why folks of note can wear my coat, yet say to me 'you vermin'?"

299 Their furniture went back to Louis XIV because they could not pay Louis for it by the thirteenth.

300 Mustachioed keyboardist played problematic rhapsody con amore. Plaudits delight whiskery piano whiz.

Answers: Cunning Mind-Bending Puzzles

1 $4^4 + 44 = 300$

2   It would appear in column B. Divide by 7 whatever number you wish to place, and see what the remainder is. If the remainder is 1, the number goes in column A; if the remainder is 2, the number goes in column B; and so on. (If the remainder is zero, however, the number goes in column G.)

3   Audrey will reach the destination first. Suppose they cover 12 miles, both walking at a rate of 2 miles per hour and running at a rate of 6 miles per hour. Use the formula $rt = d$ (rate $\times$ time = distance) to find each person's time.

Nancy (walks half the distance and runs half the distance):

$$2t = 6 \text{ mi., so } t = 3 \text{ hrs. walking}$$
$$6t = 6 \text{ mi., so } t = \underline{1 \text{ hr. running}}$$
$$t = 4 \text{ hours total time}$$

Audrey (walks half the time and runs half the time):

$$2(\tfrac{1}{2}t) + 6(\tfrac{1}{2}t) = 12 \text{ mi.}$$
$$t + 3t = 12$$
$$4t = 12$$
$$t = 3 \text{ hours total time}$$

4   Each reads the same when held upside down.

5   Lead by example.

6   Simply add the sum of the two digits in any number to the sum of the two digits in the adjacent number to get the corresponding number in the row below. For example:

$$8 + 9 \ (89) \text{ and } 5 + 3 \ (53) = 25$$
$$5 + 3 \ (53) \text{ and } 1 + 7 \ (17) = 16$$

To find the missing number, add:

$$1 + 6 \ (16) \text{ and } 1 + 7 \ (17) = 15$$

7   His younger daughter received more—$4,000 more—than the older daughter. One way to solve this is to set up an equation that represents who received what:

$$x = \frac{1}{3}x + \frac{1}{5}x + \frac{1}{6}x + 9,000$$

$$x = \frac{10}{30}x + \frac{6}{30}x + \frac{5}{30}x + 9,000$$

$$x = \frac{21}{30}x + 9,000$$

Multiplying both sides of the equation by $\frac{30}{9}$, we get

$$\frac{30}{9}x = \frac{21}{9}x + \frac{270,000}{9}$$

$$\frac{30}{9}x - \frac{21}{9}x = 30,000$$

$$x = 30,000$$

Then

$$\frac{1}{3}x = \$10,000 \text{ (wife)}$$

$$\frac{1}{5}x = \$6,000 \text{ (son)}$$

$$\frac{1}{6}x = \$5,000 \text{ (older daughter)}$$

8   The missing number is 4. Simply add the first and second rows together to get the third row, like this:

$$
\begin{array}{r}
65,927 \\
14,354 \\
\hline
80,281
\end{array}
$$

9   If you know that 2:17 is the correct time, find the difference, positive or negative, of the other clocks:

clock 1	2:15	−2
clock 2	2:35	+18
clock 3	2:00	−17
clock 4	2:23	+6
clock 5	2:17	0
5 clocks		5 minutes

As a group, the clocks average 1 minute fast.

10 The answer is $\dfrac{1}{12}$. If each fraction is converted into to twelvths, the series looks like this:

$$\frac{8}{12} \quad \frac{7}{12} \quad \frac{6}{12} \quad \frac{5}{12} \quad \frac{4}{12} \quad \frac{3}{12} \quad \frac{2}{12} \quad \mathbf{\frac{1}{12}}$$

11 Cheaper by the dozen

12 Pages 6, 19, and 20 are also missing. Newspapers are printed double sided, two pages to a sheet. The first and second pages are attached to the second-to-last and last pages—in this case, pages 23 and 24. The rest of the pages are attached as follows:

$$\begin{aligned}
&1\text{–}2 \text{ with } 23\text{–}24 \\
&3\text{–}4 \text{ with } 21\text{–}22 \\
&5\text{–}6 \text{ with } 19\text{–}20 \\
&7\text{–}8 \text{ with } 17\text{–}18 \\
&9\text{–}10 \text{ with } 15\text{–}16 \\
&11\text{–}12 \text{ with } 13\text{–}14
\end{aligned}$$

13 The value of c is 14. To solve the problem, set up the following equations:

$$\begin{aligned}
(1) \; & a + b = 13 \\
(2) \; & b + c = 22 \\
(3) \; & a + c = 19
\end{aligned}$$

Solve for b in equation (1):

$$b = 13 - a$$

Substitute this into equation (2):

$$\begin{aligned}
13 - a + c &= 22 \\
-a + c &= 9
\end{aligned}$$

Then combine equations (2) and (3) and solve for c:

$$\begin{aligned}
-a + c &= 9 \\
\underline{a + c} &= \underline{19} \\
2c &= 28 \\
c &= 14
\end{aligned}$$

14 Rotate the first square 90 degrees to the right to obtain the second square.

	X	
X		
		X

15

MOVE
MORE
MARE
BARE
BARK

16 Sarah is the second oldest; Liz is the oldest.

17 The missing number is 14. The first and last numbers added together make 19, as do the second number and the next-to-last number. Moving toward the middle in this fashion, each successive pair of numbers adds up to 19.

18 Broken promise

19 There are 23 triangles.

20 2^{73} is larger by a long way.

21 You are out of touch.

22 e. $\dfrac{1}{10\sqrt{10}}$

23 Carrot juice (The symbol before "juice" is called a "caret.")

24 The chances are 1 in 5. The possibilities are:

$$Blue_1, Blue_2$$
$$Blue_1, Green$$
$$Blue_1, Yellow$$
$$Blue_2, Green$$
$$Blue_2, Yellow$$

25 Yardstick

26 $17\frac{1}{3}$ lbs. Calculate the answer as follows:

$$1) A + B = 50 \text{ lbs.}$$
$$\text{and } 2) \$8A + \$5B = 50 \times \$6$$

Then, multiply the first equation by −5, so:

$$-5A - 5B = -250$$

Next, combine with equation 2:

$$\$8A + \$5B = \$300$$
$$\underline{-5A - 5B = -250}$$
$$3A = 50$$
$$A = 17\frac{1}{3} \text{ lbs.}$$

27 Your cup runneth over.

28 The correct answer is 20. Don't forget that the number 33 has two threes.

29 Place "end" at the beginning of each word:

endear
endless
endanger

30 The answer is 3.

$$\frac{3}{4} \times \frac{1}{2} \times 16 = \frac{48}{8} = 6$$
$$\frac{1}{2} \times 6 = 3; 6 - 3 = 3$$

31 It will take 63 moves. For any number of discs n, the number of moves can be found by $2^n - 1$.

32   Here's a list of 15 words. Are they anywhere near the words you came up with?

> serve
> vice
> rice
> ice
> see
> seer
> veer
> sieve
> eve
> rise
> ever
> sever
> cerise
> rive
> verse

33   The last number is 625. Subtract each individual digit in the numbers from 10 to crack the code.

34   A single discount of 12 percent is greater.

$$12\% \times 100 = 12.00$$
$$\text{then}$$
$$6\% \times 100 = 6.00$$
$$100 - 6 = 94$$
$$6\% \times 94 = 5.64$$
$$6.00 + 5.64 = 11.64$$
$$12.00 \text{ is greater than } 11.64$$

35   Traffic congestion

36   The answer is zero!

37   YOU ARE A GENIUS. Move each of the letters in the puzzle back by three letters in the alphabet.

38   Draw a line from point 3 to point 12 and cut along the line to divide the figure. Turn the smaller figure upside down, then connect points 1 and 12 on the smaller figure with points 17 and 13, respectively, on the larger figure.

39   The next perfect number is 28 ($14 + 7 + 4 + 2 + 1 = 28$).

40   An upward turn in the economy

41   False. Some pibs may be rews, but it is not definite.

42   The first calculation is $\frac{1}{3} \times \frac{1}{3}$ of 12×12, or $\frac{1}{9}$ of 144, which equals 16. The second calculation is $(12 \div 3 \div 2)^3$, or $(\frac{4}{2})^3$, or 2 cubed, which is 8. The correct answer is the first calculation.

43   Milepost 900. To solve this problem, recall that rate $\times$ time = distance. Let x be the time it takes the Seneca Streamer to reach the milepost. Then:

$$60 \text{ mph} \times (x + 3) = 75 \text{ mph} \times x$$
$$60x + 180 = 75x$$
$$15x = 180$$
$$x = 12 \text{ hrs.}$$
$$75 \times 12 = 900 \text{ mi.}$$

44   The cyclist can take 96 ($4 \times 8 \times 3$) different routes.

45   The correct answer is (d). To solve this, we need to find

$$\frac{^3/_7}{^4/_9}$$

Invert the denominator and multiply:

$$^3/_7 \times {}^9/_4 = {}^{27}/_{28}$$

46   Making up for lost time

47   Because there are two sides to the coin, the chances are always one in two.

48   Place a decimal point between the two numbers to get 4.5.

49   The weight should be placed five feet from the fulcrum. First, calculate foot-pounds on the left side:

$$(5 \times 10) + (6 \times 5) = 80 \text{ ft.-lbs.}$$

The right side must equal the left side:

$$16x = 80$$
$$x = 5$$

50
P = horizontal
A = triangle
U = square
G = five
F = four
M = vertical

△ △ △ △ = PAF

MUFMAG =
□
□
□
□
△
△
△
△
△

51   Overhead projector

52   It is 212 degrees Fahrenheit at which water boils.

53   The missing letter is S. Each letter is the first letter of the preceding number when spelled out.

54
1. Unctuous	j. Oily
2. Riparian	b. Relating to the bank of a lake or river
3. Porcine	g. Relating to swine
4. Plexus	c. An interlacing network
5. Platitude	i. A trite remark
6. Cosmology	a. Study of the universe
7. Concatenation	h. A series connected by links
8. Alacrity	f. Briskness
9. Fecundate	e. Fertilize
10. Newel	d. An upright post

55   There must be at least 66 chocolates—the least common denominator for 3, 6, and 11.

56   E. There is one more circle and one less straight line inside each figure than the number of sides to the figure—except for figure E. This eight-sided figure is the odd one out, because it contains only six straight lines and only eight circles.

57   I returned on Tuesday. The day before tomorrow is today, Friday. The day after that is Saturday, and four days before Saturday is Tuesday.

58   I look up to you.

59 15 hours. The problem can be solved as follows:

$$7,500 - 150x = 4,500 + 50x$$
$$3,000 = 200x$$
$$x = 15$$

60 He is 32 years old. Here's the formula for the solution:

$$x + 4 = (x - 14) \times 2$$
$$x + 4 = 2x - 28$$
$$x = 32$$

61 D is the only figure that doesn't have a straight line dividing it in half.

62 Multiple personalities

63 The probability is 1 in 132,600.

$$\tfrac{1}{52} \times \tfrac{1}{51} \times \tfrac{1}{50} = \tfrac{1}{132,600}$$

64 It weighs approximately 1,700 pounds! One cubic foot of water weights 62.4 pounds; one cubic yard (27 cubic feet) of water weights 1,684.8 pounds.

65 It must win 90 percent of the games. This is probably best expressed as follows: If a team wins 60 percent of one-third of the games, it is the same as winning 20 percent of all the games. Therefore,

$$20x + \tfrac{2}{3}x = 80x$$
$$\tfrac{2}{3}x = 60x$$
$$2x = 180$$
$$x = 90$$

66 There are 50 stars on the United States flag.

67 It would be 4. The best way to solve this is by setting up proportions:

$$\frac{\tfrac{1}{2} \times 24}{8} = \frac{\tfrac{1}{3} \times 18}{x}$$
$$\tfrac{12}{8} = \tfrac{6}{x}$$
$$12x = 48$$
$$x = 4$$

68   Here's one way to solve the puzzle

PART
WART
WANT
WANE
WINE

69   Upper crust

70   The answer is 1,234,321.

71   Growing concern

72   Six.

$$6m = b$$
$$b = f$$
$$3f = y$$

We can find the number of bops in a yump by multiplying 8 3 3, or 24, and the number of murks in a yump by multiplying 24 times 6, or 144. So,

$$\frac{144 \text{ murks in a yump}}{24 \text{ bops in a yump}} = 6$$

73   The missing number is 448. In each triangle, multiply A times B and subtract 2 to get C.

74   It is 27 cubic yards—divide the number of cubic feet by 27 to get cubic yards.

75   A pear costs $.05. Here's one way to solve the problem. Letting p = pears and r = oranges, we have

(1) $3p + 4r = 0.39$
(2) $4p + 3r = 0.38$

Multiply equation (1) by 3 and equation (2) by −4:

$$9p + 12r = 1.17$$
$$-16p - 12r = -1.52$$
$$-7p = -0.35$$

Now we can solve for p:

$$-7p = -.35$$
$$p = .05$$

76   227. In each column, divide the top number by 3 to get the bottom number. Then, add 3 to the sum of the top and bottom numbers to get the middle number.

77 $\frac{1}{2}$ or $-\frac{1}{2}$

$$\frac{1}{5}x \times 4 \times x = \frac{1}{5}$$
$$\frac{4x^2}{5} = \frac{1}{5}$$
$$4x^2 = 1$$
$$x^2 = \frac{1}{4}$$
$$x = \frac{1}{2} \text{ or } -\frac{1}{2}$$

78   Think of it this way: If the leader receives twice as much as each of the others, that's the same as having seven members all earning the same amount, which would be $175 each. If the leader earns twice as much, he or she would therefore receive $350 per gig.

79   Double play

80   The missing number is 3. The numbers correspond to letters on the telephone keypad or dial.

81   Close encounters of the third kind

82   You would say *birta farn*. Notice that the adjectives follow the nouns.

klar = red
fol = shine
birta = apples
pirt = bicycles
farn = big
obirts = often

83 The numbers are 61, 62, and 63. To solve this, let x be the first number; then $x + 1$ is the second number and $x + 2$ is the third number. An equation can be set up as follows:

$$x + (x + 2) = 124$$
$$2x + 2 = 124$$
$$2x = 122$$
$$x = 61$$

84 It equals 26. The midpoint between 20 and 32 is 26, and the midpoint between 16_a and 36_a is 26.

$$16_a = 20$$
$$\downarrow \qquad \downarrow$$
$$\text{Midpoint: } 26_a \; + \; 26$$
$$\uparrow \qquad \uparrow$$
$$36_a = 32$$

85 Over and over again

86 The word is "geometric."

87

88 80 people. When $1/4$ of the guests left, $3/4$ of the people remained. When $2/5$ of them left, $3/5$ of $3/4$ remained. When $3/4$ of the remaining people left, $1/4$ of $3/5$ of $3/4$ remained ($9/80$). Since 9 people were left at the end:

$$(1/4 \times 3/5 \times 3/4)\, x = 9$$
$$9/80\, x = 9$$
$$x = 9 \times 80/9$$
$$x = 80$$

89 Blood is thicker than water.

90   1,000—one thousand!

91   Stop in the name of love.

92   The probability is $(1/2)^5$, or 1 in 32.

93   If you hold any of these letters up to a mirror; it will appear exactly the same as on the page.

94 $1/3$. In this series you take $1/2$ of the previous number, then $1/3$, $1/4$, $1/5$, and finally $1/6$. One-sixth of 2 equals $2/6$, or $1/3$.

95   Statement (2) is true.

96   A bird in the hand is worth two in the bush.

97   Six is the maximum number of lines.

98   The missing number is 14. Pick any piece of the pie and look directly opposite that piece: the larger of the two numbers is 3 times the smaller number minus 1.

99   The case costs $5; the binoculars cost $95. To solve this, let $b =$ the binoculars and $c =$ the case:

$$b + c = 100$$
$$b = 90 + c$$

Now substitute:

$$90 + c + c = 100$$
$$90 + 2c = 100$$
$$2c = 10$$
$$c = 5$$

100   Eight of the one-inch cubes have three blue sides—they were the corners of the four-inch cube.

101
FAST
FIST
MIST
MIND

102 It will take ten seconds. Because the first strike sounds at zero seconds, two strikes sound in one second, three strikes in two, etc.

103 Two eggs over easy

104 Sammy must be a girl.

105 I'd rather be in Philadelphia. – W. C. Fields

106 There are nine innings in a baseball game.

107 MAD

108 High hurdles

109 It might look something like this:

1, 2, 3, 4, 5, 6, 7, 8, 9, G, I, V, 10

(Almost any symbols could be used to represent the old numbers 10, 11, and 12.) Our old number 13 now becomes 10. If you choose to call this number 10, the new symbols would need new names, as would all the numbers that contain these two symbols.

110 There are 17 squares.

111 Frequency is measured in hertz.

112 Home stretch

113 Parliamentary

114 CMXLIV

115 The missing letter is R. Starting with the W in the first circle and moving counterclockwise in each successive circle, the words "What is the letter" are spelled out.

116 2,047

117 The pursuit of happiness

118 Head

119 Arc de Triomphe

120 The second number in each box is the first number cubed plus three, so the missing number is 30.

121 Your odds are 2 to 3:

$$\text{Odds in favor of an event} =$$
$$\frac{\text{Probability of favorable event}}{\text{Probability of unfavorable event}}$$
$$\frac{^2/_5}{^3/_5} = \frac{2}{3}$$

122 There are 42 triangles.

123 He went under the knife.

124 Bach. B-sharp and C are the same note.

Answers: Cryptic Crosswords

1

ACROSS
  1 ARCH (2 defs.)
  4 MIST (*missed* hom.)
  7 ROU(LET)TE
  8 E + DEN
 10 STEIN (2 defs.)
 11 PETTY (2 defs.)
 12 RIFTS (anag.)
 13 EL (C)ID (*deli* anag.)
 15 BRAN(d)
 16 S(N)UGGEST
 17 EGOS (anag.)
 18 T(R)EE

DOWN
  1 ARES (hidden)
  2 ROD SERLING (anag.)
  3 CUE + STICK
  4 M(EAT)Y
  5 STRIPTEASE (anag.)
  6 TEN + NIS (rev.)
  9 SE(AFAR)ER
 11 P + LEASE
 12 RINGS (2 defs.)
 14 ANTE (rev.)

18

ACROSS
  1 (m)ORAL
  4 RA(P)T
  7 RACKETS (2 defs.)
  8 EXETER (*exiter* hom.)
  9 IN(VADER)S
 11 T-(M)EN
 14 (l)EDGE
 15 IN THE AIR (anag.)
 16 SPUR (O)N
 17 T + REACLE
     (*cereal* anag.)
 18 S(H)AW
 19 KEYS (2 defs.)

DOWN
  1 O(R)BITS
  2 RAI(N) MAN
     (*Armani* anag.)
  3 AC(E VENT)URA
  4 (b)REEDS
  5 AT + TEN + DANCE
  6 TARS (anag.)
 10 RIG + IDLY
 12 HERMES (hidden)
 13 THREW
     (*through* hom.)
 15 IS + IS

35

ACROSS
  1 DEB + ATE
  7 IMP + ROVED
  8 ABUT (rev.)
  9 KIT + E
 10 T(he) + IN CAN
 11 ELDER (2 defs.)
 15 REFER (palindrome)
 16 P + ELVIS (ref. skater
     Elvis Stojko)
 17 ON US
 18 GROW(l)
 19 SEMINARS (anag.)
 20 BESIDE (hidden)

DOWN
  1 DIAPER (rev.)
  2 EMB(OLDEN)ED
  3 (p)ARTIER
  4 EVICT (hidden)
  5 SET A RECORD
     (anag.)
  6 EDEN (anag.)
 12 REIGNS (*rains* hom.)
 13 BROWSE (*brows* hom.)
 14 PLUMB (*plum* hom.)
 16 POST (anag.;
     ref. etiquette
     specialist Emily Post)

286

52

C	A	D	S	L	O	C	K
A	J	A	N	I	M	A	L
M	A	D	E	S	U	R	E
E	X	A	M	Z	P	V	E
R	D	I	R	T	I	E	D
A	S	S	A	U	L	T	O
W	P	M	D	P	L	I	E
H	O	T	H	E	A	D	S
O	O	L	O	N	G	L	I
A	L	E	C	K	E	E	N

69

C	A	P	P	P	O	G	O
O	N	E	D	I	S	O	N
S	T	A	L	L	O	N	E
M	I	N	G	O	M	E	S
I	C	U	S	T	A	R	D
C	A	T	C	H	E	S	E
E	R	S	U	O	W	E	N
D	R	I	B	L	E	T	S
N	O	V	E	L	S	N	E
A	W	E	D	S	T	A	R

86

P	U	S	H	E	R	S	A
L	R	C	A	F	E	E	L
A	G	O	R	A	N	S	T
G	E	N	E	R	A	T	E
I	B	F	M	I	S	E	R
A	R	I	E	S	C	T	A
R	U	D	I	M	E	N	T
I	T	E	H	A	N	O	I
S	U	N	K	L	T	S	O
M	S	T	O	L	L	E	N

ACROSS

1 C(A)DS
4 (f)LOCK
7 ANIMAL (anag.)
8 MA(DE SU)RE
(*used* rev.)
9 EXAM (*m + axe* rev.)
11 DIR + TIED (*rid* rev.)
13 ASSAULT
(*a salt* hom.)
17 P + LIE
19 HO + THE + ADS
20 (t)OO LONG
21 ALE + C
22 KEEN (hidden)

DOWN

1 CAME + R + A
2 A + JA + X
3 DA(DAIS)M
4 LISZT (*list* hom.)
5 CA(R)VE
6 KLEE (*clay* hom.)
10 P(ILL)AGE
12 DOES IN (anag.)
14 S + POOL
15 A + D (H)OC
16 WHO + A
18 IDLE (anag.)

ACROSS

1 CAPP (*cap* hom.)
4 POG + O (*GOP* rev.)
7 EDISON (anag.)
8 ST + ALL + ONE
9 MI + NG
11 CUSTAR + D
(*a crust* anag.)
13 CAT + CHE'S
17 OWEN (hidden in
first letters)
19 DRIBLETS (anag.)
20 N + OVELS
(*loves* anag.)
21 A + WED
22 STAR(r)

DOWN

1 CO(S)MIC
2 ANT + I
3 PEANUTS (anag.)
4 P(I)LOT
5 GO + NER (*Ren* rev.)
6 ONES (hidden)
10 MA(E WES)T(t)
12 D + ENSER
(*sneer* anag.)
14 AR + ROW
15 CUB + ED
16 EDNA (hidden)
18 ETNA (rev.)

ACROSS

1 P + USHERS
8 FEE + L
9 AG + OR + A
10 GEN(E) + RATE
12 M(IS)E + R
13 ARIES (anag.)
15 RU(DIME)NT
17 HANOI (hidden)
18 SUN + K
19 S(TOLL)EN

DOWN

1 PLA(G)IARISM
(*IRS mail Pa* anag.)
2 (s)URGE
3 HARE + M
4 RENAS + CENT
(*earns* anag.)
5 S(EST)ET
6 ALTERATION
(anag.)
7 CON(FI) + DENT
(*if* rev.)
11 B + RUT + US
14 S + MALL
16 NOS + E

2

S	T	I	L	E	T	T	O
T	O	T	U	P	O	E	M
U	P	E	N	D	R	J	E
C	E	S	A	R	E	A	N
C	S	T	C	S	A	N	D
O	K	A	Y	O	P	O	I
S	I	M	U	L	A	T	E
O	R	E	C	A	R	A	T
S	U	N	K	C	T	X	E
O	N	T	H	E	A	I	R

ACROSS

1 S(TIL)ET-TO (*lit* rev.)
8 POE + M
9 U + PEND
10 CESAREAN (hidden)
12 S + AND
14 O + KAY (*yak* rev.)
15 SI(MULA)TE (*alum* rev.)
17 CAR(A)T
18 SUN + K
19 ON THE AIR (anag.)

DOWN

1 STUC + CO. (*cuts* rev.)
2 TOPE (*taupe* hom.)
3 L(UN)ACY
4 TO + RE AP + ART
5 TEJANO (*on a jet* rev.)
6 OMEN (rev.)
7 TEST + AMEN + T
11 SKI R(U)N (*rinks* anag.)
12 SOL(A + C)E
13 D(I)ETER
15 SO-S + O
16 T(AX)I (*it* rev.)

19

A	C	E	S	D	I	S	C
G	O	S	S	A	M	E	R
E	M	U	S	N	M	C	U
D	P	R	A	D	I	O	S
D	A	I	L	Y	G	N	O
E	R	E	H	O	R	D	E
F	I	N	A	L	A	R	L
A	S	T	L	C	I	A	O
C	O	N	T	E	N	T	S
E	N	D	S	M	E	E	T

ACROSS

1 ACES (duplicates
   removed from *access*)
4 D + IS + C
7 GO + S(SAME)R
8 EMUS (hidden)
10 (r)ADIOS
11 DA(I)LY
12 HORDE (*hoard* hom.)
13 F + IN + A + L
15 CIAO (*chow* hom.)
16 CONTENTS (2 defs.)
17 (m)ENDS
18 MEET (*meat* hom.)

DOWN

1 A + GED
2 COMPARISON (anag.)
3 ESURIENT (anag.)
4 D AND Y
5 SECOND-RATE (anag.)
6 CRUSOE (anag.)
9 M + IGRAINE
   (ref. King Arthur
   of legend)
11 D E F A C E (six notes
   of the scale)
12 HA(LT)S
14 LO(S)T

36

C	D	P	L	A	Y	E	R
R	O	U	T	D	O	N	E
A	M	E	R	I	C	A	N
T	E	R	M	E	B	C	T
E	S	I	Q	U	O	T	A
S	P	L	I	T	D	D	I
U	R	E	R	H	E	I	R
T	O	M	O	R	R	O	W
A	M	E	N	D	E	D	A
H	O	U	S	E	K	E	Y

ACROSS

1 CD PLAYER (anag.)
7 O + U + TD + ONE
8 AMERICAN (anag.)
9 TERM (hidden)
11 Q(UOT)A (*out* anag.)
13 SP + LIT
18 (t)HEIR(s)
19 TOM + OR + ROW
20 A + M + ENDED
21 HO(USE) KEY

DOWN

1 CRATES (anag.)
2 DO(M)ES
3 PUERILE (anag.)
4 A(DIE)U
5 ENAC + T (*cane* rev.)
6 RENT (2 defs.)
10 BO DEREK (anag.)
12 AIRWAY (*wear*
   in pig Latin)
14 PROM + O
15 I(RON)S
16 DI(O)DE (*died* anag.)
17 UTAH (hidden)

53

T	U	R	B	O	F	A	N
A	P	C	A	A	R	C	S
B	R	O	N	X	A	H	T
L	O	N	D	O	N	E	R
E	S	N	Y	U	C	C	A
L	E	A	D	S	H	A	N
A	B	U	T	T	I	N	G
N	E	G	P	A	S	T	E
D	A	H	L	I	E	O	S
I	N	T	E	R	E	S	T

ACROSS

1 TURB(OF)AN
7 ARCS (anag.)
9 BRONX (*broncs* hom.)
10 LON(DON)ER
11 YUCCA (*yuck + a* hom.)
13 LEADS (2 defs.)
15 A + BUTTING
17 PASTE (*paced* hom.)
18 DAHL (*doll* hom.)
19 INTEREST (anag.)

DOWN

1 TAB + L + ELAND
2 U + PROSE
3 B + ANDY
4 FRANC(HIS)E
5 ACHE (hidden)
6 CON + NAUGHT
8 ST(RANGE) + ST
12 CANT(O)S
14 STA(I)R
16 B(E)AN

70

C	U	R	F	E	W	S	R
U	R	P	I	W	H	E	E
T	E	E	T	H	I	L	P
C	A	N	I	S	T	E	R
L	B	N	N	I	E	C	E
A	R	I	E	S	R	T	S
S	I	L	I	C	O	N	E
S	D	E	M	A	S	O	N
E	L	S	E	L	E	R	T
S	E	S	T	E	E	M	S

ACROSS

1 CUR(FEW)S
8 WHEE(l)
9 T.E. + ETH (*the* anag.)
10 CA(NI)STER (*in* rev.)
12 NIECE (*Nice* hom.)
13 (v)ARIES
15 SILICONE (anag.)
17 MA'S + ON
18 ELSE (anag.)
19 ESTE + EMS

DOWN

1 CUT (C)LASSES
2 UREA (hidden)
3 F(IT)IN
4 WHITE ROSE (anag.)
5 SELECT (hidden)
6 REP + RESENTS
7 PEN(NILES)S
11 BRID(L)E
14 SCALE (2 defs.)
16 N OR M?

87

G	A	I	N	F	I	L	E
R	B	N	A	I	L	E	D
A	L	K	A	L	I	N	E
T	E	L	L	L	S	T	N
E	B	I	G	S	H	O	T
D	O	N	E	F	O	R	U
A	Z	G	A	A	F	A	R
P	O	S	T	M	A	R	K
E	N	D	E	A	R	C	E
S	E	W	N	A	S	H	Y

ACROSS

1 G(A)IN
4 FILE (2 defs.)
7 NAILED (*Daniel* anag.)
8 AL KALINE (*alkaline*)
9 T + ELL
11 BIG SHOT (*both GIs* anag.)
13 D(ONE) FOR (*Ford* anag.)
17 A + FAR(e)
19 P + OSTMARK
20 ENDEAR (*earned* anag.)
21 S + E + W + N
22 A + SHY

DOWN

1 G-RATED (*grated*)
2 ABLE (rev.)
3 INK + LING(o)
4 F + ILLS
5 LENT + O
6 EDEN (hidden)
10 SHOFARS (*chauffeurs* hom.)
12 TUR(n)KEY
14 O + ZONE
15 EATEN (hidden in second letters)
16 (t)APES
18 ARCH (2 defs.)

3

20

37

ACROSS

1 CUFF (2 defs.)
4 DREW (2 defs.)
8 A + LAB + AMA
9 SCAR + A + B
10 PAS + SABLE
12 LIEN (rev.)
14 RI(dd)LE
16 HEIRLESS (anag.)
17 G + LEANS
18 A + T (HE)ART
19 D.A. + TA(x)
20 TSAR (anag.)

DOWN

1 CA + SPER (reps rev.)
2 F(LASH)LIGHT
3 FAR + SI (si = French for "if")
5 RABBI + T EARS
6 EMBLEM (hidden)
7 WADE (weighed hom.)
11 SIESTA (hidden)
13 NASSER (anag.)
15 B(L)EAT
16 H(E)AD

ACROSS

1 S(PACE) AGE
8 STAB (rev.)
9 ARIAS (hidden)
10 PILLAGES
   (Segal + lip rev.)
12 S + L(I)M
14 EA(S)T
15 SRI (LANK)A
   (airs rev.)
17 IN + CAN
18 DOES (doze hom.)
19 ENSNARED (anag.)

DOWN

1 STA(P)LE
2 PER + I
3 CHA(LE)T
4 A + T A G + LANCE
5 GA + VE IN (Ag rev.)
6 E + BBS
7 B(ILL S)IKES
11 PAR + TON (rev.)
12 STANZA (hidden)
13 MOANED (anag.)
15 SIDE (sighed hom.)
16 KATE (anag.)

ACROSS

1 DAM + E
4 G(L)UT
7 ON A TEAR (hidden)
8 R(ANT)ED
9 F(ATHER)LY
   (heart anag.)
11 UNIT (tin + U rev.)
14 I + VAN
15 R(EACH)ING
16 ARMADA (anag.)
17 WINS + TON
18 TES + T (set rev.)
19 CAN + E

DOWN

1 DOOF + US
   (food rev.)
2 AND + ANTE
3 MARTIN (A.M.)IS
4 GEN(E)T
5 LA T(R + A)VIA + TA
   (at rev.)
6 TIDY (yd + it rev.)
10 LEAN + S ON
12 ENGINE (anag.)
13 SCAN + T
15 RAPT (rapped hom.)

54

S	W	A	N	S	O	N	G
H	A	N	T	O	N	I	A
A	T	T	A	C	H	E	S
N	E	W	S	K	A	C	P
T	R	E	I	S	L	E	T
Y	P	R	E	S	L	G	O
D	I	P	V	P	E	E	R
E	N	D	A	N	G	E	R
N	O	O	D	L	E	S	I
S	T	R	E	S	S	E	D

71

S	A	L	I	N	G	E	R
P	C	H	N	T	A	X	I
O	C	E	A	N	R	A	C
R	E	A	L	T	I	M	E
T	D	D	L	O	B	E	S
S	E	D	E	R	A	L	K
C	O	R	D	E	L	I	A
A	H	E	M	I	D	S	T
R	I	S	K	G	I	H	E
H	O	S	A	N	N	A	S

88

P	L	A	N	C	K	F	M
R	O	P	E	O	M	O	O
O	P	A	B	O	A	R	D
D	E	T	O	N	A	T	E
A	D	I	O	S	B	I	M
M	E	T	P	E	O	N	S
O	V	E	R	D	U	B	S
R	E	M	A	I	N	R	O
A	G	E	D	E	D	A	M
L	A	M	O	U	S	S	E

ACROSS

1 SWAN SON + G
7 ANTONIA (anag.;
ref. *My Antonia*)
8 ATT + ACHES
9 NEWS (anag.)
11 ISLET (anag.)
13 YPRES (hidden)
18 PEER (2 defs.)
19 END + ANGER
20 N + OODLES
21 STRESSED (rev.)

DOWN

1 SHANTY
(*chantey* hom.)
2 W + ATE + R
3 AN + TWERP
4 SOCKS (2 defs.)
5 NI(E)CE
6 G + ASP
10 AL(LEG)ES
12 TOR + RID (rot rev.)
14 PINOT (*to + nip* rev.)
15 EV(AD)E
16 GEESE (hidden rev.)
17 DENS(e)

ACROSS

1 SA(LI)NGER (ref.
Margaret Sanger)
7 TAX + I
9 OCEAN (anag.)
10 REAL TIME (hidden)
11 (g)LOBES
13 SE(D)ER
15 CORDELIA (anag.)
17 MI(D)ST
18 R + IS + K
19 HOSANNAS (anag.)

DOWN

1 S(PORTS) CAR
2 ACCED + E
(*Decca* rev.)
3 (f)IN ALL(y)
4 GA(RIBALD)I(n)
5 EX + A.M.
6 (t)HE + ADDRESS
8 ICE SKATES (anag.)
12 ELISHA (anag.)
14 REIGN (*rein* hom.)
16 OH(I)O

ACROSS

1 PLAN(C)K
7 RO(P)E
8 O + MOO
9 A(BOAR)D
10 D(ETON)ATE
12 AD(I)OS
13 PEONS (anag.)
15 OVERDUBS (anag.)
16 RE(MA)IN
17 AGED (hidden)
18 EDAM (rev.)
19 MOUS(S)E

DOWN

1 PROD (anag.)
2 LOPE D + E VE + GA
3 APATITE (*appetite* hom.)
4 CO(O)NS
5 FOR + TIN + BRAS
6 MO + DEMS
11 A(BOUND)S
12 AM + ORAL
13 PRA + DO (*Arp* rev.)
15 SOME (*sum* hom.)

4

21

38

ACROSS

1 PAN + D.A.'S
7 RIOT (hidden)
8 BRIE(f)
9 NO ON + E
11 S(EQUINE)D
12 PLUG (rev.)
15 SHOE (*shoo* hom.)
16 RUTHLESS (anag.)
18 IDEAS (anag.)
19 TEAR (2 defs.)
20 G(O)AL
21 P(EBB)LY

DOWN

1 PROSPERITY (anag.)
2 (m)AIDE(n)
3 NOT (QUIT)E
4 A + B + OIL
5 DINER + O
6 NEEDLES + SLY
10 ON THE JOB (anag.)
13 LOU + DER (*red* rev.)
14 SHARE (*Cher* hom.)
17 SEAL (2 defs.)

ACROSS

1 WE + BB
4 F(R)OG
8 B(RACE)RO
9 GRADE-A
  (*gray day* hom.)
10 WATERLOG (anag.)
12 TELL (2 defs.)
14 MO + SS
16 E(LLIP)TIC (rev.)
17 AYE, AYE (*I + I* hom.)
18 S(EVEN)TY
19 TR(A)Y
20 TEEM (hidden in
  odd letters)

DOWN

1 WIG + W + A + M
2 BRAT(IS) + LAVA
3 BADE + N
5 REAL ESTATE (hidden)
6 O(RIO)LE
7 GO(i)NG
11 GOLF + ER (rev.)
13 LYCEUM (anag.)
15 SPENT (hidden in
  first letters)
16 EAST (anag.)

ACROSS

1 PARE (hidden)
4 SO + D + A
7 OLEANDER (anag.)
8 S + TAG
10 G + ROOM
11 D + RIVE
12 S(AR)IS
13 MAG + US
15 SO + H + O
16 SELDOMER (anag.)
17 EDGE (hidden)
18 V + EST

DOWN

1 POSE (*Poe's* hom.)
2 AL(T)ERNATED
  (*de la Renta* anag.)
3 R(EA + D)INGS
4 SNARE (anag.)
5 DEMOLISHES (anag.)
6 AR(A)M + IS
9 FOURSOME (anag.)
11 DEMI'S + E
12 SUEDE (*swayed* hom.)
14 S + ORT

55

B	A	A	L	G	A	L	A
I	N	F	E	R	I	O	R
O	T	T	O	O	C	N	C
S	I	E	D	O	U	G	H
S	T	R	U	M	R	I	I
T	H	A	S	T	A	T	E
R	E	L	A	Y	T	U	P
O	T	L	C	H	I	D	E
D	I	S	C	O	V	E	R
E	C	H	O	R	E	S	T

ACROSS
1 BAAL (anag.)
4 GAL + A (*lag* rev.)
7 INFE(RIO)R
8 OTTO (palindrome)
10 DO + UGH
11 ST + RUM
12 S(T)ATE
13 REL(A)Y
15 HIDE (2 defs.)
16 D + IS + C + OVER
17 ECHO (hidden)
18 REST (*wrest* hom.)

DOWN
1 BIOS (*so + l + b* rev.)
2 ANTITHETIC (anag.)
3 AFTER ALL (2 defs.)
4 G + ROOM
5 LONGITUDES (anag.)
6 A + RCHIE (*riche* anag.)
9 CURAT(IV)E
11 STRODE (anag.)
12 SACCO (hidden; ref. Sacco & Vanzetti)
14 PER + T

72

S	H	A	M	R	O	C	K
E	O	T	T	O	M	A	N
I	S	T	H	A	T	S	O
Z	E	U	S	C	H	K	W
E	S	N	G	H	O	S	T
S	T	E	L	E	G	D	I
S	R	S	I	S	W	A	N
W	A	L	T	Z	I	N	G
A	S	P	H	A	L	T	O
T	H	R	E	A	D	E	D

ACROSS
1 SH(AMR)OCK (*arm* anag.)
7 OTTOM + AN (*motto* rev.)
8 IS THAT SO (anag.)
9 ZEUS (rev.)
11 G + HOST
13 STELE (anag.)
18 SWAN (hidden)
19 WALT + ZING
20 AS + P + HALT
21 THRE(AD)E-D

DOWN
1 S(E)IZES
2 HOSES (anag.)
3 ATTUNES (anag.)
4 ROACH (anag.)
5 C + ASKS
6 KNOW (*no* hom.)
10 HOG-WILD (anag.)
12 TIN GOD (hidden)
14 T + RASH
15 (s)LITHE(r)
16 DANTE (anag.)
17 SWAT (2 defs.)

89

M	A	T	T	R	E	S	S
E	D	I	D	E	R	O	T
A	L	F	R	E	S	C	O
G	I	F	T	V	G	K	W
E	B	A	F	E	A	S	T
R	A	N	C	H	S	B	U
C	T	Y	H	A	P	E	X
A	R	M	A	T	U	R	E
L	I	S	S	O	M	E	D
F	A	C	E	U	P	T	O

ACROSS
1 MATTRESS (anag.)
7 DID + EROT (*tore* rev.)
8 ALFRESCO (anag.)
9 GI + FT (swap FT + GI)
11 F(E)AST
13 RAN + CH
18 APE + X
19 AR(e) + MATURE
20 LI(SSOM)E (*Moss* rev.)
21 FACE UP TO (anag.)

DOWN
1 M + EAGER
2 AD LI + B (*laid* anag.)
3 TIFF + ANY
4 RE + EVE
5 SOCKS (2 defs.)
6 STOW (*Stowe* hom.)
10 GAS P + UMP
12 TUXEDO (anag.)
14 ATRIA (hidden)
15 C(H)ASE
16 BERE(f)T
17 CALF (hidden)

5

22

39

ACROSS

5

1 GROUSE (2 defs.)
7 ROSE (2 defs.)
8 TOOL (rev.)
9 TR(Y) OUT
10 WARP + LANE
12 AN + IS + E
13 DUM(b) + AS
14 SCHUBERT (anag.)
16 EL + EVEN
17 RENE (hidden)
18 PIER (*peer* hom.)
19 A + T E(AS)E

DOWN

1 GROW(l)
2 RO(MAN A CLE)F
    (*for* rev.)
3 O(ST) + RICH
    (ST = pair of STudents)
4 STYLE (*stile* hom.)
5 BOUND + ARIES
6 ALTERS (anag.)
11 AR(MEN)IA
12 A + SSERT (rev.)
13 DU(V)ET
15 TIRE (2 defs.)

ACROSS

22

1 P + IMPLY
7 A'S + EA(t)
8 I + O(u)T + A
9 ON TAP (anag.)
11 DESSERTS (rev.)
12 AC(H)E
15 AGES (rev.)
16 ENLARGES (anag.)
18 AD L(I)B (*bald* anag.)
19 ROBS (2 defs.)
20 (c)ARGO
21 L + ESSEN

DOWN

1 PAN + DA B + EARS
    (*pan* is slang for the face)
2 IS + L + E
3 MESS HALL (hidden)
4 LI(N)ES
5 S(T + AT)UE
6 RAP SESSION (anag.)
10 T + RIGGERS
13 CONDO + R
14 RAISE (*raze* hom.)
17 EDGE (hidden)

ACROSS

39

1 BRA(D) PITT
    (*bit part* anag.)
8 KNEW (*nu* hom.)
9 US + HER
10 REIN + VENT
12 (s)CRIB(e)
14 SIGH (*Cy* hom.)
15 S(T)URGEON
17 TAC + KY (*cat* rev.)
18 HEM + P
19 ODYSSEAN
    (hidden)

DOWN

1 BLUR + B.S.
2 ROSE (2 defs.)
3 D(R)ENCH
4 IN + TERSE + CT
5 TENNIS (anag.)
6 T + WIT
7 THIN + GUMMY
11 P + I + TIED
12 CIGARS (anag.)
13 B(ANY)AN
15 SOHO (hidden in
    first letters)
16 O.K. + R + A

56

I	S	O	L	A	T	E	D
N	E	M	I	S	O	D	A
G	R	A	M	S	L	I	F
R	A	S	P	I	E	S	T
I	G	S	L	D	R	O	P
D	R	A	Y	O	A	N	E
S	E	G	M	E	N	T	S
T	E	I	A	S	C	O	T
A	C	N	E	I	E	M	E
B	E	G	I	N	N	E	R

ACROSS
1 IS + OLATED
  (*lead to* anag.)
8 SODA (rev.)
9 G + RAMS
10 RA(SPIES)T
12 DR(O) + P
14 DR(A)Y
15 SE(G-MEN)TS
17 A + SCOT
18 ACNE (anag.)
19 BE + G + INNER

DOWN
1 INGRID (anag.)
2 SE(R)A
3 L + IMPLY
4 T(OLE)RANCE
5 EDISON
  (*no + side* rev.)
6 D + AFT
7 MAS + SA(GI)NG
  (*Sam* rev.)
11 GREECE (*grease* hom.)
12 DOE + S IN
13 PESTER (anag.)
15 STAB (rev.)
16 TO ME

73

S	T	E	M	M	U	S	T
C	O	N	S	O	M	M	E
A	I	D	A	V	A	A	A
N	L	A	M	I	N	T	S
S	E	N	S	E	T	T	E
C	T	G	F	L	E	E	T
A	R	E	A	S	N	R	O
M	I	R	R	S	N	I	P
P	E	N	C	H	A	N	T
I	S	L	E	L	E	G	S

ACROSS
1 STEM (rev.)
4 MUST (2 defs.)
7 CONSOMME (anag.)
8 AID + A
10 MINTS (2 defs.)
11 SENSE (*cents* hom.)
12 F(LEE)T
  (FT = FighT extremely)
13 ARE(n)AS
15 SNIP (rev.)
16 PEN + CHANT
17 ISLE (*aisle* hom.)
18 LEGS (hidden in
  first letters)

DOWN
1 S + CAN
2 TOILETRIES (anag.)
3 END + ANGER
4 M + O + VIE
5 S + MATTERING
6 TEA SE + T
9 ANTE + NNAE
  (*Anne* anag.)
11 SCAMPI (hidden)
12 FAR(C)E
14 OPTS (anag.)

90

A	M	P	S	O	U	S	T
W	O	R	D	P	L	A	Y
O	N	E	S	A	M	I	P
L	T	A	B	L	I	N	I
D	E	C	K	S	N	T	F
O	V	H	B	O	S	S	Y
L	E	E	R	Y	T	A	V
L	R	R	E	T	R	E	E
A	D	J	A	C	E	N	T
R	I	S	K	A	L	S	O

ACROSS
1 AM + P.S.
4 OU(S)T
7 (s)WORDPLAY
8 ONES (anag.)
10 B(el)LINI
11 DEC(K)'S
12 BO(SS)Y
13 LEERY (*Leary* hom.)
15 TREE (hidden in
  odd letters)
16 AD(J)ACENT
  (*dance at* anag.)
17 RIS + K (*sir* rev.)
18 ALSO (anag.)

DOWN
1 AWOL (*low A* rev.)
2 MONTE + VERDI
  (*met no* anag.)
3 PRE-ACHER
4 O + PALS
5 SAINT-S(A)ENS
  (*nastiness* anag.)
6 TYPIFY (*tip if I* hom.)
9 MINSTREL (hidden rev.)
11 DOLLAR (anag.)
12 BREAK (anag.)
14 VETO (anag.)

6

23

40

ACROSS
1 DELI (anag.)
4 SPAN (rev.)
9 DUE T + O
10 SP(L)IT
11 CO + L + OSSAL
(lasso rev.)
13 ROSE (anag.)
14 MOWN (moan hom.)
16 FLAME + NCO
18 CR(E)AM
19 RACES (2 defs.)
20 TRE + K
21 E + DEN (end anag.)

DOWN
1 DISCOMFOR + T
(from Disco anag.)
2 (s)EXPO(t)
3 IDIOT (anag.)
5 PER + SON + NEL
(Len rev.)
6 AT EASE (hidden)
7 NO + BLEW + OMEN
8 A + L(LOW)ANCE
12 C[(d)OLL]AR
15 V + ERSE
17 CAVE (2 defs.)

ACROSS
1 REJE + CT (jeer anag.)
7 OXEN (oven with
Roman numeral V
changed to X)
8 IN RE [rev. of ERNI(e)]
9 H(IDD)EN (did anag.)
10 F(LOWER)ED
12 C + OVER
13 SAP + OR
14 ETHEREAL (hidden)
16 TI(EPI)N (pie anag.)
17 ANTI (hidden)
18 REED (read hom.)
19 TAW + DRY

DOWN
1 (p)ROOF
2 EX(PLO)ITING
3 JEHOVA + H
(have OJ anag.)
4 CIDER (anag.)
5 FREELOADER (anag.)
6 RENDER (2 defs.)
11 R(I + PEN)ED
12 CRETAN (anag.)
13 SEPIA (anag.)
15 LAD + Y
(y is Spanish for and)

ACROSS
1 PATH (pass lisped)
4 ALPS (anag.)
8 DRACULA (anag.)
9 OBOIST (hidden)
10 MOURNING
(morning hom.)
12 INCH (anag.)
14 T(U)SK
16 AMEN-ABLE (pun)
17 A + P-PEAL
18 A(CUT)ELY (Yale anag.)
19 NE(X)T
20 S + LID

DOWN
1 PROM + P.T.
2 T(ROUSSEAU)X
3 H + AIRY
5 LUTINE BELL (anag.)
6 PLAN + C + K
(ref. Max Planck)
7 SANG (2 defs.)
11 PU + MICE (up rev.)
13 HEELED (2 defs.)
15 TAPES (anag.)
16 ALAN (hidden)

57

B	U	M	P	I	R	I	S
A	S	T	E	R	I	S	K
S	H	O	T	U	P	I	A
H	E	P	T	M	I	S	T
C	R	A	Y	O	N	P	E
O	S	P	A	S	T	O	R
M	E	A	N	U	O	W	K
E	L	Y	E	S	M	E	N
A	S	A	W	H	O	L	E
T	E	S	T	I	D	L	E

ACROSS

1 B + UMP
4 I + RIS (*sir* rev.)
8 AS(TERI'S)K
9 S(HOT) UP
11 MIST (*missed* hom.)
12 C + RAYON
14 PAST + OR
16 ME(A)N
19 YE(S)-MEN
20 A + S A W + HOLE
21 TEST (*T* + *set* rev.)
22 IDLE (*idol* hom.)

DOWN

1 B + ASH
2 US(H)ERS
3 P(r)ETTY
5 RI + P INTO
6 IS + IS
7 SKATER (anag.)
10 PAPA + YAS (*say* rev.)
12 CO. + ME AT
13 PO(WE)LL
15 S + U.S. + HI
17 ELSE (hidden)
18 K + NEE

74

B	O	B	D	Y	L	A	N
U	K	K	E	L	I	M	E
D	R	I	F	T	C	U	E
G	A	T	E	F	O	L	D
E	C	T	N	C	R	E	W
S	L	E	D	A	I	T	I
F	I	N	A	N	C	E	D
I	N	I	S	T	E	V	E
R	I	S	E	A	S	E	S
S	C	H	U	B	E	R	T

ACROSS

1 BOB DYLAN (anag.)
8 LIME (2 defs.)
9 DR + IFT (*fit* anag.)
10 G(ATE + F)OLD
12 CREW (initial letters)
14 S + LED
15 FI(N)ANCE + D
17 ST + EVE
18 RISE (*ryes* hom.)
19 S + CHUBERT
    (*butcher* anag.)

DOWN

1 BUDG(i)ES
2 O + KRA (*ark* rev.)
3 DEF + END (*fed* rev.)
4 LICORICES (anag.)
5 A + MU-LET
6 NEED (*knead* hom.)
7 KITTENISH (anag.)
11 CLI(p) + NIC(k)
12 C(ANT)AB
13 WI(D)EST
15 FIRS(t)
16 EVER (anag.)

91

R	E	F	E	R	S	T	O
E	C	L	S	S	A	A	B
D	R	O	S	S	N	L	E
S	U	S	A	N	D	E	Y
E	C	E	Y	S	Y	N	C
A	R	T	S	O	H	T	U
B	A	R	E	F	O	O	T
U	N	A	A	T	O	M	S
R	I	C	E	E	K	N	I
R	A	K	I	N	G	I	N

ACROSS

1 REFERS TO (anag.)
8 SAAB (rev.)
9 D + ROSS
10 SUSAN DEY (hidden)
12 SYNC (*sink* hom.)
14 ARTS (anag.)
15 B(A + REF)OOT
17 A + TOM'S
18 (p)RICE
19 RA(KING) IN

DOWN

1 RED SEA (anag.)
2 ECRU (hidden)
3 E + SSAYS
    (*Sassy* anag.)
4 S(ANDY) HOOK
5 T.A. + LENT
6 OBEY (*beau* in pig Latin)
7 (c)LOSE T + RACK
11 C(RAN)IA
12 S + OFTEN
13 CUTS IN (anag.)
15 BURR (*brrr* hom.)
16 OM(a)NI

7

24

41

ACROSS
1 PAR + SEE
7 ON THE SLY (anag.)
8 USER (hidden)
9 STIR (2 defs.)
10 NICENE(ss)
11 C + LIMB
15 PA(y) + PAL
16 ADO + RNS
17 SAPS (2 defs.)
18 GAL + A
19 IMP + ROVES
20 ARROYO (hidden)

DOWN
1 P + OUNCE
2 ANSEL ADAMS (anag.)
3 S(HR.)IMP
4 ESTEE(m)
5 B + LIND A + LLEY (*yell* rev.)
6 LYRE (*liar* hom.)
12 BANG + OR
13 EL PASO (anag.)
14 P(OPP.)A
16 A + S IN

ACROSS
1 P(R)OP
4 AS + PS
9 A(G)NEW
10 TINGE (hidden)
11 IN + T + EGRAL (*large* rev.)
13 W + ELL
14 SEEK (*Sikh* hom.)
16 E(AT)S CROW
18 S + AUDI
19 I + OW + AN
20 E + DNA (*and* rev.)
21 TAN + G

DOWN
1 PATISSERIE (anag.)
2 RAIN (anag.)
3 P + AGES
5 S(NA)RE DRUM (*an* in *murders* rev.)
6 PEDALS (*peddles* hom.)
7 SW(ALLOW)ING
8 ON THE TOWN (anag.)
12 SE(A) GOD (*doges* rev.)
15 SCAN + T
17 O + DIN

ACROSS
1 GO-C + ART (*cog* rev.)
7 EVAN (rev.)
8 ETON (rev.)
9 DEPOT (rev.)
11 S(LAPD)ASH
12 A + URA
15 MESA (anag.)
16 O(K COR)RAL (*rock* rev.)
18 U.N. + TIL (*lit* rev.)
19 NOEL (anag.)
20 PURR (*per* hom.)
21 CAR + PET

DOWN
1 GETS AROUND (anag.)
2 O + VAL
3 CA(TARAC)T (*carat* rev.)
4 REEDS (*reads* hom.)
5 BOO(S)TS
6 ON THE ALERT (hidden)
10 P(APER CU)P
13 (h)UNK + NOT
14 V(OIL)A
17 ACRE (anag.)

58

S	T	R	A	P	P	E	D
C	R	I	N	K	L	E	H
H	O	S	T	P	E	R	U
E	R	E	I	O	N	I	C
M	A	T	C	H	T	E	K
A	N	R	A	B	Y	S	S
T	I	A	R	A	B	T	T
I	N	G	E	L	U	T	E
C	T	I	P	S	T	E	R
S	O	C	R	A	T	E	S

75

A	M	I	D	P	A	N	E
R	E	B	E	L	L	E	D
M	A	T	T	E	L	R	I
Y	G	R	E	E	G	O	S
W	E	I	R	D	O	H	O
H	R	C	A	N	N	O	N
O	C	H	S	A	E	T	M
O	A	T	O	D	A	T	E
P	R	E	V	I	O	U	S
S	P	R	Y	R	I	B	S

92

S	C	A	M	R	A	P	T
K	A	Y	O	O	N	U	S
I	N	D	U	S	T	R	Y
M	O	W	N	E	W	I	L
A	N	A	T	H	E	M	A
S	A	N	D	T	R	A	P
K	D	T	O	W	P	L	T
P	L	O	W	I	N	T	O
H	A	U	L	S	N	A	P
H	I	T	S	T	A	R	S

58

ACROSS

1 S + TRAPPED
6 C + RIN(g) + KLE
  (*elk* rev.)
8 HOST (2 defs.)
9 PERU (anag.)
11 IONIC (hidden)
12 MATCH (2 defs.)
14 ABYSS (hidden)
16 T(I)ARA
18 (s)INGE(r)
19 LUTE (*loot* hom.)
20 TIPSTER (anag.)
21 SOCRATES (anag.)

DOWN

1 SCHEMATI + C
  (*a chemist* anag.)
2 RISE (*ryes* hom.)
3 ANTI + C
4 PLENTY (hidden in
  odd letters)
5 E(ERIES)T
7 H(UCKST)ERS
  (*stuck* anag.)
10 RAN INTO
  (*rain* anag., *not* anag.)
13 T + RAGIC (*cigar* rev.)
15 BALS + A (*slab* rev.)
17 BUTT (2 defs.)

75

ACROSS

1 AMID (anag.)
4 PANE (*pain* hom.)
8 RE(BELLE)D
9 MATTE + L
11 E.G. + (n)OS(e)
12 WEIR + DO
14 CANNON (*canon* hom.)
16 (l)OCHS
19 TO DATE (anag.)
20 P(REV)IOUS
21 S + PRY
22 R.I. + B.S.

DOWN

1 ARMY (anag.)
2 M + EAGER
3 DETER(gents)
5 ALL GONE (anag.)
6 NERO (hidden)
7 E(DI)SON
  (*ID* in *nose* rev.)
10 RICH(T)ER
12 W + HOOPS
13 H + OT TUB
  [*butto(n)* rev.]
15 NADIR (anag.)
17 CARP (2 defs.)
18 MESS (hidden)

92

ACROSS

1 SCAM(p)
4 RAPT (*wrapped* hom.)
7 KAYO (O + *yak* rev.)
8 ON + US
9 INDUS + TRY
12 AN(A)THEM + A
13 SA(ND) TRAP
18 P(LOW) INTO
19 HAUL (*Hall* hom.)
20 SNAP (rev.)
21 HI(T)S
22 TARS (anag.)

DOWN

1 SKI M + ASK
2 C + ANON
3 MOUNT (hidden)
4 ROSE (2 defs.)
5 A + N + TWERP
6 P(U)RIM
10 WAN + T OUT
11 LAPTOPS
  (*spot* + *pal* rev.)
14 ADLAI (anag.)
15 TWI(S)T
16 ALTAR (*alter* hom.)
17 (f)OWLS

8

25

42

ACROSS

1 BEEF STEW (anag.)
7 MADE + IRA
8 WAR + M OVER
9 L + IRA
11 BLOTS (2 defs.)
13 DA(N)TE
18 BE(R)G
19 ROBINSON (anag.)
20 E.B. + ONIES
   (*noise* anag.)
21 SE(A GREE)N

DOWN

1 BOW + LED
2 E-MAIL (hidden rev.)
3 E(A)RRING
4 SEOUL (*sole* hom.)
5 ERECT (hidden)
6 WARD (rev.)
10 F(ORES)EE
12 SIGN ON (anag.)
14 ADOBE (anag.)
15 THIN + G
16 PRO'S + E
17 (c)ARES

ACROSS

1 SCRIM + P
7 C(HITCH)AT
8 RAM + A
9 ELLA (hidden)
10 A + L + L-OUT
11 AD(M)IT
15 CHIN + A
16 KNAVES
   (*naves* hom.)
17 (w)INDY
18 T + HAT
19 WAR(RANT)Y
20 EASTER (anag.)

DOWN

1 S + CREAM
2 CHAR(DONNA)Y
3 ITALIC (anag.)
4 PHLOX (*flocks* hom.)
5 C + ALUMNI + ATE
6 STAT(e)
12 THE + TAS (*sat* rev.)
13 MARTY + R
14 CADRE (anag.)
16 KIWI (*key* + *we* hom.)

ACROSS

1 SP + EARS
7 L(I + N)E
8 HEIR (hidden)
9 G(E)ORGE
10 MARINARA (anag.)
12 S + N + ARE
13 EL + AT + E
14 METAL(L)IC
   (*climate* anag.)
16 B + LOTTO
17 ELS + E
18 IN + N,S
19 U.N. + REST

DOWN

1 S(L)UM
2 P(IRAN + DELL)O
3 ENG + RAFT
4 RHONE (*roan* hom.)
5 MIG + RATIONS
6 GREASE (*Greece* hom.)
11 A + BA + LONE
12 SOM(B)ER
   (*Rome's* anag.)
13 EATEN (*Eton* hom.)
15 COST (anag.)

59

K	I	N	D	T	R	A	P
L	A	N	E	W	E	L	L
I	M	P	L	I	C	I	T
N	B	A	T	N	I	B	S
G	I	G	A	N	T	I	C
E	P	I	G	R	A	P	H
R	R	T	S	O	L	A	I
H	I	A	T	U	S	E	S
T	O	T	O	S	C	A	M
B	R	E	W	T	I	N	S

76

P	L	A	Y	O	F	F	S
E	M	P	E	R	O	R	S
T	E	E	M	F	L	I	T
P	R	X	E	I	D	E	R
E	A	R	N	S	E	D	I
E	D	O	S	E	D	A	N
V	I	S	O	R	F	N	G
E	A	T	S	O	L	E	O
S	T	R	U	D	E	A	U
N	E	A	R	E	A	S	T

93

P	E	T	E	R	P	A	N
R	E	A	D	I	E	R	N
O	M	N	I	B	E	T	A
S	A	G	T	Y	L	E	R
T	R	A	S	H	E	M	R
R	C	P	M	A	R	I	A
A	S	P	E	N	J	S	T
T	I	E	R	T	O	N	I
E	N	A	B	O	K	O	V
V	E	R	O	N	E	S	E

ACROSS

1 KIND (2 defs.)
4 TRAP (rev.)
7 LANE (*lain* hom.)
8 WELL (2 defs.)
9 I'M + P + LICIT
12 GIG + ANTIC
13 E(PIG + RAP)H
  (*he* rev.)
18 HIATUSES (anag.)
19 TO + T + O
20 S(C)AM
21 B + REW.
22 TINS (rev.)

DOWN

1 K + LINGER
2 I + AM + BI
3 DELTA (*dealt a* hom.)
4 TWIN(e)
5 RECITAL (anag.)
6 ALIBI (anag.)
10 A + G(IT)ATE
11 SCH(I'S) + MS
14 PRIOR (2 defs.)
15 R(O)UST
16 PA(EA)N
17 S + TOW

ACROSS

1 P + LAYOFFS
6 EM(PER)OR
  (*Rome* around *rep* rev.)
8 TEEM (rev.)
9 F + LIT
11 EI + DER
  (*red* + *i.e.* rev.)
12 (l)EARNS
14 SEDAN (hidden)
16 VIS(it)OR
18 (m)EATS
19 O + LE + O
20 T(RUDE)AU
21 NEAR EAST (hidden)

DOWN

1 PET (PEEV)ES
  (*veep* rev.)
2 APE + X
3 YE + MEN
4 F(OLD)ED
5 FRIED + AN
7 ST(RING) OUT
10 RADIATE (anag.)
13 ROSTRA (anag.)
15 E(arlie)R + ODE
17 FLEA (*flee* hom.)

ACROSS

1 PET + (h)ER + PAN
6 READ(I)ER
8 OM + NI (rev.)
9 BET + A
11 T + YLER (*rely* rev.)
12 T + RASH
14 M + ARIA
16 A + S + PEN
18 TI(g)ER
19 TONI(c)
20 NABOKOV (anag.)
21 VERONESE (anag.)

DOWN

1 PROS(TRAT)E (*tart* rev.)
2 T + A + NG
3 E(DI)TS
4 PEE(LE)R
5 ARTEMIS (anag.)
7 N(A + RR)ATIVE
10 ARC SINE (anag.)
13 APPE(A)R (*paper* anag.)
15 AN(TO)N
17 JOKE (hidden periph.)

9

26

43

ACROSS

1 BERG (2 defs.; ref. Austrian composer Alban Berg)
4 TRAP (rev.)
7 O + VARIES
8 BE + A + VER(y)
9 ARBOREAL (anag.)
11 REIN (*rain* hom.)
14 RA(P)T
15 STEALTHY (anag.)
16 U + BANG + I
17 TRIP + OLI (*oil* anag.)
18 D(IS)C
19 ANTE (rev.)

DOWN

1 BOG + ART
2 EVE + REST
3 RABBIT EARS (anag.)
4 TIARA (hidden)
5 REV + ELATION
6 PURL (2 defs.)
10 A + SP + HALT
12 STY + MI + E
13 P(AN)IC
15 SUED(e)

ACROSS

1 CAROUSER (anag.)
7 OMIT (hidden)
9 BOO + T H(e) + ILL
10 F + ERAL (*real* anag.)
11 EI + DER (rev.)
14 GATOR (*gaiter* hom.)
15 S + T + OUT
17 EINSTEIN (anag.)
18 DAZE (*days* hom.)
19 D + ISOWNED (*in sod we* anag.)

DOWN

1 COB(WE)B
2 AMORISTIC (anag.)
3 R(I)OT
4 US + HER
5 SPIR + IT (*rips* rev.)
6 ROLL (*role* hom.)
8 GLAMORIZE (anag.)
12 DRONES (*crones* making *c* into *d*)
13 P + RUNED (*under* anag.)
14 GUST + O (*guts* anag.)
15 SEND (hidden rev.)
16 MEAN (2 defs.)

ACROSS

1 SAPS (anag.)
4 BAT + H
9 MET + RO(ad)
10 ETHIC (hidden)
11 D(IO)RAMAS
13 SIT + E
14 D + OTS
16 DU(RACE)LL
18 KOREA (anag.)
19 E + LBOW (*bowl* anag.)
20 DESI (anag.)
21 LI + FT

DOWN

1 SKED + ADDLED (*desk* anag.)
2 ANT + I
3 SMIR + K (*rims* rev.)
5 ATOMIZERS (anag.)
6 TR(EAT)Y
7 HO(USE + PLAN)T
8 SHORT RIBS (anag.)
12 CO(UP)LE
15 S + COWL
17 LEAF (hidden)

60

P	R	O	T	E	S	T	B
R	A	B	H	A	C	R	E
O	G	R	E	S	U	U	A
S	E	A	F	A	R	E	R
E	B	N	T	A	R	S	I
C	O	C	O	A	Y	T	N
U	S	H	E	R	I	N	G
T	U	O	M	I	N	E	O
O	N	U	S	E	G	T	U
R	S	T	Y	L	I	S	T

77

C	R	A	B	R	A	S	P
H	E	R	O	A	L	T	O
A	E	R	O	F	L	O	T
R	D	S	T	T	S	W	H
I	S	T	H	A	T	S	O
T	R	U	F	F	A	U	T
Y	E	N	T	O	R	L	S
M	A	G	R	I	T	T	E
A	D	U	E	L	I	R	A
L	Y	N	X	S	P	A	T

94

E	L	K	S	R	A	P	T
M	A	N	E	A	T	E	R
M	U	N	I	C	H	E	I
Y	D	A	N	S	E	R	F
G	E	N	E	V	A	H	L
R	D	D	E	G	R	E	E
E	R	A	S	E	T	R	A
E	O	N	A	T	T	E	R
C	U	T	L	O	O	S	E
E	X	E	C	N	A	Y	S

ACROSS
1 P(ROT)EST
8 AC(R)E
9 OGRES (hidden)
10 SE(A + FAR)ER
12 TAR + SI (*is* rev.)
13 CO + CO. + A
15 US(HER)ING
17 MINE + O
18 ON + U.S.
19 STY + LIST

DOWN
1 PROSE + CUTOR
  (*court* anag.)
2 R + AGE
3 THE + FT.
4 S(CURRY)ING
5 TRU(E)ST
6 BEA(RING O + U)T
7 B(RANCH) OUT
11 BOS(U.N.)S
14 AR(I)EL (*Lear* anag.)
16 NETS (anag.)

ACROSS
1 C(R)AB
4 RA(S)P
7 HER + O
8 AL + TO (*la* rev.)
9 A(EROF) LOT
  (*fore* rev.)
12 IS THAT SO (hidden)
13 T(RUFF)AUT
18 MA(GRIT)TE
19 A D + (c)UE
20 LIRA (anag.)
21 LYNX (*links* hom.)
22 SPAT (rev.)

DOWN
1 C(HAR)ITY (*rah* rev.)
2 RE(E)DS
3 BO(O)TH
4 RAFT (2 defs.)
5 AL(L + S)TAR
6 S(T)OWS
10 STUN G + U.N.
11 HOT SEAT (anag.)
14 READY (*Reddy* hom.)
15 FOILS (2 defs.)
16 ULTRA (hidden)
17 T. RE + X

ACROSS
1 EL(K)S
4 R + APT.
8 M + A + N-EATER
9 MUN(I)CH
11 SERF (*surf* hom.)
12 GENEVA (anag.)
14 DEGREE (hidden)
16 ERAS(e)
19 NATTER (anag.)
20 CUT LOOSE (anag.)
21 E(X)EC
22 NAY + S (*any* anag.)

DOWN
1 EM + MY (*me* rev.)
2 (c)LAUDE + D
3 SE(IN)E
5 A + T HE + ART
6 PEER (2 defs.)
7 T + RIFLE
10 A + N + DANTE
12 GREECE
  (*Grease* hom.)
13 HERESY (hidden)
15 G + ET ON
17 ROUX (*rue* hom.)
18 (m)ARES

10

27

44

ACROSS

1 S + COT
4 TAIL (*tale* hom.)
7 PARDON ME (anag.)
8 IRIS(h)
10 TYSON (*nosy* + *T* rev.)
11 LINGO (hidden)
12 (f)ALLEN
13 W + HELP
15 S(T)IR
16 REAR + REST
17 SLIT (anag.)
18 A + SHY

DOWN

1 SPIT (rev.)
2 CARMICHAEL (anag.)
3 ORIENTED (anag.)
4 TO(KY)O
5 IMP(OVER)ISH
6 LE + AN ON
   (LE = oiLErs' center)
9 I + SO(LATE)S
11 LOWERS (2 defs.)
12 ALERT (hidden)
14 (p)ARTY

ACROSS

1 ASTERISK (anag.)
7 HIT(A)CH + I
8 TE(L)ETH + ON
9 HALT (hidden)
11 MOOED (*mood* hom.)
13 MA(R)SH
18 B + RAT (rev.)
19 NOVELIZE (anag.)
20 INFER + NO
21 PEN + TAG + ON

DOWN

1 ANTHEM (anag.)
2 SHEAR (anag.)
3 TILLERS (anag.)
4 RATIO (anag.)
5 SHOVE (hidden)
6 KIN + D
10 SO(ARI)NG (*air* anag.)
12 DOT + E ON
14 ALONE (*a loan* hom.)
15 S(HE)ET
16 K(AZ)O + O
17 SNIP (rev.)

ACROSS

1 STAR + CH
7 CAME + LEER
8 ABE + T
9 DATE (2 defs.)
10 SANDED (anag.)
11 PEDRO (anag.)
15 D(RAM)A
16 ALUMNA (anag.)
17 POLK(a)
18 AN + NA (*an* rev.)
19 S(T)AR TRE + K
20 GNEISS (*nice* hom.)

DOWN

1 SCAMP + I
2 TABLECLOTH (anag.)
3 RETARD (anag.)
4 HEADS (hidden in
   final letters)
5 DET + ERMINES
   (*Ted* rev.)
6 BRED (*bread* hom.)
12 OR(N)ATE
13 K + A + YAK'S
14 GU + LAG
16 A + P'S + E

61

P	A	S	T	A	D	A	M
A	C	T	R	U	S	T	Y
T	H	E	I	D	I	O	T
H	E	R	O	E	I	N	H
O	P	O	I	N	T	E	R
S	L	I	N	G	E	R	O
A	E	D	E	D	R	A	M
R	A	M	A	Y	A	N	A
E	S	P	R	I	T	T	N
S	E	T	S	L	E	E	S

ACROSS

1 PAST (hidden)
4 ADA + M
7 TR(U.S. + T)Y
8 T(HE IDI)OT
9 HER + O
11 P(O)INTER
13 S(a)LINGER
17 DRAM(a)
19 RAMAYANA (hidden)
20 E + SPRIT
21 SETS (anag.)
22 LEE'S

DOWN

1 PATH(O)S
2 A + CHE
3 STEROID (anag.)
4 A + U + DEN
5 A(TON)E
6 MY + (au)TH(or)
10 (l)ITERATE
12 RO + MAN'S
14 (p)LEASE
15 N + EARS
16 (b)ARES
18 (d)ANTE

78

G	A	G	A	T	E	A	M
O	S	A	P	O	L	L	O
T	H	R	O	W	O	U	T
H	E	R	B	E	S	M	E
A	N	E	A	R	E	S	T
M	A	T	C	H	E	S	E
A	F	S	H	S	P	A	N
P	L	E	A	S	A	N	T
S	A	T	I	N	G	T	E
E	T	O	N	P	E	E	R

ACROSS

1 GAG + A
4 TEAM (*teem* hom.)
7 A + POLL + O
8 TH(ROW) OU + T
9 HER + B
11 NEAREST (anag.)
13 MATCHES (2 defs.)
17 SPA + N
19 PLEASANT (anag.)
20 SATING (anag.)
21 ETON (hidden)
22 PEER (*pier* hom.)

DOWN

1 GOT + HAM
2 ASHE (anag.)
3 GAR + RE(n)TS
   (*rag* rev.)
4 TOWER (2 defs.)
5 ALUMS (anag.)
6 MOT + E (*Tom* rev.)
10 SEE + PAGE
12 TENTER (hidden)
14 A + FLAT
15 CH(A)IN
16 APSE (anag.)
18 ANTE (hidden)

95

S	P	A	N	I	S	H	S
P	A	F	E	S	T	A	T
A	I	L	E	D	R	B	A
C	R	U	D	E	O	I	L
E	G	M	S	O	L	T	I
C	O	M	B	O	L	S	N
A	D	O	R	N	I	N	G
D	I	X	M	I	N	O	R
E	V	E	R	C	G	T	A
T	A	D	H	E	R	E	D

ACROSS

1 SPAN-ISH (pun)
8 STAT (2 defs.)
9 A + ILED (*deli* rev.)
10 C(RUDE) OIL
12 SOL + TI
   (ref. Sir Georg Solti)
13 COMB + O
15 ADOR(N)ING
17 MINOR (*miner* hom.)
18 (f)EVER
19 AD(HERE)D

DOWN

1 S(PACE + CAD)ET
2 P + AIR
3 NEEDS (*kneads* hom.)
4 S(TROLL)ING
5 HABITS (hidden)
6 STALING + R + AD
7 F(LUMMOX)ED
11 GO + DIVA
14 O + N ICE
16 NOT + E

11

28

45

ACROSS

1 CHICK PEA (anag.)
8 CHUM (anag.)
9 (n)ARROW
10 LOO(K IN + O)N
12 WE(P)T
14 TOAD (*towed* hom.)
15 CONTRIVE (anag.)
17 P + ILED (*deli* rev.)
18 FO + A.M. (*of* rev.)
19 F + OREGON + E

DOWN

1 CHA(p) + LET
2 HERO (hidden)
3 CO(O.K.)ED
4 PHONE BILL (anag.)
5 EUROPE (hidden)
6 AMEN (anag.)
7 T.R. + O.J. + AN WAR
11 BOO-BOO (2 defs.)
12 W(I)RING
13 TIE-DYE (*Tide I* hom.)
15 (s)CUFF(s)
16 VEIN (*vain* hom.)

ACROSS

1 ACES (hidden)
4 RAFT (2 defs.)
7 R(ANT)ING
8 TI(G)ERS
9 HARPISTS (anag.)
11 EVE + R
14 C + HAT
15 INTER + EST.
16 THIRST (anag.)
17 PE(SKI)ER
18 (c)HOSE
19 ACRE (*acher* hom.)

DOWN

1 ARCHER (2 defs.)
2 CA[RAV(e)]AN
3 ENTR(EA + T)IES
4 RIG + ID
5 ANESTHETIC
    (hidden)
6 TO + SS
10 TOASTER (anag.)
12 AT + TIRE
13 PER SE (2 defs.)
15 IT + CH

ACROSS

1 S(HERB)ETS
7 ALGEBRA (anag.)
8 I + N A GRO + UP
    (*organ* rev.)
9 GOSH (anag.)
11 (m)OTHER
13 A(S)IDE
18 G + RID
19 CHOW LINE (hidden)
20 A(MO)NGST
21 NOT SO HOT
    (*to* + *host* + *on* rev.)

DOWN

1 STIGMA
    (*a* + *MG* + *it's* rev.)
2 HANOI (hidden)
3 ELASTIC (anag.)
4 B(E.R.)ET
5 TRU(C)E
6 SAPS (rev.)
10 CHER-ISH (pun)
12 RO(DEN)T
14 SC + HMO
15 D + OWNS
16 P + INTO
17 S + CAN

62

T	H	E	L	O	R	A	X
A	E	L	I	D	E	N	S
L	L	A	M	A	V	O	T
L	E	T	A	L	O	N	E
O	N	E	S	U	C	R	E
R	A	R	E	R	A	I	L
D	E	A	R	A	B	B	Y
E	L	L	I	D	L	E	D
R	I	L	E	I	E	Y	A
L	A	Y	W	O	M	E	N

ACROSS

1 TH(E L)ORAX
7 DENS(e)
9 LLAMA (*lama* hom.)
10 LE(T ALON)E
11 SU(C)RE
13 R[ARE(a)]R
15 DEAR ABBY
(*deer abbey* hom.)
17 I'D + LED
18 RI(f)LE
19 LAYWOMEN (anag.)

DOWN

1 TALL ORDER
(*red + roll + at* rev.)
2 HE + LEN + A
3 LIMAS (hidden)
4 REVO + CABLE
(*over* rev.)
5 ANON (2 defs.)
6 LATE + RALLY
8 STEELY DAN (anag.)
12 R(I + B E)YE
14 R(AD)IO
16 (d)ELIA(m)
(*mailed* rev.)

79

S	C	A	T	T	E	R	S
T	O	P	R	O	V	U	M
A	A	R	O	N	A	S	A
T	R	O	U	N	C	E	S
E	S	G	T	R	U	S	T
L	E	N	D	S	A	E	O
I	S	O	L	A	T	E	D
N	A	S	C	R	E	D	O
E	V	I	L	G	D	E	N
D	E	S	C	E	N	D	S

ACROSS

1 SCATTERS (anag.)
7 OVUM (hidden in
first letters)
9 A(ARO)N (*oar* anag.)
10 TROUNCES (anag.)
11 T + RUST
13 (b)LENDS
15 I(SO + LATE)D
17 C(RED)O
18 EVIL (rev.)
19 D(ESCEN)DS
(*scene* anag.)

DOWN

1 STATE LINE (anag.)
2 COARSE (*course* hom.)
3 TRO(U)T
4 EVACUATED (anag.)
5 RUSE (*rues* hom.)
6 PROGNOSIS (anag.)
8 MAS(TOD)ONS
(*dot* rev.)
12 SEEDED (*ceded* hom.)
14 SARGE (hidden)
16 S(l)AVE

96

T	A	P	S	D	A	F	T
R	Q	A	U	R	O	R	A
A	U	S	P	I	C	E	S
G	A	T	E	V	B	T	K
I	A	D	V	E	R	S	E
C	O	U	N	C	I	L	N
I	Z	E	O	P	E	L	E
T	O	D	I	E	F	O	R
E	N	I	S	L	E	A	G
M	E	R	E	E	D	D	Y

ACROSS

1 TAPS (2 defs.)
4 DAFT (*t + fad* rev.)
7 AUR(OR)A
8 AU + SPICES
9 (a)GATE
11 AD VERSE (pun)
13 COUNCIL
(*counsel* hom.)
17 P(EL)E
19 TO DIE FOR (anag.)
20 ENISLE (hidden)
21 MERE (*Mir* hom.)
22 (t)EDDY

DOWN

1 T + RAGIC (*cigar* rev.)
2 AQUA (hidden)
3 PAST DUE (anag.)
4 DRIVE (anag.)
5 FRETS (2 defs.)
6 T(A)SK
10 BRIE + FED
12 ENERG + Y
(*green* anag.)
14 OZ + ONE
15 NO(I)SE
16 I + TEM (*met* rev.)
18 L(O)AD

12

```
R A P T S C A M
O Q U I X O T E
B A T M A N E A
O R I E N T A L
T B N S L I S P
S O W S C N E E
H O O S E G O W
A T R O D E N T
R E D C E N T E
M E S H S T A R
```

29

```
A C I D S O B S
R A N C H E R O
E N D S E B I U
S I O B E A D S
I S L E T L G E
N M E P A L E D
D I N A R Y T C
I N T T S H O E
G O E S D O W N
O R G Y W O N T
```

46

```
C R I B E T C H
H A S S L E D E
A M A N D R E W
S P A C E M A N
T A C K R I C P
E G S A K N E E
R E T R E A T S
O M E L E T O E
A P R E S E N T
D O N S A S E A
```

ACROSS

1 RAPT (*wrapped* hom.)
4 SCAM (rev.)
8 QUI(XO)TE (*ox* rev.)
9 B(ATM)AN
10 ORIENTAL (anag.)
12 L(IS)P
14 SOWS (2 defs.)
16 H(OOSEG)OW
   (*goose* anag.)
17 RO(DEN)T
18 RE(D) CENT
19 MESH (hidden)
20 S + TAR

DOWN

1 RO(B)OTS
2 PUT IN WORDS
   (*s + drown + it + up* rev.)
3 TI(M)ES
5 CONTIN(G)ENT
6 A + T EASE
7 ME(A)L
11 B(OOT)EE (*too* rev.)
13 PE(W)TER
15 CEDES (*seeds* hom.)
16 H + ARM

ACROSS

1 A(C)ID
4 SO(B)S
7 RAN + C + HERO
8 ENDS (anag.)
10 BE(A)DS
11 IS + LET
12 PA + LED
13 D(IN + A)R.
15 SHOE (*shoo* hom.)
16 GOES DOWN (anag.)
17 ORGY (anag.)
18 WON + T

DOWN

1 A(R)ES (*sea* rev.)
2 CANIS MINOR (hidden)
3 IN + DO + LENT
4 SHE + E.T.
5 BRIDGET + OWN
6 SO + USED
9 B(ALLY)HOO
   (*hobo* anag.)
11 INDIGO (hidden)
12 PA(TS)Y (*St.* rev.)
14 CENT (*sent* hom.)

ACROSS

1 C + RIB
4 ETCH (hidden)
7 HAS + SLED
8 AN + DREW
9 SPACEMAN
   (*name + caps* rev.)
11 TACK (2 defs.)
14 K + NEE
15 R(ETRE)ATS
16 O + ME + LET
17 PRESENT (2 defs.)
18 DO + N,S
19 A + SEA (*a "C"* hom.)

DOWN

1 CHAS(T)E
2 RAM + PAGE
3 ISAAC STERN (anag.)
4 EL + DER (*red* rev.)
5 TERMINATES (anag.)
6 HE(W)N
10 ACE + TONE
12 PE(SET)A
13 ARLES (anag.)
15 RO(A)D

63

S	T	I	R	S	A	P	S
P	O	R	T	U	G	A	L
R	E	A	L	G	O	R	U
Y	T	L	H	A	N	K	S
T	H	E	I	R	S	A	H
H	E	V	G	R	A	V	Y
E	L	I	O	T	F	E	R
S	I	N	T	M	A	N	E
I	N	C	H	O	R	U	S
S	E	A	S	D	I	E	T

ACROSS

1 S(T)IR
4 SAPS (rev.)
7 PORT + U + GAL
8 REAL (*reel* hom.)
10 (t)HANKS
11 T + HEIR
12 GRA(V)Y
13 ELIOT (*toil + E* rev.)
15 MANE (*main* hom.)
16 IN C. + HORUS
17 SEAS (*seize* hom.)
18 DIE + T

DOWN

1 SP(R)Y
2 TO + E THE L + IN + E
3 IRA LEVIN (anag.)
4 SUGAR (*Ragu's* rev.)
5 PAR(K + A)VENU + E
6 S(LUSH) + Y
9 ON SAFARI (anag.)
11 THE + S + IS
12 GOT + H.S.
14 REST (hidden)

80

R	E	S	T	R	A	I	N
E	R	E	Q	U	I	R	E
D	I	V	O	R	C	E	S
S	E	E	M	A	M	N	T
E	S	R	F	L	E	E	T
A	M	A	S	S	S	O	O
M	I	L	L	A	S	P	S
I	N	J	U	R	I	E	S
S	C	A	M	P	E	R	E
T	E	M	P	E	R	A	S

ACROSS

1 REST + RAIN
7 RE + QUIRE
8 DIVORCES (anag.)
9 SEEM (*seam* hom.)
11 F(L)EET
13 A + MASS
18 ASPS (anag.)
19 IN + JURIES
20 S + CAMPER
21 TEMPER + AS

DOWN

1 RED SE + A
    (*reeds* anag.)
2 (s)ERIES
3 S(EVER)AL
4 R + URAL
5 IRENE (hidden)
6 (o)NE + ST
10 MESSIER (2 defs.)
12 TOSSES (hidden)
14 MINCE (*mints* hom.)
15 SL + UMP
16 OPERA (anag.)
17 MIST (*missed* hom.)

97

W	H	I	T	E	S	E	A
O	O	O	H	C	E	N	T
N	A	V	A	L	R	Y	H
D	R	E	W	N	E	A	R
E	S	R	S	I	N	C	E
R	E	P	E	L	G	I	S
F	O	R	T	I	E	T	H
U	P	I	I	N	T	R	O
L	A	C	K	E	I	O	U
P	L	E	A	S	A	N	T

ACROSS

1 WHITE SEA (anag.)
7 CENT (*sent* hom.)
9 NAVAL (hidden)
10 DREW NEAR (anag.)
11 SINCE (hidden)
13 RE(P)EL
15 FOR(TIE)TH
17 I + NTRO (*torn* anag.)
18 (b)LACK
19 P(L)EASANT

DOWN

1 WONDERFUL (anag.)
2 HOARSE (*horse* hom.)
3 THAWS (anag.)
4 SERENGETI (anag.)
5 (k)ENYA
6 OVERPRICE (anag.)
8 TH(R)E + SH OUT
12 C + I(T)RON
14 LI(N)ES
16 O + PAL

13

K	R	A	K	O	W	E	B
R	I	N	G	P	A	C	F
U	M	O	S	T	A	L	L
G	E	R	M	I	N	A	L
E	R	I	C	C	T	I	W
R	E	E	S	F	I	R	E
R	A	S	P	I	E	S	T
A	S	T	E	R	T	O	H
N	O	V	A	M	A	L	E
D	N	K	R	A	M	E	R

30

B	A	L	I	A	D	D	S
A	F	A	N	T	A	I	L
R	A	N	D	O	M	N	O
B	A	D	I	N	A	G	E
F	G	R	A	A	S	H	E
D	R	O	P	K	C	Y	A
L	O	V	E	N	E	S	T
A	I	E	V	I	N	C	E
S	T	R	A	F	E	D	R
T	O	S	S	E	S	P	Y

47

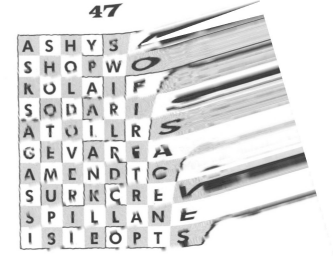

A	S	H	Y	S			O
S	H	O	P	W	O		
K	O	L	A	I	F		
S	O	D	A	R	I		
A	T	O	I	L	R		S
G	E	V	A	R	E	A	
A	M	E	N	D	T	C	
S	U	R	K	C	R	E	
S	P	I	L	L	A	N	E
I	S	I	E	O	P	T	S

ACROSS
1. KRA + KOW (rev.)
7. RING (2 defs.)
8. P + ACE
9. STALL (2 defs.)
11. GERMINAL (anag.)
12. E + RIC(h)
15. FIR + E
16. RA(SPIES)T
18. A + STER...
19. NOVA (hidden)
20. MALE (*mail* hom.)
21. KRAMER (rev.)

DOWN
1. K + RUG + FRIEND
2. RIME (*rhyme* hom.)
3. ANGRIEST (anag.)
4. OPTIC (hidden in first letters)
5. NULAIR (anag.)
6. BELL + WETHER (*belle* + *whether* hom.)
10. ANTI + ... (...*mate* rev.)
13. RE + A + SON
14. S + PEAR
17. SOLE (2 defs.)

ACROSS
1. BALI (hidden)
4. ADDS (*adze* hom.)
8. F(ANT)AIL
9. RANDOM (anag.)
10. BAD + IN + AGE
12. (...)(w)
14. DROP (hidden)
16. L(OVE N)EST (*let's* anag.)
17. F...VINCE
18. O...RA + FED (*arts* rev.)
19. TOSS (anag.)
20. ESPY (2 defs.)

DOWN
1. B + ARBED (*Debra* rev.)
2. L + AND + ... OVER + S
3. IN + DIA (*aid* rev.)
5. DAM + A + SCENE + S
6. DING(H)Y
7. SLOE (*slow* hom.)
11. GROTTO (anag.)
13. (h)EATER + Y
15. KNIFE (E + *fink* rev.)
16. LAST (2 defs.)

ACROSS
1. AS + H(osier)Y
4. SA...PU (...rev.)
. ...(HOP)WORN
8. KO(a)LA
10. ARISE (hidden)
11. A + TOLL
12. ARE(A)S
13. A + M + END
15. CREW (2 defs.)
16. S(PILL)ANE
17. ISLE (*I'll* hom.)
18. O + RTO

DOWN
1. AS(K)S
2. S(HOO) 'EM-UPS (*spumes* rev.; ref. Hoot Gibson)
3. H(OLD)OVER
4. SWIRL (hidden in even letters)
5. PRES(S AG)ENT
6. S(N)EERS
9. FIRETRAP (*parter* + *if* rev.)
11. AGASSI (*I's* + *saga* rev.)
12. (r)ANKLE
14. (t)EWES (ref. Lauren Tewes as Julie McCoy)

63

S	T	I	R	S	A	P	S
P	O	R	T	U	G	A	L
R	E	A	L	G	O	R	U
Y	T	L	H	A	N	K	S
T	H	E	I	R	S	A	H
H	E	V	G	R	A	V	Y
E	L	I	O	T	F	E	R
S	I	N	T	M	A	N	E
I	N	C	H	O	R	U	S
S	E	A	S	D	I	E	T

ACROSS

1 S(T)IR
4 SAPS (rev.)
7 PORT + U + GAL
8 REAL (*reel* hom.)
10 (t)HANKS
11 T + HEIR
12 GRA(V)Y
13 ELIOT (*toil* + E rev.)
15 MANE (*main* hom.)
16 IN C. + HORUS
17 SEAS (*seize* hom.)
18 DIE + T

DOWN

1 SP(R)Y
2 TO + E THE L + IN + E
3 IRA LEVIN (anag.)
4 SUGAR (*Ragu's* rev.)
5 PAR(K + A)VENU + E
6 S(LUSH) + Y
9 ON SAFARI (anag.)
11 THE + S + IS
12 GOT + H.S.
14 REST (hidden)

80

R	E	S	T	R	A	I	N
E	R	E	Q	U	I	R	E
D	I	V	O	R	C	E	S
S	E	E	M	A	M	N	T
E	S	R	F	L	E	E	T
A	M	A	S	S	S	O	O
M	I	L	L	A	S	P	S
I	N	J	U	R	I	E	S
S	C	A	M	P	E	R	E
T	E	M	P	E	R	A	S

ACROSS

1 REST + RAIN
7 RE + QUIRE
8 DIVORCES (anag.)
9 SEEM (*seam* hom.)
11 F(L)EET
13 A + MASS
18 ASPS (anag.)
19 IN + JURIES
20 S + CAMPER
21 TEMPER + AS

DOWN

1 RED SE + A
   (*reeds* anag.)
2 (s)ERIES
3 S(EVER)AL
4 R + URAL
5 IRENE (hidden)
6 (o)NE + ST
10 MESSIER (2 defs.)
12 TOSSES (hidden)
14 MINCE (*mints* hom.)
15 SL + UMP
16 OPERA (anag.)
17 MIST (*missed* hom.)

97

W	H	I	T	E	S	E	A
O	O	O	H	C	E	N	T
N	A	V	A	L	R	Y	H
D	R	E	W	N	E	A	R
E	S	R	S	I	N	C	E
R	E	P	E	L	G	I	S
F	O	R	T	I	E	T	H
U	P	I	I	N	T	R	O
L	A	C	K	E	I	O	U
P	L	E	A	S	A	N	T

ACROSS

1 WHITE SEA (anag.)
7 CENT (*sent* hom.)
9 NAVAL (hidden)
10 DREW NEAR (anag.)
11 SINCE (hidden)
13 RE(P)EL
15 FOR(TIE)TH
17 I + NTRO (*torn* anag.)
18 (b)LACK
19 P(L)EASANT

DOWN

1 WONDERFUL (anag.)
2 HOARSE (*horse* hom.)
3 THAWS (anag.)
4 SERENGETI (anag.)
5 (k)ENYA
6 OVERPRICE (anag.)
8 TH(R)E + SH OUT
12 C + I(T)RON
14 LI(N)ES
16 O + PAL

13

30

47

ACROSS

1. KRA + KOW (rev.)
7. RING (2 defs.)
8. P + ACE
9. STALL (2 defs.)
11. GERMINAL (anag.)
12. E + RIC(h)
15. FIR + E
16. RA(SPIES)T
18. A + STER(n)
19. NOVA (hidden)
20. MALE (*mail* hom.)
21. KRAMER (rev.)

DOWN

1. K + RUG + ERRAND
2. RIME (*rhyme* hom.)
3. ANGRIEST (anag.)
4. OPTIC (hidden in first letters)
5. ECLAIR (anag.)
6. BELL + WETHER (*belle* + *whether* hom.)
10. ANTI + ETAM (*mate* rev.)
13. RE + A + SON
14. S + PEAR
17. SOLE (2 defs.)

ACROSS

1. BALI (hidden)
4. ADDS (*adze* hom.)
8. F(ANT)AIL
9. RANDOM (anag.)
10. BAD + IN + AGE
12. (c)ASHE(w)
14. DROP (hidden)
16. L(OVE N)EST (*let's* anag.)
17. E + VINCE
18. STRA + FED (*arts* rev.)
19. TOSS (anag.)
20. ESPY (2 defs.)

DOWN

1. B + ARBED (*Debra* rev.)
2. L + AND + R + OVER + S
3. IN + DIA (*aid* rev.)
5. DAM + A + SCENE + S
6. DING(H)Y
7. SLOE (*slow* hom.)
11. GROTTO (anag.)
13. (h)EATER + Y
15. KNIFE (E + *fink* rev.)
16. LAST (2 defs.)

ACROSS

1. AS + H(osier)Y
4. SA + P.S. (*as* rev.)
7. S(HOP)WORN
8. KO(a)LA
10. ARISE (hidden)
11. A + TOLL
12. ARE(A)S
13. A + M + END
15. CREW (2 defs.)
16. S(PILL)ANE
17. ISLE (*I'll* hom.)
18. O + PTS.

DOWN

1. AS(K)S
2. S(HOOT)-'EM-UPS (*spumes* rev.; ref. Hoot Gibson)
3. H(OLD)OVER
4. SWIRL (hidden in even letters)
5. PRES(S AG)ENT
6. S(N)EERS
9. FIRETRAP (*parter* + *if* rev.)
11. AGASSI (*I's* + *saga* rev.)
12. (r)ANKLE
14. (t)EWES (ref. Lauren Tewes as Julie McCoy)

64

E	X	T	R	U	D	E	D
X	A	R	C	S	I	N	E
O	X	I	D	A	T	E	S
D	I	C	E	G	S	M	K
U	S	K	P	E	P	Y	S
S	A	L	S	A	A	V	A
W	N	E	U	E	R	I	C
A	N	C	E	S	T	O	R
N	E	W	D	E	A	L	A
E	X	T	E	R	N	A	L

ACROSS
1 EXTRUDED (hidden)
7 ARCSINE
   (*ark* + *sign* hom.)
8 OXIDATES (anag.)
9 D + ICE
11 PEPYS (*peeps* hom.)
13 S(A + L'S)A
18 ERIC (anag.; ref.
   Lassie creator
   Eric Knight)
19 A + N(C)ESTOR
20 NEW DEAL
   (*nude* + *eel* hom.)
21 EXTERNAL (anag.)

DOWN
1 EXODUS (anag.)
2 X - A + X + IS
3 TRICK + LE
4 U.S. + AGE
5 (r)ENE + MY
6 (o)DES + K
10 SPAR + TAN
12 SACRAL (anag.)
14 ANNE + X
15 SUED + E
16 VI(O)LA (ref. Bob Vila
   of *This Old House*)
17 WANE (*Wayne* hom.)

81

E	L	L	E	T	O	G	A
L	E	A	N	O	V	E	R
S	A	W	N	I	L	R	R
A	D	R	F	L	A	M	E
G	E	E	S	E	M	I	S
R	R	N	P	A	I	N	T
A	S	C	O	T	N	A	M
S	H	E	S	C	A	T	O
P	I	L	E	A	T	E	D
S	P	U	R	C	E	D	E

ACROSS
1 EL + LE
4 T + OGA (rev.)
7 L[(j)EAN(s)] OVER
8 SAW + N
10 F + LAME
11 GEESE (anag.)
12 P + AIN'T
13 A + SCOT
15 CATO (anag.)
16 PILEATED (anag.)
17 SPUR(t)
18 CEDE (hidden)

DOWN
1 ELSA (hidden)
2 L + EADERSHIP
   (*diapers he* anag.)
3 LA(WREN)CE
4 TOILE(d)
5 GERMINATED (anag.)
6 A(R)REST (*tears* anag.)
9 LA(MI)NATE (*I'm* rev.)
11 G(R)ASPS
12 P(O'S)ER
14 MODE (*mowed* hom.)

98

M	A	R	I	N	A	S	R
A	U	C	R	A	C	H	E
T	R	A	I	N	C	I	D
C	A	P	S	T	O	N	E
H	M	A	H	A	R	E	S
S	Y	R	I	A	D	S	I
T	R	I	P	P	I	N	G
I	T	S	S	P	O	O	N
C	L	O	G	L	N	T	E
K	E	N	T	E	R	E	D

ACROSS
1 MARINAS (anag.)
8 A + CHE
9 TRAIN (2 defs.)
10 CAPSTONE (anag.)
12 H(ARE)S
13 S(Y)RIA (*sari* anag.)
15 T + RIPPING
17 SP + O + ON
18 CLOG (2 defs.)
19 EN(TERE)D
   (*Erté* anag.)

DOWN
1 MATCH + STICK
2 (l)AURA
3 IRIS + H
4 A + C + CORD + I + ON
5 SH(IN)E'S
6 REDESIGNED (anag.)
7 C(A + PARIS)ON
11 MYRTLE (anag.)
14 APPLE (hidden)
16 NOTE (rev.)

311

14

31

48

ACROSS

1 A'S + TRAY
7 T + WIN
8 MACE (2 defs.)
9 DRAMAS (anag.)
10 PA + INTERS
12 TREVI (hidden)
13 BEGIN (anag.)
14 MOT + I(VAT)E
16 CRATER (2 defs.)
17 ADZE (*ads* hom.)
18 IDEA (anag.)
19 ASSES + S

DOWN

1 A TO P
2 S(WEAR) WORDS
3 TIDIEST (anag.)
4 A + MAT + I
5 SCAR + CITIES
6 LESS + ON
11 EN GARDE (anag.)
12 TO(MC)AT
(perfectly = TO A T)
13 BITES (*bytes* hom.)
15 ETAS (rev.)

ACROSS

1 LAC(ROSS)E
(ref. Harold Ross)
8 PIT + Y
9 MALT + A
10 B(REACH)ED
12 G + ALL
14 A + SHE
15 SPAN + IE + L + S
17 UNSET (anag.)
18 CREE(d)
19 KEYBOARD (anag.)

DOWN

1 LAMB + D.A.
2 A + JAR
3 ROT(A)TE (*T tore* anag.)
4 S + INHALES + E
5 S(TEE)LY
6 EYED (*I'd* hom.)
7 AL(EX HALE)Y
(*lay* anag.)
11 ASP + IRE
12 G(RING)O
13 LASTED (anag.)
15 SOCK (2 defs.;
Oxford = shoe)
16 (c)LEAR

ACROSS

1 BA(LANCE)D
8 TON + Y (*not* rev.)
9 D + RAIN
10 DE(RANG)ED
12 SAAB (*sob* hom.)
14 ANNE (*an* hom.)
15 SAT + IRIS + T
17 (b)RANCH
18 AC(N)E
19 THOU + SAND

DOWN

1 BUD + DHA
(*had* anag.)
2 ACRE (*acher* hom.)
3 AVIATE (hidden)
4 CON(GA L + IN)E
5 END + EAR
6 DYED (anag.)
7 T.A. + RAN + TINO
(*into* anag.)
11 SNATCH (anag.)
12 SCRAPS (2 defs.)
13 BAT + HE'D
15 SPAT (2 defs.)
16 S + CAN

65

S	W	A	L	L	O	W	S
A	A	J	I	S	N	A	P
G	R	A	F	T	A	G	A
E	N	D	E	A	V	O	R
S	B	E	R	C	E	N	T
T	A	G	S	I	R	S	E
S	U	R	I	N	A	M	E
H	B	E	B	E	G	A	N
O	L	E	S	M	E	I	S
D	E	N	T	A	L	L	Y

ACROSS
1 SWALLOWS (2 defs.)
8 SNAP (rev.)
9 GRAFT (*graphed* hom.)
10 ENDEAVOR (anag.)
12 CENT (*sent* hom.)
14 TAGS (2 defs.)
15 SUR(I)NAME
17 B(E.G.)AN
18 (p)OLES
19 DEN + TALLY

DOWN
1 SAGEST (hidden)
2 WAR + N
3 LIFERS (anag.)
4 O + N AVE + RAGE
5 WA + GO + N + S
6 SPAR(e)
7 JA(DE GREE)N
11 BAUBLE (*bobble* hom.)
12 CINEMA (anag.)
13 TEENS + Y
15 S(H)OD
16 MA + IL

82

C	O	M	E	U	P	O	N
R	S	D	S	B	A	S	E
A	L	O	H	A	P	I	W
D	O	W	A	G	E	R	S
L	D	N	R	P	R	I	M
E	A	R	P	A	T	S	O
C	H	I	T	C	H	A	T
A	L	V	S	M	I	T	E
M	I	E	N	A	N	O	L
P	A	R	S	N	I	P	S

ACROSS
1 CO(ME) UPON
8 BASE (2 defs.)
9 ALOHA (hidden)
10 DO + WAGERS
12 P + RIM
14 EAR + P
15 C(HITCH)AT
17 S(M)ITE
18 MIEN (*mean* hom.)
19 PAR + SNIPS

DOWN
1 CRADLE (anag.)
2 O + SLO(w)
3 E SHARP (hidden)
4 PA(PER-TH)IN
5 O + SIR + IS
6 NEWS (*gnu's* hom.)
7 D(OWN)RIVER
11 DAHLIA
   [(G)ail + *had* rev.]
12 PAC-MAN (anag.)
13 M(OT)ELS (*to* rev.)
15 CA(M)P
16 A + TO + P

99

S	P	A	M	C	I	A	O
A	R	I	D	N	E	S	S
P	O	R	T	O	S	T	I
S	V	E	S	T	O	R	E
W	E	D	G	E	M	O	R
A	N	A	E	V	E	N	S
B	A	L	L	S	M	O	L
A	N	E	A	R	O	M	A
S	C	E	N	A	R	I	O
H	E	A	D	P	E	C	S

ACROSS
1 SPAM (rev.)
4 CIAO (*chow* hom.)
7 ARIDNESS (anag.)
8 PORT (2 defs.)
10 STORE (hidden)
11 W + EDGE
12 EVENS (anag.)
13 BALLS (2 defs.)
15 (a)ROMA
16 SCENARIO (anag.)
17 HEAD (hidden)
18 PECS (*pecks* hom.)

DOWN
1 SAPS (2 defs.)
2 PR(OVEN)ANCE
3 AIRED + ALE
4 C-(NOT)E
5 (g)ASTRONOMIC
6 OSIERS (anag.)
9 SO(ME MO)RE
11 W + A + BASH
12 E + LAND
14 L + A(O)S

15

W	A	R	D	D	A	T	A
H	N	S	I	M	P	E	L
O	T	T	E	R	P	R	L
L	E	A	T	H	E	R	Y
E	L	R	S	L	A	O	S
W	E	L	L	B	L	R	H
H	A	I	R	L	I	N	E
E	N	G	C	A	N	O	E
A	T	H	O	S	G	O	D
T	O	T	E	T	O	N	Y

ACROSS
1 WAR + D
4 DATA (*a tad* rev.)
9 I'M + P + E + L
10 (p)OTTER
11 LEA(THE)RY
13 L.A. + OS
14 WELL (*we'll*)
16 H + AIRLINE
18 CANOE (anag.)
19 ATHOS (hidden)
20 TOT + E
21 TO + N.Y.

DOWN
1 W + HOLE + W + HEAT
2 ANTE (*auntie* hom.)
3 DIETS (2 defs.)
5 AP(PEAL)ING
6 T + ERROR
7 ALLY S + HEED + Y
8 S(TAR)LIGHT
12 LE(A)N-TO
15 B + LAST
17 NOON (palindrome)

32

Q	U	A	R	R	Y	S	F
U	R	N	S	I	N	T	O
I	G	A	H	O	M	E	R
N	E	G	A	T	I	V	E
T	E	R	N	S	L	E	C
U	Q	A	O	U	L	N	A
P	U	M	P	K	I	N	S
L	I	S	T	S	N	O	T
E	P	E	E	F	E	T	E
D	S	A	D	O	R	E	D

ACROSS
1 QUARRY (2 defs.)
7 URNS (*earns* hom.)
8 (p)INTO
9 HOMER (2 defs.)
11 NEGATIVE
   (*Evita* + *gen.* rev.)
12 TERN (*turn* hom.)
15 ULNA (hidden)
16 PUMP(KIN)S
18 LISTS (2 defs.)
19 EPEE (hidden rev.)
20 FE(T)E
21 ADO + RED

DOWN
1 QUINTUPLED (anag.)
2 (p)URGE
3 A + NAG + RAMS
4 R(I)OTS
5 STEVEN (anag.)
6 FORE(CA)STED
10 M(ILL)INER
13 E + QUIPS
14 OPTED (anag.)
17 NOTE (rev.)

49

A	W	O	L	M	E	E	T
M	A	K	I	N	G	D	O
P	R	O	N	T	O	G	U
S	C	M	E	S	T	E	P
T	R	A	D	E	R	P	E
R	Y	S	I	M	I	L	E
O	B	O	E	I	P	A	C
O	O	N	O	D	I	C	E
P	O	R	T	S	A	I	D
S	T	Y	X	T	I	D	E

ACROSS
1 A + WOL (rev.)
4 MEET (rev.)
8 MAKING DO (hidden)
9 PRONTO
   (letter shift in *proton*)
11 STEP (rev.)
12 TRADER (*red* + *art* rev.)
14 S(I)MILE
16 (h)OBOE(s)
19 NO D + ICE
20 P(ORT SA)ID
   (*Astro* in *dip* rev.)
21 STYX (*sticks* hom.)
22 TIDE (*tied* hom.)

DOWN
1 A + M.P.'S
2 W(AR C)RY
3 L(IN)ED
5 E + GO T + RIP
6 EDGE (hidden)
7 TOUPEE (*two pay* hom.)
10 MA(SON)RY
12 TRO(O)PS (*sport* rev.)
13 PLA(C)ID
15 MI(D)ST
17 B + OOT (*too* rev.)
18 CEDE (*seed* hom.)

66

S	E	E	S	R	H	O	S
A	N	A	T	H	E	M	A
V	O	Y	E	U	R	I	L
E	U	C	L	B	E	T	A
A	G	H	A	S	T	A	A
D	H	I	N	F	I	R	M
V	A	S	T	L	C	E	H
I	W	E	Q	U	I	N	E
C	O	L	O	S	S	A	L
E	L	S	A	H	A	S	P

ACROSS

1 SEES (*seize* hom.)
4 RHOS (*Rose* hom.)
8 ANATHEMA
(*a + Mehta + N.A.* rev.)
9 VOY(age) + EUR.
11 BET + A
12 AGHAST (hidden)
14 IN FIRM (pun)
16 VA(S)T
19 (s)EQUINE(d)
20 CO(LOSS)AL
21 ELSA (anag.)
22 HAS + P

DOWN

1 S + AVE.
2 ENOUGH (anag.)
3 STEL + A (*lets* rev.)
5 HERE + TIC
6 OMIT (hidden)
7 SALAAM
(*ma + alas* rev.)
10 CHIS + ELS
12 AD + VICE
13 ARENAS
(*saner + a* rev.)
15 FLUS + H
17 AWOL (*a wall* hom.)
18 HE + LP

83

S	T	E	M	F	E	T	A
T	O	R	I	A	M	O	S
A	P	O	L	L	O	G	T
G	E	N	A	S	T	A	R
B	R	U	N	E	I	D	A
E	S	D	I	S	N	E	Y
C	O	N	E	O	G	B	C
A	P	I	N	N	A	T	E
M	A	K	E	G	O	O	D
E	L	S	E	S	O	R	E

ACROSS

1 STEM (rev.)
4 FETA (*ate + F* rev.)
8 TORI AMOS (hidden)
9 A + POLL + O
11 S + TAR
12 BRUNEI (anag.)
14 DISNEY
(*yens + I'd* rev.)
16 C + ONE
19 INNATE (anag.)
20 M(A + KE G)OOD
21 ELSE (hidden)
22 SORE (*soar* hom.)

DOWN

1 S + TAG
2 TOPERS (anag.)
3 M(IL)AN
5 EMO(TI)NG
(*it* in *gnome* rev.)
6 TOG + A (*got* rev.)
7 AS + TRAY
10 NU(DNIK)S
(*kind* in *sun* rev.)
12 BECAME
(*beak aim* hom.)
13 DEBTOR
(*rot + bed* rev.)
15 SON(G)S
17 O + PAL
18 CEDE (*seed* hom.)

100

S	R	I	L	A	N	K	A
T	O	F	E	M	A	I	M
O	W	L	E	T	T	D	E
R	E	A	D	J	U	S	T
E	N	U	S	A	R	G	E
R	A	N	C	H	A	O	R
O	N	T	H	E	L	A	M
O	O	I	V	I	L	L	A
M	O	N	K	R	Y	I	I
I	N	G	E	S	T	E	D

ACROSS

1 SRI (LANK)A
(*airs* rev.)
7 (i)MAIM (rev.)
9 OW + LE + T
10 READ + JUST
11 SA(R)GE
13 RANCH (hidden)
15 ON THE LAM (anag.)
17 VI(L)LA
18 M + ON + K
19 INGESTED (anag.)

DOWN

1 S(TORERO)O + M
2 ROWENA (anag.)
3 LEEDS (*leads* hom.)
4 N + AT + U + RALLY
5 KIDS (2 defs.)
6 FL(AUNT)ING
8 ME + TER M + AID
12 GO + ALI + E
14 (t)HE + IRS
16 NO ON(e)

16

A	S	C	O	T	S	H	K
S	P	A	C	E	M	A	N
H	U	G	E	R	O	L	E
C	R	R	A	N	K	L	E
A	R	E	N	A	Y	O	B
N	I	S	S	C	I	F	I
I	N	P	A	R	T	F	L
O	G	L	E	O	P	A	L
T	O	I	L	S	O	M	E
A	N	T	A	S	T	E	D

ACROSS

1 A + SCOT'S
7 SPAC + EMAN (rev.)
8 HUG + E
9 ROLE (*roll* hom.)
10 RAN + KLE (*elk* rev.)
11 ARE(N)A
15 SC + I-F + I
16 IN PART (anag.)
17 O + GLE (*leg* anag.)
18 O + PAL
19 T(OILS)OME
20 TASTED (hidden)

DOWN

1 A + S(H)CAN
  (ref. Ashcan School)
2 SPUR(RING O)N
3 OCEANS (anag.)
4 S(MO)KY
5 H(ALL) OF FA + ME
6 K + NEE
12 ACROSS (anag.)
13 BILLED (*build* hom.)
14 SP + LIT
16 I(O)T + A

33

B	A	S	K	E	D	C	A
E	T	C	H	L	A	O	S
A	T	H	O	V	E	R	S
K	H	O	M	E	I	N	I
H	E	L	M	S	C	F	S
O	W	A	D	W	E	L	T
T	O	R	E	A	D	O	R
A	R	A	F	A	T	W	E
I	S	L	E	S	E	E	N
R	T	A	R	C	A	R	O

ACROSS

1 B(ASK)ED
7 ETC. + H
8 LA + OS (rev.)
9 H + OVER + S
10 K(HOME)IN + I
12 HELMS (2 defs.)
13 DWEL + T (*lewd* rev.)
14 TO(READ)OR
  (*root* rev.)
16 A + RAF(A)T
17 IS + LE
18 SEEN (hidden)
19 ARC + AR + O

DOWN

1 BEA + K
  (ref. Bea Arthur)
2 AT THE WORST
  (hidden)
3 S(CH)OLAR
4 E(L)VES
5 CORN(FLOW)ER
6 (b)ASSIST
11 ICED TEA (anag.)
12 H(OT) AIR (*to* rev.)
13 DEFER (rev.)
15 R + ENO (*one* rev.)

50

A	C	H	I	L	L	E	S
S	H	A	D	I	E	R	M
T	A	L	E	T	A	R	A
R	C	E	S	O	N	A	R
O	R	A	T	E	E	T	R
D	O	T	M	A	R	I	A
O	N	T	A	P	S	C	K
M	I	E	N	R	A	C	E
E	E	S	C	O	R	T	S
A	S	T	O	N	I	S	H

ACROSS

1 ACH(ILL)ES
6 SHADIER (anag.)
8 TALE (*tail* hom.)
9 TAR + A
11 SON + A + R
12 O + RATE
14 M + ARIA
16 ON TAP (*pat* + *no* rev.)
18 MIEN (*mean* hom.)
19 (t)RACE
20 ESCORTS (anag.)
21 AS(TONI'S)H

DOWN

1 A + ST + RO(DO)ME
2 HALE (*hail* hom.)
3 ID EST (anag.)
4 LEANER (2 defs.)
5 ERRATIC (anag.)
7 MAR(RAKE)SH
10 CR(ON)IES
13 AT(TES) + T (*set* rev.)
15 A(PRO)N
17 SARI (*sorry* hom.)

67

S	T	O	N	E	A	G	E
A	G	R	E	E	T	O	I
L	I	Z	A	P	E	O	N
A	S	O	T	R	A	D	E
D	E	F	O	E	S	D	A
B	R	R	S	P	E	A	R
O	P	E	R	A	L	Y	N
W	I	S	E	P	I	N	E
L	C	C	L	A	M	P	S
G	O	A	L	L	O	U	T

84

R	E	D	W	I	N	G	S
E	T	E	R	N	A	L	S
M	E	M	O	T	R	O	T
B	R	I	N	U	R	S	E
R	E	I	G	N	O	S	E
A	T	N	R	A	W	E	R
N	I	C	E	R	M	S	S
D	R	A	W	G	U	A	M
T	E	S	T	O	N	I	A
A	D	H	E	S	I	O	N

17

F	L	A	M	B	E	E	D
I	I	M	P	R	O	V	E
S	P	A	C	E	M	E	N
H	I	D	E	A	G	N	T
E	D	E	O	D	E	T	S
D	R	U	M	S	N	A	L
M	O	S	I	M	O	D	E
A	D	A	M	B	E	D	E
R	E	V	E	R	S	E	P
S	O	L	D	I	E	R	Y

ACROSS

1 S(TONE) AGE
6 A + GREE T + O
8 LIZA (hidden)
9 PEON (anag.)
11 TRADE (anag.)
12 DE-FOE (pun)
14 SPEAR (anag.)
16 OPERA (anag.)
18 WISE (*whys* hom.)
19 PINE (2 defs.)
20 C-CL + AMPS
21 GO AL + L OUT

DOWN

1 SALAD BOWL (anag.)
2 ORZO (hidden)
3 NEATO (anag.)
4 A + T EASE
5 G(O + OD D)AY
7 I + N EAR + NEST
10 SERPICO (anag.)
13 FRES(C)A (*a + serf* rev.)
15 P(A + P)AL
17 LIMO (anag.)

ACROSS

1 RED WINGS (anag.)
6 E + TERNAL
  (*rental* anag.)
8 ME + MO
9 TRO(u)T
11 NURSE (anag.)
12 REIGN (*rein* hom.)
14 RAWER (hidden)
16 NICER (*rec + in* rev.)
18 DRAW (rev.)
19 GU(A)M
20 ESTONIA (anag.)
21 ADHESION (anag.)

DOWN

1 RE(M)BRANDT
  (*Bertrand* anag.)
2 DEMI(t)
3 WRONG (anag.)
4 N + ARROW
5 GLOSSES (2 defs.)
7 STEERSMAN (anag.)
10 RE-TIRED (pun)
13 IN CAS + H
15 (w)AR(GO)S
17 MUN + I (*num.* rev.)

ACROSS

1 F(LAMB)EED
7 IMP + ROVE
8 SPA + CEMEN(t)
9 HIDE (2 defs.)
11 ODETS
  (*owe debts* hom.)
13 D + RUMS
18 MODE (hidden)
19 A + DAM (BED)E
  (ref. George Eliot
  novel)
20 RE + VERSE
21 SOLDIERY (anag.)

DOWN

1 FI + SHED (*if* rev.)
2 LIP + I'D
3 AMADEUS
  (*sued + AMA* rev.)
4 BREAD (*bred* hom.)
5 EVEN + T
6 DEN + T
10 GE(NO)ESE
12 S(LEE)PY
14 RODE + O
15 M + IMED (rev.)
16 ADDER (2 defs.)
17 MARS (2 defs.)

34

S	A	N	G	A	M	E	S
P	M	C	A	B	O	D	E
R	E	A	L	M	U	W	I
I	N	F	E	R	N	O	S
N	H	E	S	A	T	O	M
G	A	T	E	S	A	D	O
T	R	E	A	T	I	N	G
I	B	R	S	O	N	A	R
M	O	I	R	A	S	P	A
E	R	A	S	T	R	A	M

ACROSS

10 SANG (hidden)
4 A(M)ES (*sea* rev.)
9 ABODE (anag.)
10 REAL + M
11 INFERNOS (anag.)
13 A + TOM
14 G + ATE
16 TRE + ATING (*giant* anag.)
18 SO(N)AR
19 MOIRA (anag.)
20 ERAS (2 defs.)
21 T + R(A)M (rev.)

DOWN

1 SP + RING + TI + ME
   (*it* rev.)
2 AMEN (hidden)
3 GALES (anag.)
5 MOUNTAINS (anag.)
6 (r)ED WOOD
7 SEISMOGRAM (anag.)
8 CA + FETE + RIA (*air* rev.)
12 H + ARBOR
15 STO(A)T (rev.)
17 NAP + A

51

M	U	G	S	S	T	A	Y
U	N	D	O	H	Y	M	N
S	I	G	N	A	L	E	D
T	O	M	I	Q	E	N	P
A	N	A	C	O	N	D	A
R	E	X	S	T	O	U	T
D	Q	I	O	R	L	T	R
B	U	M	P	I	N	T	O
T	A	U	T	P	E	E	L
A	L	M	S	E	A	R	S

ACROSS

1 MUGS (anag.)
4 ST(A)Y
7 UNDO (hidden)
8 HYMN (*him* hom.)
9 SIGNALED (anag.)
12 ANACONDA (anag.)
13 RE(X) ST + OUT
18 BUM + P INTO
19 TAU + T
20 P + EEL
21 AL(u)MS
22 (h)EARS

DOWN

1 MU(STAR)D
2 UNION (*no* + *in* + *U* rev.)
3 SONIC (anag.)
4 SHAQ (*shack* hom.)
5 TYLENOL (*lonely* + *T* rev.)
6 AMEND (anag.)
10 MA(XI), MUM
11 PATROLS (anag.)
14 EQUAL (hidden)
15 TRIPE (anag.)
16 UTTER (2 defs.)
17 OPTS (anag.)

68

C	A	D	S	C	A	W	S
A	L	I	T	A	W	O	L
R	O	S	E	M	A	R	Y
N	U	B	A	E	R	L	T
A	D	A	M	B	E	D	E
G	O	T	O	T	O	W	N
E	N	H	T	H	F	H	A
D	A	I	R	Y	M	A	N
M	I	N	I	M	E	L	T
A	R	G	O	E	W	E	S

ACROSS

1 C + ADS
4 CAWS (*cause* hom.)
7 ALIT (anag.)
8 A + WOL (*owl* anag.)
9 ROS(EM)ARY
12 A + DAM (BED)E
13 GO (TO TO)WN
18 DAIRYM + AN (*myriad*
   rev.)
19 MINI (anag.)
20 ME(L)T
21 ARGO (hidden)
22 EWES (*use* hom.)

DOWN

1 CAR(NAG)E
2 ALOUD (*allowed* hom.)
3 STE(A)M
4 CA + ME
5 A + WARE (O)F
   (*wafer* rev.)
6 WOR(L)D
10 BA(THIN)G
11 TEN + ANTS (*net* rev.)
14 O + N AIR (*rain* anag.)
15 THYME (*time* hom.)
16 W + HALE
17 T + RIO

85

ACROSS

1 ERIC (hidden)
4 CAFE (anag.)
7 LE(N)O
8 OWED (*ode* hom.)
9 G(LEND)ALE
12 EX + P + ONE + NT
13 CALLIOPE (anag.)
18 KEYN(OT)ES (*to* rev.)
19 F(R)EE
20 LOCO (anag.)
21 HYDE (*hide* hom.)
22 SE(v)EN

DOWN

1 EL (G)RECO
   (*Creole* anag.)
2 R + ELAX (*axle* anag.)
3 CONDO(r)
4 COD + A
5 A + WAR + E OF
   (*foe* rev.)
6 FE(LO)N
10 SPLAYED (anag.)
11 STEPS ON
14 A + VERY
15 IDOLS (anag.)
16 PIECE (*peace* hom.)
17 KNEE (hidden in
   odd letters)